SOCIAL WORK PRACTICE WITH THE ELDERLY

Second Edition

edited by
Michael J. Holosko
Marvin D. Feit

Canadian Scholars' Press   Toronto   1996

Social Work Practice with the Elderly, Second Edition
Edited by Michael J. Holosko and Marvin D. Feit

First Published in 1996 by
Canadian Scholars' Press Inc.
180 Bloor Street West, Ste. 402
Toronto, Ontario
M5S 2V6

Canadian Cataloguing in Publication Data
Main entry under title:
Social work practice with the elderly
2nd ed.
Includes bibliographical references.
ISBN 1-55130-070-2

1. Social work with the aged.
I.   Holosko, Michael J.   II.   Feit, Marvin
D. (Marvin David), 1942-   .

HV1451.S62   1996   362.6 C96-931395-0

Page layout and cover design by Brad Horning

For our parents,

Joseph John Holosko, Maria Mary Klochko
and
Abraham Feit, Sara Gleicher

We thank you for not only dispelling
but shattering the societal myths
associated with old age.

TABLE OF CONTENTS

WITHDRAWN

Section I
Direct Practice Elements

Section III
Future Considerations

ACKNOWLEDGEMENTS

As one might imagine, the preparation of such a manuscript involves a cast of many. We would like to thank the following for their utmost support in this endeavour, from its inception to its conclusion: Dean Zbigniew Fallenbuchl, Professor Emeritus, Faculty of Social Science, University of Windsor; Ingrid Sands, typist extraordinaire; Jack Wayne at Canadian Scholars' Press; Sandy Van Zetten, Secretary, University of Windsor; and, Mary Lou Simon, Secretary, University of Akron.

We sincerely thank all of you for your assistance in completing this project and appreciate your contributions immensely.

CONTRIBUTORS

AUSTIN, CAROL D., Ph.D., Professor and Assistant Dean, Faculty of Social Work, The University of Calgary, Calgary, Alberta.

BECK, IRENE, BSW, Social Worker, Luther Senior's Centre, Saskatoon, Saskatchewan.

DICKS, BARBARA , Ph.D., MPH, Associate Professor, School of Social Work, University of Connecticut, West Hartford, Connecticut, U.S.A.

FABIANO, LEN, BA, RN, President, ECS Publishing and Consulting Service, Seagrave, Ontario, Canada.

FEIT, MARVIN, Ph.D., Director and Professor, School of Social Work, University of Akron, Akron, Ohio, U.S.A.

FEIT-CUEVAS, NURIA, Ph.D., Northeast Ohio Universities College of Medicine, Rootstown, Ohio, U.S.A.

FITCH, VIRGINIA, Ph.D., Associate Professor, Department of Social Work, University of Akron, Akron, Ohio, U.S.A.

GIANNETTI, VINCENT, Ph.D., Professor of Social and Administrative Studies, School of Pharmacy, Duquesne University, Pittsburgh, Pennsylvania, U.S.A.

GREEN, JANICE, MSSA, Social Work Supervisor, Edwin Shaw Hospital, Akron, Ohio, U.S.A.

GRIEVE, JANE, MSW, Coordinator, Grandside Psychogeriatric Clinic, Cambridge Memorial Hospital, Cambridge, Ontario.

HARDINA, DONNA, Ph.D., Assistant Professor, School of Social Work, California State University, Fresno, California, U.S.A.

HINKSON, DEBRA, MSW, Social Worker, Edwin Shaw Hospital, Akron, Ohio, U.S.A.

HOLOSKO, ANN, MSW, The Child's Place, Windsor, Ontario, Canada.

HOLOSKO, MICHAEL, Ph.D., Professor, School of Social Work, University of Windsor, Windsor, Ontario, Canada.

KINDIAK, DARLENE H., MSW, Program Manager, Seniors Mental Health Program, Stratford General Hospital, Stratford, Ontario.

KOPSTEIN, RHODA, MSW, Director, Day Care Services, Baycrest Centre for Geriatric Care, North York, Ontario, Canada.

MACKENZIE, PATRICIA, MSW, Assistant Professor, Faculty of Social Work, University of Regina, Regina, Saskatchewan, Canada.

MARINO, SUSAN, MSW, Supervisor, Department of Social Work, London Psychiatric Hospital, London, Ontario, Canada.

MARTYN, RON, MA, Associate, ECS Publications and Consulting Services, Seagrave, Ontario, Canada

NICHOLS, SALLY, LSW, Social Worker, Rockynol Retirement Community, Akron, Ohio, U.S.A.

PATCHNER, LISA, MSW, Doctoral student, School of Public Health, University of Pittsburgh, Pittsburgh, Pennsylvania,U.S.A.

PATCHNER, MICHAEL, Ph.D., Associate Dean, School of Social Work, University of Pittsburgh, Pittsburgh, Pennsylvania, U.S.A.

ROSSITER, CHARLES, Ph.D., Project Director, Caregiver Support Project, School of Social Welfare, and the Ringel Institute of Gerontology, University at Albany, State University of New York, Albany, New York, U.S.A.

SCHENK, CATHERINE, BSW, Croton, Ontario.

SLIVINSKE, LEE, Ph.D., Associate Professor, Department of Sociology, Anthropology and Social Work, Youngstown State University, Youngstown, Ohio, U.S.A.

SOIFER, AHUVA, MSW, Associate Professor, School of Social Work, McMaster University, Hamilton, Ontario, Canada.

TOSELAND, RONALD, Ph.D., Associate Professor of Social Work and Principal Investigator, Caregiver Support Project, School of Social Welfare, and the Ringel Institute of Gerontology, University at Albany, State University of New York, Albany, New York, U.S.A.

URMAN, SORELE, MSW, Director of Central Intake, Baycrest Centre for Geriatric Care, North York, Ontario, Canada.

VENTURINI, VINCENT, MSW, Coordinator of Social Services, Boswell Retardation Center, Sanatorium, Mississippi, U.S.A.

WATT, SUSAN, DSW, CSW, Director and Associate Professor, School of Social Work, McMaster University, Hamilton, Ontario, Canada.

WHITE, LINDA, M.S.W., EAP Coordinator, Customs and Immigration Canada, Windsor, Ontario, Canada.

PREFACE

The text was written primarily by experienced practitioners working in the field of gerontology in North America and is intended for use by undergraduate and graduate social work students and other helping practitioners. It attempts to confront and address current and important practice issues for social workers working with the elderly in a variety of practice settings.

In the past 25 years or so, we have been deluged with demographic trends and statistics that clearly project the stark reality that the elderly population is growing at a rapid rate and that existing health and human service agencies cannot adequately serve their immediate, let alone future, needs. Indeed, health and social service institutions have largely been extending their mandates and organizational parameters to serve this population. The long-standing North American notion of 'out-of-sight, out-of-mind,' reflected in reactive (rather than proactive) policy-making, and a 'symptom-disease' orientation to helping the elderly is slowly changing. Social workers have been quick to respond to this by being in the forefront in developing creative approaches to caring for the elderly, by initiating and using more holistic interventions in treatment, by injecting liberal doses of humanism into the overall care process, and being flexible in working 'within the contradictions' of these agencies and their existing policies and procedures. The profession of social work has once again shown that its malleability and adaptation is its greatest single asset, and in this evolution it has never lost sight of its mission — to help serve the needs of its clients. Certainly, all of the chapters in this text serve as testimony to this legacy.

The revised text is organized in two main subsections: *Direct Practice Elements (I)*; and, *Selected Practice Settings (II)*. The former provides the context for understanding generic practice issues that cut across all practice settings. Feit and Feit in Chapter 1 set the stage for understanding both the dynamics of practice with the elderly and also the multi-faceted aspects of such work by providing an overview of salient trends and practice issues confronting workers in this field. Holosko and Holosko then attempt to distill elements of the uniqueness of social work practice with the elderly by 'seeking the difference that makes the difference.' In Chapter 3, Watt and Soifer present in detail both the rationale for conducting psycho-social assessments with the elderly and a prescription for how to conduct them. Along the same line, Marino (in Chapter 4) diligently articulates four genetic cornerstone practice issues that social workers need to address if they are to be successful in counselling the elderly. Further, Giannetti, in Chapter 5, clearly describes an important practice issue confronting gerontological social workers, that being medication utilization problems and their implications. Hardina and Holosko then present a case for social workers becoming more actively involved in policies that influence practice with the elderly. Their chapter, (6), outlines and then analyzes all of the social policies affecting the elderly in North America by using a common-sense typology. Schenk and Holosko identify a unique niche for gerontological social work practice — identifying the elderly alcoholic. Austin then presents a comprehensive overview of the emergency field of case management practice with the elderly.

Section II presents ten chapters formatted in the same way: The Clientele, Practice Roles and Responsibilities, Potential for Role Development, Concluding Remarks and Case Examples. Indeed, these chapters reflect the diverse practice settings in which gerontological social work is practiced, and they range from urban to rural, institutional to community-based care, acute to chronic, and wellness to disease orientations. They are all written by (and for) front-line practitioners, the 'fighter pilots' of the profession, and are all blatant reminders of the integral role social work plays in serving the elderly in health and human service organizations. In each of these settings, social workers have carved out unique niches in caring for the elderly, and their creativity, initiative and ability to be effective in these respective settings is profound.

In Chapter 9, Fabiano and Martyn present the full range of practice issues confronting social workers practicing with the growing numbers of frail elderly. Patchner and Patchner then enlighten us about the realities and conduct of social work practice in nursing homes in America. In Chapter 11, MacKenzie focuses on practice in specialized geriatric assessment units prevalent in hospitals in both Canada and the U.S. Then, MacKenzie and Beck describe the intricacies of practice with dementia patients in a unique adult day care programme in Saskatoon, Saskatchewan. Kopstein and Urman (in Chapter 13) describe the realities of practice with the frail elderly in another adult day care programme in a well-regarded, Toronto-based facility, the Baycrest Centre for Geriatric Care. Toseland and Rossiter then provide an insightful overview of issues related to practice with the much neglected cohort of family caregivers of frail older persons. Dicks and Venturini describe the nuts and bolts of rural practice with mentally retarded elderly in Mississippi. Fitch, Slivinske and Nichols (in Chapter 16) describe and analyze practice roles and responsibilities in a unique private retirement community. Subsequently, Fitch, Slivinske, Green and Hinkson shift settings in order to describe practice issues affecting geriatric patients in a rehabilitation hospital. Section II concludes with Kindiak and Grieve presenting an overview of practice in community psychogeriatric programmes.

Finally, Section III, written by Holosko, White and Feit, projects the realities of practice with the elderly in the future pointing to the new challenges and exciting frontiers for the profession. They conclude, as do many chapters in this text, by pointing out that the future is now for gerontological social work and the profession has an important role to play in the future of service delivery for the elderly.

Each of the chapters in this revised text are both descriptive and analytic and are intended to enhance an understanding of the realities of front-line social work practice with the elderly. We have learned much about practicing with the elderly and it is only by sharing our knowledge that we can enhance our skills. One fact that underscores the 'critical mass' of these chapters is that our education and training has lagged far behind our practice initiatives, and the profession has much work to do in this regard. Another is that much more research of a clinical, theoretical and empirical nature is needed to discover, refine, test out or verify some of our cherished practice wisdom. Finally, this is not a book which is about 'what's wrong' with social work practice (which may feed the fragile insecurity of some social workers), but moreso 'what's right' with social work practice! But alas, we would prefer you to be the judge of that.

M.J.H.

About the Editors

MICHAEL J. HOLOSKO is a Professor at the School of Social Work, University of Windsor. He has taught social work and nursing and been a consultant in the human service and health field for the past 17 years in Canada, the United States, Europe, Asia and Australia. His speciality areas are clinical and programme evaluation, administrative skills and stress management. He has published numerous monographs, chapters and articles, and conducted research studies in the areas of health care, social policy and evaluation. His published texts include the *Evaluation of Employee Assistance Programs* published by the Haworth Press in 1988 and *Social Work Practice in Health Care Settings*, with Canadian Scholars' Press in 1989. He is also on the editorial board for the *Journal of Health and Social Policy* and the *Journal of Human Behavior in the Social Environment*. He has served on numerous boards of directors for a variety of local, provincial, federal and international human service agencies including Health and Welfare Canada's Research Advisory Committee.

MARVIN D. FEIT is a Professor and Head of the Department of Social Work at the University of Akron. He has taught social work graduate and undergraduate courses in administration and treatment and served as a consultant to a variety of health and human service organizations for the past 27 years. His areas of expertise are financial management, administration, group work, substance abuse and health care. He has published many chapters, articles, monographs and books over the years including *The Management and Administration of Drug and Alcohol Programs*, *Evaluation of Employee Assistance Programs*, *Adolescent Substance Abuse*, *Capturing the Power of Diversity* and *Health and Social Policy*. He is also the founding editor of the *Journal of Health and Social Policy* published through the Haworth Press.

Section 1

Direct Practice Elements

CHAPTER 1

AN OVERVIEW OF SOCIAL WORK PRACTICE WITH THE ELDERLY

MARVIN D. FEIT, PH.D.
NURIA M. CUEVAS-FEIT, PH.D.

*T*his chapter assesses social work practice with the elderly by identifying seven trends useful for practitioners and social work students. These are: 1) more people are getting older, particularly in the over-85 age group, and they are likely to be more active politically, economically capable, independent and mobile; 2) older people will both need and demand more social, health and medical services; 3) they will be hit hardest by chronic illnesses and diseases; 4) many 'unique' situations will arise requiring attention; 5) despite possessing more resources than their predecessors, a greater share of the economic pie will be consumed by costly medical and health care; 6) benefits will continue to be provided unevenly; and, 7) for many people, old age will be the first time they have had any contact with health, social and/or medical services. Finally, the effects that these trends are likely to have on social work practice with the elderly are discussed.

I. Introduction

The focus of this introductory chapter is on identifying emerging trends to better understand social work practice with the elderly. One must be able to look beyond numbers and statistics and react to the present or immediate needs of the elderly in providing meaningful services. Thus, in order to prepare practitioners for work with this clientele, one must start with the present and offer suggestions about the future direction of practice.

Two fundamental premises of this overall text have long been accepted by our society. One is that there will be more elderly people in the United States and Canada during the next 20 to 30 years than ever before. Indeed, no one doubts this reality nor its importance. Less clear is the precise impact that this population will have on the social, economic and political structures of the respective societies of each country.

The second premise is that as people age they require and use more health and social welfare services. It should, therefore, be of no surprise to learn of the continuous increases in Medicaid and Medicare costs resulting from increased provider costs, the increase in the number of senior citizen programmes, and the increased costs of basic goods and services to this population.

Based on these factors, one is able to provide an overview of the salient issues, problems and concerns likely to be faced by social workers as they engage in practice with the elderly during the next 20 to 30 years. The purpose of this chapter, then, is to identify these particular trends and discuss ways that they may influence gerontological social work practice. Certainly one must start with the present, and in many chapters of this text practitioners provide, in exceptional detail, their current practice realities in various social work settings. Thus, these chapters taken together, provide quite a 'picture of the landscape' and offer a better understanding of the range of agencies and services provided to the elderly. They also reveal some interesting gaps in services and disparities in programmes and offer insights about very important practice and policy issues.

However, as social workers continue to practice in this emerging field, it is likely that changes will occur as a result of, or in response to, several factors. For instance, current programmes are likely to be modified or changed, new or different programmes are likely to be developed (as well as specialized services), the political infrastructures and resulting policies most certainly will be different, and the character of social work practice with the elderly is likely to be profoundly affected.

Seven significant trends identified in this regard are as follows:

- While many people are getting older, they are likely to be more politically sophisticated and active, more economically capable, more mobile and independent than ever before;
- Older people will need and demand significantly more social, health and medical services, and these services will have to be integrated in order to be most effective;
- Older people will continue to be hit hardest by illnesses and diseases that require chronic care, despite periodic acute medical and psycho-social problems;
- Many 'unique' subpopulation situations and their problems will emerge and require attention, such as minority elderly not living to age 65, the 'sandwich' or 'squeezed' generation, etc.;
- While the elderly as a group may possess more resources than their predecessors, a greater share of the economic budget is likely to be consumed by costly medical and health care;
- Benefits will continue to be provided unevenly to the elderly, i.e., those with money and/or insurance will have better health care than those without money or insurance. In turn, many elderly are likely to receive no care or inadequate care; and,
- For many people, old age will be the first time in their lives that they or their families have had to formally access and engage health, social and medical programmes and their services on a regular and continuing basis. These people, predominantly from the private sector, will inevitably find these programmes not what they expected.

1. The Politics of Aging in North America

While many persons are getting older, the largest increases among the elderly are projected to be in the 75-and-over age group. Specifically, the population of adults aged 65 and older has increased by 24 percent, while the population under age 65 has increased by only six percent in the past 20 years. Further indications are that this population will more than double in North America by 2020, and by the year 2030, 21 percent of the elderly population will be 65 years of age or older.

However, the largest relative proportionate growth of the elderly population is projected to be in the 85-and-older group in the next 20 years. This age category is estimated to grow three to four times faster than the population aged 65 to 84. The primary reason given for this is the high birth rates prior to 1920 and during the post-World War II period between 1945-1959. A number of other factors such as improved diets and better nutrition, better personal health care, better health care services, advances in medical technology, etc., have also contributed to these longevity patterns (Fitch and Slivinske, 1989).

There appears to be some disagreement in the literature regarding when actual aging begins. The definition ranges from those aged 65 years of age and older, as defined by government agencies such as Medicare or the Canadian Pension Plan, to those 50 years of age and older as defined by the American Association of Retired Persons (AARP). The most widely used definition associated with the development and implementation of age-specific programmes for older adults appears to be 65 years of age or older, which is the retirement age established in the original U.S. Social Security legislation of 1935. (This is the same age for receipt of benefits in Canada.)

It is our contention, consistent with many authors in this field, that the elderly will be more politically active, more mobile and independent than ever before. One reason for their being more politically active is the decline in the number of labour force workers supporting persons receiving Social Security retirement benefits. For example in the U.S.A. in 1960, 20 workers supported one retired person. Currently in the U.S.A., three workers support one retiree (Dobelstein and Johnson, 1985). Thus, the growing political significance of older persons is likely to focus on the Social Security debate even moreso in the future. Preferences for the living styles of older adults and their ability to maintain the standards of living for which they worked all of their lives, when contrasted with the uncertainty of future Social Security retirement benefits, will likely trigger sharp debate in America.

Future elderly will also be more economically viable and have more financial security than the elderly of today. Pension plans, stocks and bonds and other non-wage-related income serve as the cornerstone of the various pre-retirement plans of today's 30- to 60-year-old group. For example, Feit and Tate (1986) reported that in one company the financial aspect of one pre-retirement programme accounted for 75 percent of its content and emphasis.

At the same time, this population will also be more mobile. First, with 'aged' starting at 50 years of age for membership in the AARP, and one of their services being discounts at many service establishments (e.g., hotels, restaurants, car rental agencies, etc.) throughout the country, significantly greater numbers of these 'elderly' will be mobile and able to travel. Programmes that define elderly at younger ages such as 50 generally attract persons who are 'in the prime of their lives' and are physically and mentally healthy. Also, in North America, many elderly live independently until age 75 to 80 when they then require assistance. Should the current emphasis on illness and health continue, it is conceivable that considerably more elderly will live independently and perhaps extend their independence to 90 years of age.

2. Service Demands

Older people need more social, health and medical services. The vulnerability of this population includes issues related to a series of life-cycle processes and adjustments identified by a number of authors in this text. These adjustments include: educational and cognitive issues, e.g., quality of life, the ability to remain active and to maintain personal interests, and mental and intellectual functioning; emotional and psychological issues, e.g., isolation, depression, anxiety, loss of friends and spouses, unfulfilled expectations, and communication abilities; physical health concerns, e.g., how vision, illness, mobility, etc., affects social and financial resources; family dynamics, e.g., is the family helpful or do they exacerbate problems; financial realities, e.g., a high percentage of their income, about 20-25 percent is 'out-of-pocket' expenses and go to health care and long-term care in the U.S.A.; leisure and recreational, home and living environment, home maintenance issues, e.g., shopping, household chores, preparing meals, managing money, etc., and; personal care, e.g., walking, going outside, bathing, dressing, using the toilet, getting in and out of bed or a chair, eating, etc.

As individuals age, they undergo gradual changes in most of their psychological and physical areas of functioning. Most of these are hardly noticeable except when greater than average exertion is required. For example, one may need more time to complete tasks or to remember things, or not be able to more as quickly as before. Cognitive changes reflect an actual slowing down of functioning rather than a loss of functioning. For instance, new learning can occur; however, one must allow adequate time to learn various tasks, information and/or skills. Further, in this regard, sexual functioning may reflect the same slowing of response mechanisms rather than the actual loss of functioning, libido or physiologic response (Edinberg, 1985).

While medical and health services play a prominent role in the lives of many elderly, the need for social services will be enormous. Although case management may be the most utilized service, there will be need for services such as home-based care, family treatment, substance abuse counselling and mental health counselling (with an emphasis on depression and suicide). Such services will inevitably require a baseline knowledge in other health and medical related disciplines, such as pharmacology, medicine, dentistry and so forth, for effective social work practice (see Giannetti, Chapter 5, for a good example for this).

Finally, in this regard, increased age brings on increased susceptibility to illness and disease. The majority of older adults have at least one chronic impairment in their lives, yet it is remarkable that most can manage on their own with appropriate supports. Thus, many problems are often overlooked because medical symptoms are similar to each other, complaints can be incorrectly thought of as signs of aging and, also, older persons may be reticent to discuss their actual problems for a variety of reasons.

3. The Impact of Chronic Illness

The elderly suffer more from illnesses and diseases, and a substantial proportion are chronic in nature. While the perceived self-reported health status of the elderly is generally 'excellent' or 'poor' for most, 20 percent of older adults report their health status to be 'only fair' or 'poor.' By contrast, older adults make up 12 percent of the general population yet use 40 percent of all prescription drugs in the U.S.A. Further, they account for approximately 31 percent of the total health care expenditures nationally in America (Myers, 1989).

About 80 percent of older persons can carry out and manage their daily lives without assistance despite chronic problems. In North America, they can generally live independently and in good health until at least age 75, although by age 85 most need some form of assisted living. As indicated previously, most can cope with physical limitations and chronic illnesses and maintain independence despite chronic conditions, which are usually debilitating in nature, such as arthritis, hypertension, hearing and vision impairment, heart disease, diabetes, etc. However, blanket assumptions about chronic health care needs can be misleading as such needs include either acute, transitional or long-term care. For instance, acute care involves a hospital stay, which is needed when an episodic flare-up occurs or when certain health and medical problems don't respond to treatment. Transitional care usually involves a period of 90 days or less, which follows a hospital stay, and is necessary before an elderly person can return to regular community living. Long-term care involves continuous care in a facility in which the elderly person resides. Thus, while chronic health care needs imply symptomatic treatment of a condition that remains with people for a long time, other types of continuing care will be needed from time to time in the course of one's life.

Arthritis, gout, gastritis, gall bladder disease, hiatus hernia, Alzheimer's disease, nutritional and vitamin problems, hypertension, coronary artery disease, diabetes, prostatitis, certain cancers (e.g., stomach, testicular, cervix, uterine) are just a few of the frequent and major medical problems among the elderly. Generally, those elderly with money and insurance usually receive care and those without either go without attention or seek service at emergency facilities.

However, there are many problems that reimbursement usually doesn't cover or is limited. For example, Medicare in the U.S.A. doesn't cover the cost of sensory-correcting devices such as glasses, hearing aids or corrective shoes. Similarly, American medical insurance coverage for eye care is limited; however, vision problems among the aged are common and may be severe. For example, 50 percent of the population of blind Americans is over 65 years of age, 55 percent of the new cases of blindness each year occur among older people, and 25 percent may be using incorrect lens prescriptions (AARP, 1990). Similarly, foot and dental care needs are often neglected and/or not addressed at all.

In regard to functional disorders, depression seems to be the most common. As well, alcoholism affects ten to 15 percent of the elderly, suicide is three times more likely to occur among the elderly and elder abuse is increasing rapidly in every urban centre in North America. The exacerbating reality of isolation and loneliness contribute greatly to these frequently occurring disorders (Edinberg, 1985). Finally, in this regard, older adults use more than twice as much medication as younger people, and 75 percent of the American elderly regularly use prescribed and 'over-the-counter' medications.

In summary, the future health picture of the elderly may seem cloudy. Ironically, at the same time many elderly need more services to address their increase in health and medical problems, they consume a larger portion of national health care costs and many are better able to function independently for many years despite having one or more chronic illnesses. The realities of the impact of such illnesses on care providers and programmes has profound implications for social and health care institutions in general, and social work practitioners in particular.

4. Emerging 'Unique' Situations

Many 'unique' population situations and their problems will inevitably emerge and require attention in the future. In one such situation many minority people do not live to age 65. For example, in an American study by Watson et al., (1986-87) approximately 90 percent of persons aged 65 and over were white, 8 percent were black, and 2 percent were categorized as 'other'. In the same vein, the life expectancy of Native Americans is approximately 63 years of age (Gelfand, 1982), and the life expectancy for black men is 60.1 years of age, about 7.5 years less than the life expectancy of white men (and this has been steadily declining) (Lowy, 1979).

Another interesting observation about our contemporary society is that more couples have elected to remain childless. Specifically, almost 5 percent of older American adults are married and have remained childless, and 5 percent are single and childless. With lower fertility rates, and an increased possibility for outliving their children, it seems that 10 percent of future older U.S. adults will have no children to help with their needs and/or to support them (Myers, 1989).

One spin-off effect of this is that new roles emerge for both older adults and their children. For instance, children may provide assistance to older adults in housework, financial assistance, transportation and caring for them in their homes. Older adults may, in turn, help with children, financial assistance, advice on business or other matters, running errands and taking in grandchildren or other relatives to live with them.

These new roles certainly assume a different character when the older adult requires extensive care, attention and, in some cases, financial help. Some children then may become part of the 'squeezed' or 'sandwiched' generation, in that they must choose between financial help for their parent(s) or their own family or spend considerable time being a caregiver to their parent(s) and spending time with their own family. Being part of the squeezed generation is becoming much more common in our society and will emerge as a major problem in the near future.

Further, family and in-home caregivers and services will continue to grow in numbers and importance as elderly persons live longer and suffer more debilitating illnesses and diseases that require 'round-the-clock' care e.g., Alzheimer's disease, chronic depression, stroke victims, etc. As a result, these caregivers will also demand help and support services as they try to regain some control over their own lives (see Chapter 14 by Toseland and Rossiter for a good example of this). Part of this effort is very likely to be an increase in many social, health and some medical support services provided in the home.

5. The Costs of Care

The future population of the elderly may have more money than their previous counterparts, yet a greater share of the overall economic pie will be taken by increasing health and medical care costs. Currently, retirement benefits, including Social Security benefits, and public and private pensions make up almost half of the income for older adults in the U.S.A. Further, one-third of their income comes from employment earnings and the remainder comes from savings, investments and gifts. Presently, the overall income of older adults may be greater than at any time before; however, poverty rates remain high among certain subgroups of the elderly, in particular Native and black men and women, and white women.

In addition, living on a fixed income poses serious problems for a number of elderly. In general, any increases or adjustments in their fixed incomes fall far below the national increases in the cost of living and/or inflation. Moreover, expenditures change dramatically for many older adults. Specifically, older adults comprise 11 percent of the total U.S. population but account for over 30 percent of public health expenditures (AARP, 1989). Further, older adults tend to spend more of their household incomes on food and medical care, less on shelter and recreation, and more on household assistance and maintenance, which they usually cannot do for themselves (Dobelstein and Johnson, 1985).

When their incomes do not allow for paying for household assistance and maintenance, many elderly simply 'do without,' and their domiciles often go unattended and/or fall into disrepair. Most older adults are forced into lowering their accustomed standards of living when they retire (Dobelstein and Johnson, 1985). They also tend to be squeezed out of the workforce due to failing health, biases against older people, public policies and practices, and retirement incentives such as income support plans. In general, most experience as much as a one-half drop in annual income upon retirement (Dobelstein and Johnson, 1985). Since health and medical costs have continued to increase annually at at least a two digit rate, the pressure to maintain themselves in their homes while continuing to pay for escalating costs for such care will become tremendous. At some point in the not too distant future, this situation will become intolerable for many elderly and changes in the system will be necessitated. Unfortunately, many elderly are likely to get caught in this dilemma and will suffer needlessly.

6. Discrepant Benefits

Benefits received by the elderly in North America tend to be uneven. Poverty proportions among various subgroups are unequal, e.g., American blacks are 1.5 times as likely as whites to be included among the older adult poor in 1990. Similarly, American Hispanics represented 5 percent and blacks represented 20 percent of the elderly poor in 1980, despite accounting for 3 percent and 5 percent, respectively, of the over-65 population. As one might assume, older blacks and other minorities are among the least able to afford private health insurance (Watson, et al., 1986-87). These authors also noted that as a result of past and recent discrimination practices in hiring, promotions, firing and underemployment, it is expected that older blacks will also have lower rates of Social Security benefits, few if any union pensions and will be more dependent on Supplemental Social Insurance, Medicare and Medicaid than their older adult white counterparts in the U.S.A. Furthermore, we concur that much is yet to be learned from future research about the ways to defray 'out-of-pocket' health care costs, the effects of Diagnostic Review Groups (DRGs) on social class and ethnicity and other problems faced by the elderly, in particular the minority aged, in either financing their health care and/or living on an annual fixed amount.

Further complicating the disproportionate benefits received by many elderly subgroups, will be their place of residence. Specifically, the American black elderly population is projected to migrate and have high concentrations living in central U.S. cities while the white elderly are likely to remain in the suburbs with only a very slight increase migrating to less costly central corridor cities. Thus, some projections estimate that elderly blacks may come to constitute one-fourth of the population living in central cities in the 1990s, instead of the current 16 percent (Watson, et al., 1986-87).

The picture is essentially not different when gender is considered in this formula. For instance, Hispanic elderly females in the U.S. were twice as likely as elderly white females to live in poverty. And black females were almost three times as likely as white women to be considered impoverished (Stone, 1985).

Elderly persons with incomes between the poverty line and 12.5 percent above the poverty line (the 'near poor') are the most vulnerable because they most often run the risk of not qualifying for public support programmes (e.g. Supplemental Security Income, Medicaid, Food Stamps, etc.), but they do not have enough income to provide for their basic needs. Further, most cannot afford the cost of insurance to supplement Medicare and they do not have the financial resources to offset the costs of a sustained illness in the U.S. (Stone, 1985).

Another significant change lies in the sociodemographic characteristics of the ethnic aged. Specifically, there has been a decline in the number of European-born American older adults, an increase in American-born ethnic older adults and also ethnic older adults immigrating from Indo-China, Asia and Latin America. The median educational level of older adults should continue to rise to 12 years by 1990, although the median educational level for blacks and Hispanics is likely to remain almost five years below that of whites in the U.S. While the overall economic situation of older adults has improved since 1970 (over the past 20-25 years), the median income of older adult whites continues to be twice that of black and Hispanic older adults (Gelfand, 1982).

In the U.S.A., slower advancement of blacks, other minorities and ethnic populations due to inadequate education, difficulties with English, unfamiliarity with American culture and discrimination generally restrict their economic opportunities, advancement and social mobility. As a result, there is a large discrepancy between white and black older adults in the availability of unearned income. For example, Gelfand (1982) noted that in 1976 two-thirds of white older adults have incomes from dividends, pensions and/or investment interest. This source of income was found among one-sixth of all older adult black families. Black older adults, therefore, are more likely than whites to depend on Social Security, current earnings and SSI for their incomes. Finally, in this context, the lower incomes and educational backgrounds of older American adult blacks are shared by other minority aged. Lower educational levels and relegation to poor-paying positions have prevented many minorities from obtaining maximum benefits available from Social Security, pensions and unearned income or quality services, which higher income older adults generally expect.

7. The First Contact with Services

For many people, old age is the first time that either they or their families will have to contact and engage social, health and/or medical services on a regular and/or continuing basis. These families are likely to need help to understand and sort through the various programmes and services that they require. As one might assume, they usually do not understand the social, health and medical system, how it functions, the roles of its personnel, how to obtain services and/or the extent of care needed. Specific information on what to expect from such agencies as Social Security, home health care, public welfare, Medicaid and Medicare, rehabilitation facilities, community mental health facilities and others will be needed as well as basic information about accessing and using such services. Case management, a relatively new service covered by financial reimbursement, is the most likely form of service the elderly and their families are most likely to use in America. A case manager works to see that needed services are provided and coordinated on behalf of elderly clients and their families in their respective communities. However, case management is limited by the extent of available community services. For instance, discouragement and frustration are two common outcomes many families realize when needed community services do not exist, are inadequate in number, have waiting lists or are poorly funded or staffed, etc. In other words, the public policies of the 1980s, which were usually supported by these 'baby boomers,' will make for frustrating encounters with the service providers. Our contention is that many elderly will conclude that these policies and services are inadequate and not quite what they expected.

II. What do the Trends Mean?

These trends provide a backdrop for understanding the certain challenges for social workers as they confront gerontological social work practice in the next generation. The major question for the field is, of course, what are these trends likely to mean and what impact are they likely to have in the preparation and practice of its professionals.

One way to initially grasp the meaning of these trends is by categorizing their effects or outcomes in two aspects: 1) those that have a direct effect on social work practice; and, 2) those that have to do with the environments in which the practice occurs. In other words, we should think of how these trends are likely to change or alter social work practice and also how they are likely to shape the political climate and human service organizations in which social workers are employed.

As indicated, social work practice with older adults is very likely to be quite different. As it evolves over time, these changes may seem modest; however, when examined from one time period to another, these changes may become dramatic. For example, it is obvious that there will be a need for more social workers in this field and employment opportunities will be plentiful. However, social work practice with older adults will also become more highly specialized. In turn, the education and training of personnel will be dramatically altered due to the specialized knowledge requirements and requisite skills needed to be effective with this population.

Foremost, the concept of the 'older adult' will be expanded to include several subgroups. The age range of 'older adults' is likely to be from 50 to 90 years of age, and workers will be called upon to understand the lifespan needs and unique characteristics of the 'young' older adults as being distinct from 'old' older adults. Thus, the universality of the aged concept will give way to a body of unique knowledge; that is, the identification of needs translated into client services, which reflect these age specific subgroups. At the same time, a greater knowledge of the social, emotional and physical problems of these subgroups is also likely to be required. Such knowledge is likely to occur in at least such areas as: pharmacology (drug interaction and substance abuse), chronic and debilitating illnesses and the problems they cause for an individual, family and society; mental health (depression and isolation); domestic relations (older adult abuse); family interaction and caregiving; and, developing community resources.

A critical component of social work practice will inevitably involve the interweaving of social services with medical care and health services. To be effective in this regard, a social worker must be able to move fluidly from one system to the other in an integrated community-based service network. Thus, as the chapters in Section II of this text exemplify, social work practice with older adults will include being able to work effectively in health and mental health care, being a hospital social worker, being skilled in individual, group, family and community practice, being a substance abuse worker and so forth. This type of worker is very different from today's generic social worker.

The case management approach to service delivery will continue its prominence and become even more important in serving elderly clients. Case management, with its emphasis on connecting clients with community resources, will probably be the major conduit for identifying gaps in service and, at times, bring public attention to many issues for resolution (e.g., advocacy-in-action). Such community resources as hospices, long-term care facilities and home care services are a few of the services likely to be brought to public attention in this regard. Some issues likely to be highlighted are the need to deplete economic resources before obtaining public services, the high costs of insurance despite the availability of Medicare and the lack of public support (in both Canada and the U.S.) for needed programmes.

It seems clear that the nature of social work practice, i.e., what we do, will be affected greatly by the seven trends previously identified. However, another variable influencing social work practice is the agencies themselves, and each author in Section II of this text projects how their social work role may potentially develop over the years from their own organizational setting and perspective.

Probably one of the more obvious and important reasons why social work practice will be different with this clientele has to do with the clients themselves. They will be very different indeed. The population we are talking about is today in the age range of 35 to 65. As a group, they are likely to have more education, more resources, more mobility, live longer and have the characteristics previously mentioned. As equally important, they are likely to have been part of the 60s generation, with its social consciousness, be more technically and technologically competent and may have been part of the individual human growth and development effort. They will have been a part of the computer age, an age where rapid technologic advances replaced the factories and foundries of the Industrial Revolution hangover. In short, many more will be used to working with their minds rather than their hands.

This scenario suggests that much of today's social work practice and the activities of the organizations in which they work *must* change if they expect to meaningfully serve tomorrow's clients. Future activities must be challenging, have relevancy to their clients' lifestyles, be needs appropriate to a computer-age population and reflect the age-specific and unique needs of these different older adults. It seems safe to assume that senior citizen day care centres, with such activities as ceramics, quilting, knitting, arts and crafts and the like, will have to change more than they imagine, if they expect to attract and service future clients.

III. The Environmental Context

The environmental context shaped by these trends is likely to produce at least four powerful outcomes: 1) political clashes between older and younger adults; 2) increased hostility among the serviced population and their families; 3) problems associated with accessing medical and health technology; and, 4) complex ethical decision-making.

Future older adults will inevitably become more politically active, in part to protect their economic resources as well as to lobby for equitable public policies and much needed services. Their competition is likely to come from fewer younger workers supporting Social Security, for example, with the majority of these younger workers expected to be minorities. A sizeable portion of the older adults will also have private pensions, Individual Retirement Accounts (IRAs), etc., which they will fight to protect through changes in public policies. It is quite possible that medical, health and social services for chronic illness will be financially underwritten by insurers in the U.S.A. due to shifts in public attitudes and policies.

Increased hostility may be one consequence of future older adults who require service but find these services inadequate. In this regard, they may not connect the current national fiscal policies, which they supported, with the inadequate provision of services. In addition, they may be forced to participate in an unfamiliar system of care on a long-term basis for the first time in their lives. While one cannot predict with certainty how each client will respond, there is much evidence to support that these future clients will behave much differently than their predecessors.

North American society is already witnessing a raft of ethical decisions, which are coming to the public's attention, that are complex. Such decisions are likely to continue and will be difficult to make and/or understand. For instance, euthanasia, cryogenics, genetic splicing and transplants are just some of the problems that the society in general will face for which decisions regarding the allocation of resources will be very difficult to make.

Likewise, it is our contention that the accessibility of available technology will continue to plague public policy and negatively affect care of many elderly. Unless major changes are made, the financial means to pay or live close to major medical and health centres will determine who receives the benefits of a highly technological and exclusive system. People lacking these resources may find themselves receiving a poorer quality of services or no services at all.

This scenario regarding the environmental context of social work practice largely depends on the current situation continuing to endure without major changes. The whole picture would change radically in America should universal health insurance become public policy, as it is in Canada. In that case, social work practice would adjust accordingly in order to be an integral part of a comprehensive service system. While difficult to accurately predict each situation, it is important to remember the fundamental point made in this chapter and throughout this text — *social work practice with the older adults will be very different in the future as a result of current trends and public policies.*

IV. Concluding Remarks

The future practice of social work with older adults will change significantly as a result of the interaction of the seven trends previously described. These trends will directly affect the actual practice of social work by making it more specialized, requiring greater knowledge and improved training, by understanding the various age-specific subgroups and their unique characteristics and needs, by identifying and developing needed services, and by emphasizing case management as a major service component.

These trends will significantly alter the environmental context within which social work is practiced. Public policy will be affected dramatically as a result of legislative clashes between numerous future older adults and fewer, mostly minority, younger working persons. Many more people and their families are likely to enter the care system with and on behalf of older adults for the first time and remain in it due to chronic illness or loss of economic resources.

Most important, social work practice will change because the client population it is likely to serve will be quite different. A rule of thumb would be to project that the characteristics of future clients are likely to reflect today's 35- to 60-year-old group, for these will be tomorrow's older adult clients. Of central concern to this issue is whether social work will react to these trends, as it has done too often in previous situations, or will it respond proactively and be ready for these future challenges? We hope the latter.

References

American Association of Retired Persons. (1989). *Perspectives in health promotion and aging*, 4(3), Washington, D.C.

American Association of Retired Persons. (1990). *Perspectives in health promotion and aging*, 5(2), Washington, D.C.

Bloom, M. (1985). *Life span development* (2nd ed.). New York: Macmillan Publishing Company.

Dobelstein, A. W. and Johnson, A. B. (1985). *Serving older adults: Policy, programs and professional activities.* Englewood Cliffs, N.J.: Prentice-Hall Inc.

Edinberg, M. A. (1985). *Mental health practice with the elderly.* Englewood Cliffs, N.J.: Prentice-Hall Inc.

Feit, M. D. and Tate, N. P. (1986). Health and mental health issues in preretirement programs. *Employee Assistance Quarterly*, 1(3), 49-56.

Fitch, V. L. and Slivinske, L. R. (1989). Situational perceptions of control in the aged. In P. S. Fry (ed.), *Psychological perspectives of helplessness and control in the elderly* (Chapter 6). North-Holland: Elsevier Science Publishers.

Gelfand, D. E. (1982). *Aging: The ethnic factor.* Boston, M.A.: Little, Brown and Company.

Lowy, L. (1979). *Social work with the aging.* New York: Longman.

Myers, J. E. (1989). *Adult children and aging parents.* Dubuque, I.A.: Kendall/ Hunt Publishing Company.

Stone, R. (1985). *The feminization of poverty among the elderly.* Washington, D.C.: U. S. Department of Health and Human Services.

Watson, W. H., McGhee, Jr., N. and Reed, W. (1986-87). Health policy and the black aged. *The Urban League Review*, 10(2), 63-71.

Chapter 2

What's Unique About Social Work Practice with the Elderly?

Michael J. Holosko, Ph.D.
D. Ann Holosko, M.S.W.

*T**his chapter attempts to answer the question — what is unique about social work practice with the elderly? It describes general practice issues related to this uniqueness from the standpoint of: 1) attitudes toward the elderly; 2) practice modifications; and, 3) educational issues. The main contention put forward is that the profession has made great strides in this area but has a long way to go in 'seeking the difference that makes the difference.'*

I. Introduction

Any attempt to answer the question posed in the title is by its very nature limited because, foremost, it is impossible to delineate all of the unique attributes of such social work practice and/or the elderly. Common sense tells us that the elderly are unique and the literature acknowledges the fact that the profession has evolved to accepting the position that practice with the elderly is unique. Indeed, the chapters in this text serve as testimony to the fact that social work practice with the elderly is decidedly unique and requires description and specification. However, the profession has had a long history of identity-anxiety about its uniqueness (Lubove, 1973). William James' (1906) classic essay on pragmatism makes the point more succinctly as: "seeking the difference that makes the difference." Since *Part II* of this text describes specific practice issues about the elderly (in attempting to 'seek the difference'), this chapter will present some of the general social work practice issues that transcend these various settings.

Since the inception of social work practice (generally thought to be around the 16th century with the advent of the Elizabethan Poor Laws in England), the profession has generally treated and cared for the elderly in the same way that society at large has. The socio-political structures and governments of the Western world have generally assumed that the elderly were 'taken care of' through the major institutions and mechanisms of social welfare, e.g., the church, state, health care system, social and family agencies, social policies and programmes, etc. After all, how could a society (North America), which evolved a social welfare system founded on the principles of Judeo-Christian ideology, not consider the elderly to be as important as say for example, children, families, the sick, the poor, the destitute or the needy? Well, we have failed miserably in providing minimally adequate care for the elderly, however one examines this issue.

The demographic realities of better health, nutrition and lifestyle coupled with no world wars, plus having the economic means and social supports to endure, has caused an accelerated population growth and increased longevity among the elderly, making them the fastest growing cohort in our society in the past 30 years. Neither society at large or the institutions of care have been able to keep up with their needs. For example, as indicated by Hardina and Holosko (1990), with the exceptions of old age security benefits for the elderly (in North America), which arose after they served their country in at least one world war, the elderly has not been deemed as a distinct group for social policy consideration until about 1955. This is about the same time that their visibility in numbers became more viable to both politicians and policy-makers. Since then, a proliferation of social policies emerged to provide programmes and services to this group in society (Klemmack and Roff, 1981).

Concurrently, social work practitioners anxious to serve their clients when their needs arose adapted the institutions of care, their policies and programmes as well as their interventions, to the elderly in a reactive (rather than proactive) fashion, based almost exclusively on the medical model with its orientation on symptomology of acute illness. Thus, from an interorganizational perspective, for example, when elderly clients showed up with greater frequency in general hospitals in the late 50s and early 60s, the nursing home movement was launched. In turn, when nursing homes could not adequately care for the frail elderly (who were living longer than ever), chronic care institutions (or facilities within institutions) arose in the 1970s. When these became too expensive to operate, there was a renewed emphasis on community-based caregivers and day care programmes in the early 1980s. Thus, the various programmes, policies and services were always one step behind the needs of the elderly, were medically determined and were always incremental or short-term in nature.

In this regard, a review of the literature on social work practice with the elderly reveals that, up until 1970, very little clinical, theoretical or empirical attention was devoted to practice issues with this group. And it was about this same time that the profession gave up trying to impose their traditional practice assumptions on the elderly and began modifying them accordingly to suit their differential needs. Indications of specialized education and training to further meet the needs of the elderly generally paralleled this knee-jerk reaction by the profession. It was really not until about 1980 that the profession fully acknowledged the extent and nature of their specialized needs. Louis Lowy (1987) a respected social work author in this field noted that:

> Although still debated to what extent specialized geriatric or gerontological expertise for working with older people is required, there is increasing consensus that people in their later years have needs and problems that are associated with particular biological, physiological, psychological, social or cultural conditions which are correlated with aging processes or with an interface of personal and social situations, such as retirement, widowhood, or status and role deprivations. As health and social care providers frequently find it hard to come to terms with

their own aging, they must learn to cope better with these feelings in order to be effective in their professional roles. (p. 40)

As indicated in this quotation, social workers have made considerable changes in understanding how to care for the elderly. The primary reasons for this have been attributed to their acquiring a better understanding of the elderly and their needs, adapting and modifying their interventive repertoires to suit these needs and formalizing their education and training. In short, the profession has been actively engaged in 'seeking the difference that makes the difference.' These general practice issues will be discussed according to: 1) attitudes toward the elderly; 2) practice modifications; and, 3) educational issues.

II. Attitudes Toward the Elderly

Two areas in which social work practitioners have changed their attitudes toward the elderly are: 1) accepting that the elderly have unique needs, and, 2) dispelling negative myths and stereotypes.

The clinical literature on the elderly has clearly indicated that old age is a stage-specific part of the life-cycle complete with diverse biological, physical, emotional and psychological changes within it. In order to understand the aetiology of any mental and physical disorder, therefore, a social work practitioner must consider fully: 1) the individual's health status, including her or his ability to cope; 2) the challenges and difficulties experienced with the stage the person is in; 3) the nature of the disorder itself — as some, such as neurosis, insomnia, broken hips, depression, somatic complaints, sexuality, cancer, dementia, circulatory problems, Alzheimer's disease, alcoholism, stress reactions, etc., have been shown to be highly clinically unique to the elderly; 4) their prognosis for recuperation and rehabilitation; 5) the social, familial and financial supports available; 6) their consequences and sequelae; and, 7) the capacity for self-determinism, independence and autonomy. As one might assume, gerontological social work practitioners have had to learn much about medicine, pharmacy, physiology and biology in addition to changing their attitudes toward how certain problems are unique to the elderly. Acknowledging their uniqueness has helped immeasurably in facilitating such an attitude change.

The other area of attitudinal change that came about within the profession has to do with dispelling societal myths about the elderly, which have trickled down to front-line practitioners. Whether we wish to admit it or not, North American society has generally promoted a negative attitude toward the elderly, which has permeated caregivers for centuries. Such stereotypes are largely perpetuated by: 1) social institutions, which are usually age-segregated e.g., schools, hospitals, mental health centres, alcohol treatment centres, the United States social welfare system, etc.; 2) political-legal structures, which formulate laws that preclude the elderly from participation in avenues of society, e.g., mandatory retirement laws; and, 3) economic institutions, which promote youthful employees, e.g., commercial and financial institutions, the service, fashion and entertainment industries, etc.; and, all of these stereotypes have been fuelled by a sometimes merciless media industry. For example, a recent article in *Rolling Stone* magazine written by P. J. O'Rourke (April 19, 1990), opened by stating the following title and text: "Octogenarians at the Gate — Old people have more money and power these days, and what's worse, they're living a lot longer. The geezers are everywhere — arteriosclerosing around and filling us with duffer dread" (p. 42).

The extent to which such stereotypes have affected practitioners may be understood by exploring a series of myths, which have contributed to such 'ageism,' or the prejudices and stereotypes that are applied to older people solely on the basis of their age (Butler, 1969). R. Greene (1986) has listed some of these major myths and facts as follows:

Myth: Being 'old' is merely a matter of chronological age.
Fact: Aging refers to the processes of change in individuals that occur after maturity. Not all aspects of the human organism show the same age-related changes as the person advances in chronological age. Therefore, it is well to distinguish three aspects of aging: biological age, referring to organic changes and life expectancy; psychological age, referring to adaptive capacities; and sociocultural age, referring to social roles and expectations of the group. These are interrelated and together comprise an individual's functional age (Birren and Sloane, 1980, p.4).

Myth: Older people talk about the good old days because they are garrulous or 'senile.'

Fact: The introspective qualities of older people are a result of a naturally occurring return to past experiences, reassessing them in an attempt to resolve and integrate them. This provides the opportunity for the ego to reorganize these events and come to terms with past conflicts and relationships. The process of reminiscing can occur at any age, particularly at times of transition. However, this takes place more frequently in some elderly who are not as actively involved in the present and may not be able to draw upon interesting current experiences. The tendency to reminisce also increases as the older person begins to deal with his or her own mortality. This process can be tapped as a therapeutic tool in life review (Butler, 1963).

Myth: Older people do not develop or grow.

Fact: Lifespan theorists reject the view that growth ends with adulthood. They point out that, while there may be growth limits for attributes such as height, other qualities such as creativity and abstract reasoning do not fit this model. In this context, growth refers to differentiation, increased complexity, and greater organization, and can occur at every age (Schell and Hall, 1979).

Myth: Older people cannot learn new roles, skills or competencies.

Fact: Unfortunately, mature individuals are usually thought of as having reached a stage when no further socialization takes place. However, research on aging and the life-cycle indicates that, as people mature, they must "continually learn to play new or altered roles and to relinquish old ones" (Riley et al., 1969). It is now understood that at every stage of life the individual must master certain developmental tasks requiring new skills and competencies.

Myth: Older people are not suitable candidates for insight therapy.

Fact: Because of their introspective qualities, capacity for growth, and lifelong coping styles, many elderly clients have great adaptational skills to draw upon in a crisis. Butler (1968) suggests that "the possibility for introspective change may be greater in old age than at any period in life" (p. 237).

Myth: Older people are alienated from their families.

Fact: The family continues to be the primary source of social support in old age. While most Americans do not live in three- or four-generation households, the family continues to be the primary caregiver for the frail and impaired elderly. Research affirms that there is frequent contact between the elderly and their families, particularly at times of illness. "Exchange of services and regular visits are common among old people and their children whether or not they live under a single roof" (Shanas, 1979).

Myth: Older people are cared for by their families but do not give anything in return.

Fact: Survey data suggest there is a high degree of interdependence between generations in today's families. There is generally ongoing contact between adult children and their parents in the form of shared social activities and the mutual exchange of material and emotional support (Bengston and Treas, 1980).

Myth: When older people experience a biopsychosocial crisis, they are best helped without the involvement of the family.

Fact: A family system is composed of interrelated members who constitute a group. A change in the life of one of the members brings about change throughout the system. Therefore, a biopsychosocial crisis in one of the members can be expected to result in change affecting everyone in the family system. An awareness of this phenomenon can enhance casework services to the aged and their families. (Greene, 1986)

In addition to the profession largely being responsible for confronting and shattering these myths (perceived of as barriers to service delivery), the literature points out that social workers have: 1) worked creatively within existing institutions and structures of care (sometimes stretching their boundaries) to provide for the differential needs of the elderly; 2) consistently promoted the uniqueness of the elderly; 3) attempted to fulfil their rights for self-determinism and autonomy; and, 4) as will be discussed, have modified many of their practice interventions to suit the needs of their clients. Such initiatives have taken time, but all of them have been driven by a pervasive positive attitude toward the elderly on behalf of the profession. As one might assume, all of these types of activities have assisted in socializing not just social work but other helping professions and the general public toward creating more favourable attitudes toward caring and helping the elderly.

III. Practice Modifications

It wasn't until about the 1960s that social work practitioners gave up trying to fit the elderly into their existing practice ideologies and began to modify their assumptions and frameworks to fit the unique needs of the elderly. Two areas where such modifications took place were assessments and interventions.

A. Assessments

Other helping professions (e.g., medicine, psychiatry, psychology, nursing, etc.,) have realized the importance of modifying their assumptions regarding how to assess elderly clients, and as a result have adapted their assessment protocols and technologies accordingly. Generally, such adaptations have been more comprehensive and holistic in nature, have included a biological and health status appraisal, and have included considerations for more continuity of care, rather than being acutely episodic in nature. For instance, medical doctors working in the field of geriatrics and psychogeriatrics have acknowledged the necessity for taking more comprehensive biopsychosocial histories (Shulman, 1984), more age trend and family support assessments (Freedman, Bucci and Elkowitz, 1982), and the need for determining functional status, quality of life and health status (Rubenstein et al., 1989). Functional status in this regard includes physical, mental and social functioning in daily life; quality of life includes socioeconomic or environmental factors (financial security, availability of food, quality of housing); and health status includes physical, mental and social health.

As well as adapting their actual test items for conducting assessments, professionals working in this field have critiqued and adapted a number of standardized measures for this purpose and have also broadened the role that the interviewer (or assessor) must play in conducting them. For instance, Volans and Levy (1982) found major flaws with the Picture Matching Test when administered to elderly psychiatric patients calling for its revision. Thus, they concluded that there was no evidence to suggest that the method of controlling for practice effects, as suggested by the test's distributors, would be effective. Similarly, Granick (1983) presents a case for the importance of psychological assessments of the elderly be expanded to assist in the diagnosis of psychiatric and neurological disturbances, psychosomatic disorders, circulatory diseases, diabetes, chronic pain, sexual dysfunctions and gastrointestinal problems. He suggests that the outlook for the future of including such content in the standard psychologic assessments is highly probable.

Since there is an entire chapter in this text devoted to conducting social work assessments toward the elderly (see Chapter 3), making a case for their uniqueness here seems redundant. Suffice to say that the issues previously dealt with by other helping professionals (noted earlier) have been confronted by social work practitioners working in this field. For instance, issues such as including biosocial histories; modifying protocols, assessment tools; and, modifying the role of the assessor have been used with much success by social workers. A review of literature in this area suggests that such techniques have been further expanded by social workers to include: 1) developing a personal assessment style conducive to elderly clients e.g., using two to three sessions rather than one for conducting an assessment; 2) using an assessment framework that extends beyond psychopathology or a straight problem-solving approach e.g., individual capacity assessments (finances, housing, etc.), personality assessments, medication appraisals, family and/or social support network assessments, biographical or ecological considerations, etc.; 3) accepting the principle of multiple symptomology among the elderly in the assessment process, e.g., one symptom interacts with a subsystem, which in turn influences another symptom and subsystem; 4) using significant others directly in the assessment process e.g., family, friends, physicians, etc., to obtain a more complete and accurate appraisal; 5) reiterating the importance of social work principles such as self-determinism and client autonomy in the assessment process; and, 6) adapting assessment procedures in ways to suit the variety of health and human service organizations that care for the elderly. Indeed, the profession has modified how they conduct assessments with the elderly based on their uniqueness and needs.

B. Interventions

Social workers, like other helping professionals working in this field, have developed practice approaches to intervention based on the unique needs of the elderly whether focusing on mental health needs, individual needs, family needs, institutional needs, case management needs or the elderly in general (Lowy, 1979). In examining the actual content of such treatment, Tobin and Gustafson (1987) posed the question — what do we [social workers] do differently with elderly clients? They then surveyed 541 subscribers to the *Journal of Gerontological Social Work* and reported that the five unique intervention activities were:

1) **Touching**	— which reflected a worker's active approach to the elderly's needs;
2) **Activities**	— which were perceived to be greater in frequency including providing more concrete assistance, more reaching out to families and more talking by the worker in sessions;
3) **Reminiscence**	— or the use of the past which helps clients to develop ego strength (by noting past coping) and adaptation capabilities, as well as helping to recapture and reaffirm the current self;
4) **Transference**	— referring projections onto the worker of meaning, wishes and thoughts that are redirected from other persons; and,
5) **Countertransference**	— or specific concerns evoked by the worker to the client (e.g., dependency, helplessness, death, concerns with aging parents, etc.) (pp. 116-119).

These authors concluded here and in a related publication (Smith, Tobin and Gustafson, 1987), that despite worker differences, within group differences of the elderly, the settings in which they were located or percentage of time spent with them, these interventions were the differences between how social workers practiced with the elderly rather than younger clients. Based on our experiences in working in this field, as well as through a series of in-depth interviews with other gerontological workers and a review of the literature in this regard, we believe these to have empirical and clinical justification.

All of these intervention modifications, therefore, have profound implications for a growing role being expected by social workers working in this field. It is inevitable that the profession of social work will become more involved in the care for the elderly in a variety of community and institutional-based settings. The profession's hallmark trait of being malleable and adaptable to client's needs, which then shape its roles and responsibilities, will in our judgment be a plus in this regard.

IV. Educational Issues

Although the institutions of social welfare and health care are slow to change, educational institutions are slower. The training and education for social work practitioners that has come about on-site in gerontological institutions has generally been more significant than that offered in educational institutions. When one considers the extensive knowledge expectations of social workers practicing in this field (e.g., biological, physiological, psychological, sociological, life-cycle, etc.) this is not surprising (see Lowy, 1979, pp. 155-204 for a good example of this). As well, when considering the overall objectives of BSW and MSW programmes, the issue of how to successfully integrate gerontological content into the curriculae without overwhelming it is indeed a critical question (Schneider et al., 1984).

Since about 1980 onward, university-based social work degree granting programmes have taken the initiative in attempting to infuse gerontological content into their curriculae. Generally, such efforts have been more successful at the graduate level than undergraduate level, and have taken one of two avenues, either by developing speciality concentrations or by promoting such content in a more broad-based fashion across the entire curriculum.

As well, the use of speciality field practica, research projects, multi-disciplinary training, case vignettes and certificates have been instrumental in helping to educate and train professional social workers (MSWs or BSWs) in these settings (Schneider et al., 1984; Rathbone-McCuan and Hurwitz, 1988; Schneider and Nelson, 1984).

An area where social work educators have not progressed as much as possible in this regard has been in research, publication and speciality teaching. As one administrator of a Canadian school of social work remarked, however: "As a faculty begins to age or experience aging as an issue in their lives, more attention may be given [in the curriculum] to aging. . . when it takes on a less abstract dimension" (Rathbone-McCuan, 1988, p. 32). In an effort to bolster geriatric education programmes, Macfadyen (1989), who conducted an international study on the subject for the World Health Organization, offered the following suggestions:

1. Identification and training of key faculty to act as institutional stimuli for curriculum development.
2. Development of regional and/or national resource centres to strengthen multidisciplinary training, faculty development, continuing education and mid-career retraining.
3. Development of clearing houses on curricula and resources.
4. Stimulation of research efforts in the field of aging both to strengthen the knowledge base and increase the level of faculty awareness and interest. One approach is the provision of traineeships and fellowships for research.
5. Development of links between teaching institutions and community care facilities (p. 6).

He goes on to state that to fulfil the teaching and learning objectives that have been identified for care of the elderly, schools must develop teaching networks beyond the traditional institutions and teaching hospitals, which have conducted the bulk of clinical teaching so far. The processes of teaching must also allow maximum opportunity for active involvement and personal interaction of students with elderly people (pp. 7-8).

Of all the careers in gerontology, social work, without exception, provides the greatest variety of employment opportunities for working with the elderly. The profession, by its very nature, has an ethical responsibility to promote the dignity of all human beings, elderly or otherwise. Its training and educational facilities offer rich learning experiences for advancing knowledge and research in this field. As indicated previously, we have made considerable strides in educating professionally trained BSWs and MSWs to work in this unique field. We still have, however, a long way to go in helping professionals in 'seeking the difference that makes the difference.' The future in this regard is nothing less than promising.

V. Concluding Remarks

This chapter attempted to answer the question — what is unique about social work practice with the elderly? — by examining general practice issues related to: 1) attitudes toward the elderly; 2) practice modifications; and, 3) educational issues. The main contention put forward was that the profession is rapidly evolving in 'seeking the difference that makes the difference' in working in this field, however it still has a long way to go. The demographic reality that the elderly will constitute the largest minority group in North American society by the year 2050 has resounding implications for social work and other professions. To attempt to meet the challenges of caring for this group in society, this chapter has indicated that the profession has to continue to be creative, take initiative, advocate for change and adapt its attitudes, assumptions and interventions accordingly — as the unique needs of this group warrant such modification. Certainly, the time is now for social work to take proactive measures in enhancing its knowledge, values and skills related to care for the elderly.

References

Bengston, V. and Treas, J. (1980). The changing family context of mental health and aging. In J. E. Birren and R. B. Sloane (eds.), *Handbook of mental health and aging* (pp. 400-428). Englewood Cliffs, N.J.: Prentice-Hall.

Birren, J. E. and Sloane, R. B. (eds.). (1980). *Handbook of mental health and aging*. Englewood Cliffs, N.J.: Prentice-Hall.

Butler, R. N. (1963). The life review: An interpretation of reminiscence in the aged. *Psychiatry, 26*, 65-76.

Butler, R. N. (1969). Directions in psychiatric treatment of the elderly: Role of perspectives in the life cycle. *Gerontologist, 9*(2), 134-138.

Butler, R. N. (1968). Toward a psychiatry of the lifecycle: Implications of socio-psychologic studies of the aging process for the psychotherapeutic situation. In A. Simon and L. Epstein (eds.), *Aging in modern society* (pp. 233-248). Washington, D.C.: The American Psychiatric Association.

Freedman, N., Bucci, W. and Elkowitz, E. (1982, June). Depression in a family practice elderly population. *Journal of the American Geriatrics Society, 30*(6), 372-377.

Granick, S. (1983, December). Psychologic assessment technology for geriatric practice. *Journal of the American Geriatrics Society, 31*(12), 728-742.

Greene, R. (1986). *Social work with the aged and their families.* New York: Hawthorne, Aldine de Gruyer.

Hardina, D. and Holosko, M. (1990). Social policies which influence practice with the elderly. In M. Holosko and M. Feit (eds.), *Social work practice with the elderly.* Toronto: Canadian Scholars' Press Inc.

James, W. (1906). What pragmatism means. *Pragmatism and other essays.* New York: Washington Square Press, 22-28.

Klemmack, D. L. and Roff, L. L. (1981, December). Predicting general and comparative support for governments' providing benefits to older persons. *The Gerontologist, 21*(6), 592-599.

Lowy, L. (1979). *Social work with the aging.* New York: Harper and Row Publishers.

Lowy, L. (1987). Major issues of age-integrated versus age-segregated approaches to serving the elderly. *Journal of Gerontological Social Work, 10*(3-4), 37-47.

Lubove, R. (1973). *The professional altruist.* New York: Harvard University Press.

Macfadyen, D. (1989, March). *Training professionals in health care of the elderly.* Hamilton, Ontario: McMaster University Faculty Health Sciences.

O'Rourke, P. J. (1990, April). Octogenarians at the gate. *Rolling Stone,* 42-43.

Rathbone-McCuan, E. and Hurwitz, E. (1988). *Crossroads: A report on Canadian gerontological social work education trends.* Burlington, Vermont: University of Vermont — Canadian Studies Program.

Riley, M., Foner, B., Hess, B. and Toby, M. (1969). Socialization for the middle and later years. In D. A. Goslin (ed.), *Handbook of socialization, theory and research.* Chicago: Rand McNally College Publicating Co.

Rubenstein, L. V., Calkins, D., Greenfield, S. and Jette, A. (1989, June). Health status assessment for elderly patients: Report of the society of general internal medicine task force on health assessment. *Journal of the American Geriatrics Society, 37*(6), 562-569.

Schell, R. and Hall, E. (1979). *Developmental psychology today*. New York: Random House.

Schneider, R., Decker, T., Freeman, J. and Syran, C. (1984). *The integration of gerontology with social work educational curriculum*. CSWE Series in Gerontology. Washington, D.C.: Council on Social Work Education.

Schneider, R. and Nelson, G. M. (1984). *The current status of gerontology in graduate social work education*. CSWE Series in Gerontology. Washington, D.C.: Council on Social Work Education.

Shanas, E. (1979). The family as a social support system in old age. *The Gerontologist*, 19, 169-174.

Shulman, R. (1984, October). What should be taught in psychogeriatrics: A personal viewpoint. *Journal of the American Geriatrics Society*, 32(10), 758-761.

Smith, G., Tobin, S. and Gustafson, J. (1987, Spring). Perceptions of geriatric practice: The role of theoretical orientation, age and gender. *Clinical Gerontologist*, 6(3), 29-46.

Tobin, S. and Gustafson, J. (1987). What do we do differently with elderly clients? *Journal of Gerontological Social Work*, 10(3-4), 107-120.

Volans, P. and Levy, R. (1982, June). A re-evaluation of an automated tailored test of concept learning with elderly psychiatric patients. *British Journal of Clinical Psychology*, 21(2), 93-101.

Chapter 3

Conducting Psycho-social Assessments with the Elderly

Susan Watt, D.S.W., C.S.W.
Ahuva Soifer, M.S.W., C.S.W.

P *sycho-social assessments of elderly persons by social workers require
the full range of knowledge and skills used in the assessment of
any adult coupled with particular sensitivities to the biological,
cultural, social and psychological factors, which shape the lives of
the elderly. Particularly, social workers must recognize the purposes
to which the assessment may be used, which may lead to major
life changes for elderly persons. The importance of history, obtained
from the elderly person and collateral sources, is discussed. Two
case examples illustrate some of the challenges of obtaining and
interpreting information for such psycho-social assessments.*

In our changing Canadian demography, social workers are
increasingly being called upon to assess the ability of elderly persons
to function in their environments. There are several aspects of psycho-
social assessments of elderly persons that distinguish them from other
types of assessments.

It should be noted that the elderly are not a homogeneous group.
Some are physically well, some are frail, some are competent in all

spheres, and some cannot remember the names of their children. Each has an individual history of life experiences and relationships with a unique meaning and importance to him or her.

We (the authors) reject the notion of 'cookbook assessments,' which are popular in many disciplines. We believe that social work brings to human caring the unique perspective of individuals in their social environments. Unlike the researcher who seeks to discover the commonality among disparate individuals, patterns of behaviour, common perceptions, shared difficulties, etc., the social worker focuses on the individual's strengths, deficits and coping strategies in the unique environment. Thus, we depend upon the patterns established through the insights of practice wisdom and research to evaluate and predict outcomes in individual cases.

I. Implications of a Psycho-social Assessment

Assessments for the elderly, as for all other age groups, touch upon complex psychological and social factors and composites, relative to the individual in the context of social environment. For the elderly, there is additionally, a precarious, delicate balance of a number of biopsycho-social components. For instance, particular factors of and responses to time, relationships, of losses and of vulnerabilities, as well as entrenched attitudes and a history of experiences, make this balance particularly fragile. Therefore, a change in any one component is likely to result in a more profound effect upon the others and, in turn, upon the balance, than would be expected among the non-elderly. For example, a broken hip that results in temporary hospitalization is more disorienting, alarming and dependency producing in the elderly than would be the same condition in a non-elderly person and may even lead to symptoms of cognitive impairment and social dysfunction. These consequences, which are most often transient, may lead caregivers to arrange alternative care without including the elderly in the decision process.

Similarly, social changes such as the death of a spouse or changes in a living arrangement, may lead to a response (e.g., withdrawal, apprehension, depression, 'stubbornness,' etc.), which is considered disproportionate and dysfunctional by others. This response may also express itself in physical symptoms (e.g., loss of appetite, sleeplessness, chest pain, fatigue), which may then be interpreted as decrepitude.

Any involvement, therefore, which may imperil the balance, is fraught with potential disturbance for the elderly person. Psycho-social assessments are frequently used as a tool. Commonly, an assessment is related to a decision to make a major change in the environment of the elderly person. Rarely does the elderly person seek the assistance of the social worker. More often family members, health care professionals, facility management or other service providers instigate the assessment process. Although the assessment is often used by others as an end in itself (to determine entitlement or access), social workers see assessments as dynamic undertakings, the first part of a process that feeds back on itself as indicated in Figure 1.

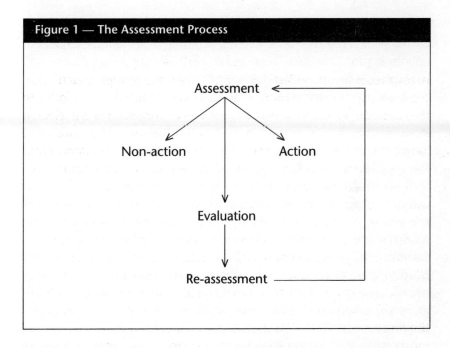

Figure 1 — The Assessment Process

II. How to Conduct a Psycho-social Assessment

Social work assessments of the elderly are always guided by the reason for the assessment and the context in which it is being undertaken.

Thus, both conducting the assessment and interpreting it requires specialized skills and knowledge on the part of the social worker. Particular attention needs to be paid to the following:
1. the purpose of the assessment;
2. the circumstances under which the assessment is done;
3. the capacities and skills of the elderly person and of caregivers;
4. cultural factors; and,
5. fears.

Each of these will be discussed accordingly.

A. Purpose of the Assessment

The most common reason for the referral of an elderly person to a social worker is to determine 'what should be done with her or him.' For instance, there is an external demand to develop, confirm or negate a plan that has been made for the care of an individual, most often at a time following significant functional or social loss.

Often the assessment is initiated by trusted others, with the purpose being concealed from the elderly person. Although the intent is usually viewed by such concerned persons as necessary and in the 'best interest' of the elderly person, the social worker must understand the investment, and suspicion about the outcome of the assessment not only of the elderly person but also on the part of these significant others. In this regard, some may wish to be relieved of their responsibilities, while others may view the assessment as an attempt to intrude on, or be critical of, family or institutional caregiving. For example, some children may believe that a psycho-social assessment is an evaluation of their concern for an aging relative, or hospital personnel may believe the same assessment is merely the first step in institutionalizing an elderly patient whose treatment hospital bed they want to free.

In part, both are correct in their perceptions, since one of the major reasons for an elderly person undergoing a psycho-social assessment is to determine his or her capacities to cope and to determine the supports that are required. Thus, the gate-keeping role of the social worker in conducting such assessments is important. It is often on the basis of such assessments that the elderly individual is admitted to institutional care or transferred from one level of care to another.

The purpose of the assessment is frequently misidentified as 'medical' (i.e., part of the prescribed treatment or consequences of a specific medical condition). Hence there is often an association of social work assessments with major medical disorders such as strokes, hip fractures, kidney failure or heart attacks. It would be a mistake to link the medical condition per se with the rationale for assessments. It is rather the impact of the illness on the life situation, on the ability of the individual and his or her environment to cope with the need for a new arrangement of interdependencies that inspires such assessments.

B. Circumstances of the Assessment

The circumstances under which the assessments of elderly individuals are conducted are important to understanding the type and meaning of the information that the social worker is able to obtain. Usually, the social worker who is attempting to assess the elderly individual will be a stranger to the client, arousing many concerns about 'talking to strangers,' telling family secrets and revealing the last vestige of privacy; one's secret thoughts, hopes and fears, left to the elderly.

Further, it is quite common in institutional settings to disrupt the individual by changing his or her locale for the purpose of the assessment. Well-intentioned relocation to an interviewing room or social work office may result in an individual appearing disoriented. Thus, the move removes the cues in the already strange environment by which the elderly person orients himself or herself and creates subtle barriers of turf and power.

To minimize the hurdles to conducting the assessment, the social worker needs to pay particular attention to the problems of personal comfort of the client, including seating comfort (e.g., well-padded chairs that may suit an agile adult will become a 'trap' for the elderly who are unable to get out of the chair), issue of language compatibility (including figurative speech related to era and gender as well as fluency) and hearing (e.g., although an individual may be able to hear you on a one-to-one basis, the background noises of a hospital, screened out by staff, give garbled auditory input when using a hearing aid).

Also of major importance in conducting such assessments is the significance of the presence, or absence, of caregivers and significant others. Reticence, fear of offending and 'allowing' others to answer are among the problems inhibiting an honest assessment.

Further, the elderly person may be suspicious about the goals of the assessment, sensing that the results of the assessment may have a profound, yet unspecified, impact on the rest of his or her life. Thus, they may be hesitant to initiate discussion about such issues, retreating instead into passive resistance, which may be misconstrued as cognitive and/or personality deficits.

C. Capacities and Skills of the Individual and of the Caregivers

Any psycho-social assessment of the elderly must pay particular attention to the capacities of the individual as well as to any limitations they may have. It is tempting to see only the limitations of the elderly and to give these issues inordinate prominence. To what degree are the activities of daily living (ADL) managed by the individual and with what type and amount of help? How does this management, by this person, differ from his or her previous standards, and why? — are a few of the more salient questions that should be considered in this regard.

Similarly, it is important to evaluate the skills and capacities of significant others in the life of the client as they relate to possible caring options. For instance, do others provide direct service to the client? What is the nature of the care provided? How able and willing are they to continue to provide these or additional services? How does the elderly dependent feel about the care that she or he is receiving and the possibilities for continuing assistance? Has there been, or will there be, a major transfer of assets, and under what conditions? Are there relationship issues being denied or protected by the emotionally, physically or financially vulnerable elderly person? Is there fear? Is there a realistic plan preferred by the person being assessed?

D. Cultural Factors

The concept of culture must include socioeconomic, geographic, gender, age, racial, religious, minority status and ethic components.

Such factors are of particular importance to the psycho-social assessment of the elderly and include communication and language, role relationships and the past and present expectations about aging, including the anticipated behaviour of others.

What needs to be remembered in this context is that both the worker and the elderly person are grounded in his or her own set of age-related cultural values and assumptions. The elderly, often very conscious of these age-generated differences, are often distrustful of the willingness and the ability of the social worker to understand them and, therefore, are frequently not very disclosing. In addition, the current generation of elderly has a view of social workers and their functions that is quite different (e.g., dispensers of charity, welfare workers and priers into privacy) from a professional social worker's view and practice.

Similar differences may be well disguised within family units, especially between the elderly person and some family caregivers, which may create additional tensions and ambivalence. In addition, there is frequently an overlay of cultural dissonance created by intermarriage and the accrual of extended family members deriving from distinctly different cultures. For instance, in a three-generational situation these interrelationships are particularly complicated 'sandwiched generations.'

Finally, in this regard, the predominant culture of the agency, in addition to the specific expectations of staff from a variety of cultural backgrounds, further complicates and colours what is expected from the behaviour of the elderly person and from the psycho-social assessment. Such differences may be extreme enough actually to precipitate the request for a psycho-social assessment. Certainly, these differences will influence the way in which the assessment is conducted, interpreted, conveyed and used.

E. Fears

Implicit for the elderly person undergoing a psycho-social assessment are a number of fears, often unvoiced, which threaten his or her well-being and may undermine the entire assessment process. Interrelated and interdependent of each other, these fears are truly psycho-social in nature because they represent emotional, practical, relationship and situational changes. These fears most often include the following:

a. displacement (the loss of decision-making and lifestyle as well as familiar setting);
b. self-doubt (questions raised about memory, cognition, capability and power);
c. social value conflicts (compromise of social role and image both as perceived by the individual and by others; the sense of being discardable);
d. abandonment (rejection by significant others, not being understood or appreciated, including by the social worker doing the assessment); and,
e. finality (ultimate helplessness and the real beginning to the end of self).

Within the process of the assessment, not only awareness of the worker of these fears is important, but also the opportunity to express and discuss their implications are crucial to developing a meaningful assessment. This is an area often shunned by social workers and others. It is difficult for the elderly person to discuss their fears, and this is often used as a reason by the social worker for not pursuing them. Excuses such as irrelevance, lack of time, concern about being hurtful are often used to cover for the potential distress in workers confronting these feelings in others and, significantly, in themselves.

III. Skills

The skills required to evaluate and interpret the information obtained for a psycho-social assessment of an elderly person are in accordance with the best traditions of social work practice and require competent social work practitioners. In short, this is not an arena for beginners. In addition to understanding a wide range of theoretical constructs concerning the biological, psychological and social aspects of adulthood and aging, the social worker must understand complex cultural and interpersonal structures that transcend several generations.

Although the skills required to undertake a psycho-social assessment of an elderly person are the same skills required in any adult assessment, the vulnerability and fragility of balances for the elderly demand highly competent social workers for obtaining, interpreting and conveying the information, which reflects an accurate and sensitive true picture of the life of these individuals. Particular awareness is required in the obtaining of information and deriving meaning from it, including the need to allocate sufficient time in shorter, more frequent contacts and to grasp the significance of discrepancies in language and communication issues (previously noted).

As well, special sensitivity is needed to explore areas that the elderly often view as sacrosanct (e.g., financial disclosures, family problems, etc.). Elderly persons often believe that problem solving is a matter of honour, something one does on one's own; and the concept of asking strangers for help is viewed as an abrogation of responsibility by many. Similarly, the elderly commonly view professionals as possessing authoritative knowledge — 'the truth' — and thus may feel obligated to follow the 'prescription' even if the options presented are not viewed as necessary or desirable. Self-determination, a cherished social work value, can easily be set aside in such situations.

Many of the elderly who are assessed by social workers have moved, as a result of physical, psychological and social losses, toward increased dependency upon other family members and formal caregivers. Thus, a central issue in any psycho-social assessment becomes at what point in the dependence and independence spectrum the individual finds himself or herself at that particular time and how he or she perceives the exchanges involved in caregiving and getting. For example, the very presence (hovering, answering for, being 'betrayed' or offended) or absence of family members (anxiety, lack of confidence) may change the whole tone, course or even content of an assessment.

The complexity of relationship histories, which are remembered in idiosyncratic ways by the elderly persons and significant others in their lives, produces a potential situation in which the taking of histories is neither straightforward or subject to objective confirmation. It is how that history is remembered, rather than any objective 'fact' that is critical to it, that becomes the issue. Often, there are mutually agreed to or unilateral 'protection' of one or the other of these issues that may distort facts. Thus, the inexperienced social worker is often led by conflicting stories to conclude degrees of memory loss and incompetence on the part of the elderly person when, in fact, it may be evidence of the complexity of perception and the meaning attached for different individuals about the same event. Sorting through these differences and drawing carefully considered professional conclusions is indeed an advanced professional skill.

Conveying the results of psycho-social assessments of the elderly is often more complex than it is for other adults. There is a sometimes overwhelming temptation to take sides, to advocate for, to wish to protect and to oversimplify a lengthy history of experiences and relationships. In such situations, there is a need for skill in succinct reporting of significant conclusions that can, and will, be read and understood within the framework of the host setting and the context of the elderly person's life situation.

It is important to note that much of the data received by the social worker will not be transmitted to others, but is used to form the basis of the professional assessment. Further, it should be remembered that the transmission of raw, descriptive data, out of context, is potentially more harmful than useful. Sharp analytic conclusions, briefly documented, are essential in this regard.

In summary, while recognizing the highly refined skills consonant with all social work practice, psycho-social assessments of the elderly demand additional knowledge, sensitivity and methodology. The fragility of the balance of biological, psychological and social factors for the elderly is compounded by the fact that such assessments are usually instigated by others and are perceived as leading to major change and loss of self-determination. Differences in the meaning of time, and intergenerational differences in values, expectations and communications, as well as the lack of understanding or acceptance (by host agencies and involved others) of essential social work values and criteria for making an assessment further complicate the issue. The requirements of a well-trained and highly skilled social worker to conduct such assessments are essential if the profession is to grow and develop in this area.

IV. Role

In a situation where the particular expertise and skills of social work are so clearly essential, the actual roles and responsibilities filled by trained social workers vary greatly from setting to setting. The involvement of a social worker in the process of psycho-social assessments of the elderly depends on several factors: 1) whether the task itself and/or the position of the social worker is community or agency-based; 2) whether it is part of an ongoing job description (e.g., intake, discharge planning) or is an occasional part of other expectations; and, 3) on the status accorded social work in the specific setting, as well as the agenda (official and covert) of those requesting the assessment. Depending on the mandate of the host agency, the assessment process may limit the social worker to:

1. conducting only an assigned part of the assessment, as part of a team, within prescribed criteria, as a delegated assistant to another professional (e.g., psychiatrist, admissions officer, head nurse) or one aspect (e.g., the family, living conditions);
2. a limited time frame for the whole process;
3. reporting within a prescribed format including a checklist, and/ or lack of interest in diagnostic or even any written report;
4. pro forma performance, with predetermined conclusions, to suit a family or interested agency, with resistance to advocacy or differing recommendations; and,
5. no allowance for follow-up, with the elderly person, family, and/or involved agencies.

Most requests for assessments come to social workers as a response to:

1. concern about functioning of the elderly person, which has been judged to be inadequate or poor, and concern for the future of the elderly person in his or her present situation — based on 'observation,' complaints and the value system of the observer who sometimes represents family (or some part of it, not always in agreement with the others), or by a professional, or a 'neighbourhood;' and a referral is made to a professional or agency with the expectation that a change in situation (e.g., removal to a more protected setting) will be made — preferably quickly.
2. concern for caregivers — based on 'observation, complaints and/or suppositions about 'what is best for everybody' or 'what is best for the caregivers;' requests made by 'other family member' often not the primary caregiver; professional care providing 'visitor' (e.g., public health nurse) or a social work

agency working with all or part of the family; and a referral is made to a professional (e.g., physician) or to an agency expected to admit the elderly person for relief of the family (e.g., a home).

3. as part of a discharge process — based on institutional priorities and needs as perceived by identified personnel whose observations and training may depend upon disciplines foreign to social work's view of assessment; or by family members who may or may not be aware of relationship, responsibility and respite issues; and a referral is made to an institution/agency with request for placement/service — preferably quickly (and often directly from hospital).

4. as part of admissions process (including transfer) — based on decisions usually by family members and/or institution staff often with the approval of a physician and/or other professional care providers; the information on the formal application is often suspect (i.e., 'fudged' to ensure acceptability of elderly person); often 'networking' (in all its forms) is used to jump queues or obtain preferred accommodation. Thus, a referral is made directly or by a 'brokering agency' (e.g., placement and co-ordination services); a re-assessment is often made by the accepting agency.

5. to establish competency for legal and financial purposes — based on request, usually by family members, or by an interested professional (e.g., physician, lawyer, hospital administrator); often controversial; application often suspect. Then a psycho-social assessment is occasionally made by a lawyer or based on uninvestigated appraisal by other personnel (e.g., appraisal by a lawyer to determine if someone is competent to sign a power of attorney or to make out a will or appraisal by a nurse of a patient's competency to give medical consent).

6. to remove nuisance and responsibility — based on complaints or concerns of neighbours; and a referral is usually to police, church or visiting professional (e.g., public health nurse) with expectation of quick resolution.

7. Finally, to assess for a course of treatment and/or adjustments in lifestyle — based on concern for changing functional ability or life situation by individuals; and a referral is made to a specialized clinic (e.g., gerontological assessment clinic).

V. Advanced Psycho-social Assessments

Particular assessment difficulties arise in circumstances that may be significantly more fraught for the elderly than for other adult populations. Ironically, many of these involve what appear to be maladaptations to problems or dysfunctions but are actually ways to maintain an individual's homeostasis, relationships and/or abilities to function.

Common examples include individuals who live alone in disreputable, unhygienic or dangerous areas, such as abandoned buildings, unserviced apartments or even outdoors. Elderly persons who talk aloud to themselves or even to 'unseen others' may not be hallucinating but rather merely externalizing the dialogues most people participate in internally or have aloud only in private situations such as driving a car.

Further, in this regard, marriage and companionships that may appear bizarre, or even destructive, to others may be the product of the well-worn habits and patterns that serve the most important needs of the partners. Often a sense of propriety or a desire to protect a relationship with a spouse, with a child or other caregiver or with a 'buddy,' are such that the elderly person denies truths, concocts or colludes in fictions or purposefully obfuscates. Perceived danger of retribution (even elder abuse), pride, shame, guilt or a desire to deny all may inform what is reported by the elderly person, family members or other caregivers. Professionals who wish to avoid entanglement or responsibility may participate in hiding or changing such important truths to these elderly clients.

Even in cases of persevering and confabulation, the skilled social worker needs to assess the significance of the uses to which these are put and weigh their part of the total biological-psychological-social context. A vital part of every assessment is consideration of the costs as well as the gains and losses to the elderly of removal or change of those components that comprise their present lifestyle, given their own attachment to them. When such components appear to be linked to the elderly person in a pathological way, it will also require that an experienced clinician make a well-reasoned judgment about the relative costs of intervention. In these situations, the risk of harm is at least as great as the possibility of benefit.

In addition to the acquisition (and practice) of the complex skills required, there are general, realistic and political issues for the social worker who wishes to engage in legitimate, thorough psycho-social assessments of the elderly. One challenge is to establish the significance of the complexities of psycho-social assessments and move toward changes in understanding and use of the assessment on the part of those with access to them.

Thus, social workers should push for changes in role definitions for social work, including specialized training, authority, status, adequate time and follow-up allotments. Always, the social worker should insist that attempts be made for prior involvement of the elderly person, including open discussion of risks, choices and consequences. Social workers should be willing to risk the support of social work principles, seeing the elderly person as a client even when this concept is not understood or supported by referring agencies or persons. Finally, social workers should advocate for changes in agencies and community services serving the elderly and in their eligibility criteria. They should also participate in creating appropriate policies and innovative community facilities and services, as desired and required by the elderly and their caregivers.

VI. Case Examples

Case #1

An elderly woman is admitted to hospital following a stroke. She has been left with a functionally useless left arm and some difficulty in locating objects in space. At times, she appears to be confused about the time of day and where she is. A social worker is called in to determine where she should go following hospitalization. Prior to her stroke the lady lived alone in an apartment, which she had shared with her husband of 40 years. He had died suddenly six months before her stroke. Her family had wanted her to leave the apartment at the time of her husband's death fearing for her safety and her ability to manage on her own. The physician was concerned that the patient's time in acute care was coming to an end since nothing more could be done for her. The nurses, who had become quite fond of the patient, worried about her being alone and about what they viewed as her confusion. The patient wanted to go home to her apartment and appeared not to understand the concerns of the staff or her family: "I've done all right until now and I'll manage just fine."

Case Comments

In this instance, the social worker is required to develop an understanding of this individual in her social context including the concerns of the significant others in her life. The views of family members, health care professionals and alternative care providers cannot be ignored. They form part of the environment in which the elderly must function.

Social workers employed in settings providing care for the elderly are engaged in assessing individuals to establish appropriate levels of care and of service provision. For example, social work assessment may play a role in determining intervention programmes geared toward improving functioning such as re-establishing ADL skills. Similarly, community-based programmes such as Home Care rely on social work assessments in establishing complex in-home care programmes. In such cases, the assessment of the environment of the individuals, especially the human environment of the home, will determine not only the suitability of home as the place of care but also the degree to which the home environment can tolerate the intrusive nature of support services that provide direct care.

Generally, social work assessments are called for when the person-in-environment nexus is seen to be either very complex or problematic in the provision of service, which is believed by someone — the client, the family, or any one of a myriad of care providers — as impinging upon, impeding or preventing the otherwise desired plan of care.

Case #2

Mr. and Mrs. M have lived on the fifth floor of a high-rise, subsidized, senior housing development for ten years. Mrs. M, a petit woman, speaks no English; though she smiles and nods to neighbours as a greeting she never invites anyone in nor has visited anyone in the apartment. Mr. M, a tall, heavy man with a marked limp and awkward gait, speaks a simple, often crude English, and is often loud, argumentative and, when drunk, belligerent.

Their country of origin is not known, and the Ms have no visitors. Rumour, passed along among neighbours is that Mr. M used to work at heavy labour but was badly injured on the job and spent over a year in hospitals and in rehabilitation and has lived, for the past 20 years (he is thought to be 70) on disability and old-age pension. It is also rumoured that there was a daughter who married, moved away and died in childbirth.

The superintendent of the building reports that Mr. M has always been angry, bitter and verbally abusive but that Mrs. M, when she was with him, could quiet him with a touch or a few soft spoken words. They always looked immaculately groomed and formally dressed. Lately, however, the neighbours have noted that Mrs. M hardly goes out, and when she does there are spots on her dress, clothing colours do not match and she seems to stumble. Some neighbours have mentioned to each other that they think she drinks now, too — others wonder whether she is loosing vision.

Recently, the neighbours have reported what sounds like loud arguments in a foreign language, occasional weeping and some loud thuds coming from the M's apartment. Unpleasant smells have also been reported on the floor, seeming to emanate from the M's apartment. Some neighbours say that Mr. M's drinking has become more frequent than the former regular, monthly binges.

The neighbours held a meeting of tenants without inviting the Ms to discuss them. Some expressed anger and irritation at the Ms. Others expressed concern for Mrs. M's safety and for the possibility of fire threatening them all. Others felt that for the sake of everybody, 'the matter' should be looked into. By unanimous vote a call alerting the police was made.

On the basis of the formal complaint of disturbing the peace, two police officers demanded admission to the M's apartment. They issued a warning and, despite Mr. M's rage, made a referral to Home Care.

Case Comments

The social worker, to make a valid assessment, must acquire basic information about the language, country of origin and some of the values/customs at the time of Mr. and Mrs. M's youth. Access to the Ms must be made gradually and with their permission if at all possible, especially to counteract the effects of the neighbours' and police intrusions. Help from a compatriot, a public health nurse or someone who is involved with the disability benefits should be used, if possible, and notice of intended visits (repeated patiently) should always be given.

It is essential, once contact has been permitted, that the assessment include the nature and nuances of the marital relationship and the investment each has in it. Further, questions about health and safety need to be explored, and the kind of assistance the Ms might be willing to accept (e.g., doctor, nurse, tests, surgery, medication, clinics, pamphlets, etc.) offered, leaving the door open for change.

Assessment should be made with both — and if possible separately with each partner — of their perceptions of their present lifestyle and relationships; important changes they see and react to; consideration and preferences for their futures; difficulties they identify for which there may be acceptable solutions, etc., as well as an updated appraisal of their living conditions, interdependencies, attitudes, cognitive function and emotional liabilities.

CHAPTER 4

SELECTED PROBLEMS IN
COUNSELLING THE ELDERLY

SUSAN MARINO, M.S.W., C.S.W.

*T*his chapter outlines four major problems that social workers encounter in counselling the elderly. These are: attitudes and countertransference in the counselling relationship; the dependence/independence conflict; dealing with issues of loss; and, intergenerational conflict. A discussion of each problem is followed by practice suggestions and a case example. Particular attention is devoted to the multiple nature of problems and high levels of stress in the lives of aging clients. The chapter concludes with a consideration of those counselling interventions that cut across problem areas and practice settings.

I. Introduction

Counselling the elderly presents social workers with both unique challenges and serendipitous rewards. The rewards come in many ways. There are individual positive experiences in encountering the spirited dispositions of older people who at first glance seem frail and overwhelmed by stress and change. The normal stresses of aging present problems themselves and are always there as undercurrents to the additional crises caused by illness, social circumstances, multiple losses and relationship conflicts. The challenges too are unique because aging sets up a more complex relationship between life-cycle issues, individual psycho-social dynamics, and disease than for younger age groups. The gerontological social worker, therefore, needs to have a way to untangle this web, to assess and respond to what is the most important issue facing their clients without denying their other problems.

In this chapter, four major problems experienced by the elderly who are counselled by social workers will be discussed. They were chosen because they are almost always present in some way in all problems brought by the elderly and their families to the counselling process, regardless of the precipitating event. Further, they seem universal in nature and cut across a variety of practice settings. While it is helpful to have an integrated practice model for working with the elderly, there are specific interventions for specific problems. Therefore, the discussion of each problem is followed by some practice suggestions and a case example.

II. Attitudes, Countertransference and the Counselling Relationship

i) The Problem

As social workers, we are consciously and unconsciously affected by a variety of attitudes toward the aged, which are maintained by our lack of knowledge and life experiences with the elderly. These attitudes often block accurate assessment and diagnosis, the direction of counselling to appropriate goals and the choice and time frame of interventions. The concept that best explains how one brings these attitudes to the therapeutic relationship is countertransference.

Countertransference is the therapist's emotional reactions to a patient, based on the therapist's past relationship history rather than the 'real attributes of a patient.' These are usually distortions that occur in a worker's perceptions as a result of conflicts within him or herself (Greene, 1986). They are also the result of a set of attitudes workers bring to their roles due to having stereotypic views of a particular client group that causes them to see their clients in biased and incomplete ways.

Aging is associated with decline in all areas of a person's functioning. Social work's belief in the potential for growth and development is challenged and compounded in the struggle to help older clients value themselves in a culture that does not accord them a meaningful place. Often, unconsciously, we agree with this view of aging and react in one of two ways.

We may ascribe helplessness to our clients and rejection by society and thus become inadvertently paternalistic. As well, we may offer solicitous sympathy, believing that they have been abandoned and, therefore, fail to seek out and mobilize the potentially available resources within their families and the larger community. Secondly, one may deny the impact of older peoples' functional difficulties and push for a stoic acceptance of their losses, demanding too quickly that they adapt to a compromised existence (at a pace that is sometimes beyond their capacities). These behaviours from social workers can flow from their own anxieties and fears of aging and an unconscious wish to deny its impact. Such attitudes have generally led to unrealistic expectations of rehabilitation of elderly patients, and decisions by professionals to stop treatment when they don't recover quickly enough (Becker and Kaufman, 1988).

Most social workers have not had the benefit of exposure to the special dimensions of life and life review that elders hold by virtue of their position in the life-cycle. As well, most workers have probably been trained in professional schools that offer little specific gerontological content in their curriculae. Previous social work experience with the elderly is usually insufficient to learn about the unique characteristics and life view of the elderly population. Aging is one life stage social workers have not passed through themselves at the time they practice (Monk, 1986). Younger workers may bring a sense of energy and optimism about life, but it may be difficult to understand those who measure life in terms of 'time left' and by past accomplishments (Monk, 1986). Indeed, such notions can feel threatening to a worker's own sense of well-being and feelings of optimism. This altered sense of time is crucial to the elder's preservation of self (Tobin, 1988), for by respecting this life view is in direct contrast to one's tendency to pathologize those who 'dwell in the past.' It is only in recent years, and by professionals who have learned in clinical relationships with the elderly that the process of life review has been reunderstood as a 'legitimate' one. As a consequence, reminiscence has become an essential tool in counselling.

Because aging bears a stigma, so does social work with the elderly. The belief that elders are unable to change usually leads to the assumption that working with elders entails practical resourcing for people, or 'supportive' work only, or a 'job that no one else wants.' Thus, some social workers working with the elderly may unintentionally devalue their work and be reluctant to engage them in psychotherapy directed at change when it is warranted.

Another problem is generated by the medical model inherent in professional social work training, which defines problems as the result of pathology (Miller, 1987). This view is further reinforced by having most services for the elderly as hospital-based ones. Indeed, there are problems caused by disease processes and also problems associated with aging. There are also problems and conflicts that are a reflection of neither — because they are part of a lifelong pattern of coping. Thus, if a worker sees aging as pathological and the problems of aging as being due to disease, his or her ability to separate out the processes of aging from disease and personality and social circumstances is obfuscated.

ii) A Practice Framework

Most social workers understand that attitudes and experiences directly affect their work. Social workers with the elderly, however, are more likely not to have had the 'corrective experience' related to their own attitudes toward aging prior to entering this field of practice (Greene, 1986). The lack of education/training and lack of personal and professional experience previously noted above are two reasons for this. An additional one is that most attitudes are outside of one's awareness until we experience them within the context of a therapeutic relationship with the elderly themselves, the process in which the concept of countertransference finds its embodiment.

In this context, social workers need to accept that uncovering such attitudes and feelings is one of the most difficult, and yet most important, aspects of counselling, as it enables them to identify countertransference issues. As adult children themselves, they also need to be aware of particular opinions they have about dependency and family responsibilities. This will usually protect them from making the error of overidentification with, or judgment of, the adult children of their clients.

Of prime importance in this regard is a social worker's feelings about loss, grief and dying. 'Death anxiety' (Greene, 1986) can affect a worker's assessment and willingness to handle issues such as living wills, pre-arranged funerals, discussions about quality of life, life-threatening illnesses and spiritual matters, which may be a primary source of support for their clients. The problem presents itself most vividly to the beginning gerontological social worker at a time when she or he is also experiencing the greatest anxiety about bonding with clients and being helpful. Paradoxically, it is such anxiety and discomfort with clients in counselling that are the most useful tools for identifying countertransference issues.

Supervision is a primary process for identifying countertransference so that one may see and respond to elderly clients as they really are. More accurate assessments and relevant treatment planning can then occur. Social workers should make this a goal of supervision, if it is available. If not, they should find a colleague in the field whose work, experience and/or relationships with elderly clients are known to be good and consult them.

As well, social workers can make a special effort to reformulate their understanding of growth and development and client self-determination, and the possibilities for its expression in later years. The recent literature on the psychological tasks of aging can be quite helpful in this regard as it reflects acknowledgement that aging, as different from other stages of the life-cycle, includes tasks of integration, finding meaning and preserving rather than expanding a sense of self (Tobin, 1988).

Further, social workers need to value their work with the elderly and have it valued by their colleagues. They should ask themselves questions such as, "What can I learn from the elderly that no other client group can teach me?" and "What unique role in family and community life do the elderly perform?" They should also spend time with other colleagues in this field who value this practice even if they have to go outside their agencies to do so.

Most importantly, social workers need to consider their clients as their primary teachers. Aging, although it carries some universal themes, has many stages. Subgroups of the young, middle and frail elderly have decidedly different stresses and adjustment issues (Hartford, 1985), and the experience and reality of aging has particular significance to each individual. Despite our own sensitivity and knowledge, we should not assume that we know what clients have not told us because we failed to ask them.

iii) Case Example

Mrs. L, an experienced social worker, began work in a geriatric hospital, a job change of her own choosing. Her first client, Mr. M, a 74-year-old gentleman, had been in long-term care for a year because of an unstable diabetic condition and repeated dizzy spells. His behaviour and self-care in the hospital was erratic and uncooperative. Staff believed he could never be managed outside hospital, although he desperately wanted to live independently. The social worker advocated for an alternative plan to try him living in a nursing home in the community. Finally, the doctor agreed.

Mr. M listened impatiently to the social worker's plan. The social worker cited it as a better alternative to hospitalization and talked of new opportunities available. Suddenly, Mr. M became very angry, accusing her of having no respect for him. Taken aback, the social worker sensed she had missed something. So she apologized, and asked. "You should know better than to tell me what I should like," said Mr. M, "and you should also know that neither I, nor anyone else would want to live in a nursing home."

The social worker wondered how she had missed remembering that no elder ever wants to be institutionalized, and how she had failed to empathize with the loss of self-esteem that accompanies such a move. Later, in discussion with her supervisor, she talked of her eagerness to be helpful and her assumption that her advocacy for discharge would be appreciated by her client. She felt that the 'bad' attitudes were held by other team members — not her.

When she examined her own feelings about institutionalization, however, she admitted that they matched Mr. M's. Unable to accept this reality, she was reconstructing an image of new possibilities in nursing home life, so that she would not see herself as an agent in helping the client toward an uninviting future. With this new awareness in her next session with Mr. M, the social worker empathized with his fear of institutionalization and facilitated a discussion of some of the negative aspects of nursing home life. These were compared with Mr. M's experiences of the negative aspects of hospital living. The criteria of continuing care that were crucial to Mr. M's sense of dignity and self-esteem were then identified. Mr. M agreed to visit a number of nursing homes to evaluate them as potential placements on the basis of those criteria. Eventually, he was placed voluntarily in a nursing home that least offended him and his world view.

III. Dependence-independence Conflicts

i) The Problem

Dependence-independence conflicts are present in some form in almost every counselling situation with an elderly client. This is an issue in the worker-client relationship because many elderly are involuntary clients. Such conflicts can be the primary contributing factor to a client's presenting problem of being faced with growing dependency and the consequent losses of self-esteem and morale needed for recovery. They can also threaten the relationship between the client and his or her caretakers, the family and the community. They also present ethical dilemmas to the worker who may wish to control and direct treatment plans and, often times, they place a worker in conflict with his or her agency and its mandates.

Western culture values independence, and it is a primary source of self-esteem for persons of all age groups. Productivity and financial self-sufficiency, emancipation from one's parents and the ability to care for oneself are benchmarks of self-worth. Thus, dependence, vulnerability and the acknowledgement of such needs are often judged, especially by the elderly themselves, as weaknesses.

Our society has vigorously supported the rights of individuals to maintain autonomy and to retain control of decision-making affecting their own lives. Indeed, the social work ethic of client self-determination is partly founded on this principle. Yet the processes of aging inevitably place elders in a position of growing dependency. For most, beginning with retirement and/or the death of a spouse, financial resources, especially for women, diminish. Widowhood brings with it the loss of companionship, a caretaker and the surfacing of 'new' emotional needs. Physical and mental illnesses and health decline make it difficult for an elderly person to care for himself or herself independently. In addition, the stresses of loss and changes in the aging process can overwhelm an elder person's capacity to adapt accordingly. They can lower his or her morale and motivation to make use of opportunities to maintain some degree of independence. The lack of fit between an elder person's partial but not totally dependent lifestyle needs (e.g., assisted mobility, 'one stop shopping,' simplified bureaucratic procedures for service eligibility, etc.,) and his or her environment can cause him or her to withdraw into isolation.

When we are young children, we are expected to be dependent and are supported by institutions of change (e.g., family, friends, church, school system, etc.,) to be as such. However, the dependency that accompanies aging is not as facilitative. Faced with the lack of resources to help elders maintain some degree of independent living, the community often feels obligated to turn to institutionalization to solve the problem. Paradoxically, this is the most feared experience for the elderly client, and often the process of institutionalizing a parent causes guilt that tears families apart. What must be understood here is that elders often regress temporarily as the result of the lowering of self-esteem that accompanies loss of, or even partial, dependency.

Helpers, including social workers, may inadvertently reinforce this regression by being overprotective and/or by mobilizing too many services too quickly for their clients. A classic example occurs when families move too soon to institutionalize a parent in difficulty after the death of a spouse as they see their parent's difficulty in coping as a permanent reality rather than a grief or immediate stress reaction. They are frightened by their parent's loss of capacity and feel unable to be their caretakers.

The elderly's resistance to dependency can be functional, as the experience of dependency can be debilitating. Research indicates that institutional living is deleterious and that the less residents have control over their lives the more they tend to lose control of their faculties. Alternatively, the feeling of being in control over what happens in one's life can improve physical and mental functioning (Lowy, 1989). In fact, aggressiveness (seen in younger people as pathological) and unrealistic beliefs in environmental mastery are associated with positive outcomes in the very old in adaptation to stress (Lieberman and Tobin, 1985).

Because of their resistance to dependency, the elderly have become a unique group of involuntary clients. Often they have not initiated contact for help and they do not see a need for services but are pressured to do so by others — usually a family member or health agency (Burstein, 1988). Additional factors are that they have been socialized to see seeking help as a weakness or stigma, and they may have had previous experiences of controlling interventions in their lives. Thus, not used to seeking help, they may be unaware of eligibility for service or become overwhelmed by the maze of bureaucratic tasks involved to gain eligibility (Burstein, 1988). Often times, in this regard, they may truly come to believe that they are without choices.

The social worker then has a dilemma in engaging the elderly at all in the counselling process, not to mention persuading them to utilize services they may need for their own protection and welfare. Additional ethical dilemmas are present for social workers when working with the frail elderly in the community. They are caught between the belief in the client's right to self-determination and the responsibility to protect him or her. Thus, the worker may be ambivalent about his or her own need to be in control of the treatment plan and about being responsible for another person's safety (Burstein, 1988). It may be difficult to decide who the client is in the face of conflicting demands of the elderly client who doesn't want the worker there and the family, who does.

Such problems are made more complex by the fact that there are still no clear guidelines on the issue of rights and freedoms and protective service for the elderly in North America. Traditional medical models of health care delivery emphasize protection and solutions that would be 'in the best interests' of patients. Resistance to such orientations is seen as negative. At the same time, the ever-expanding human rights movement in our society emphasizes an adversarial approach, which can pit worker/agency vs. client or the family vs. client, especially in situations of incompetence (Parsons and Cox, 1989). Neither of these approaches offer social workers a viable way to maintain their ethical stance of preserving relationships. In short, the adversarial model does not lessen conflict and can reinforce isolation. The social worker must somehow find a working relationship between the client's right to and need for self-determination, proper social work practice, the mandate of the agency and the opinions of family members and other professionals working with the client. This is a delicate issue that should not be minimized by practitioners working in this field.

ii) A Practice Framework

A worker needs to understand that the elderly must maintain dignity and some control of their lives. Elders must participate, if possible, in all decisions about their present and future circumstances. Even if older people have lost the capacity to do some things for themselves, many still know what they want. Thus, all interventions should include some options.

A social worker's assessment of problems and behaviours should include an attempt to understand what function they play in the maintenance of independence. Even a lack of motivation or interest in coping by a client may be due to his or her belief in a lack of capacity or opportunity for recovery to some level of independence. Behaviours seen as 'problematic' among other age groups (e.g., aggression, magical thinking, etc.,) must be reassessed in elders as to their functional merit for coping (Tobin, 1988). Thus, an astute assessment of remaining capacities and strengths should be undertaken. As such, initial interventions should be directed toward enlarging a sense of competence and problem-solving abilities (Monk, 1986). Treatment objectives should be simplified and achievable and counselling goals should be aimed at the alleviation of stress rather than personality change.

Engaging elderly clients in counselling requires the use of non-traditional methods and a willingness to be flexible in one's professional role. For instance, home visits rather than office interviews are suggested. The worker must be willing to be patient, to relinquish control and to begin a therapeutic relationship on the client's 'turf' or his or her terms (Burstein, 1988). Helping the client with tasks they choose (e.g., filling out income tax or rent subsidy forms, etc.), even if it does not constitute the worker's purpose in being there, is also recommended. For if the worker succeeds in engaging the client, the worker must be willing to be proactive in a case management as well as psychotherapeutic capacity.

A worker also needs to have thought out the conflict between a client's self-determination and protective service, and be clear about when she or he must intervene despite a client's refusal of service (e.g., extreme self-neglect, malnutrition, suicidal risk, clear danger to others) (Burstein, 1988). The worker should clarify this mandate with the agency for which she or he works and the worker should expect to face many case situations in which the preferred course of action is not clear and be willing to live with such ambivalence. Obtaining support from, and sharing the responsibility with, the agency in this regard is important.

The worker should remember that a client may be incompetent in one area but not in others. Thus, a client may not be competent to care for him or herself but may be competent to choose who he or she wishes to care for them from among viable alternatives. Assuring integrity in the face of protective service can prevent the spiralling effect of loss of some, but not all, independence.

Paternalistic and adversarial models of conflict resolution about issues in independence should be avoided. Rather, interventions should be directed toward preserving relationships and fostering communication and interaction between elders and others in their lives. Family mediation and helping organizations need to be more flexible to meet elders' needs and wishes is preferable, as it helps elders to maintain rather than be separated from needed ongoing support.

Finally, social workers must be willing to accept elderly clients as permanent clients with fluctuations in service needs. This is the reality of working with the chronically frail elderly in the community — that clients, although stabilized, will return at a later date, when in need, to the agency and worker with whom they are familiar and whom they trust.

iii) Case Example

Miss G, 85 years old, was admitted to the hospital due to recurrence of a drinking problem. Medical assessment revealed several physical problems — severe arthritis, malnutrition and a significant hearing deficit. She had no family and had discontinued attendance at a community day care programme three months ago. Doctors, concerned about her frailty, were recommending nursing home placement. Miss G adamantly refused. She was referred to the hospital social worker for discharge planning. The social worker was advised that doctors were considering a declaration of incompetency in order to place her.

After initial assessment, the social worker concurred that Miss G was becoming too frail to live on her own much longer. In the absence of family, no one was available to help on a regular basis and Miss G did not have the financial means to hire a part-time caretaker. The social worker, lacking time and a mandate to provide ongoing support, could not be involved beyond Miss G's hospital stay.

Miss G refused to sign the applications for nursing home placement, which she said would also deny her financial independence because of the high cost of care. The social worker decided to 'buy time' and deferred placement planning. Further discussion with Miss G revealed that the pain of her arthritis had demoralized her and she had started drinking again to cope with the pain. She had stopped going to day care because of social problems arising from her hearing deficit. The social worker persuaded the doctor to refer Miss G to a pain clinic. Medications were prescribed that relieved the pain and improved her mobility. A hearing aid was obtained with the help of a government subsidy.

Subsequently, Miss G's morale improved and she was more than ever determined to return home. The grounds for incompetency decreased with her improved functioning and her doctor had no choice but to discharge her home. Before she left hospital, the social worker proposed that Miss G visit several nursing homes in her area as a preparation for the future possibility of being unable to live independently. Surprisingly, Miss G agreed to this plan and also to return to the day care programme she had previously attended.

In this case, the social worker's initial assessment indicated a need for institutional placement. The client's strong resistance moved the worker to alternative interventions, which improved the patient's competence and the chances of a better quality of life wherever she would ultimately reside. The social worker's efforts to delay adversarial action (declaration of incompetency) were productive. Creative solutions not present in the initial assessment arose and the need for placement against the client's wishes was lessened.

IV. Dealing with Issues of Loss

i) The Problem

Loss is a central theme of aging. It is intrinsic to other stages of life, but is experienced differently when successful grieving can more easily lead to new roles, relationships and opportunities. Loss for the elderly is much more difficult. Aging is characterized by a multitude of changes, matched in number and intensity probably only to those experienced in childhood. Changes are stressful at any age, and in later years many changes are experienced as loss. These losses often follow each other in rapid succession, such that the elderly have little time to adapt to one before they face another. While many elderly have learned to adapt to change throughout their lives, they are often without the resources, vigour and supports that were available to them in earlier years.

Some losses lead to other losses. For example, the death of a spouse (loss of companionship, intimacy) can lead to a reduction in income and a change in residence (loss of familiar surroundings, lifestyle), especially for women. If the spouse was also a caregiver, his or her death may lead to the institutionalization of the widow(er) (loss of home, financial flexibility, privacy, independence). For young elderly, the experience of initial losses, especially in physical functioning, may precipitate an awareness of aging, expectations of impending frailty and fears of future losses. Some of these fears are realistic; others are not. In any event, these fears can be immobilizing.

Grief reactions are different for the elderly. Grieving for prior losses may not be complete before additional loss is experienced. Further, loss provokes memories of earlier losses and additional grieving tasks. Grief and loss reactions in the elderly can be so pervasive that they precipitate other problems — depression, excessive preoccupation with self, ill health, self-imposed isolation and, in some cases, even death by suicide or 'failure to thrive' (Garrett, 1987). This is sometimes referred to as 'bereavement overload' — overwhelming grief reactions related to multiple successive losses with little or no separate grieving time (Garrett, 1987). Losses experienced by the elderly may be categorized according to five main areas outlined as follows (Freeman, 1984).

Loss of some physical and mental functioning is experienced by most elders at some time. Physical losses can be life-threatening (e.g., cancer, heart conditions, etc.), or those whose chronic nature necessitate living with ongoing pain, diminished energy and mobility and the curtailment of some social activities (e.g., arthritis, sight and hearing loss, etc.). These losses may represent the onset of old age, the end of usefulness, depletion of strength and vigour, and result in a lowering of self-esteem.

Mental losses include loss of cognitive abilities (memory, concentration, ability to integrate new learning) and are most often due to stroke or senility. In this regard, the diagnosis of organic brain syndrome (e.g., Alzheimer's disease) is the one most feared by the elderly. Its significance is indeed profound, for this disease inevitably leads to a loss of memory, orientation, perception, communication and ultimately a loss of identity and all forms of independence. The reality of this diagnosis is different from the fear of it. A primary defence for the maintenance of hope and self-esteem for cognitively impaired individuals facing further deterioration is denial. Paradoxically, this attitude is functional through the phase of the illness when the patient is aware of his or her impaired capacities and is a defence against depression. The fear of senility is another matter. It is not uncommon for depressed elderly to suffer memory problems and to resist treatment because of the fear of the diagnosis of senility. Residing in treatment facilities and institutions with cognitively impaired individuals generally compounds this fear.

Losses in status and role in aging occur with retirement and changing marital and family role, e.g., when the last child leaves home or with the chronic illness of a spouse. These have significance for many elderly persons.

Losses of relationship are profoundly felt because relationships are the primary source of connectedness, for the expression of caring and fulfilment of needs for companionship and intimacy (Powell, 1988). Opportunities for close relationships are lost through death, separation, divorce, the relocation of friends, colleagues, neighbours and adult children. One of the most painful losses is the death of one's child, as it is experienced as a 'death out of time' (Conway, 1988).

Loss of lifestyle and familiar surroundings occur when one is no longer able to participate in activities formerly enjoyed due to physical decline, or reduction in income or relocation occur. Such losses are compounded if the elderly person has no choice in these changes and is unable to maintain a sense of continuity during a move.

Loss of hope and self-esteem are usually the consequence of multiple losses and the meaning attributed to these losses. They can occur if one's identity is primarily tied up in a lost relationship or role, or if the loss seems to signal decline and further losses.

The intensity of these loss experiences varies with the individual and his or her place in the late life-cycle — whether one is in the early, middle or later stages of aging (Hartford, 1985). For instance, the younger elder responds by adapting quite well. Of those who experience difficulties some become depressed but respond quite well to treatment. It is the frail elderly and, for the most part, those in institutional care who have experienced the most losses, are isolated and present more serious emotional and behavioural problems. The most common fears of loss held by the elderly are the fear of losing independence, the fear of loss of one's mind though senility (mentioned earlier), the fear of abandonment and isolation and the fear of dying, particularly of dying alone.

Normal grief reactions of elders may seem quite pervasive. Grieving may initially be overwhelming for many and they may find even the most basic activities difficult to do. This is not a permanent incapacity as much as it is the initial response of anxiety. In turn, they may withdraw temporarily, experience somatic complaints or express anger toward family members or friends. Further, they may seem unduly resistant to problem-solving and to making even the smallest, practical change or to accept new opportunities. These grief reactions are normal and stem from the need to minimize change and maintain continuity in their lives in the aftermath of loss. Generally, grieving for elders takes longer than for younger people, often for a period of up to two years.

Some grief reactions are more serious and require radical and prompt intervention. These include rapidly deteriorating physical health, alcohol and substance abuse, excessive feelings of unworthiness and guilt, refusal to eat, a pervasive and prolonged sense of hopelessness and/or anxiety that prevents the person from functioning at all. These are also symptoms of clinical depression, which if left untreated can be life-threatening.

Finally, some of the influences affecting an elder person's ability to cope with grief are his or her age, the number of losses within a short period of time, past experiences coping with loss, the existence of other relationships and a support system, the ability to maintain control over related factors, one's state of health and belief in a power greater then oneself (Garrett, 1987).

ii) A Practice Framework

Helping the elderly deal with loss involves four main practice principles: 1) a comprehensive assessment; 2) mobilization of resources to reduce stress, minimize change and maintain continuity during the grieving process; 3) assisting in grief resolution; and, 4) instillation of hope.

The assessment of loss includes its perceived and real consequences to the griever. A history of previous losses should be obtained with information about how such losses were dealt with in the past. As well, fears of future losses should be uncovered. The extent of a person's support system should be explored — including the state of health, financial and social resources, and the attitudes and availability of family, friends and other caregivers. Attempts should be made to understand the person's belief system about loss, what causes it, how one is 'expected' to cope and express grief and what is necessary for resolution, e.g., religious beliefs and/or ritual, etc. A 'before loss' picture of the person's personality and lifestyle should be obtained in this regard.

An evaluation of the person's grief reactions should be undertaken, and assessment as to whether they seriously impede the person's capacity to function or not should occur. Even some bizarre behaviours (e.g., acting as if a dead person is there, repeated and numerous grave site visits, etc.) should be tolerated. Particular attention should be given to the potential presence of clinical or acute depression.

As indicated previously, social workers need to explore their own feelings and reactions to loss and be aware of attitudes and feelings they bring with them to the counselling relationship. This will allow them to identify issues of countertransference and to more sensitively and accurately respond to the client's reality rather than their own.

Initial interventions should be aimed at reducing stresses and minimizing change. Most behaviours of the elderly associated with coping with loss are directed toward preserving self-esteem and continuity of lifestyle. What is most needed is to maintain connectedness with others. All interventions, especially initial ones, should be in concert with these goals. This means that interventions should be scaled down to the minimum to solve immediate problems caused by the loss (Monk, 1986). Because self-esteem is so closely tied to the issue of independence, those interventions that will allow an elder as much choice and autonomy as possible are recommended. There are exceptions, of course, but very few. Even faced with the necessity of institutionalization, an elder can be offered some options and some involvement in decision-making, which are crucial to successful adjustment. If possible, no major life changes should be contemplated at the initial stage of grieving, especially against a person's will.

Efforts should also be made to communicate with family members and to encourage them to refrain from moving too quickly to assume control of an older person's affairs. In this context, the family needs to understand that an elder's incapacities provoked by loss are often normal grief reactions, and temporary. The social worker should understand that the family's own stress load may make it difficult for them to become primary caregivers. Social workers can mediate between the conflicting sides of adult children and their aging parents or relatives and point out alternative sources of support for both the grieving elder and his or her caretakers.

Models of grief resolution have been presented by experts in death and dying. Most more or less follow the stages outlined by Kübler-Ross (denial, anger, bargaining, depression, acceptance). These models are helpful in assisting elders with grief resolution. However, the grieving process does not always occur the same way for elders. In some cases, only partial grief resolution is possible if losses occur in rapid succession. Sometimes, final resolution is delayed, for example in the case of the institutionalized widow(er) whose spouse is institutionalized or of a marital partner who becomes the caretaker of a chronically ill spouse over a period of several years.

Special counselling interventions may include:

a) Normalizing grief: Helping the elderly understand that their grief, associated anxiety, fears and impulses are normal and are not pathological and, that they are not 'crazy.' Helping them express feelings of anger and guilt are important, especially for a spouse caretaker who may have felt exhausted and resentful during the long illness of his or her partner.

b) Separating present losses from the fear of further ones: This process sometimes reduces the overwhelming nature of current adjustment tasks. Discussions of fears can identify realistic from unrealistic worries and pave the way for later counselling aimed at preparation for future losses. Interventions for cognitively impaired individuals differ in this regard. It is not always advisable to directly challenge their impaired perceptions because of their inability to integrate reality and recover accurate memories. Empathizing with feelings and responding to the purpose behind their behaviours is preferable.

c) Reviewing present and past losses: Discussing the significance of these attachments is a useful way to identify their meaning and value in the life of an elderly person. This process affirms their past and contributes to a sense of worth. Such review should include a gentle uncovering and validation of both positive and negative aspects of those relationships. Loosening bonds with the past only occurs when it can be accepted in its true perspective (Schwartz-Borden, 1986).

Social workers should learn about the transformational possibilities of loss experiences in order to communicate hope to their clients. This includes exploring existential dimensions of loss and grieving. Petersen (1985) has identified spiritual counselling as a crucial component to grief resolution. Grieving involves spiritual dimensions as well, and such faith can provide a solution to the dilemma of guilt, a means to maintain a sense of worth beyond what one can do and provide a sense of love and relatedness beyond loss. Older people often refer to their faith as a source of hope for grief recovery.

Social workers without the appropriate training should not act as experts in pastoral matters. However, they need to respond with some understanding and compassion to reflections about faith as a support in the face of loss. Information and workshops for professionals working in death and dying are prolific and are good sources of counselling support.

iii) Case Example

Mr. P's 45-year-old son called a family counselling agency for help with his 73-year-old father. Mr. P had relocated a year ago to be closer to this son. However, he had been miserable since the move and was becoming excessively demanding of his son's time. Ever since a heated argument between them a week ago, Mr. P had been hallucinating but refused to see a doctor.

A social worker visited Mr. P in his apartment. During their first interview, she discovered he had suffered a series of major losses over the past ten years, beginning with the death of his wife and followed by the death of two siblings and the deaths of two other adult children. Consequently, he had moved to town to be closer to his only remaining son. The relocation had involved the sale of his home of 40 years and leaving his church congregation, which constituted his main social network.

The move had not gone as positively as he had hoped. His adolescent grandchildren in the new setting were uninterested in him. Unsure of his way around, he was dependent on his son for transportation everywhere. After their argument the previous week, he had been seeing his dead wife in his apartment at night. Believing his father was psychotic, his son had suggested he be admitted for psychiatric treatment.

Mr. P refused the social worker's suggestion of a joint interview with his son to discuss his feelings and the issue of dependency. The social worker, therefore, met alone with Mr. P's son, identifying the issues of loss and grief. She agreed to remain involved and Mr. P's son agreed to delay a referral for psychiatric treatment if his father would attend a day care programme. Mr. P reluctantly agreed to a referral for day care for three months and began attending.

During the next eight weeks, the social worker undertook individual counselling sessions with Mr. P. An extensive review of his losses was carried out. Mr. P had a very close relationship with his deceased wife. He acknowledged that probably he had 'imagined her presence' in the nights that followed the argument with his son, as she had always been a support to him. The social worker explained this as a grief reaction and affirmed that he was not crazy. Mr. P also talked of the years following his first son's death, during which he helped to raise his grandson, and felt proud of his contribution as a grandparent. The social worker affirmed Mr. P's close bond with his grandson and encouraged him to correspond with him.

Mr. P's hallucinations disappeared. He began to take an interest in day care activities. Alternative ways of solving his transportation and shopping difficulties were organized through community agencies so that Mr. P would not be so dependent on his son for daily outings. Mr. P transferred to a church-based activity group from the day care programme. His son reported that their visits were more amicable.

However, Mr. P continued to resist discussing any conflict issues with his son for fear of alienating him and losing the relationship with his only remaining child. The social worker did not push him to do so but reminded him of her availability to mediate should conflict arise in the future. After two months, visits were decreased to monthly contact and Mr. P continued to function well.

V. Intergenerational Conflicts

i) The Problem

Every family has within it an issue of aging. This statement has emerged in recent years as a reminder to social workers, and especially family therapists, of the impact of aging on family life. The social work literature generated from practice experience is emphasizing the changing nature of intergenerational relationships occurring in families as a result of people living longer and pointing to new problems experienced between these generations.

Because of technological advances that have increased life expectancy and population behaviour patterns begun earlier in the century, the nature of the extended family has changed. The lower average age of marriage, earlier parenthood and the decrease in the number of large families in that mothers are younger when they have their last child, have contributed to the advent of the four, and sometimes five, generation extended family (Miller, 1981). There are often generations in childhood, early adulthood, middle age, those in their early to middle elder years and elders at an advanced stage of frailty.

These generations, for the most part, live separately and studies of the very old indicate that they prefer it this way (Berman, 1987). However, numerous studies are validating the existence of, the importance of and the frequency of contact between these generations. It is well known that family members turn to each other first for economic and financial help, emotional and social support, and assistance in crisis situations (Miller, 1981).

The myth that families abandon the elderly, or are alienated from them, has been put to rest. It is known that family members are the primary caretakers for the elderly, and particularly significant are findings that emotional involvement with others may increase in relative importance after the middle years, probably because losses in aging remove other sources of gratification (Brody, 1974). As well, the mental health of older people is linked with family relations (Kirschner, 1985). While generational ties are strong, there are new stresses and strains between the generations, which underlie family problems presented to the gerontological social worker.

In life-cycle terms, one of the primary reasons for conflict is that the developmental tasks and needs of each generation are no longer complementary. In the aging family, the most prevalent tensions occur between the elderly and their adult children. The middle aged, or young elderly, are facing major changes in their own lives — including preparation for, or adjustment to, retirement. Their adolescent or young adult children may not quite be independent. If they have successfully launched their children from home, they face adjustment to the 'empty nest' and attendant changes to their marital relationships. The young elderly are faced with the task of placing some boundaries between themselves and their adult children, which is difficult for parents whose primary source of identity and satisfaction was found in raising their children. Problems at this stage are mediated by the energy and wellness of most young elders who have opportunities for new freedom and the pursuit of new interests. They also gain new roles as grandparents. In this regard, conflict occurs if children have difficulty leaving the parental home or if their parents cannot let them go. In recent years, a new problem has been presented to the young elderly by the returning home of their adult child, often with their own young children, after separation or divorce.

Early widowhood of a parent often presents adult children with first concerns about the potential dependency of their parents. A common reaction is for these children to mobilize prematurely to take control of their parent's lives, unaware that their own fears and grief are affecting their judgment about the ability of their remaining parent to adjust successfully to living alone.

The most prevalent conflicts, however, occur because of the real and increasing dependency needs of frail elderly parents and the high stress load already being carried by their middle-aged adult children. Terms such as 'the sandwich generation' (Miller, 1981) and 'women in the middle' (Brody, 1981) explain the particular dilemmas of this middle-aged generation who become caretakers of their parents. Most studies have revealed that the bulk of caring is by women — adult daughters, daughters-in-law, a female spouse — often a single woman, unmarried or divorced and, therefore, is seen as the one most able to provide support. The sons and daughters of these elderly are in the middle, squeezed by the competing demands for their resources and caregiving to generations above and below them, to their spouses, and by their responsibilities to work outside the home. This problem is particularly felt by women, many of whom have returned to the workforce. They highly value the care of the elderly as a family responsibility, and also their financial contribution to the marriage and the new opportunities for personal development and freedoms their own children's departure from home has brought them. The culture in which they were raised assigned to the daughters the principal caregiving role, yet their ability to carry this out is profoundly affected by lifestyle changes. The strain is usually felt in terms of competing roles, financial resources, fatigue and personal relationships (Brody, 1981).

The particular position of adult children becoming caregivers to their frail elderly parents is not helped by the fact that there are no models for behaviour for the aging multigenerational family because it is a relatively new phenomenon. In addition to problems created by competing interests for time and resources, there are individual emotional issues experienced by each generation — both the givers and receivers of help.

As well, there is a culturally supported notion that 'one has a duty to one's parents.' Indeed, one of the prevalent dilemmas facing adult children is their belief that they 'can never do enough' for their parents, indebted as they are for the gift of life and the care they received as children (Berman, 1987). Most adult children do what they can do willingly and out of love for their parents, but the issue of 'what is enough' usually causes them significant anguish as they make decisions about how to, and how much to, care for their frail parents. Certainly, it is a guilt-inducing dilemma, and because adult children have difficulty negotiating this conflict they are often unable to place limits on their caretaking and present to social workers as suffering from extreme exhaustion and stress.

Their elderly parents, on the other hand, are suffering themselves. They have probably experienced a series of irreplaceable losses (e.g., health, spouse, work, home) and come to their children with additional losses in hope and self-esteem (Berman, 1987). In turn, they feel guilty at not being able to maintain themselves independently and may be afraid of losing the support of their children because of their immediate needs. Some authors are predicting trends whereby it will not be unusual for adult children to share their home with a frail parent despite their desire to live independently (Berman, 1987; Parsons et al., 1989). In one study, frail elderly women living with their adult children reported most frequently their wish not to be a burden (Parsons et al., 1989). Elders may, therefore, be afraid of openly discussing their problems with adult children for fear of alienating them, and as a result may become more isolated. In addition, the frail elderly have fewer opportunities to reciprocate the care given by adult children, and thus their sense of usefulness diminishes.

Some mention must be made of the vulnerability of this particularly stressful relationship to elder abuse. The problem of elder abuse is now recognized as a family issue whose victims are both the elderly and their exhausted caretakers. In this context, some elderly feel the only thing they have left to give is money, and the risk of adult children in financial need taking financial advantage of their parents, or being perceived as doing so, is well known.

How can adult children and their parents resolve their own personal emotional conflicts in the shifting balance of dependency as their parents grow old? A new relationship is needed, and it is inadequate to explain the change in terms of role reversal that children need to become parents to their parents, or parents need to become children to their children (Brody, 1974). The concept of filial maturity attempts to explain this relationship shift, suggesting that it is a maturational task of the adult child to be depended upon, to relinquish childhood roles and to decide, without extreme guilt, how much they can do, and that it is enough. Their ability to do so generally depends upon many factors — facing their own fears of aging, accepting separation from, and the future death of, their parents and resolving or putting aside previous conflicts with their siblings and parents. The onset of the dependency of aging parents is certain to reactivate old wounds among all family members. Frail parents need to be willing to depend upon their children and to accept that there are limitations to their children's resources.

Conflicts are most dramatically evident in families facing the crisis of institutionalizing a parent. Paradoxically, at this time, it is the giving up of the caregiving role, rather than maintaining it, which can be the problem. Also, at this time, the parents' fears of abandonment and the children's sense of guilt are exacerbated because of the attendant losses in relationships that are anticipated. Unfortunately, institutionalization is often considered an urgent matter by families, hospitals and placement agencies by whom social workers are employed, affording little time to carry out the interventions that result in a successful adjustment process.

ii) A Practice Framework

Most families who seek help from gerontological social workers are coping with the issue of intergenerational conflict arising out of the perceived or real increasing dependency needs of an older, sometimes frail, member. More often, it is the adult children who initiate the referral rather than the elderly person themselves. Sometimes, the problem is not initially presented as a family issue but as an individual referral by a hospital or health agency concerned about the ability of an elderly person to care for himself or herself.

Some professionals suggest the utilization of a family systems approach to all issues facing the elderly because of the belief that problems in one generation inevitably effect other generations. In my experience, there are problems facing elderly individuals and couples that should be treated individually, and the boundaries between the generations should be honoured. However, as standard practice, all assessments of elderly problems should include an inquiry about the nature of the extended family network, their availability for support, the relationships among the generations and whether changes in the life of one generation have had an impact on the problem presented for help (e.g., divorce, death, financial setbacks or illness of adult children). As well, the importance of relationships with grandchildren should not be ignored.

It is particularly important in cases of elderly spouses where one is a caretaker to inquire about the emotional and other support they receive or do not receive from other friends, relatives and adult children. In addition, in all cases where problems of an elderly person involve increased caretaking or alternative placement needs, a strong effort should be made to contact and involve other family members. Other relatives may already be providing support and need to have their effort confirmed. It is important to remember that caretakers, especially siblings, may have differing perceptions about the problem and personality of their parent, and this difference is a reflection of their own relationship history and the stresses and strains of caretaking they may be experiencing. For example, reports of an elder's uncooperativeness may be exaggerated because of current relationship stress.

Adult children, faced with making decisions about care for their parents who don't want to, often need help to understand the dependence/independence conflict and loss and grief issues from the elder's point of view. Further, they should be helped to refrain from assuming control over their parents' lives unless they really need it, and encouraged to become willing to assume a nurturing role. Helping adult children to know about community support services for themselves and their parents, and how to access them, is useful counsel.

As a matter of course, major decisions involving competence and institutionalization should involve meetings with all the adult children, even if it entails them coming from considerable distances. Adult children need to feel consulted and invited to contribute to such major changes in their parents' lives. Further, a family gathering gives the social worker the opportunity to assess family dynamics. Family meetings reveal the existence of conflicts and supportive networks and the family's style of problem-solving. Children should be invited to share their fears about their parent's frailty and the stresses they are experiencing in their own lives related to their capacities and motivation to assume responsibilities.

At such family meetings, it is the social worker's responsibility to have assessed the functioning of the parent and to have some opinion regarding his or her capacities and needs, especially related to placement in an institutional setting or the potential for continued independent living. These issues should be realistically interpreted to the family. Social workers should be aware of the tendency of families to assign the caretaking role to a particular member — often a daughter or the sibling living closest — and for that person to assume it. It is here that work can be done to prevent the future problems of resentment, exhaustion and caretaker breakdown that occur when one family member carries the total responsibility. All siblings should be encouraged to offer help, even if they live at a distance.

Problem-solving and family cooperation is the primary goal of family meetings, not the resolution of previous long-standing relationship issues (Parsons and Cox, 1989). The presence of conflict should be identified and recognized as legitimate suffering, but family members should be encouraged to put this aside for the time being. The elderly parents should be present if possible. They should *always* be asked to contribute their opinions and be involved in decision-making if they are competent. If the social worker has time, subsequent counselling can be offered to individual family members to help them understand and resolve rivalry and conflicts arising from their earlier history.

Special problems arise around decisions of competence and managing finances. Adult children are very sensitive to the issues of disenfranchisement and inheritance, and if a parent's finances are to be managed by one or more of their adult children, they must have a relationship of trust and cooperation and the blessing of the rest. Otherwise, a third party trustee is advisable.

Social workers also need to help adult children identify how much care is enough and empathize with the guilt and sense of loss that is felt by them, especially if the need is for institutionalization. Helping elders and their children find a suitable placement acceptable to both, interpreting institutional care issues, mediating between families and staff during the initial phase of placement when adjustment problems are most prevalent are important counselling tasks. Social workers can be of great assistance in helping institutions understand that families' initial complaints about care are often a reflection of their grief reactions and in finding ways for families to continue in a supportive role in caretaking after placement.

The elderly, especially the frail elderly, may have a more difficult time resolving conflict with their adult children if they perceive them as abandoning them or not doing enough. Thus, they must be encouraged to refrain from making them feel guilty. Individual counselling, utilizing life-review aimed at recovering one's history as parent and grandparent, validating and finding meaning in these roles, past and present, identifying feelings of failure and needs for forgiveness is very helpful in this regard. It is also important to remember that the elderly and their adult children yearn for reconciliation, and sometimes joint sessions can be arranged to provide both the opportunity to ask for and offer forgiveness. Finally, parents provide counsel and emotional support to their children at all stages of the life-cycle. Social workers can be creative in helping both generations identify ways the elderly can continue to be parents, even in the last stages of life.

iii) Case Example

Mrs. G, a 79-year-old widowed woman, lived alone and seldom went out. She was visited regularly by her 50-year-old daughter, B and a public health nurse who was concerned about her failing memory. During one of her visits, the public health nurse found Mrs. G in bed crying. After much effort, she was finally able to determine that Mrs. G had had an argument with her daughter, whom she said had shouted and pushed her. The public health nurse contacted a social worker at a psychogeriatric outpatient clinic, which had a mandate to investigate concerns of elder abuse. The social worker and nurse visited Mrs. G together. After a prolonged interview, the social worker determined that Mrs. G had extensive cognitive problems. She then contacted B, her daughter.

Over the phone, B burst into tears. She told of how she had been visiting her mother three times a week for two years, looking after her banking, meals, laundry and housekeeping. She wanted her mother to see a doctor because of her memory problems, but Mrs. G refused. On the night of the quarrel, Mrs. G accused B of stealing her money and was refusing to pay her rent. B admitted to exhaustion, frustration and fear of losing control again with her mother's lack of cooperation. An office interview with B allowed the social worker to determine in more detail Mrs. G's history of progressive mental deterioration, the probability that she was not competent and that it was unsafe for her to continue living alone. A family meeting including B and two siblings, a brother and sister living in towns nearby, was subsequently arranged. At the meeting, B's brother accused B of wanting to institutionalize their mother and of being an unwilling caretaker. The younger sister expressed guilt at her unavailability to help out because of job and family responsibilities.

The social worker explained Mrs. G's problem as one of possible senility and not neglect. She outlined B's great caretaking efforts and explained the phenomenon of caretaker stress. She suggested that placement in a nursing home was probably required, pointing out how difficult this process is for adult children and their parents. A plan was suggested whereby Mrs. G would be referred immediately for respite care and a psychiatric assessment undertaken to clarify questions of diagnosis, competency and further ability to live independently. Mrs. G was unable to participate in the family meeting because of her confusion. The family agreed to this plan. Respite care was organized. A psychiatric assessment revealed the probability that Mrs. G was suffering Alzheimer's disease and required nursing home placement.

Three weeks later, a second family meeting was held. The social worker discussed the diagnosis of Alzheimer's disease and its implications for further mental deterioration, providing the family with written educational information about the disease. All three siblings outlined their inability to take their mother into their own homes. The social worker advised placement and offered to assist. The siblings agreed to visit several nursing homes and to return to the social worker with their selections and for assistance with the application process.

At this meeting, the question of Mrs. G's money management was also raised as the psychiatric assessment indicated financial incompetence. The siblings decided to apply for committeeship together and to delegate B to make day-to-day decisions regarding spending to which B agreed. Unfortunately, Mr. G was not well enough to participate in the planning. She was advised of the plan and given an opportunity to share her wishes, which she was unable to do. During her weeks in respite care, she remained very confused but seemed more secure. She could not understand why she was unable to return home and was unable to participate in the placement process.

After Mrs. G was admitted to a nursing home, the social worker met with the family again to talk about institutional care, to encourage all to visit regularly and to offer suggestions about communication strategies with nursing home staff. She also provided information about Alzheimer support groups. During the next year, B remained the primary adult child involved in her mother's life. She called the social worker from time to time for advice and to gain support for her feelings of loss as her mother gradually became unable to recognize her. A year later, all three adult children were able to decide together on issues of heroic measures after their mother was admitted to general hospital.

VI. Concluding Remarks

It is evident from the preceding that, while specific problems require a special focus, many counselling interventions with the elderly transcend the boundaries of practice settings and problem areas. This is because all elders are coping with the experiences of aging, which challenge their capabilities to adapt to multiple changes and diminished opportunities, especially in the later years. As such, all problems of the elderly are experienced within this context. Regardless of the specific manifestations of difficulty, their paramount motivation is to maintain continuity, identity and self-esteem as they reluctantly move in the direction of dependency.

Because of the complex nature of these problems, initial counselling interventions with an elderly person should be aimed at the assessment and reduction of stress in his or her life. This process often calls on the gerontological social worker to have and assume a variety of case management functions in addition to counselling. The complex interplay of difficulties of an aging person also affects the timing of social work interventions and expectations for recovery. Treatment goals should be realistic and achievable and, where dependency is an issue, oriented to the minimum amount of change needed to solve the problems at hand. At the same time, social workers should persist with assistance and rehabilitation efforts beyond the time required for younger populations to recover.

Aging is a family affair, and families are primary caretakers of the elderly. They suffer in a complementary fashion and need to be consulted, involved and supported. The processes of life-review and reminiscence are gaining widespread acceptance in individual, marital and group work with the elderly. These counselling tools offer special therapeutic qualities of bringing one's history to the present and affirming continuity, meaning and identity in one's life. While the methods of life-review have developed with special reference to the elderly, they may prove to be a gift to the work with other client populations as well.

Finally, social workers, especially at the beginning stages of their gerontological practice, should become consciously aware of their own attitudes and feelings about aging, loss, dependency and family responsibility. Doing so will ensure that they respond more accurately and sensitively in therapeutic relationship with the elderly and their families.

References

Becker S. and Kaufman, S. (1988). Old age, rehabilitation and research: A review of the issues. *The Gerontologist*, 28(4), 459-468.

Berman, Harry H. (1987). Adult children and their parents: Irredeemable obligation and irreplaceable loss. *Journal of Gerontological Social Work*, 10(1/2), 21-33.

Burstein, Beth. (1988). Involuntary aged clients: Ethical and treatment issues. *Social Casework*, 69(10), 518-524.

Brody, Elaine M. (1974). Aging and family personality: A developmental view. *Family Process*, 13(1), 23-37.

Brody, Elaine M. (1981). Women in the middle and family help to older people. *The Gerontologist*, 21(5), 471-480.

Conway, Pat. (1988). Losses and grief in old age. *Social Casework*, 69(11), 541-549.

Freeman, Edith. (1984). Multiple losses in the elderly: An ecological approach. *Social Casework*, 65(5), 287-296.

Garrett, Jean E. (1987). Multiple losses in older adults. *Journal of Gerontological Nursing*, 13(8), 8-12.

Greene, Roberta R. (1986). Countertransference issues in social work with the aged. *Journal of Gerontological Social Work*, 9(3), 79-88.

Hartford, Margaret. (1985). Understanding normative growth and development in aging: Working with strengths. In G. Getzel and J. Mellor, (eds.), *Gerontological Social Work Practice in the Community*. New York: The Haworth Press.

Kirschner, Charlotte. (1985). Social work practice with the aged and their families: A systems approach. In G. Getzel and M. Mellor (eds.), *Gerontological Social Work Practice in the Community*. New York: The Haworth Press.

Lewis, Harold. (1984). The aged client's autonomy in service encounters. *Journal of Gerontological Social Work*, 7(3), 51-63.

Lieberman, M.A. and Tobin, S.S. (1985). *The experience of old age*. New York: Basic Book Inc.

Lowy, Louis. (1989). Independence and dependence in aging: A new balance. *Journal of Gerontological Social Work*, 13(3/4), 133-145.

Miller, Dorothy. (1981). The Sandwich Generation: Adult children of the Aging. *Social Work*, 26, 419-423.

Miller, Leo. (1987). The professional construction of aging. *Journal of Gerontological Social Work*, 10(3/4), 141-153.

Monk, Abraham. (1986). Social work with the aged: Principles of practice. In C. Meyer (ed.), *Social work with the aging* (2nd ed., pp. 9-16). Silver Spring, MD: National Association of Social Workers.

Parsons, Ruth J. and Cox, Enid O. (1989). Family mediation in elder caregiving decision: An empowerment intervention. *Social Work*, 34(2), 122-126.

Parsons, Ruth J., Cox Enid O. and Kimboko, Priscilla J. (1989). Satisfaction, communication and affection in caregiving: A view from the elder's perspective. *Journal of Gerontological Social Work*, 13(3/4), 9-19.

Petersen, Elizabeth. (1985). The physical, the spiritual: Can you meet all of your patients' needs? *Journal of Gerontological Nursing*, 11(10), 23-27.

Powell, William. (1988). The ties that bind: Relationships in life transitions. *Social Casework*, 69(11), 556-562.

Schwartz-Borden, Gwen. (1986). Grief work: Prevention and intervention. *Social Casework*, 69(8),499-505.

Tobin, Sheldon S. (1988). Preservation of self in old age. *Social Casework*, 69(11).

Tobin S. and Gustafson, J. (1987). What do we do differently with elderly clients? *Journal of Gerontological Social Work*, 10(3/4), 109-121.

CHAPTER 5

MEDICATION UTILIZATION PROBLEMS AMONG THE ELDERLY: IMPLICATIONS FOR SOCIAL WORK PRACTICE[1]

VINCENT J. GIANNETTI, PH.D.

T *he improper use of medication can frequently threaten the health and well-being of elderly persons. This chapter alerts social work practitioners to the possible dangers of drug utilization among the elderly and explains the factors commonly associated with the inappropriate use of drugs.*

I. Introduction

Demographic trends in the United States over the past century have necessitated shifts in the emphasis of the health care system to accommodate the special needs of increasing numbers of people surviving beyond age 65. One area of health care delivery to the elderly that has received increased attention is the use of medication. Older people frequently suffer from multiple chronic diseases and they are often prescribed several medications. It is not surprising then, that an increased risk of adverse reactions to drugs has been documented among this age group (Hurwitz, 1969; Holloway, 1974;

Krupka and Verer, 1979; Seidl, Thornton and Smith, 1966; U.S. Dept. of Health, Education and Welfare, 1976a). Because of physiological, social and psycho-social factors, the elderly tend to use medication more often than younger people do, and they also tend not to comply with medication regimens more frequently (Wallace and Watanabe, 1977).

The social work practitioner working with elderly clients may be confronted with a variety of medication-related problems. These problems may manifest themselves as exaggerated or less-than-optimal responses to medication, symptoms of drug-induced illness and a lack of therapeutic response to medication because of noncompliance with a regimen. In general, medication utilization problems common among the elderly may be divided into four basic categories: (1) problems related to over-prescribing; (2) dose-related complications caused by the unique manner in which drugs are metabolized by and distributed in the body of the elderly patient; (3) adverse drug interactions related to a lack of coordination among the prescribing practices of the medical professionals treating the elderly and to self-medication among the elderly; and, (4) noncompliance with medication regimens, which may result in the exacerbation of illness.

II. Overprescribing

The extent to which medication is overprescribed for the elderly is difficult to analyze because the appropriateness of a particular drug regimen is related to individual factors and dependent on the individual physician's clinical expertise. However, U.S. federal Medicare regulations require the review of drug regimens in extended-care facilities, and the results of drug utilization reviews by clinical pharmacists offer some evidence that a tendency toward overprescribing exists in regard to the institutionalized elderly.

Estimates of the use of medication among elderly people in institutions have revealed that an average of seven to eight drugs are taken per patient and that 33 percent of this population receive eight drugs daily (U.S. Dept. of Health, Education and Welfare, 1976b; U.S. Senate, 1975). In a study reported by Cheung and Kayne, 122 potential adverse reactions to drugs were identified and corrected as a result of a drug utilization review conducted by clinical pharmacists, and this prevented the development of more serious illness among nursing home residents (Cheung and Kayne, 1975). In another study, a decrease from 6.8 to 5.6 prescriptions per month was realized per patient after a drug regimen review (Hood, Lemberger and Stewart, 1975). Other evidence of overprescribing has been offered. During a review of 13,081 medical charts at ten skilled nursing facilities, clinical pharmacists identified 928 potential or actual medication problems, which represented 7.1 percent of all the prescriptions reviewed (Witte et al., 1980). Approximately 60 percent of these problems stemmed from the prescription of medication without reference to a patient's laboratory test results or other documented indications for the drug or a lack of data concerning a medication's effectiveness.

In a study conducted over an eight-year period in three long-term care facilities, Strandberg and his associates have also described some indications of overprescripting (Strandberg et al., 1980). As a result of consultation in the facilities by clinical pharmacists who reviewed 4,004 medical records, a significant decrease took place in the number of prescription drugs taken, accompanied by a reduction in dosage for selected drugs. An interesting by-product of the pharmacists' review was a reduction of 28.9 percent in medication costs per patient, after adjustments had been made for inflation over the eight years. In addition, the findings of a recent epidemiological study suggest the overuse of psychotropic medication in nursing homes (Ray, Federspiel and Schaffner, 1980). Finally, limited evidence for excessive dosing of elderly patients in office-based medical practice has been suggested (Manning et al., 1980).

III. Dose-related Complications

The second category of medication utilization problems among the elderly relates to improper dosage. The absorption and distribution of drugs in elderly people and their elimination or clearance from the body are altered as a result of specific physiological changes that take place during aging. These changes place the elderly at higher risk than younger people of developing various adverse reactions to drugs. One such change is a modification in the ratio of fat to lean tissues, which is altered significantly in aging. The fat content of tissues doubles in elderly men and increases by 1.5 percent in elderly women. This significant change in fat composition affects the concentration of fat-soluble drugs in the elderly because it increases the storage of such drugs in fat tissues, thereby making them less immediately available in the blood. Because the elderly also lose approximately 10 to 15 percent of the water in their bodies as a result of aging, the distribution of water-soluble drugs is also affected. Specifically, the reduction of water in the body increases the concentration of such drugs in the blood.

The clearance of drugs in the elderly is also changed as a result of aging. The kidney and liver basically accomplish the clearance of drugs in the body. Because of changes in the liver's ability to modify drugs, total drug clearance may be affected in elderly people. Furthermore, the glomerular filtration rate, the rate at which the kidney filtrates and secretes substances, tends to decrease with aging, thus slowing down the rate at which drugs are excreted by the kidney. This can also result in higher levels of drugs in the bloodstream.

Finally, when in the body, some drugs tend to bind to proteins. Because of the decline in plasma albumin in elderly people, it is hypothesized that when such a drug is taken by an older person, there may be an increased amount of unbound, protein-binding medication in his or her bloodstream. This may increase the likelihood that the individual will develop adverse reactions and that drug interactions will take place (Vestal, 1982; Schmucker, 1979).

Other changes in the physiological status of older people have also been suggested as possible factors affecting drug distribution in the body. Because cerebrovascular disease results in reduced blood flow to the brain, antihypertensive agents that cause hypotension (or reduced blood pressure and blood flow) may also cause cerebral hypoxia (a lack of oxygen to the brain) in elderly persons with cerebrovascular disease. Both coronary artery disease and decreased cardiac output in the elderly may reduce blood flow to organ systems and thus affect the distribution of drugs to target areas. Elderly people who have chronic respiratory disease may also be especially vulnerable to medications that depress the respiratory rate. Finally, changes in intestinal function and motility in the elderly may result in changes in the rate at which drugs are absorbed if their primary site of absorption is the intestines (Wallace and Watanabe, 1977).

Although all these changes in drug distribution in the elderly may be caused by aging or by chronic illnesses common in aging, the disposition of any particular drug in the body is dependent on many complex factors. Some of these pertain to the specific physiochemical properties of the drug; others pertain to patient-related variables such as the individual's body composition and weight, the presence of disease, altered physiological functions and other drugs present in the body. The field of clinical pharmacokinetics is specifically concerned with the distribution and disposition of drugs in the body and is a relatively new subspeciality within the pharmaceutical and medical sciences. Many hospitals are now developing clinical pharmacokinetic services to assist physicians in prescribing medication for special populations, such as children and the elderly, and certain drugs whose range between therapeutic and toxic levels is extremely narrow, such as digitalis and theophylline. It has been suggested that physicians in general do not receive adequate training in the special pharmacokinetic considerations important in prescribing medication for elderly patients and tend to prescribe for the elderly as they would for younger patients, thus increasing the possibility that medication-related problems may develop (National Academy of Sciences, 1978).

One example of drug-related problems affecting the elderly is the use of benzodiazepines, or tranquillizers, including Valium and Librium. The use of these drugs is not without difficulties for older people. Certain types of benzodiazepines have been associated with an increase in the frequency of drowsiness (specifically, diazepam and chlorodiazepoxide) and with impaired psychomotor performance (specifically, nitrozepam) in the elderly. These reactions are apparently caused by heightened central nervous system depression, which occurs among elderly as compared to non-elderly subjects who are administered these drugs at equal doses, and which leads researchers to caution against the drugs' use with the elderly (Bender, 1979; Wilkinson, 1979). Mental confusion and falling may already be problems for some elderly people, and the use of certain benzodiazepines may exacerbate these problems and create a potentially dangerous situation.

However, in a survey in Great Britain of drug-prescribing patterns for the elderly, 50 percent of the psychotropic medications prescribed were found to be one of the benzodiazepines (Freeman, 1979). In 40.5 percent of the cases, psychological conditions such as anxiety, insomnia, depression and drug habituation were cited as the primary reason for prescribing the medication. Interruptions in social functioning caused by such factors as bereavement, marital problems and a seriously ill spouse and nonspecific ailments such as headache, dizziness and general malaise were given as the reason for the prescription in 20 percent of the cases. Organically related problems such as cardiovascular disease and musculoskeletal ailments were the primary factor in 39.5 percent of the cases. In addition, in a study of the use of tranquillizers by elderly people in Texas, an increased use of both tranquillizers and sleeping pills was influenced by social stress caused by such factors as unemployment, divorce, widowhood, inadequate income and loneliness as well as by a lack of social supports (Eve and Friedsam, 1981). Although this study used secondary data and was based on a nonrandom sample, which limits the extent to which its findings can be generalized, it did suggest that the use of psychotropic drugs varied directly with the number of stresses related to health, social and emotional problems in the elderly person's life. In light of findings indicating that the use of benzodiazepines and other tranquillizers is not uncommon among the elderly, it should be repeated that the efficacy and wisdom of the pharmacological management of complex psycho-social problems with tranquillizing drugs have been frequently and widely criticized (Illich, 1975; Koumsian, 1981).

IV. Drug Interactions

In addition to drug-related problems having to do with the physiological processes of aging, drug interactions can be a major problem for the elderly. Older people living in the community may be taking many different medications while under the care of various physicians who may not coordinate their prescribing practices for chronic diseases, and the risk of adverse drug interactions is increased under such circumstances (Lamy, 1980). Also, because many elderly people medicate themselves with over-the-counter drugs, there is an increased risk of interactions taking place between these drugs and prescribed medications (Lamy, 1980).

Both the extent and the pharmacological complexities of drug interactions in the elderly are well beyond the scope of this article. However, two specific problems may be discussed here: drug-related hypothermia and self-medication among the elderly. Each year, many thousands of elderly people die from accidental hypothermia, the loss of body heat leading to illness or death. The elderly are especially vulnerable to hypothermia because they have decreased physiological capabilities that result in reduced blood circulation and because they are often subject to financial constraints that cause an inability or reluctance to use enough heat to keep warm in severe weather. Certain psychotropic medications that are commonly used by the elderly can increase the risk of hypothermia. The phenothiazines, minor tranquillizers, and tricyclic antidepressants affect the central nervous system in such a way as to decrease the perception of cold. Moreover, alcoholic beverages will potentiate the affects of these drugs in addition to increasing heat loss by the body. The use of alcohol in combination with any of the drugs described can therefore significantly increase the risk of hypothermia for elderly individuals. In addition, vasodilating agents used in the treatment of cardiovascular disease will inhibit vasoconstriction, which is the body's normal response to cold and which is intended to decrease peripheral radiant heat loss and increase internal temperature. The elderly who live alone, who are having financial difficulties and who may be using any combination of the drugs mentioned should be considered at risk for accidental hypothermia (Avery, 1982).

Self-medication is fairly common among the elderly, and a variety of problems involving over-the-counter drugs may result from this practice. For example, aspirin in high dosages is often used by elderly people who have rheumatoid arthritis. If taken in large enough doses, aspirin may cause toxicity that is manifested as confusion; irritability; tinnitus, or ringing in the ear; blurred vision; and vomiting and diarrhea. Moreover, aspirin taken in combination with alcohol can result in gastrointestinal bleeding. Because the long-term use of aspirin may result in bleeding of this kind, elderly patients with a history of anemia may exacerbate their problem if they medicate themselves with large doses of aspirin.

Antacids are another kind of over-the-counter preparation whose use by the elderly can lead to unforeseen difficulties. Antacids may cause constipation and may interfere with the absorption of certain drugs by causing acid-base imbalances in the intestines. Also, because many antacids have a high sodium content, they may cause problems for elderly patients who must restrict their intake of salt. Cough and cold preparations contain alcohol (the content of some is 40 percent) and may expose the elderly who use them to drug-alcohol interactions, such as those in which the effects of sedatives, barbiturates and tranquillizers are heightened. Many products also have a high sugar content, and this can be a problem for elderly diabetics or other elderly persons who should restrict their intake of sugar. The use of laxatives can result in harm as well. Reliance on laxatives may be frequent among the elderly because of common misconceptions concerning irregularity and the necessity of a daily bowel movement. Overuse and dependence on laxatives can cause constipation by reducing muscle tone and reflexes in the large bowel, whereas many nonpharmacological approaches to the treatment of constipation can be effective. Increased dietary fiber in the form of such foods as bran, whole grains, fresh vegetables and fruits, an increased intake of water and increased activity and exercise have all been suggested as methods for overcoming constipation. Vitamins are another substance whose use by the elderly may entail complications. Self-medication with high doses of vitamins, especially fat-soluble vitamins, can lead to adverse reactions such as vitamin toxicity and organ damage (Lamy, 1980).

V. Noncompliance

Noncompliance represents a final category of medication utilization problems among the elderly. Both the sophistication of pharmaceutical technology and the individual physician's expertise are of little value if the patient does not take medication that is prescribed or fails to take it correctly. Noncompliance may lead to the exacerbation of illness as the patient consumes dosages insufficient to prompt a therapeutic response or suffers toxic reactions from taking unprescribed drugs in dosages that are too high.

Estimates indicate that noncompliance in the ambulatory population may vary from as much as 25 to 50 percent (Blackwell, 1973). Because of various physiological, social and psychological processes common in aging, many elderly people may tend not to comply with medication regimens and may consequently be subject to negative effects on their health. In addition, financial constraints may lead a number of older people to delay seeking treatment while medicating themselves, to share medication with other elderly friends or to save leftover medication for another episode of illness when taking the full prescription of the drug is indicated. Overall, five primary factors are associated with noncompliance among the elderly:

1. Polymedicine: As the older person is prescribed an increasing number of drugs with different purposes and dosing schedules, the probability increases that he or she will fail to take medication or will confuse instructions (Fletcher et al., 1979; Haynes, Sackett and Taylor, 1980; Hulka et al., 1976; Wandless and Davis, 1977).

2. Inadequate knowledge: Communication among physicians, pharmacists and elderly patients regarding the purpose and proper use of drugs tends to be incomplete. Furthermore, many elderly people do not ask questions of health care providers concerning the use, purpose and side effects of medication (Lunden, 1980; Lunden, et al., 1980; Schwartz et al., 1962).

3. Financial constraints: Delays in filling and refilling prescriptions, premature discontinuance of drug therapy and the saving of medication for subsequent self-medication may result from the inability of many elderly people to afford drugs (Brand, Smith and Brand, 1977; Smith, 1976).

4. Poor memory: Because of the effects of aging, a number of older people may have difficulty remembering instructions regarding medication (Waugh et al., 1978).

5. Social isolation: Many of the elderly lack a significant other who expresses concern about their medications or monitors whether they are following regimens.

VI. Social Work Implications

Problems involving the usage of medication can significantly affect the health and well-being of many of the elderly. Because social work practitioners work with elderly clients in both institutions and the community, they should have a basic knowledge of medication-related problems that are common among older people and the ability to refer clients for medical intervention. This ability is especially critical for the social worker in the community, for in many cases the worker comes into contact more often than any other health care professional with the older person who is living in the community.

This places the social worker in a unique position for monitoring drug-taking behaviour and adverse effects among elderly clients, and it may be helpful for workers to familiarize themselves with the variety of sources of information available on drug utilization problems.[2]

Although physicians are generally accustomed to consulting with pharmacists and nurses about the medication problems of patients, they are not accustomed to doing so with social workers. Traditionally the social worker has not been trained to act as a source of information on drugs. However, it would be within the worker's recognized province to play the role of advocate for the elderly by recognizing medication-related problems and helping to resolve them and by encouraging health practices that could reduce medication utilization problems.

Because periodic reviews of drug regimens are essential for coordinating the prescribing of drugs for elderly patients, it may be beneficial for social workers to encourage the elderly to patronize pharmacies that keep medication profiles of their clients and that screen these profiles for drug interactions and other medication-related problems. A medication profile is a list of medications that an individual is taking, and many pharmacies compile such lists, often computerizing them. Elderly people may tend to patronize pharmacists on the basis of the price they charge for drugs and may therefore not consistently use one pharmacy that offers medication profile reviews as a service to clients. If at all possible, the elderly should be helped to choose a pharmacist with whom they can communicate and who offers consultation and medication reviews, even if they must pay slightly higher prices for their medication. If maintaining a medication profile in a pharmacy is not possible for an individual, he or she should be encouraged to keep a record of all prescription and nonprescription medications taken on a regular basis. Ideally, physicians should take a drug history before prescribing new medications for a patient, and when the elderly person visits a physician who changes a prescription or initiates new medication, he or she should inform the physician of any medications being taken and the medical conditions for which they are being prescribed.

Elderly people who live alone should be closely monitored for medication utilization problems and for compliance with drug regimens. Social workers can take an active role in this important area. It would not be inappropriate for workers to speak with physicians and pharmacists about the medications their clients are taking. In this way, they can become familiar with standard dosages, major side effects and adverse reactions, which in turn would help them monitor drug regimens more effectively. If noncompliance or medication-related complications are suspected, most physicians would appreciate being informed of this by the social worker. In such cases the worker can simply state the problem and ask for intervention by the physician. Examples of such problems would include a client's complaints of tiredness and lethargy after the initiation of diuretic therapy, symptoms of depression after the initiation of steroid therapy, or increased episodes of falling and dizziness after psychotropic medication has been prescribed. Observing and interviewing elderly clients about the medication they take and applying basic knowledge on drugs or consulting with a pharmacist should enable workers to detect medication-related problems.

In addition, social workers can adopt a number of specific strategies for reducing noncompliance with medication regimens among the elderly. For example, in many cases in which financial considerations may be contributing to noncompliance, generic drugs can be substituted for more expensive brand-name drugs. Although there is considerable controversy concerning bioequivalency and bioavailability of generic drugs, pharmacists and physicians who are knowledgeable about them and whether they are as effective as their brand-name counterparts can evaluate their appropriateness for the individual and recommend quality products that can reduce costs for the elderly patient.

A variety of procedures can also help reduce confusion for the older person taking more than one medication. Typewritten instructions in large type can be developed, and colour-coded charts matching the pills taken and showing the amount prescribed and time of day of consumption can be particularly helpful when multiple medications are involved. Ideally, the elderly patient should understand the disease being treated, how the prescribed medication alleviates or controls the disease, what the major side effects of the medication are, the proper manner of taking the medication, any special instructions for the storage of the medication and what adverse effects should be reported to the physician. The social worker can help elderly clients become well-informed consumers by encouraging them to ask questions of physicians and pharmacists and by telling them where they can obtain further information about drugs. In some instances, if properly trained, social workers can undertake educational efforts with elderly clients regarding certain diseases and the proper use of medication.

Finally, older people should be encouraged to take a list of their current medications with them when they are purchasing over-the-counter drugs. Buying over-the-counter preparations should be done in consultation with a pharmacist who knows about the medications an elderly person is taking. Pharmacists are trained to assist their clients with the selection of nonprescription medication and with the identification of the symptoms of serious disease and this may be particularly important for an older person who is experiencing distressing symptoms. Nonprescription medication is frequently not indicated for the serious symptoms of disease, and self-medication may actually mask these symptoms or cause a delay in the seeking of treatment. For example, it is not uncommon to interpret the chest pain of angina as an upset stomach and through self-medication with antacids to delay the diagnosis and treatment of potential heart disease.

Finally, by acting as an advocate for the coordination of prescribing practices for the elderly in the community, as a resource for monitoring medication utilization problems and as an educator of patients, the social worker can greatly increase his or her effectiveness in the delivery of health and social services to the elderly. The advocacy role is especially critical in work with elderly people living alone, who may not see a physician or pharmacist regularly and whose contact with helping professionals other than the social worker may be limited. In filling this gap in service delivery, social workers can become an important resource for the elderly in need.

Endnotes

[1]   A version of this article appeared in *Journal of Health and Social Work,* 8(4), 1983, pp. 262-270, and was reprinted with the permission of The National Association of Social Workers, Washington, D.C.

[2]   The following are a number of drug information resources useful for social workers; addresses where they may be obtained are also listed: *Medication Teaching Manual: A Guide for Patient Counseling,* 2d ed., 1980, available from American Society for Hospital Pharmacists, 4630

Montgomery Ave., Bethesda, MD 20814; Dorothy Smith, *Medication Guide for Patient Counseling*, 2d ed., 1981, available from Lea and Febinger, Washington Square, Philadelphia, PA, 19106; *About Your Medicine*, published annually, available from U.S. Pharmacopeial Convention, Publications Department, 12601 Twinbrook Parkway, Rockville, MD 20852; Joe and Teresa Graedon, *The People's Pharmacy*, Vol 1 (1977) and Vol. 2 (1980), available from Avon Books, 959 Eighth Ave., New York, NY 10019 and in bookstores; *Handbook of Non-Prescription Drugs*, 7th ed., 1982, available from American Pharmaceutical Association, 2215 Constitution Ave. NW, Washington, D.C. 20037; William Poe and Donald Holloway, *Drugs and the Aged*, 1980, available from McGraw-Hill Book Co., 1221 Avenue of the Americas, New York, NY 10020 and in bookstores; and Peter Lamy, *Prescribing for the Elderly*, 1980, available from PSG Publishing, Littleton, Mass.

References

Avery, W. M. (1982, February). Accidental hypothermia, drugs and the elderly. *American Pharmacy*, 22, 14-16.

Bender, A.C. (1979). Drug sensitivity in the elderly. In J. Crooks and I. H. Stevens (eds.), *Drugs in the elderly: Perspectives in geriatric clinical pharmacology* (pp. 147-153). Baltimore, MD: University Park Press.

Blackwell, B. (1973, August). Patient compliance. *New England Journal of Medicine*, 237, 49-63.

Brand, F., Smith, R.T. and Brand, P.A. (1977, January-February). Effect of economic barriers to medical care on patient compliance. *Public Health Reports*, 92, 72-78.

Cheung, Alan and Kayne, R. (1975, September). An application of clinical pharmacy services for extended care facilities. *California Pharmacist*, 22-26.

Eve, S.B. and Friedsam, H.J. (1981, April-June). Use of tranquilizers and sleeping pills among older Texans. *Journal of Psychoactive Drugs*, 13, 165-173.

Fletcher, S. et al. (1979, Spring). Patient understanding of prescribed drugs. *Journal of Community Health*, 4, 183-189.

Freeman, G.K. (1979). Drug prescribing patterns in the elderly — A general practice study. In J. Crooks and I. H. Stevens (eds.), *Drugs in the elderly: Perspectives in geriatric clinical pharmacology*. Baltimore, MD: University Park Press.

Haynes, R.B., Sackett, D.L. and Taylor, D.W. (1980, January). How to detect and manage low compliance in chronic illness. *Geriatrics*, 35, 91-97.

Holloway, Donald A. (1974, November). Drug problems in the geriatric patient. *Drug Intelligence and Clinical Pharmacy*, 8, 632-642.

Hood, J.C., Lemberger, M. and Stewart, R.B. (1975, January). Promoting appropriate drug therapy in a long term care facility. *Journal of the American Pharmaceutical Association*, 15, 32-34.

Hulka, B. et al. (1976, September). Communication, compliance, and concordance between physician and patients. *American Journal of Public Health*, 66, 847-853.

Hurwitz, N. (1969, February). Predisposing factors in adverse reactions to drugs. *British Medical Journal*, 536-539.

Illich, Ivan. (1975). *Medical Nemesis*. London: Clader and Bayers Ltd., pp. 31-110.

Koumsian, K. (1981, February). The use of valium as a form of social control. *Social Science and Medicine*, 15E, 245-250.

Krupka, L. and Verer, A. (1979, February). Hazards of drug use among the elderly. *Gerontologist*, 19, 90-95.

Lamy, Peter P. (1980). *Prescribing for the elderly*. Littleton, MA: PSG Publishing Co.

Lunden, Dorothy V. (1980, May-June). Must medication be a dilemma for the independent elderly? *Journal of Gerontological Nursing*, 4, 25-27.

Lunden, Dorothy V. et al. (1980). Education of the independent elderly in the responsible use of prescription medications. *Drug Intelligence and Clinical Pharmacy*, 14, 46-71

Manning, P.R. et al. (1980, September). Determining educational needs in the physician's office. *Journal of the American Medical Association*, 244, 1112-1115.

National Academy of Sciences. (1978). *Aging and medical education*. Washington, D.C.

Ray, W.A., Federspiel, C.F. and Schaffner, W. (1980, May). A study of antipsychotic drug use in nursing homes: Epidemiologic evidence suggesting misuse. *American Journal of Public Health*, 70, 489-491.

Schmucker, D.L. (1979). Age related changes in drug disposition. *Pharmacological Reviews*, 30, 445-456.

Schwartz, D. et al. (1962, December). Medication errors made by elderly, chronically ill patients. *American Journal of Public Health*, 52, 3018-2029.

Seidl, Lawrence G., Thorton, G.T. and Smith, F.W. (1966). Studies on the epidemiology of adverse drug reactions, III: Reactions in patients on a general medical service. *Bulletin of Johns Hopkins Hospital*, 119, 299-315.

Smith, M.C. (1976). How drug costs affect compliance. *Drug Therapeutics*, 6, 12-15.

Strandberg, L.R. et al. (1980, January). The effects of comprehensive pharmaceutical devices on drug use in long term care facilities. *American Journal of Hospital Pharmacy*, 37, 92-94.

U.S. Senate, Subcommittee on Long-Term Care of the Special Committee on Aging. (1975, January). Drugs in nursing homes: Misuse, high costs and kickbacks [mimeographed].

U.S. Department of Health, Education and Welfare. (1976a, October). *Drugs and the elderly* (Publication No. (NIH) 78-1449). Washington, D.C.: National Institute on Aging.

U.S. Department of Health, Education and Welfare. (1976b). Physicians' drug prescribing patterns in skilled nursing facilities (Publication No. 76-50050, p. 27). Rockville, MD: Office of Long-Term Care.

Vestal, R. F. (1982, March). Pharmacology and aging. *Journal of the American Geriatrics Society*, 30(3), 191-202.

Wallace, D. E. and Watanabe, H. S. (1977, October). Drug effects in geriatric patients. *Drug Intelligence and Clinical Pharmacy*, 11, 597-603.

Wallace and Watanabe. (1977). Drug effects in geriatric patients. *Drug Intelligence and Clinical Pharmacy*, 11, 597-603.

Wandless, I. and Davis, J.W. (1977, February). Can drug compliance in the elderly be improved? *British Medical Journal*, 359-363.

Waugh, N.C. et al. (1978, September). Retrieval time from different memory stores. *Journal of Gerontology*, 33, 718-724.

Wilkinson, G.R. (1979). The effects of aging on the disposition of benzodiazepines in man. In J. Crooks and I. H. Stevens (eds.), *Drugs in the elderly: Perspectives in geriatric clinical pharmacology* (pp. 103-116). Baltimore, MD: University Park Press.

Witte, K.W. et al. (1980, June). Drug regimen review in skilled nursing facilities by consulting pharmacists. *American Journal of Hospital Pharmacy*, 37, 820-824.

CHAPTER 6

SOCIAL POLICIES WHICH
INFLUENCE PRACTICE WITH THE ELDERLY[1]

DONNA HARDINA, PH.D.
MICHAEL J. HOLOSKO, PH.D.

T his chapter's purpose is to identify social policies in North America related to the elderly and suggest ways that social workers can be more directly and actively involved in policy formulation and implementation. It discusses: the complexities involved in understanding the relationship between macro policy and front-line practice; a comparison of social welfare policies for the elderly in Canada and the United States; and, practice and policy development issues in terms of an 'advocacy-in-action' model. The profession's Code of Ethics and practice values espouse the importance of social policy development, and the authors contend that social workers have a responsibility to do something more than simply being aware of policies related to the client groups they serve.

I. Introduction

Our contention in this chapter is to unravel some of the complexities inherent in a consideration of social policy so that practitioners may be better informed about what policy has to do with practice as it relates to the elderly. Thus, some generalizable issues about the nature of social policy need to be addressed so that the more substantial practice issues can be understood. These general issues relate to: 1) its definition; 2) its rationale; and, 3) its evolution in the field of social work practice.

Every text or literature source that attempts to convey information about social policy defines it differently (while reviewing literature for this chapter, we found some 47 different definitions of social policy). The reasons for this reality are less important than the resultant effect, which is, 'what definition should practitioners use?' A fairly simple consensus definition is: social policies are directives (which are usually written) which are the basis to provide services for people's needs. As such, social policies are intended to reflect social welfare programmes or services within a framework of humanistic values (Barnes, 1983).

Social policy in this perspective, may be considered on a continuum from macro to mezzo to micro. For instance, at the macro level, some authors explicitly maintain that social policies require formal authority or legitimation and are solely social legislative acts or regulations. At the mezzo level, social policies are guidelines, procedures or mandates that human service organizations use to operationalize their missions. At a micro level, policies may be formal or informal ways of doing things on the front-line by direct service practitioners. In this regard, all social policies eventually start at an external source, e.g., either through laws, acts, mandates, operational procedures, policy manuals, and trickle down to front-line practitioners and eventually clients they serve. Thus, as one might assume, most policy changes are usually effected at administrative levels beyond the day-to-day concerns of direct service practitioners (Titmuss, 1974).

While tabling some of these definitional issues, it is important to note that social policies are distinct from, yet interrelated to, economic and political policies. Further, all social policies are derived or are the result of broader and more priorized economic or political agendas. This usually renders such policies and their related social welfare concerns to a vulnerable power-dependency relationship in most Western world countries. For instance, it is well known by students of policy science in many fields (e.g., economics, public policy, political science, law, etc.,) that social policy initiatives are usually based on the residuals left over after economic and/or political concerns have been taken care of. Some Western countries, most notably Sweden, Norway, Canada and West Germany, have attempted to push social concerns to the forefront of their national priorities, but the reality is that economic and political imperatives, their infrastructures and power positions in society, supersede and generally inhibit the potential for social policies and programmes to become priorized as such.

There are basically four rationales (some more altruistic than others) for the formulation of social policies in North American society. The first is that policies are developed in order to respond to needs (e.g., child abuse, domestic violence, income maintenance, etc.). As we well know, however, there are more social needs than policies, needs often change and common sense tells us that one would be naive to assume that all social needs are being met by social policies (just look around you).

The second rationale for social policy formulation relates to the humanitarian and universal notion that social policies are developed in order to close the gap in society between the 'haves' and 'have nots,' that is, reduce social inequalities. This redistribution notion couched in a social responsibility imperative has been questioned by numerous authors and theorists in the fields of economics, political science, business and social welfare. Their consensus conclusion is that social policies do indeed help some groups of 'have nots,' e.g., through income supplementation, in-kind services or programmes, but they *do not* reduce the social inequalities existing in our society, they perpetuate them! (See Piven and Cloward, 1974 for a good example of how public welfare serves as a social control mechanism to regulate the poor).

The third rationale for the development of social policies has to do with the fact they attempt to provide guidelines, regulatory mechanisms, plans of action, and/or criteria for social welfare concerns. Social policy analysts stress that the content of these policies should be examined in terms of: the rationale for the policy; how it was formulated; what is says; how it will be interpreted and implemented; and, who will be affected by it. Such questions are not trite and often times serve as the impetus for policy change, modifications, revisions, amendments and clarifications. Clearly, this rationale reminds one both about: 1) the importance of understanding the policy-making process and whether those who formulate policy understand the needs of those who implement it (Majchrzak, 1984); and, 2) the content of the actual policies themselves, e.g., intents, acts, legislated policies, regulations, service documents, implicit vs. explicit policies, etc.

The finale rationale for how social policies emerge in our society is that they are the direct result of appeasing a political agenda. A study of some of the more profound social policies in North America that have emerged in the past 100 years would suggest that many of these have been largely politically motivated. That is, individual politicians or political parties have been the driving force behind their formulation. The consideration of social policy in a political context as such certainly causes one to be mindful about the larger sociopolitical context of policy formulation. For instance, at a very simple level, front-line practitioners may ask, 'How can the needs of my clients get to the agenda of policy-makers?' At another level, one may certainly wonder about whether political agendas mesh with the social welfare concerns of citizens. In any event, to try and understand social policy without a consideration of the political context is erroneous.

The history of the social work profession has been intertwined with social policy throughout its evolution (Lubove, 1973). Essentially, both the practitioners and educators of social work consider social policy as the cornerstone impetus for the development of the profession. Indeed, the profession's inception was deemed to be launched when the Elizabethan Poor Laws (in Britain) of the 16th century set down a series of legislative acts to 'help the poor, sick and indigent' and then the church, state and charitable organizations became recognized as the main institutions of social welfare. Thus, social policy determined the character of social welfare practice as much then as it does today. However, as history reminds us, the profession was (and is) more concerned and better able to implement policies than it is to influence, develop or analyze them (Lubove, 1973).

Schools of social work in North America virtually gave lip service to the study of social policy science until about 1960, at which time there was both a proliferation in social policy development (in society at large), as well as a shift in social welfare service delivery (from the voluntary to the public sector). The working definition of practice espoused by the National Association of Social Workers (NASW) in 1958 implicitly acknowledged the importance of policy in the configuration of social work practice (Bartlett, 1958). However, its later revised Code of Ethics had three sections (IV, V and VI) explicitly operationalizing policy concerns affecting all practicing social workers (NASW, 1980). As well, both North American accrediting bodies for social work education, the Council on Social Work Education (U.S.A.) and the Canadian Association of Schools of Social Work (CAN.) presently require policy courses taught in all BSW programmes of study. In this regard, social work educators have finally 'claimed' social welfare policy science as their domain and have moved beyond the previous awareness and policy consciousness stages into more proactive educational concerns such as ways to influence policy formulation, implementation and analyses.

We (the authors) are particularly optimistic and encouraged by the profession's (both practitioners and educators) investment in social policy issues and concerns to date. Indeed, the primary assumption put forward in this chapter is that social work practitioners have a responsibility to ensure that they are not only aware of social policies directly related to the elderly but also have a role to play in developing and implementing such policies.

The purpose of this chapter is to provide a framework for understanding social welfare policies in Canada and the United States that guide the provision of income security, medical care and social services to the elderly. The content of these policies in terms of how benefits are allocated, what benefits are provided, how services are delivered and how benefits are finances are discussed. The value assumptions underlying the development of social welfare policies are also presented and the policies in both countries are compared. In the final section, the relationship between social work practice and policy development is explored.

We as social workers need to first understand the 'process' of becoming a client in social welfare organizations. For instance, the elderly may be made to feel confused or humiliated by bureaucratic red tape and procedures established by the government agencies that implement social welfare policies. Although worthy of assistance by virtue of their past contributions to society, some elderly may not be treated with the respect they deserve when they attempt to obtain income or medical assistance.

We also need to realize that there is a wide difference between policy and practice in government programmes. For example, social welfare legislation often reflects the conflicting goals and values of a number of interest groups in society. The resulting policies are not always beneficial to the elderly but may prove to reflect the policy preferences and values of other interest groups as well (such as the medical profession or corporations). In addition, policies may be implemented in a discretionary manner by government bureaucrats (Lipsky, 1980). Although services are designed to be standardized by legislative mandate, elderly persons may have difficulty obtaining services to meet their needs. By understanding the content of these policies and the value assumptions that contribute to the design of social welfare programmes for the elderly, we as social workers can develop the capacity to help elderly consumers gain access to the benefits to which they are entitled. Our knowledge as to the impact of various policies on the elderly people we serve can also be utilized to successfully intervene in the policy development process in order that programmes are effective, equitable, preserve self-determination and enhance the quality of life for senior citizens. Thus, policy practice not only empowers elderly clients to receive their benefits as citizens but empowers social workers to have a direct impact in shaping these policies.

II. Comparing Social Welfare Policies in Canada and the United States

Social workers often use policy models to examine the content of social welfare policies and the effect of these policies on the consumers of service, and such models offer specific frameworks for analyzing policies. For example, Gilbert and Specht (1986) identified several characteristics common in all social welfare policies. These are: 1) allocation (Who receives the service?); 2) provision (What benefits are offered?); 3) service delivery (How are the services delivered to clients?); and, 4) financing (Who pays for the service?) (p. 37).

In examining social welfare policies related to the elderly, each of these characteristics is important in understanding the manner in which these policies interact with the needs of elderly consumers. More specifically, allocation of resources can be made either on a universal basis (almost every citizen has access to the benefit) or a selective basis (specific groups of citizens having special needs). As a consequence of resource allocation decisions, social welfare organizations may establish eligibility criteria that exclude clients without specific needs or income above a specified level from the service delivery process. Government programmes in North America have historically selected beneficiaries based on their 'moral worth,' and people needing assistance have been categorized as: 1) the worthy poor (children, the disabled and others who cannot be expected to work for benefits); and 2) the able-bodied or undeserving poor (people who could work if jobs were available and are regarded as choosing not to work).

As well, benefit provision may involve compensation for past contributions to the workforce (social insurance) or income assistance (welfare) for the very poor. However, welfare participation often carries a stigma, in that recipients may be viewed by other members of society as incapable of helping themselves. Generally, people will be more likely to apply for a benefit regarded as a universal 'right' based on past contributions in the workforce than a benefit associated with socially stigmatized groups of people (the unemployed, low wage earners) who have been 'selected' as requiring a special service (Rein, 1983; Hasenfeld, 1985).

Although the elderly have primarily been perceived as 'worthy' to receive social welfare benefits, income security programmes seldom provide equal benefits to all elderly citizens. Programmes for the elderly almost always differentiate between those eligible for adequate levels of social insurance benefits based on past work contributions and others who need additional assistance to meet their needs. The Old Age Security (OAS) programme is the only programme for the elderly in North America that provides an equal monthly cash benefit for all Canadian residents age 65 or over. The current Conservative Canadian Federal government plans to tax or 'claw back' OAS benefits for individuals with incomes over $50,000 per year, eliminating this 'universal' benefit.

Service delivery also reflects assumptions about worthy vs. unworthy beneficiaries. For benefits can be provided in ways that enhance the dignity of recipients (direct bank deposit of social insurance checks) or in a manner that reinforces the social stigma associated with assistance — a cumbersome application process and a long wait for service (Prottas, 1981). Further, the use of a 'means-test' to determine who will receive the service often requires that applicants submit proof of income, living expenses and savings. Such procedures often discourage applications and are associated with income assistance rather than social insurance programmes.

The financing of the programme also determines how the benefit will be allocated, provided and delivered. For example, a benefit system funded through past contributions of recipients will be more generous than one funded through general tax revenues and is less vulnerable to government cutbacks (Starr, 1988). Although government expenditures for both income security and medical care rose rapidly during the 1970s and 1980s in both Canada and the U.S., government policy-makers have been relatively unsuccessful in limiting the growth of social insurance programmes. These programmes provide benefits to almost all adults over 65 years of age and have a much larger political constituency than programmes targeted specifically to the poor. Income assistance programmes, on the other hand, are more likely to be subject to reductions in government funding and consequently attempts have been made to contain costs by decreasing access to services for all but the most needy.

In addition to the examination of policy content, policy analysis also requires that policies be evaluated in terms of specific social values. Social workers may ask whether policies as implemented promote such key social work values as confidentiality, client self-determination and equality (Flynn, 1987). Government's purpose in establishing a new programmes or restructuring current programmes may be to reflect changing societal attitudes about programme operation and beneficiaries. For example, the U.S. Medicare programme, first implemented in 1965, was designed to provide equal access to hospital and medical services. However, after the election of conservative president Ronald Reagan and a tremendous growth in programme costs, the government began to emphasize medical cost containment (Starr, 1986). Thus, 'efficiency' in service delivery became a primary policy value.

Van Gunsteren and Rein (1985) have identified two value criteria primarily associated with social welfare policies for the elderly: equity and adequacy. Equity is associated with social insurance programmes, in which benefit levels are proportional to the past work-related contributions of beneficiaries. Adequacy refers to whether the benefit is sufficient to meet the needs of recipients. In both Canada and the U.S., adequacy is assessed in terms of the 'poverty line,' or the amount of income considered to be sufficient for individuals, couples or families to meet minimum basic needs. Income assistance programmes are primarily designed to help low-income people increase their total income to an amount equivalent to the poverty line.

Income assistance programmes for the elderly were developed in both Canada and the U.S. as a consequence of the design of social insurance programmes. Social insurance programmes were never intended to 'lift' retired wage earners out of poverty but to provide income to supplement retirement savings and private pensions (Burtless, 1986). Consequently, both the U.S. and Canada developed three-tiered income security policies that emphasized self-reliance on income from wages, insurance to supplement lost income during retirement and income assistance programmes to help the elderly poor obtain an adequate income. (Canada also has a fourth tier, the Old Age Security programme providing universal and equal benefits to all residents over the age of 65) (Health and Welfare Canada, 1988; Social Security Administration, 1990).

Although most elderly social welfare beneficiaries have made a contribution to social insurance programmes, benefits are not always sufficient to provide adequate support.[1] In Canada, benefits provided through the Canadian Pension Plan are equivalent to only 25 percent of the individual's pre-retirement earnings (National Council on Welfare, 1990). Length of work history and employment determine work-related contributions and future benefit levels. Thus, minimum wage workers will not receive the Canadian Pension Plan or U.S. Social Security benefits equivalent to individuals with a greater amount of income from work. Further, women who have remained out of the workforce while raising a family will also receive lower benefits based on their own work history or will receive benefits by virtue of their marital status that may not be equivalent to that of the male wage earner (Eichler, 1987).

Programmes such as Supplement Security Income and Food Stamps in the U.S. and Guaranteed Income Supplement and Spouse's Allowances in Canada are designed to help people obtain an adequate level of benefits. Because these programmes are means-tested and selective, access to benefits often proves difficult for some elderly consumers.

Social welfare policies for the elderly in the U.S. and Canada deal primarily with two types of benefits: income security and medical care. The content of income security policies (allocation, provision, access and service delivery, and financing) and the values underlying these policies are illustrated in Table 1 (Social Insurance) and Table 2 (Income Assistance). Social insurance programmes are clearly differentiated from income assistance programmes in terms of basic value assumptions and the universal/selective dichotomy but also vary significantly in terms of access. Verification of past work contributions and age are the only requirements for participation in social insurance programmes. That is, assistance programme applicants must often supply proof of income, marital status, assets (home, savings account, investments) and living expenses. Access to services also varies greatly by country. U.S. residents are subject to more stringent income and asset tests than Canadians, suggesting that income security is much more likely to be regarded as an 'universal entitlement' in Canada than a selective programme provided only for the neediest (or least worthy) citizens.

Medical programmes in the U.S. and Canada are described in Table 3. Again these programmes are dichotomized as social insurance and medical assistance for the poor or 'medically needy.' Canada's health programme provides universal access to medical and hospital insurance for nearly all Canadian residents regardless of income. Although premium payments are required from members of the workforce, all Canadians age 65 and older receive free medical services (some co-payments are required for nursing home care). The U.S. insurance programme provides medical care only for those elderly who make premium payments both prior to and after retirement. Co-payments and deductible are required for most services, and nursing home care is not covered under this programme. Many of the elderly must apply for medical assistance from state Medicaid programmes to cover the costs of nursing home care. Applicants are subject to a means-test, and eligibility is determined by the proportion of an individual's or couple's income spent on medical care. A focus on cost-containment in both Medicare and Medicaid programmes has reduced the accessibility of medical services for many beneficiaries regardless of income (Marmour, 1988). U.S. federal and state governments now ration services with the use of prospective payment systems that limit the amount of money paid to hospital and physicians for services to individual clients. Similarly, Canada has also initiated cost containment measures resulting in the rationing of some specialized medical services.

A final category of social policies for the elderly involves the actual provision of social services. Social services designed to help seniors remain independent are funded by federal governments in both Canada and the U.S. (see Table 4). The Canadian Assistance Plan (1966) provides 50 percent of the funding for counselling, homemaker, food and other social services for every individual over 65 in each of the provinces and territories. The Older Americans Act (1965) provides federal funding to state governments for meals-on-wheels, congregate dining, transportation, recreation and other social services to income eligible people over 65 or others receiving benefits through the Supplemental Security Program (SSI). In some instances, people with incomes above the poverty line are required to make a co-payment in order to receive the service. All of these tables reflecting these policies are presented at this point.

III. Social Welfare Practice and Policy Development: 'Advocacy in Action'

For many social work practitioners, the connection between policy and practice is unclear. Policies seem to be made by government officials with little input from social workers or the people they serve. Social workers are the essential linkage between policy-makers and the people served by government programmes, however. Not only do social workers have direct knowledge of how policies impact on their clientele, they are also responsible for the implementation of many government policies in both public and voluntary social welfare organizations. Further, social workers often develop policy in the course of everyday practice. Dolgoff (1981) defined one of the primary social policy roles of social workers as the: "individual discrete decisions by workers [that] are policy choices that affect, for the time being, only the immediate situation and are ideological choices determining sources or plans of action." Individual decision-making by front-line workers also contributes to the formulation of agency policies. Social workers help to influence community policies and practices through networking with other social workers, helping professionals, consumer groups and government officials. Social

Table 1 — Social Insurance — United States and Canada

Policy	Date	Allocation	Provision	Service Delivery and Access	Financing	Basic Assumptions	Values
Social Security (OADSI) See (a) below (U.S.A.)	1935	Individuals 65 or over. Previous work-related contributions. Surviving or divorced spouses at age 62; or disabled surviving spouses between ages 50 and 64. Retirees between ages 62 and 65 can receive 80% of their monthly benefit. Late retirees can receive increased benefits. Ten year minimum contribution required for participation.	Monthly cash benefit. Amount determined by past contributions, age and quarters of coverage. Adjusted annually for cost of living.	Application at age 65 or upon disability, death of spouse or early retirement. Verification required: birth certificate, proof of recent earnings, and for surviving spouses, proof of the worker's death. Medical verification of disability for surviving spouses, ages 50-64.	Worker and employer contributions from payroll taxes. Income tax on 50% of Social Security benefits for beneficiaries receiving income from other sources over $25,000 per year.	Supplements retirement income for contributors; income protection for low income wage earners.	Equity; universal coverage.
Old Age Security Program (Can.)	1952	Age 65 or over and Canadian citizen or landed immigrant who has lived in Canada for 10 years past the age of 18. Retirement is not a requirement.	Monthly cash benefit for cost of living quarterly. Maximum: $343/mo (1990). Partial benefits for those who have lived in Canada less that 40 years after the age of 18. (1/40 of full pension for each year of residence.)	Application at age 65. Proof of age and Canadian residency. Portion of benefits to be taxed or 'clawed' back for persons with income over $50,000/ year. No income or asset test.	Consolidated Revenue Fund. Federal government.	All seniors should have a minimum level of income to meet their needs. Compensation for past social and economic contributions.	Adequacy Equality Universal coverage. Full implementation of the claw-back change will make the program selective in intent, means-tested.

Table 1 (continued)

Policy	Date	Allocation	Provision	Service Delivery and Access	Financing	Basic Assumptions	Values
Canada Pension Plan and Quebec Pension Plan See (b) below	1965	Age 65 or anyone over 60 who has ceased pensionable employment and who has made at least one valid contribution above minimum. Surviving spouses. Divorced spouses split credits earned by both spouses.	Monthly cash benefit equal to 25% of contributor's average monthly pensionable earnings. Maximum $543 (1988). Benefit decreases if taken before age 65 and increases if taken after age 65. Surviving spouses over 65 receive 60% of the worker's pension. Benefits adjusted annually for inflation. See (c) below.	Application at age 65, disability, death of spouse. Proof of age (birth certificate or baptismal record).	Worker, employer, and self-employed make contributions.	Protection against loss of income due to retirement, disability, and death. Supplements private pensions and savings.	Equity; universal coverage.

(a) The U.S. maintains separate pension systems for Federal government employees and Railroad workers.

(b) Both Canada and the U.S. provide pension benefits and medical services for veterans.

(c) Canada provides a "lump sum" retirement benefit to anyone age 65 and older who has worked and paid Unemployment Insurance premiums for at least 20 weeks in the previous year regardless of whether the individual continues to work. The weekly payment is equal to 60% of the person's weekly insurable earnings for the last 20 weeks of employment. The payment is intended to provide income while the worker is waiting to receive other pension benefits.

Table 2 — Income Assistance — United States and Canada

Policy	Date	Allocation	Provision	Service Delivery and Access	Financing	Basic Assumptions	Values
Supplemental Security Income (SSI) (U.S.A.)	1972	Individuals or couples, 65 and older. Any adult who is blind or disabled. Individual assets many not exceed $2,000. A couple's assests may not exceed $3,000. Assets do not include home, a car, burial plots or funds.	Monthly cash benefits. Maximum: $38 /mo. for individuals and $579/mo. for couples. Reduced if beneficiaries have other income or are living in institutions. Additional benefits are provided in 26 states.	Application through Social Security office. Verification: birth certificate, income assets, living expenses (mortgage, rent, food, utilities). Changes in income must be reported annually.	General Revenues, Federal Government.	Minimum monthly benefit to needy aged, blind and disabled people. Uniform benefit standard in all 50 states.	Adequacy; Selective assistance program, Means-testing.
Food Stamp Program (U.S.A.)	1964	Households with less than $3,000 in disposable assets if one member is age 60 or over (in two person households). Net household income cannot exceed 100% of the poverty line after deducing mortgage, rent, and utility costs.	Coupons that are to be used to purchase food. Benefit level is determined by household size, income, and expenses. Average monthl benefits: $50.04 person.	Households in which all members receive SSI or Social Security may file Food Stamp applications at their local SS Office. All other households must apply through state public assistance offices. Households with elderly or disabled members may be certified for Food Stamps over the phone or through office visits once the application has been received. Verification: income, assets, medical expenses, proof of mortgage or rent and utility payments. A new application is required each year.	General Revenues, Federal Government.	Diet Supplements for low income households. Recipients are expected to use one-third of their income exclusive of Food Stamps to purchase food.	Adequacy. Selective assistance program. Means-testing.

Table 2 (continued)

Policy	Date	Allocation	Provision	Service Delivery and Access	Financing	Basic Assumptions	Values
Guaranteed Income Supplement (Can.)	1966	Persons who receive Old Age Security Pension and little or no other income.	Monthly cash benefit. Amount determined by marital status and combined net income for couples. Maximum benefit is $407/mo. for a single person or a married person whose spouse does not receive OAS payments or spouse's allowance and $263/mo. for each married person whose spouse receives OAS payments or spouse's allowance. Benefits indexed quarterly at full rate of inflation. Benefit may be increased for people receiving partial OAS benefits.	Beneficiary must reapply each year. Proof of marital status. Applications are mailed to all OAS beneficiaries by Health and Welfare Canada each January. Eligibility based on previous year's income. No asset test. Benefits are not taxable.	General Revenues, Federal Government.	To compensate those whose only source of income is OAS.	Adequacy Selective program. Means-testing.

Table 2 — (continued)							
Policy	Date	Allocation	Provision	Service Delivery and Access	Financing	Basic Assumptions	Values
Spouse's Allowance (Can.)	1975	All low income widows and widowers or spouses of pensioners age 60 to 64. Must be a Canadian resident for at least 10 years after age 18.	Monthly cash benefit. Amount based on combined yearly income of both spouses exclusive of OAS and GIS benefits. Maximum: combination of full OAS and GIS at the married rate. Indexed to inflation quarterly. Benefit ceases when spouse reaches 65, leaves the country for more than 6 months, or is separated or divorced.	Beneficiary must reapply each year. Proof of marital status.	General Revenues, Federal Government.	Designed to recognize difficulties of couples living on the pension of one spouse and widowed persons.	Adequacy Selective program. Means-testing.

Table 2 (continued)

Policy	Date	Allocation	Provision	Service Delivery and Access	Financing	Basic Assumptions	Values
Provincial Supplements to GIS (Can.)	Varies by Province.	"Top-up" benefits to OAS/GIS/SPA beneficiaries. Available in Alberta, British Columbia, Manitoba, Nova Scotia, Saskatchewan, Yukon and Northwest Territories. Alberta also provides assistance to widows and widowers, aged 55-64. Manitoba provides supplemental benefits to low income individuals, age 55 and over. Persons aged 65 and over who are ineligible for OAS/GIS because of residency requirements can receive enhanced income assistance under regular social assistance legislation in all provinces.	Monthly cash benefits. Amount varies by province but is less than $100/mo. Nova Scotia provides one lump sum payment each May. Maximum: $219. Cost of living adjustments are made on an "ad hoc" basis.	Automatic eligibility for OAS/GIS/SPA beneficiaries. Annual application for Federal programmes necessary. Application must be made in Alberta and Manitoba by persons not categorically eligible. Nova Scotia also requires a separate application for lump sum payments. All provincial supplements are nontaxable. Income reduction rates are similar to GIS rates.	Provincial general revenue funds.	Ensures that income of the elderly does not fall below minimum levels.	Adequacy.

Table 3 — Medical Care — United States and Canada

Policy	Date	Allocation	Provision	Service Delivery and Access	Financing	Basic Assumptions	Values
Medicare, Part A (U.S.A.)	1965	Age 65 and older who have made payroll contributions. Spouse, divorced spouse, or surviving spouse. Individuals who have received disability benefits for more than 24 months.	Hospital insurance. Reimbursement for inpatient care after beneficiary pays an annual deductible ($592 for first 60 days, 1990). Skilled nursing facility for up to 100 days. Beneficiary pays co-insurance of $74/day for 21-100 days of skilled care. Unlimited approved home health and hospice care.	Benefits automatic at age 65 for Social Security beneficiaries. Individuals who continue to work after age 65 or government employees must apply for benefits. Prospective payment system limits the length of hospital stay.	Worker and employer contributions through payroll taxes. Non-contributors may "buy" into the system ($175/mo. in 1990).	Partial payment of hospital expenditures for the aged. Increased access to health care. Cost containment.	Equity Efficiency.
Medicare, Part B (U.S.A.)	1965	Age 65 and older. Anyone who is eligible for hospital insurance. (Part A) Previous Social Security credits not necessary for enrolment.	Medical insurance. Reimbursement for 80% of doctor's services, out-patient hospital services, home health visits and other medical services and supplies after $75 deductible (1987).	Automatic enrolment for most beneficiaries.	Beneficiaries pay a monthly premium of $28.60. Must also be enrolled in Part A. States must pay premiums and deductibles for people with incomes at/below 100% of the poverty line by 1993.	Partial payment of medical expenses for the aged. Increased access to health care. Cost containment.	Equity Efficiency.

Table 3 (continued)

Policy	Date	Allocation	Provision	Service Delivery and Access	Financing	Basic Assumptions	Values
Medicaid. (U.S.A.)	1965	Based on state discretion. Elderly persons assessed by the state to be SSI eligible. At state option, persons needing long-term care and "medically needy" individuals and households who "spend down" to Medicaid eligibility through accumulation of medical expenses that reduce income below income guidelines. 1990 Medicare provisions permit elderly couples to retain up to 50% of income and their homes while qualifying for Medicaid coverage for nursing home care for one spouse.	Basic medical, doctor and hospital services. Many services such as intermediate care services for the aged are state optional.	Reimbursement for services is made to providers. States may limit hospital stays or number of doctor visits per year. States may also "cap" provider reimbursement levels. This can result in Medicaid patients being transferred to low cost hospitals. Inner city and rural hospitals have also been forced to shut down due to high number of Medicaid patients and unrealistic reimbursement levels.	General revenues, Federal and state government. Federal government paid between 50-78.5% of state medical costs and 50% of adminis- trative costs. Wealthier states are reimbursed at lower levels. States required to pay for "Medicap" coverage i.e., Medicare premiums and deductibles for individuals and couples with incomes at or below 90% of the poverty line.	Federal/state partnership to provide medical services to the needy. Cost control.	Adequacy, Selective program. Means- testing.

Table 3 (continued)

Policy	Date	Allocation	Provision	Service Delivery and Access	Financing	Basic Assumptions	Values
Canada Health Act 1) Hospital Insurance and Diagnostic Service Act 2) Medical Care Act	1957 1966	Federal mandate to provide comprehensive hospital and medical insurance to 90-95% of the population in each province and territory at little or no cost to the consumer.	Hospital and medical services. Including: medically necessary services in nursing homes, homes for the aged and hospitals; portion of ward costs in nursing home, physician services, rehabilitative services, home care, ambulance services, prescription drugs and medical devices. Some services are provided at provincial discretion. For example, Ontario's insurance program (OHIP) only covers prescription drugs for the elderly.	Provinces pay insurance premiums for the elderly, social assistance recipients and other low income individuals. Some individuals pay own premiums if not covered through employer plans. Specialized services such as coronary care may not be available in some localities. There may also be a waiting period for some services. Available services are often supplemented by the purchase of private health plans by individuals and employers.	Employers pay insurance premiums for most employees. Provinces pay premiums for low income or elderly. Some individuals buy into the system. Under the Established Program Financing Act, provinces receive Federal block funding for health care. Canada Health Act (1984) prohibits extra billing by physicians for services rendered. Co-payments are required for some services such as nursing home care.	Health services should be universal and accessible to all.	Equality of access.

Table 4 — Social Services — United States and Canada

Policy	Date	Allocation	Provision	Service Delivery and Access	Financing	Basic Assumptions	Values
Older Americans Act (Title III) (U.S.A.)	1965	Over 65 or SSI beneficiary. Some benefits contingent on income or co-payments.	Social services, senior centres meals on wheels, congregate dining, transportation and recreation services.	Proof of income. Services such as meals on wheels have income guidelines and co-payments.	General revenues, Federal government. Funding provided through state and local government for non-profit organizations. Some fee for service. Service delivery through State or Area Councils on Aging.	Preserve quality of life and independence for retired persons.	Adequacy.
Canadian Assistance Plan (Can.)	1966	Individuals age 65 and over.	Food, shelter, clothing, fuel, utilities, repairs to property, care in nursing homes, homemaker and counselling services.	Service provision is not contingent on income.	Federal government pays 50% of all provincial, territory and municipal expenditures for social services. Ceiling put on CAP expenditures in 1991 Federal budget in 3 provinces: Ontario, British Columbia and Alberta.	To provide appropriate and accessible services to help seniors remain in their own communities. Also, promotes gerontological education and public awareness of the needs of the elderly.	Equity.

workers also engage in social action in order to change macro level policies (pp. 288-289).

Pierce (1984) identifies a number of policy roles for social workers. For instance, outreach workers, advocates and brokers help link clients with needed resources. Social workers can also be catalysts, organizers or activists working with community groups to effect change. Social workers may undertake research to document existing problems, engage in community planning and networking to develop programmes and work as administrators and evaluators of programmes. In addition, social workers may provide testimony at public hearings, analyzing the effects of legislation on client groups (p. 178).

Many of the social work roles defined by Pierce are familiar to social workers as part of the profession's commitment to advocacy. Thus, policy practice can be thought of as advocacy on behalf of individual clients or client groups. According to Sauber (1983) there are two basic types of advocacy: 1) general case advocacy and follow-up services by staff; and, 2) consumer advocacy education and investigation of complaints (p. 386). *Case advocacy* involves increasing client access and utilization of social welfare services. Consumer advocacy, on the other hand, involves the use of influence or the mobilization of pressure to achieve changes in service quality. Case advocacy is provided by professional social workers who have obtained information about social welfare policies and benefits. Thus, the social worker acts as a broker, linking people with available resources. However, advocacy in social welfare organizations is often confined to action on individual cases rather than addressing the root causes of the problem (such as government policies or organization practices). Organizations (and individual workers) may also choose not to practice advocacy due to the commitments of time and resources required to sustain such activities (Lipsky, 1980).

In consumer or *self-help advocacy*, the involvement of service consumers and the dissemination of information about services is essential to the advocacy process. Self-help advocacy has been associated with efforts to increase access to services for the mentally or physically disabled (Gould and Ardinger, 1988; Rose and Black, 1985). Self-help advocacy can also be used as a strategy to help powerless groups obtain other assistance such as emergency food, shelter, welfare benefits or social insurance payments. This type of intervention requires not only that the social worker provides information to client groups about service availability and social welfare policies but also assists them in learning the skills necessary to obtain benefits from public organizations. The purpose of self-help advocacy is to empower clients by developing their capacity to advocate for themselves. Solomon (1976) argues that empowerment should be the goal of any social work intervention because: "power and control are energizing magnets, drawing the client into the redefinition of his own self-worth, competence, and ability to affect his social and physical worlds" (pp. 342-343).

A third type of advocacy commonly practiced by social workers is *legislative advocacy* or lobbying for laws or regulations that will benefit either the profession or service consumers. Legislative advocacy is conducted not on behalf of individuals but involves issues affecting a group or class of individuals having similar needs (Paul, 1977). For instance, a caseworker may find it necessary to help several people receiving income assistance who have problems meeting their basic needs by organizing a legislative campaign to increase income assistance grant level.

Patti and Dear (1975) defined legislative advocacy as an attempt "to influence the course of a bill or legislative measure" (p. 108). Kramer (1981) identifies four such advocacy activities: securing tax exemptions or benefits for clientele; obtaining voluntary agency funding; improving governmental service programmes; and, influencing legislation or regulations (p. 214). Legislative advocacy requires the utilization of a number of social work skills: defining problems and needs, research to document needs, community organization to build public support, development of recommendations for changes in service delivery or policy, testimony at public hearings and lobbying public officials.

Mayer (1982) stated that advocacy practice on the part of social workers is insufficient to shape the development of social welfare policies:

> The mission of the profession and the methods in which its recruits have been trained tend to focus on changing the public agenda or the ends to which public programs are directed. This mission is consistent with the profession's involvement in social reform. . . . From such a perspective, the concern for

how one achieves those reform goals, or for assessing the availability of resources for their attainment is defined as the responsibility of other professions. (p. 58)

Mayer believes that social workers should be involved in the development of social welfare policy. Thus, not only do social workers have access to information about the impact of policies on clients, but they also have the power to implement policy at the agency level. The value base of social work (our emphasis on equality, self-determination and confidentiality) makes it preferable that social workers formulate policy rather than economists, public administrators or government officials.

Table 5 — Policy Formulation and Social Work Roles*	
Tasks	Professional Roles
Identification of the programme	Practitioner
Analysis	Researcher
Informing the public	Community organizer
Development of policy goals	Planner
Building public support	Community organizer
Legislation	Legislative analyst
Implementation, administration	Administrator, practitioner
Evaluation, assessment	Practitioner
* From Specht (1968), p. 44.	

In this regard, Specht (1968) identified eight policy formulation tasks that correspond to social work roles (see Table 5).

Social workers as practitioners, researchers, community organizers, planners, legislative analysts and administrators can influence the development of social welfare policies at the case, agency or governmental level. Policy development requires the identification and analysis of problems, providing information to the public and building support, the development of policy goals, the approval of legislation, programme implementation and evaluation of the programme (achievement of policy goals). The role of the direct service practitioner is crucial in the policy development process. Practitioners help define the needs of the people they serve and can communicate these needs to policy-makers in agencies and government bureaucracies. For instance, our involvement in the policy development process is essential if programmes for the elderly are to promote the dignity and independence of all senior citizens. Current efforts by the federal governments in both Canada and the United States threaten to dismantle current programmes and limit access to both income security and medical services for many elderly.

IV. Concluding Remarks

Social workers have to become more concerned with understanding the relationship between policy formulation, implementation, practice and how this affects the clients they serve. This chapter does not attempt to minimize the complexities involved in this issue, but discusses how workers can better serve their elderly clients if they move beyond an awareness level of policy consciousness to a more proactive 'advocacy-in-action' orientation. After a comparison of policies that influence practice with the elderly in Canada and the United States, we presented a three-tiered advocacy model for practice, which involves case advocacy, self-help advocacy and legislative advocacy. Each type of advocacy is not beyond the roles and responsibilities of front-line practitioners — indeed, we contend they should be part of their practice. Our ability to empower our clients rests clearly with our ability to empower ourselves in the policy process. The sooner we understand how to assist elderly clients in this regard, the better we will be able to serve them.

Endnotes

1   We would like to acknowledge the assistance of Robin Perry, M.S.W. in the preparation of this chapter.
2   Social insurance programmes in both Canada and the U.S. provide low income wage earners with benefits that are proportionately larger than their past contributions. High wage earners receive slightly less in benefits proportionate to past contributions. Hence the programmes somewhat adjust for disparities in past income.

References

Barnes, J. (1983). *Welfare: An overview.* Windsor, Ontario: University of Windsor Press, The Research and Development Unit.

Bartlett, H. (1958, April). Toward clarification and improvement of social work practice. *Social Work,* 3(2), 3-9.

Begin, M. (1988). *Medicare: Canada's right to health.* Ottawa: Optimum Publishing International.

Burtless, G. (1986). The policies of elderly Americans. In S. H. Danzinger and D. H. Weinberg (eds.), *Fighting poverty: What works and what doesn't.* Cambridge: Harvard University Press.

Center for Budget and Policy Priorities. (1987). *Holes in the safety net: Poverty programs and policies in the States.* Washington, D.C.

Davison, N. (1989). *Guide for older adults. . . community services in the greater Windsor area.* Windsor: Community Information Services.

Dolgoff, R. (1981, May). Clinicians as social policymakers. *Social Casework,* 62, 284-292.

Eichler, M. (1987). *Families in Canada today.* Toronto: Gage Education Publishing Company.

Flynn, J. (1987). *Social agency policy.* Chicago: Nelson Hall Publishers.

Gilbert, N. and Specht, H. (1986). *Dimensions of social welfare policy.* Englewood Cliffs, N.J.: Prentice-Hall.

Gould, M. and Ardinger, R. (1988). Self advocacy. *Journal of Voluntary Action Research,* 17, 46-53.

Government of Canada. (1988). *Senior's guide to federal programs and services* (Cat. No. H71-3/8-1988E ISBN 0-662-16261-7). Ottawa: Minister of National Health and Welfare.

Government of Ontario. (1988). *Guide for senior citizens.* Toronto: Minister for Senior Affairs.

Government of Ontario. (1989). *GAINS for seniors: The guaranteed annual income system for Ontario senior citizens.* Toronto: Ministry of Revenue.

Hasenfeld, Y. (1985). Citizens' encounters with welfare state bureaucracies. *Social Service Review,* 59, 623-635.

Health and Welfare Canada. (1988). *Senior citizen's financial benefit programs in inventory of security programs in Canada* (Cat. No. H75-161 1988E ISBN 0-662-17178-9). Ottawa: Minister of Supply and Services, Canada.

Kramer, R. (1981). *Voluntary agencies in the welfare state.* Berkeley: University of California Press.

Lipsky, M. (1980). *Street-level bureaucracy: Dilemmas of the individual in public service.* New York: Russell Sage Foundation.

Lubove, R. (1973). *The professional altruist.* New York: Harvard University Press.

Majchrzak, A. (1984). *Methods for policy research.* Beverly Hills, CA: Sage Publications Inc.

Marmour, T. (1988). Coping with a creeping crisis. Medicaid at twenty. In T. R. Marmour and J. L. Mashaw (eds.), *Social security: Beyond the rhetoric of crisis.* Princeton, NJ: Princeton University Press, 119-148.

Mayer, R. (1982). Social planning as social work practice. *Administration in Social Work,* 9, 49-60.

National Association of Social Workers. (1980). *Code of ethics.* Washington, D.C.

National Council of Welfare. (1990). *Pension reform* (Cat. No. H68-24 1990E ISBN 0-662-17514-X). Ottawa: Minister of Supply and Services, Canada.

Paul, J. (1977). A framework for understanding advocacy. In J. L. Paul, G. R. Neufeld and J. W. Pelosi (eds.), *Child advocacy within the system* (pp. 11-31). Syracuse, NY: Syracuse University Press.

Patti, R. and Dear, R. (1975). Legislative advocacy: One path to social change. *Social Work,* 20, 108-114.

Pierce, D. (1984). *Policy for the social work practitioner.* New York: Longman.

Piven, F. F. and Cloward, R. A. (1971). *Regulating the poor: The functions of public welfare.* New York: Vantage Books Inc.

Prottas, J. (1981, September/October). The cost of free services. *Public Administration Review,* 41, 526-534.

Rein, M. (1983). *From policy to practice.* New York: Armonk.

Rose, S. and Black, B. (1985). *Advocacy and empowerment.* Boston: Routledge and Kegan Paul.

Sauber, R. (1983). *The human service delivery system.* New York: Columbia University Press.

Social Security Administration. (1989). Social security programs in the United States. *Social Security Bulletin,* 52. Washington, D.C.: Department of Health and Human Services.

Social Security Administration. (1990). *Social security facts and figures.* Washington, D.C.: Department of Health and Human Services.

Solomon, B. (1976). *Black empowerment.* New York: Columbia University Press.

Spears, G. (1990, March 21). Benefit gains offer hope to the elderly. *Detroit Free Press.*

Specht, H. (1968). Casework practice and social policy formulation. *Social Work, 12,* 42-51.

Starr, P. (1986). Health care for the poor. In S. Danzinger and D. Weinberg (eds.), *Fighting poverty: What works and what doesn't* (pp. 119-148). Cambridge: Harvard University Press.

Starr, P. (1988). Social security and the American public household. In T. Marmour and L. Mashaw (eds.), *Social security.* Princeton, NJ: Princeton University Press, 177-199.

Titmuss, R. (1974). *Social policy: An introduction.* Abel-Smith and K. Titmuss (eds.). New York: Pantheon Books Inc.

Van Gunsteren, H. and Rein, M. (1985). The dialectic of public and private pensions. *Journal of Social Policy, 14,* 129-149.

CHAPTER 7

IDENTIFYING THE ELDERLY ALCOHOLIC: A NICHE FOR GERONTOLOGICAL SOCIAL WORK PRACTICE

CATHERINE SCHENK, B.S.W.
MICHAEL J. HOLOSKO, PH.D.

*T*his chapter presents a case for social workers practicing in this field to become more actively involved in the assessment and detection of alcoholism among the elderly. The chapter rests on the assumption that early detection and assessment serves as a perfect niche for gerontological practice. This issue is discussed from the standpoint of: 1) the profile of the elderly alcoholic; 2) prevalence rates; 3) methodological issues; 4) early identification issues; and, 5) direct practice suggestions.

I. Introduction

Alcoholism is a multi-faceted problem, both for the addicted individual and society at large. Many elderly citizens who could be potentially enjoying their 'golden years' are caught in the web of alcohol addiction, and instead lead lives of misery and unhappiness (Aims Media Source, 1990). Social workers are in an ideal position to help identify elderly alcoholics, as the nature of social work is helping persons to cope and adjust to their life situations in timely and effective ways.

This chapter begins by providing a profile of the types of elderly alcoholics identified in the literature and some examples of prevalence data. Identification of elderly alcoholics remains somewhat of a professional enigma as the gerontological social worker must have specific assessment knowledge and skills in order to ask the right questions. She or he also needs to identify the various aspects associated with treating addicted clients in this unique age group. Our experience has shown that there is an opportunity for both direct and indirect social work practitioners to be effective in this field; however, this ability rests foremost on developing a specialized approach to performing assessments that are reliable and valid. This chapter ostensibly builds upon Chapter 3 (by Watt and Soifer) and makes a case for showing how the assessment and detection of problems of the elderly are inextricably linked to treatment.

II. Profile of the Elderly Alcoholic

In the early 1970s researchers in this field differentiated older problem drinkers into early-onset and late-onset/reactive categories (Schonfeld and Dupree, 1991). While these two typologies remain widely accepted, other researchers and clinicians maintain that not all elderly persons with problematic drinking patterns fit one of these categories. For instance, an early- or late-onset diagnoses is based solely on age of onset, whereas those proposing additional typologies also take other factors into account.

I. Early-onset

The early-onset elderly alcohol abuser typically begins an excessive drinking pattern in mid-life and has managed to survive to old age. Usually concerns about drinking are not new to them, as they have had significant alcohol-related problems for many years (Schonfeld and Dupree, 1991). Further, earlier onset has been related to a family history of alcoholism and more severe alcohol problems (Graham, 1993). When compared to late-onset drinkers, they generally have more psychological problems: higher levels of depression, greater trait anxiety and lower levels of life satisfaction (Schonfeld and Dupree, 1990; Graham, 1993). As well, Zimberg (1984) has suggested that early-onset drinkers have personality characteristics that are similar to younger alcoholics.

Other variations found between the early- and late-onset groups are the quantity and frequency of drinking as well as their receptiveness to treatment. Generally, the early-onset group also consume more liquor on a typical day of drinking and have twice as many drinking days as late-onset drinkers. They are also more resistant to treatment with a 56 percent drop-out rate, compared to 26 percent for late-onset individuals (Schonfeld and Dupree, 1990).

II. Late-onset or Reactive

In contrast to the early-onset alcoholic, the late-onset drinker usually reacts to the stresses of aging with a pattern of heavy drinking. Typical age-related stressors include: depression, bereavement, retirement, loneliness, marital stress and physical illness (Zimberg, 1984). In general, one-third of elderly alcoholics are reactive drinkers, but the distribution varies across study or region. For example, in Toronto, the Community Older Persons Alcohol Program reported a prevalence rate of 29 percent to 68 percent in programmes for older people (Graham, 1993). Ironically, no empirical evidence of late-onset alcoholism was reported in elderly skid row communities, as a study of alcoholic patients in private hospital found 88 percent had begun excessive drinking later in life (Atkinson, 1984). There is also some evidence to suggest that late-onset alcoholism is more common among women and persons of higher socioeconomic status (Graham, 1993). Apparently, although late-onset alcoholics have less emotional and social problems than early-onset drinkers, they also tend to have more physical problems (Gulino and Kadin, 1986).

Recent research focusing on the similarities between the two groups warrants some acknowledgement at this point. Although age of onset has been used as a distinguishing factor separating types of drinkers, antecedents for current drinking behaviour have been found to be similar for both groups. Specifically, "most were steady drinkers, who drank at home and alone, and in response to such negative emotional states as sadness, loneliness, depression, and boredom"

(Schonfeld and Dupree, 1990, p. 7). Further, many of them were widowed, divorced, retired, and had a limited social support network. These authors, among others, have suggested that the early-onset drinkers may have caused some of their losses by drinking, whereas the late-onset alcoholics drank in response to such losses.

III. Additional Typologies

Age for late-onset alcoholism is not clearly defined, and as a result some researchers have used age 50 to define the so-called 'late drinker' (Liberto, Oslin and Ruskin, 1992). As gerontological practitioners acknowledge, there is a generation of difference between mid-life and old age. For instance, at a national conference in Toronto, Graham (1993) presented data that differentiated drinkers into three 'age-of-onset' categories. In this typology, early-onset drinkers, those who began before age 40, represented 38 percent of the elderly alcoholics who showed up in treatment. Mid-life onset drinkers were those who began drinking between ages 41 and 59, and made up 47 percent, while the remaining 15 percent were in the late-onset group, or those who began drinking after age 60 (Graham, 1993). These figures may lead to a much clearer picture of cohort differences, lifestyles and reasons for drinking than the previous two-age differentiation dichotomy.

Others have proposed alternate typologies to differentiate elderly alcoholics. A recent study in Ontario used the early- and late-onset model, as well as a category for persons with inter-related alcohol abuse and cognitive/psychiatric problems (Graham et al., 1990). Persons in this category were mainly young-old women who displayed irrational thinking patterns, denied excessive drinking and could not comprehend that drinking might be related to their physical, psychological and/or social problems. Further, some had long histories of drinking and others had begun as a reaction to grief (Graham et al., 1990). Finally, in this regard, Sumberg (1985) proposed a third type of alcoholic, the binge drinker, as one who abstains between periods when drinking gets out of control. His evidence suggests the whole notion of that assessment may be more complex than slotting all 'other alcoholics' into either one of two traditional groups.

III. Prevalence Rates

While it is commonly accepted that rates of drinking among elderly cohorts are lower than those of younger populations studied (Graham, 1986), it is difficult to determine the scope and nature of the problem of alcoholism among the elderly population. Some reports suggest there is little cause for concern, while others contend that alcohol abuse affects a high proportion of elderly persons. (The reasons for variation in these statistics will be examined in a subsequent subsection of this chapter that addresses the applicability of current screening instruments when applied to this population.)

The Addiction Research Foundation's (ARF) (1991) statistics for the province of Ontario indicated that 27.5 percent of people age 65 and over reported consuming five or more drinks at a single sitting and 3.6 percent had two or more alcohol-related problems. In a comprehensive review of cross-sectional population studies of drinking patterns of people over age 60 living in the community, significant variance in prevalence of problem drinkers was found by ARF. When the threshold criteria of 'heavy' drinking was consumption of 12 to 21 drinks per week, 3 percent of these older persons were considered to have 'problematic' drinking behaviour. Dropping the classification criteria down to five to seven drinks per week resulted in identifying 11 percent to 25 percent of the older population as so called 'heavy' drinkers. Similarly, in a study of one-month prevalence rates that used the *Diagnostic and Statistical Manual of Mental Disorders, Third Edition Revised (DSM III-R)* criteria, 3.1 percent of men and 0.4 percent of women were considered to be 'problem' drinkers (Liberto, Oslin and Ruskin, 1992).

In an earlier study that reported the overall prevalence of alcoholism in the population over age 21 to be 19 per 1,000, elderly widowers' rates were the highest of all groups at 105 per 1,000 (Zimberg, 1984). Although these data are limited, it appears that elderly hospital and nursing home residents have increasingly high rates of alcohol-related problems. For instance, prevalence of alcoholism was reportedly as high as 40 to 60 percent for nursing home residents in a study by Gulino and Kadin (1986). Among older hospital patients, some research reported rates of 17 percent, while others ranged up to 63 percent (Blazer and Pennybacker, 1984). The variation in these hospital rates was explained as the result of different clinical samples (i.e., medical wards, mentally ill patients and veterans' hospitals) used as a basis for such research.

Canada's shifting demographic profile of elderly persons, if nothing else, will result in increased rates of alcoholism among elderly persons. From all accounts it appears that the problem may become even more predominant in future years. Alcohol consumption patterns vary within cohorts, and today's elderly tend to view drinking with more restrictive pre-Prohibition mores (Graham, 1986). For instance, those elderly who recently became late-onset alcoholics were found to already have moderate, habitual drinking patterns prior to later life, and since those cohorts who approach old age usually have a higher incidence of moderate drinking patterns (Holzer et al., 1986), we anticipate seeing problematic drinking, particularly the late-onset type, become an increasing concern in the future.

IV. Methodological Issues

The variation in prevalence rates indicates that there are factors, other than actual drinking patterns of elderly people, that distort the picture of what is really happening in the lives of many of these older men and women. Although these are research-oriented concerns, they are intertwined with practice realities and interventions. A critique of methodological issues related to assessment makes it obvious that social workers need to learn to ask the right questions when conducting psychogeriatric assessments, and that they should not necessarily take statistical data at face value when planning interventions or services for such clients.

I. Operational Definitions

There is no apparent consensus on operational definitions for 'elderly' or the older 'alcoholic,' hence how each researcher individually defines these terms in the literature is different. As a result, such data are not readily comparable. The prevalence rates cited in this chapter are extrapolated from studies that used either age 60 or 65 to define elderly. As gerontological social workers are aware (see Chapter 1 of this text), the within group variability of elderly cohorts presents its own particular dilemmas for practitioners. Coupled with this, the lack of a singular operational definition for 'alcoholism' (a long-standing and perennial problem in the addictions field) results in the use of differential identification criteria, which compounds data interpretation of incidence, occurrence or prevalence. Traditional criteria frequently used to define alcoholism among the elderly are: quantity, frequency and volume of drinking, social and behavioural problems, tolerance and withdrawal symptoms, and physical health problems (Blazer and Pennybacker, 1984). Addictions workers are mindful that these criteria in and of themselves present an incomplete operational definition.

II. Variations in Measurement Instruments

Closely related to the definitional dilemma is the lack of a consistent measurement instrument used to identify alcohol abuse among the elderly. As indicated, the *DSM III-R* uses fairly stringent criteria to diagnose alcoholism per se (American Psychiatric Association, 1987). Other common instruments used are *The CAGE Assessment* (Saunders and Conigrave, 1990), *The Michigan Alcoholism Screening Test (MAST)*, and it's shorter version (Gullno and Kudin, 1986). All of these rely on younger males as a normative reference group to determine alcohol abuse. However, the effects of alcoholism on social, behavioural or psychological functioning (Liberto, Oslin and Ruskin, 1992), factors that are usually relevant to elderly persons, are not normally considered in such assessments.

III. Quantity and Consumption Measures

Although overall rates of 'heavy' drinking are lower (than the general population) for elderly persons, it does not mean that drinking among the elderly is any less of a problem. Indeed, physiologically, alcohol consumption may decrease because of disabilities related to aging or due to increased effects of alcohol related to a poorer ability to metabolize alcohol (Graham, 1986). Further, many medications are seriously contraindicated when alcohol is consumed concurrently, and the effect of alcohol is amplified (Willenbring and Spring, 1988). Thus, alcoholism detection can be obscured by using gross quantitative measures of drinking. In this regard, Sumberg (1985) offered an example where an elderly client repeatedly insisted she had only two drinks of vodka a day. It was only when she was asked what size the glass was, and she produced her eight-ounce tumbler, that her alcohol problem was uncovered.

IV. Self-report Data

Similarly, Graham (1986) pointed out the unreliability and invalidity of standardized questionnaires when indiscriminantly applied to elderly persons. For instance, most valid instruments require a degree of self-report, and such data rely on an accurate memory and a willingness to provide truthful information. For many elderly, without jobs to structure their days or concurrent drug use that may impair their mental ability, our experience has shown that they may be confused about reporting drinking behaviours. Additionally, given that denial is part of the pathology of alcoholism, many elderly often do not respond accurately on self-report or inventories.

V. Health Criterion

Alcohol-related health problems are easily confounded with those that are a natural consequence of aging (Graham, 1986). While alcoholism normally intensifies physiological changes of the aging process, signs of alcoholism such as slurred speech, poor coordination and visual disturbances, are different from specific age-related changes (Gulino and Kadin, 1986). Even when elderly alcohol abusers formally enter the health-care system, their addiction is frequently undiagnosed because it is not the presenting problem. In general, diagnoses using health indicators do not focus on those health problems that are exclusively alcohol related in elderly patients (Blazer and Pennybacker, 1984).

VI. Lifestyle Data

Indicators of alcohol abuse on standardized questionnaires (e.g., employment difficulties, spouse abuse, drinking and driving, etc.,) often do not realistically reflect the lifestyle issues of elderly persons.

For instance, these questionnaires are not only biased toward younger, active, employed persons, but they also tend to characterize a male gender bias (Graham, 1986). Further, the elderly are less likely to enter the legal system because of public disturbances, arrests, drunk driving or the social/behavioural consequences of drinking, which are ways many alcoholics become detected (Blazer and Pennybacker, 1984). In short, often times due to their lifestyles (i.e. not working, isolated from family, friends or neighbours, not driving, etc.,) the elderly are less likely to exhibit problems with alcohol that could be readily detected.

V. Early Identification Issues

The point of departure for this chapter rests on the common-sense and well-known social work assumption that early identification and assessment leads to more effective treatment. Therefore, social workers have a vital role to play in that they often serve as the gatekeepers to the variety of institutional and community-based settings (see Section II of this text) in which the elderly are treated. It is necessary for the profession to realize its potential and act more proactively in providing prudent early identification of this problem. The role of the social worker in this early identification process will be discussed with respect to: 1) assessment, 2) dispelling myths, 3) transference and countertransference, and 4) using support systems.

I. Assessment

Weinberg (1983) clearly stated the importance of assessment to uncover alcohol problems among adult clients, and his warnings should be heeded by the social workers practicing in this field:

> The most important potential contribution that social workers might make in the treatment of alcoholism would be to move from intellectual recognition that alcoholism is a prevalent problem to direct application of appropriate helping strategies in clinical practice. First and foremost, social workers

should systematically screen all adult clients, prior to launching into treatment of the presenting problem, to see whether they can rule out a diagnosis of alcoholism. The alcoholic will derive little or no benefit, and much time will be wasted if his treatment focuses on secondary or interdependent individual, family, or marital problems. (p. 209-210)

If accurate diagnosis is not made, there is little, if any, chance that either the problem drinker or the members of the family will be helped by any subsequent interventions (Ehline and Tighe, 1977). Indeed, it has been well acknowledged that "assessment is the cornerstone of good psychogeriatric care. Careful, systematic examination is essential for accurate diagnosis and appropriate treatment decisions" (Health and Welfare Canada, 1988, p. 8). Acknowledging that alcoholism is a problem facing many elderly and that often it is the social worker who is responsible to uncover its presence, leads to the issue of scrutinizing the assessment process as a whole.

Social workers may facilitate such awareness by routinely conducting comprehensive biopsychosocial intakes and assessments where they become acutely aware of the many physical symptoms, which may appear to be age related but are associated with drinking, and by asking direct and detailed questions about drinking-related behaviours (Sumberg, 1985). When a problem is suspected at intake, one of the simplest and most frequently used instruments is *The CAGE Assessment*. This acronym is derived from four questions: "Have you felt you should Cut down on your drinking?" "Have people Annoyed you by criticizing your drinking?" "Have you felt Guilty about your drinking?" "Have you ever had a drink first thing in the morning (an Eye-opener) to steady your nerves or get rid of a hangover?" (Jacobson, 1989, p. 22). *The CAGE Assessment* has high face validity and sensitivity in that it purportedly identifies 76 percent of positive cases and has a specificity rate of 94 percent among general populations of various adult age groups (Health and Welfare Canada, 1988). Its reliability and validity for elderly clients has not yet been determined; however, our experiences have shown it to be a useful detection instrument when used with other assessment devices.

Another relatively simple and useful assessment device recommended to social workers is *The WART Assessment*. This acronym developed by Ehline and Tighe (1977) means "With Alcohol, Repeated

Trouble." The assumption put forward here is not to determine how much, when, where or what an elderly person drinks, but focuses on the trouble (i.e., social, behavioural, familial, etc.) drinking may be causing and the role that drinking plays in the person's life. Either of these quick assessments, or similar ones, could easily become incorporated into a more comprehensive, diagnostic assessment protocol.

II. Dispelling Myths

The stereotypical image of an alcoholic as a person who drinks daily, sneaks drinks, drinks in the morning and drinks only hard liquor is still pervasive among both clinicians and the general population. It may be difficult for a social worker to imagine that a sweet grandma who says she has a glass of sherry to stimulate her appetite before supper may have a serious problem with alcohol dependency. For instance, she does not have delirium tremens, is not dishevelled, drinks less than others in her environment and is open about her drinking. Thus, she may not fit the image of an alcoholic. As indicated in Chapter 2 of this text, myths get in the way of identification and can only be dispelled by facts. Further, as indicated in this earlier chapter, we concur with the suggestion offered in Chapter 2 that it is the responsibility of social work practitioners to dispel myths whenever they can, as this is a way of creating awareness about problems such as alcoholism. In turn, knowledge, skills and behaviour change of practitioners will only come about when such awareness is fully realized. Although we only cited an example of one myth here to make the point, the field of addictions is prone to myth perpetuation and, as a result, is fertile ground for the promulgation of such fabrications. Some of the more frequent ones that prevail and relate to the elderly are: "she or he is old and will die anyway — so let her or him drink," "alcohol is needed to aid the digestion" (this is synonymous with — it is only for medicinal purposes), "if you only drink beer or wine you can't be an alcoholic," "if a person has never been in trouble with the law or at work — how can you say she or he is an alcoholic?", "she or he is not hurting anyone by their drinking," "alcohol helps one to sleep," "studies show it helps the heart and circulatory system," "I don't wish to change my drinking behaviour as any radical change in my habits may result in death," "it helps as a laxative," and "they've worked hard their whole life — they are entitled to drink now that they are old."

III. Transference and Countertransference Issues

Social workers with elderly alcoholic clients need to become aware of a number of transference and countertransference issues peculiar to this group. Sumberg (1985) defined four such issues. First, even when drinking seems to be one of the remaining pleasures in the life of an elderly person, the worker must be aware of the potentially devastating effects of the addiction for the client and be prepared to enable the client to give up drinking. Second, the frustration when a client relapses and drinks after much work was completed, and the resultant tendency is to see that client as a 'hopeless case.' Third, if a worker attempts to help a client work through issues of loss and/or death (prevailing themes with this clientele), and the client uses this as an excuse to drink, the effect on the worker may be frustration. Fourth, elderly clients may be using alcohol to cope with other losses, and it is difficult to ask them to relinquish the 'only comfort' they have left, even though it is blocking their normal grieving process (Sumberg, 1985, p. 172-73).

In this regard, self-awareness is critical for the worker so that personal apprehension is not projected into the relationship. For example, a social worker untrained in this specialized field may feel inadequate to deal with alcoholism and is unreasonably pessimistic about it; she or he avoids or minimizes the problem and subsequently her or his feelings become a self-fulfilling prophecy as the treatment fails to help (Weinberg, 1983, p. 204).

Beginning with the first contact with the client through to follow-up, social work practitioners must always be mindful of the impact of self and how personal attitudes and values relate to the therapeutic relationship (Strean, 1993). For instance, personal views on drinking and life experience of the worker may have a detrimental effect on a worker's capacity to recognize and bring to light an elderly person's excessive drinking. Our culture gives us decidedly mixed messages about drinking, both glamorizing and condemning it, making it difficult to clearly know how to evaluate its use and abuse. Further, some practitioners may be uncomfortable about drinking, perhaps because of their own use or because of negative experiences with drinking (Willenbring and Spring, 1990). In turn, such negative experiences may be particularly pertinent to direct practitioners as they constantly interact face-to-face with their clients. For instance, one study of MSW students found that almost half (49.7 percent) of the sample reported the existence of alcohol abuse as a problem in their families of origin compared to 28.2 percent and 23.1 percent respectively for education and business students (Russel et al., 1993). Thus, awareness, peer support, education, therapy and supervision are all avenues through which social workers may resolve countertransference issues should they arise.

IV. Using Support Systems

Elderly alcoholics are unlikely to refer themselves for services because of reluctance to use services, lack of experience with social service agencies and the denial element that is part of alcoholism. When they are referred for services, the social worker will often be working with others in addition to the identified client. When a referral for an elderly person is made by another professional, the referent may be a resource for the assessment process and be part of an inter-disciplinary team that will combine resources to assess the client's problems. Some clients, because of their degree of isolation, will lack a social support network and a social environment will need to be developed (Sisson and Azrin, 1989). Thus, the impact of other professionals with whom the elderly person has had contact may be very significant for these individuals.

Graham (1986) explicitly recommended that "those interested in identification should exploit other sources of information (i.e., family, neighbours) concerning drinking patterns of the elderly person" (p. 325). If a worker preliminarily screens a problem (by using The CAGE or another type of assessment) and is concerned that the elderly persons' memory may not be accurate, that he or she is confused, is denying the existence of a problem, or fears stigmatization, altering the questions for corroborating information from family and friends is probably necessary (Jacobson, 1989).

Further, when elderly alcoholics enter the health or social service system for help, their spouses and adult children often feel guilty, responsible, exasperated and helpless, as well as angry, fearful, frustrated and resentful. These feelings seem to be more intensified (particularly the feelings of guilt), when the person drinking is older and the condition is critical and life-threatening (Dunlop, 1990). Further, when the family recognizes that the client's drinking is a problem, but the client does not, the family system may provide useful information about the problem and establish contingencies that require the alcohol abuser to seek help (McCrady, 1986), rather than inadvertently enabling drinking patterns by interfering with the natural consequences of his or her drinking because of mistaken beliefs they are helping. In short, workers must use whatever available supports they can, namely other professionals, families, neighbours or friends in assisting with this identification process.

Finally, in this regard, one of the best known and effective supports available is Alcoholics Anonymous (AA). Ehline and Tighe (1977) recommended that social workers working with alcoholics and their families attend an open AA meeting. AA has groups specifically for elderly persons, and attending a meeting may increase an understanding of alcoholism in elderly persons and provide first-hand experience of their rehabilitation needs. Further, classic-style intervention, where many friends and family gather together to confront the alcoholic, has been found to have a profound negative impact on an elderly person's self-worth. A mini-confrontation, with one person and/or a counsellor, presented in a supportive and educational manner emphasizes an elderly person's freedom of choice and enhances his or her dignity or self-respect (Dunlop, 1990). The importance of AA as a proven and beneficial support should not be underestimated, in particular for those elderly who have a limited social support network.

VI. Direct Practice Suggestions

Since social workers are often the gatekeepers to service elderly clients, in that their assessments must look beyond the obvious for underlying problems that, when resolved, will enhance a client's functioning. Detection of alcohol abuse, through early, comprehensive assessments, leads to early, prompt intervention. In order to create a therapeutic environment that is conducive to detection of alcohol abuse in elderly clients there are a number of suggestions workers should be mindful of.

1) Just as there is no typical older person, there is no stereotypical older person who abuses alcohol.

2) All social workers in gerontology need to learn at least the rudiments of alcoholism education (Sumberg, 1985, p. 176).

3) Social workers need to hone their assessment skills so that, with older clients, they are alert and attentive to the possibility that alcohol abuse may be present even when at first appearance it may seem unlikely. In order to accomplish this, general intake tools with elderly clients should include questions that screen for alcohol abuse. Even when alcohol problems are apparent, the focus of the assessment should also consider factors of current medical condition, mental status, domestic situation, financial status and extent of family or social support (Dunlop, 1990).

4) Alcohol-related concerns may very well not be the presenting problem nor the primary concern of the client. More often they present with health concerns, and assisting clients to recognize the impact of drinking on their physical condition can be a valuable starting point toward helping them to accept that their drinking is problematic (Gulino and Kadin, 1986).

5) Social workers working in this field require knowledge of normal physiological, age-specific changes in order to identify and distinguish symptoms of alcohol abuse.

6) One should acknowledge that drinking patterns differ — for some it has been a lifelong pattern and for others it is a problem that begins later in life. Thus, with early-onset drinkers, an assessment may likely focus on losses incurred because of drinking, whereas late-onset drinkers may need to discuss losses that occurred that triggered drinking.

7) Regardless of when the drinking began, in addition to all other losses that an older person faces (a main issue with the elderly), giving up the bottle will be another serious loss issue for such clients.

8) Drinking occurs within different contexts, and although normally most elderly people drink alone and at home, there is an increasing concern that the extent of social drinking

occurring in retirement communities is placing retirees at risk for alcoholism (Sumberg, 1985).

9) It is very likely that family members will also need to be supported, educated and worked with in order to assist the older person to recognize a problem exists. (A list of recommended reading material and resources for families is given at the end of this chapter.)

10) Other professionals and agencies may be involved in the client's care; this may mean arranging for concrete needs such as meals-on-wheels, transportation or home care services. In the event that a client is referred to another agency, the social worker may be required to make the initial appointment, arrange for someone to meet the client there or obtain releases for the transfer of information.

11) Continuing to support the alcoholic elder by following up and staying in touch may be essential for a positive outcome for that person (Blazer, 1990). Ensuring that treatment is received and that an older person does not get lost in the system may require a liaison person (Gulino and Kadin, 1986).

12) An awareness of personal values and attitudes regarding not only the elderly in general but also in relation to alcohol abuse is necessary.

13) Finally, social workers require a sincere belief in the client in his or her recovery because: "Above all, treating the elderly alcoholic client requires faith on the part of the worker that recovery from alcoholism is possible. Such faith can feed the recovery of an alcoholic as nothing else can" (Sumberg, 1985, p. 180).

Suggested Reading/Resources for Families and Friends

Beattie, M. (1987). *Codependent no more*. Center City, MN.: Hazelden Foundation.
Black, C. (1982). *It will never happen to me*. Denver: MAC Publishing.
Johnson, V. (1980). *I'll quit tomorrow*. Scranton, PA: Harper and Row.
Marlin, E. (1987). *Hope: New choices and recovery strategies for adult children of alcoholics*. New York: Harper and Row, Publishers.

Woititz, J. (1983). *Adult children of alcoholics*. Deerfield Beach, FL: Health Communications.

Self-help groups are available in your community, such as Alanon for adult family members and friends of alcoholics, Adult Children of Alcoholics (ACOA), or Alafam for alcoholic families.

Contact the local AA group for information or assistance, there are some localities that have groups specifically for older adults. AA also has publications available, including information regarding older alcoholics, that can be ordered from the General Service Office of Alcoholics Anonymous, Box 459, Grand Central Station, New York, NY 10163.

References

Addiction Research Foundation. (October/November 1991). Stats · facts: Older. *The Journal,* p. 13.

Alcohol, drugs and seniors: Tarnished dreams. (1990) The Educational Media Producers and Distributors Association of Canada [Aims Media]. Film.

American Psychiatric Association. (1987). *Diagnostic and statistical manual of mental disorders* (3rd ed., rev.). Washington, DC: American Psychiatric Association.

Atkinson, R.M. (1984). Substance use and abuse in later life. In R.M. Atkinson (ed.), *Alcohol and drug abuse in old age* (pp. 2-21). Washington, D.C.: American Psychiatric Press, Monograph Series, 1-22.

Blazer, D. (1990). *Emotional problems in later life: Intervention strategies for professional caregivers.* New York: Springer Publishing Company.

Blazer, D.C. and Pennybacker, M.R. (1984). Epidemiology of alcoholism in the elderly. In J.T. Hartford and T. Samorajski (eds.), *Alcoholism in the elderly: Social and biomedical issues* (pp. 25-34). New York: Raven Press.

Crook, T. and Cohen, G. (1984). Future directions for alcohol research in the elderly. In J.T. Hartford and T. Samorajski (eds.), *Alcoholism in the elderly: Social and biomedical issues* (pp. 277-282). New York: Raven Press.

Dunlop, J. (1990). Peer groups support seniors fighting alcohol and drugs. *Aging,* 361, 28-32.

Ehline, D. and Tighe, P.O. (1977). Alcoholism: Early identification and intervention in the social service agency. *Child Welfare,* 56(9), 584-591.

Graham, K. (1986). Identifying and measuring alcohol abuse among the elderly: Serious problems with existing instrumentation. *Journal of Studies on Alcohol,* 47(4), 322-326.

Graham, K. (1993). *Interventions with older people who have alcohol or drug problems: Recent developments.* Paper presented at a national conference on Misuse of Alcohol and Other Drugs by the Older Person: Community-

Based Prevention and Intervention, Toronto, Canada, November 25-26, 1993.

Graham, K., Zeidman, A., Flower, M.C., Saunders, S.J. and White-Campbell, M. (1990). *A typology of elderly persons who have alcohol problems.* Manuscript submitted for publication. The University of Western Ontario and Addiction Research Foundation: Programs and Services Research Department and Community Older Persons Alcohol Project, Toronto, Ontario.

Gulino, C. and Kadin, M. (1986). Aging and reactive alcoholism. *Geriatric Nursing*, 7(3), 148-151.

Health and Welfare Canada. (1988). *Guidelines for comprehensive services to elderly persons with psychiatric disorders.* Department of National Health and Welfare.

Holzer, C.E., Robins, L.N., Myers, J.K., Weissman, M.M., Tischler, G.L., Leaf, P.J., Nathony, J. and Bednarski, P.B. (1986). Antecedents and correlates of alcohol abuse and dependence in the elderly. In G. Maddox, L.N. Robins and N. Rosenberg (eds.), *Nature and extent of alcohol problems among the elderly* (pp. 217-244). New York: Springer Publishing Company, Inc.

Jacobson, G.R. (1989). A comprehensive approach to pretreatment evaluation: I. Detection, assessment, and diagnosis of alcoholism. In R.H. Hester and W.R. Miller (eds.), *Handbook of alcoholism treatment approaches* (pp. 17-53). Toronto: Pergamon Press Canada Ltd.

Jayck, W.R., Tabisz, E., Badger, M. and Fuchs, D. (1991). Chemical dependency in the elderly. *Canadian Journal of Aging*, 10(1), 10-17.

Liberto, J.G., Oslin, D.W., and Ruskin, P.E. (1992). Alcoholism in older persons: A review of the literature. *Hospital and Community Psychiatry*, 43(10), 975-984.

Marino, S. (1991). Selected problems in counselling the elderly. In M.J. Holosko and M.D. Feit (eds.), *Social work practice with the elderly* (pp. 47-74). Toronto: Canadian Scholars' Press.

McCrady, B.S. (1986). The family in the change process. In W.R. Miller and N. Heather (eds.), *Treating addictive behaviours: Process of change* (pp. 305-329). New York: Plenum Press.

Robertson, N. (1988). *Getting better inside Alcoholics Anonymous.* New York: William Morrow and Company, Inc.

Russel, R., Gill, P., Coyne, A. and Woody, J. (1993). Dysfunction in the family of origin of MSW and other graduate students. *Journal of Social Work Education*, 29(1), 121-129.

Saunders, J.B. and Conigrave, K.M. (1990). Early identification of alcohol problems. *Canadian Medical Association Journal*, 143(10), 1060-1068.

Schonfeld, L. and Dupree, L.W. (1991). Antecedents of drinking for early- and late-onset elderly alcohol abusers. *Journal of Studies on Alcohol*, 52(6), 587-591.

Sisson, R.W. and Azrin, N.H. (1989). The community reinforcement approach. In R.H. Hester and W.R. Miller (eds.), *Handbook of alcoholism treatment approaches* (pp. 242-258). Toronto: Pergamon Press Canada Ltd.

Strean, H.S. (1993). *Resolving counterresistances in psychotherapy.* New York: Brunner/Mazel Publishers.

Sumberg, D. (1985). Social work with elderly alcoholics: Some practical considerations. *Journal of Gerontological Social Work,* 8(3/4), 169-180.

Watt, S. and Soifer, A. (1991). Conducting psycho-social assessments with the elderly. In M.J. Holosko and M.D. Feit (eds.), *Social Work Practice With the Elderly* (p. 47-74). Toronto: Canadian Scholars' Press.

Weinberg, J. (1983). Counselling recovering alcoholics. In F.J. Turner (ed.), *Differential diagnosis and treatment in social work* (3rd ed.) (pp. 193-206). New York: The Free Press. (reprinted from *Social Work,* 1973, *18*(4), 84-93).

Willenbring, M. and Spring, W.D. (1990). Evaluating alcohol use in elders. *Aging,* 361, 22-72.

Zimberg, S. (1984). Diagnosis and the management of the elderly alcoholic. In R.M. Atkinson (ed.), *Alcohol and drug abuse in old age* (Chapter 4). Washington, D.C.: American Psychiatric Press, Monograph Series, 23-34.

CHAPTER 8

CASE MANAGEMENT PRACTICE
WITH THE ELDERLY

CAROL D. AUSTIN, PH.D.

*B**y using the frail elderly as an example, this chapter presents a comprehensive overview of the state-of-the-art of case management. Discussion about case management centres around: its origins, definition, various components, goals, role conflicts, models, client-centred issues, caregiving and ethical issues. Given the demographic realities of the elderly population and their demands for increased and cost-effective services, quality case management seems inevitable for social workers practicing in this field.*

The growth of the older population has stimulated more attention to their functional disabilities and to their capacity to live independently in the community. As indicated in Chapter 1 of this text, it is the increase of the oldest old, those over the age of 85, which most dramatically demonstrates the need for health and social services that can assist frail elders to continue to remain independent.

Since the early 1970s, public policy-makers have become more aware of future population shifts and developed a variety of responses to a range of complex and critical issues. These concerns illustrate the profound social changes that will be present in an aging society and demonstrate the far-reaching effects of public policy on the daily lives of the elderly and their families.

A number of questions/concerns emanate from these changes. Who will care for the large and growing number of elders who are no longer able to care for themselves? When, if at all, should publicly funded services replace or substitute for the care that family members might provide? Should public policy encourage the use of nursing homes to serve the larger numbers of frail elders who can no longer live independently in the community? Institutional care is costly — how much of it should be provided and to whom? Can community-based services provide enough to support frail elders and enable them to remain in the community? What kinds of services should be available and who should authorize their provision? How will these policy directions affect the lives of elders, their autonomy, their integrity and the quality of their lives?

As public policy-makers have designed programmes, funding strategies and delivery systems, case management has been a consistent and central component. Over the last two decades, a massive investment has been made in North America on the development of community-based services and delivery systems with the aim of helping frail elders to remain in their own homes or in the community. In this regard, case management has become ubiquitous in community-based, long-term care programmes for the elderly. Although it is frequently given another name (i.e., case coordination, care management) the case management role and function are virtually universally present. Case management is presently and will continue to be an important part of social work practice with frail elders and their families.

I. Origins

Case management has been hailed as a cure for the ills of any type of long-term care service delivery. Although it has enjoyed considerable popularity recently, it is not new. Its origins are found in the early 1900s and the beginnings of social work practice. It is rooted in early social work activities designed to arrange and coordinate care for clients. Case management activities were identified in both the early settlement house movement and in the operations of the charity organization societies. As such, case management is closely related to social casework, a basic social work practice method.

Early caseworkers adopted what is now known as the 'person-in-environment' perspective, directly working with and indirectly working on behalf of their clients.

> The concern to provide carefully coordinated services for clients...and to account for service provision and the use of resources has its roots in the record keeping methods developed in these early movements.... Through its history, case management has had a dual sets of goals — one set related to service quality, effectiveness and service coordination, and the other set related to goals of accountability and cost effective use of resources. (Weil et al., 1985, pp. 5,2)

Contemporary case management practice rests on these roots and is based on a commitment to address both client and system issues.

This dual emphasis is also apparent in the current delivery of case management in community-based, long-term care programmes. A wide range of goals has been associated with case management, those regarding direct service, system development and cost containment. Direct service goals are primarily focused on clients, caregivers and family members, with attention to improving service coordination, access, quality and efficiency. In the area of system development, case managers assess the local delivery system to identify, develop and expand needed services. Case managers also function as resource allocators, service authorizers and system gatekeepers in pursuit of cost containment goals. This is an extremely complex role that requires extensive expertise, diverse skills and comprehensive knowledge.

II. What is Case Management?

Various definitions have been advanced (Steinberg and Carter, 1983; Capitman, Haskins and Berstein,1986; Cline, 1990; Grisham, White and Miller,1983; Applebaum and Austin, 1990; Quinn, 1993; National Association of Social Workers, 1992). Perhaps the most general definition has been offered by Kane (1988) who stated, "case management is the coordination of specified groups of resources and services for a specified group of people" (p. 5). Another broad definition is included in the National Association of Social Workers standards for social work case management: "Social work case management is a method of providing services whereby a professional social worker assesses the needs of the client and the client's family, when appropriate and arranges, coordinates, monitors, evaluates and advocates for a package of multiple services to meet specific client's complex needs" (NASW, 1992, p.5). Further, Quinn (1993) stated

> that case management for long term care is based on three tenets: it is a holistic approach to the client; it is a problem-solving strategy for the client; and, it is a dynamic process involving the interactions among the case manager, the client and the providers of care (including the family, and other informal supporters, formal agencies and physicians if necessary). (p.3)

Applebaum and Austin (1990) identified three features that distinguish long-term care case management: intensity, breadth of services encompassed and duration of case management service provision: "Intensity refers to the amount of time case managers spend with their clients....Breadth of services refers to how broadly case managers view the problems of clients.... Duration refers to how long case managers remain involved with clients" (pp 5,6).

Indeed, the question "What is case management?" has been hotly debated. Although the discussion has abated recently, there is still considerable variation in how case management is defined and implemented. It is not safe to assume that all participants share the same definition, philosophy or approach. Over time, however, considerable consensus has developed regarding the core components of the case management role and function.

III. Components of Case Management

Case management is recognized as having a common set of core components: 1) outreach, 2) screening 3) formalized assessment, 4) care planning, 5) service arrangement, 6) monitoring, and 7) formalized re-assessment. In the following discussion, the target population for case management services will be frail elderly, specifically individuals who require a nursing home level of care, as it is this group that might be diverted from nursing home placement. This is only one of several possible target populations served by community-based, long-term care programmes that provide case management.

i. Outreach

Outreach activities include efforts to publicize the services offered by an agency and to identify persons likely to qualify for and need case management and supportive services. 'Case finding' and 'locating the target population' are other terms for outreach. Older persons experiencing high levels of disability may have the most difficulty gaining access to services. Outreach efforts help to locate these persons and connect them with appropriate services. Outreach mechanisms may include listing the programme with an informal referral agency and negotiating agreements with provider agencies to make accurate referrals and public information campaigns.

Outreach activities represent the first step toward reaching the programme's target population in locations where screening is required before nursing home admission. These case finding efforts are designed to ensure that only individuals who clearly meet eligibility criteria are served. Others are referred to more appropriate programmes. Caseloads will be more heterogeneous than desired since outreach, screening and targeting efforts are not foolproof. In fact, providers have come to understand that "not all consumers require full levels of case management, and not all consumers desire it … self-directed or reduced case management [may be more appropriate] for consumers who may need no or minimal case management" (Connecticut Continuing Care Inc., 1994, p.ii).

ii. Screening

Screening is a preliminary assessment of clients' circumstances and resources in order to determine presumptive eligibility. In many community-based, long-term care programmes screening criteria are designed to target those clients at risk for institutionalization. Screening criteria are applied to determine whether the clients' needs and circumstances match the target population definition(s) in the programme. A standard instrument, considerably shorter than one used for a comprehensive assessment, is generally used to screen potential clients.

It is critical that screening procedures accurately identify appropriate clients. This is particularly important since once a client is screened into a programme, s/he will receive a comprehensive assessment. The comprehensive assessment process is time consuming, labour intensive and costly. Comprehensive assessment is an expensive service that should not be provided to individuals who do not meet a programme's target criteria. Effective outreach and screening are necessary for efficient programmes operations and management. If individuals who do not meet target population criteria are accepted, the programme will experience difficulty in meeting its goals and managing its operations. Outreach and screening are critical gatekeeping tasks.

iii. Comprehensive Assessment

Comprehensive assessment is "a method of collecting in-depth information about a person's social situation and physical, mental and psychological functioning which allows identification of the person's problems and care needs in the major functional areas" (Schneider and Weiss, 1982, p.12). The areas commonly evaluated in the comprehensive assessment include physical health, mental functioning (both cognitive and affective), ability to perform activities of daily living, social supports, physical environment of the home and financial resources. Because frail elderly usually have multiple health problems, functional disabilities and social losses, a comprehensive multi-dimensional assessment is required for effective care planning and service arrangement.

Comprehensive assessments are conducted for every client who is screened into a programme, and optimally the assessment interview is conducted in the client's home. The benefit of an in-home assessment is having the opportunity to observe the client and her caregivers in their own environment. Assessments can also be conducted in hospitals and nursing homes, although these are limited by the lack of information regarding the home environment. Family members are typically interviewed as well to assess the state of the client's support system and the family's interest and capacity to provide care to the client. In many cases, caregivers have overextended themselves and are physically and emotionally spent. Here the assessment becomes even more comprehensive, including the caregiver more directly as a client. Thus, assessments must attend to the caregivers' capacity to effectively continue in that role in light of her physical and emotional status.

Many provinces and states have developed their own standardized assessment instruments, protocols and formats used throughout their jurisdictions. These instruments are normally comprehensive in nature, including extensive health and social history data. Although some programmes design their own instruments, many have adapted standardized multi-dimensional instruments, which have been rigorously developed and previously administered to large numbers of clients. For example, *The Sickness Impact Profile (SIP)*, or *Older Americans Resource Survey (OARS)* are multi-dimensional assessment tools designed to measure capacity among the elderly in all functional areas. Less comprehensive tools may be used to assess specific domains. For example, *The Mental Status Questionnaire (MSQ)* measures cognitive functioning and *The Beck Depression Inventory* provides a measure of affective functioning.

Comprehensive assessment is characterized by consumer involvement and input. As a result, it should focus on strengths not solely on disabilities and deficits. The assessment is designed to identify and support the client's ability to live independently. Thus, in collecting assessment data, a case manager obtains consumer permission to request information from other sources (i.e., health providers, family members, neighbours). The quality of relationship established during assessment often influences the nature of contact between the client and case manager in the later stages of the relationship.One common observation is that these instruments are lengthy and demand considerable attention and energy from frail elderly. Often, it is necessary to make more than one home visit to complete the assessment. Thus, case managers must remain sensitive to client fatigue and its impact on the quality of assessment data.

Quality assessment services demand that case managers possess broad knowledge and well-honed skills. The knowledge base is so comprehensive that inter-disciplinary teams and consultation models have been developed and implemented. Nelson (1987) observed that quality assessments require expertise in technical competence, interpersonal competence and the amenities of service encounters with older persons (i.e., privacy, confidentiality and dignity).

iv. Care Planning

Information gathered during a comprehensive assessment is used by the case manager in developing a care plan. Care planning is perhaps the most demanding case management activity. It requires clinical judgment, creativity and sensitivity as well as knowledge of community services and the ability to create a care plan within the fiscal limits imposed by budget requirements.

Schneider (1988) has identified components that she asserts should be present in all care plans. These are:

> a comprehensive list of problems; a desired outcome
> for each problem; the types of help needed to achieve
> each desired outcome; a list of the services and
> providers that will be supplying help; an indication
> of the amount of each service to be provided; a
> calculation of the costs of providing the listed services
> for a specific periods of time and an indication of the
> sources of payment; an indication of agreement by
> the client and, when appropriate, the informal
> caregiver. (p.16-17)

Care plan development takes into account the willingness and availability of informal caregivers to provide care. Most care plans include a combination of formal services and informal care. It is the mix of formal and informal that is often a central issue in the care planning process. The significance of available and able caregivers cannot be overestimated.

The case manager can assist in stimulating and enhancing their clients' independent functioning and providing support to clients' caregivers. Caregiver support services may become a significant component of the care plan. Thus, the case manager may be able to identify new sources of informal support and strengthen existing sources by expanding the existing support network. Case managers often find that clients are referred when their caregivers have reached the point of burnout. In these cases, the case manager's client is both the older person and her primary caregiver.

Elders lacking a support system in the community are more likely to be admitted to institutional care. The balance between formal and informal service provision continues to be a central public policy issue. Two key questions emerge: What should families be expected to provide and what kinds of support should be available to assist caregivers in this key role?

A guiding principle in the development of care plans is the direct involvement of the client and her caregivers. The NASW *Standard for Social Work Case Management* states that "the social worker shall ensure that clients are involved in all phases of case management practice to the greatest extent possible" (NASW, 1992, p. 10). Involvement and participation are essential, and client autonomy and independence must be enhanced and protected. Clients and caregivers are critical care plan decision-makers as, without their participation, case managers will not likely develop care plans that can be successfully implemented. Client self-determination remains a core social work practice requirement, and is a commitment that is honoured in care plan decision-making.

Finally, through care planning, the case manager performs an important resource allocation function. The care plan is a service prescription that identifies what services are to be delivered, by which providers and with what frequency. Thus, care plans can specify the costs of individual services and the total cost of the entire service package.

v. Service Arrangement

The service arrangement function is a process of contacting both formal and informal providers to arrange for services identified in the care plan. Service arrangement is really care plan implementation and it involves negotiating with providers for services when the case manager makes referrals to other agencies. It also involves ordering services from providers when the case manager has the authority to directly purchase services on behalf of their clients. The process of arranging for care plan implementation serves the function of distributing resources to the various formal providers in the delivery system. This is clearly the case when the case manager can directly purchase services on behalf of her clients.

A key aspect of service arrangement involves sharing client assessment and care plan information with relevant family members and formal providers. Although families provide the majority of services, family members may not be adequately informed about what formal services are to be provided or what they are expected to do as part of the overall care plan. Accurate and clear communication are essential for the successful implementation of care plans, and persons involved in care plan decision-making must be adequately informed.

The process of implementing care plans provides important information about the capacity of the local delivery system to meet service demands. Case managers can identify service gaps and services that are in short supply, and this information is necessary for case managers to pursue their system-level activities.

vi. Monitoring

Monitoring is a critical case management task that enables the case manager to respond quickly to changes in the client's situation and increase, decrease, terminate or maintain services as required. The frequency of monitoring varies depending on the intensity of client needs and the type of services being delivered. For example, a client who has been discharged from a hospital after an acute illness and is temporarily receiving home health care from two shifts of in-home workers may need substantial monitoring. Occasional case monitoring may be all that is required by a client who is stable and whose care plan has not changed. Indeed, careful attention to changes in client needs can have significant effects on service costs. Clients may experience changes in their functional capacity, in their living arrangements, in the availability of caregivers and/or in their health status. Systematic monitoring allows the case manager to identify such changes and to alter care plans to more adequately meet clients' current needs. Ongoing monitoring combined with appropriate changes in care plans increase confidence that programme expenditures reflect current client needs and are not based on out-of-date assessment data.

vii. Re-assessment

Re-assessment can be routinely scheduled or precipitated by specific events. In either case, it involves a systematic examination of the client's current situation and functioning. The goal here is to identify whether changes have occurred since the initial or most recent assessment and to determine how much progress has been accomplished toward the outcomes specified in the care plan. Re-assessment often takes the form of a partial re-evaluation of the most significant client problems. In some programmes, re-assessment is a modified form of the original assessment, focused primarily on changes since the last re-assessment.

Dates for routine re-assessments can be written into the care plan and are often based upon a case manager's judgment of an appropriate time frame. Other programmes require re-assessments at specific intervals (i.e., six months, annually). Major events in a client's life can trigger a re-assessment such as: loss of a major caregiver through death or relocation; death of the client's spouse or member of the household; acute medical crisis; major deterioration in physical or mental status; placement in a hospital, lodge or nursing home and forced relocation of the client. Re-assessment can also be triggered when the initial problem has been resolved, alleviated or re-defined; when a planned service is terminated by the client or service provider; or when there is the need to prepare clients for a planned withdrawal of services. Often re-assessments are conducted when the client is terminated from the programme and when a new worker is assigned.

This final task creates a feedback loop back to the overall care planning process. As a result, case management becomes an ongoing process. Re-assessment can result in substantial changes in care plans, which can have a substantial impact on programme costs. Finally, re-assessment provides an important opportunity to ensure that the most appropriate clients are being served by the programme and that their care plans reflect their current status and situations. In this respect, re-assessment is a major gate-keeping function.

IV. Case Management Goals

Although there is considerable consensus on the core components that constitute case management, there appear to be multiple goals or expectations concerning these core activities (Applebaum and Austin, 1990; Quinn, 1993; Kane 1988; Radol-Raiff and Shore, 1993; Weil, et. al., 1985; Steinberg and Carter, 1983). An examination of goals that have been associated with case management practice reveals role conflicts — conflicts which make case management simultaneously challenging and frustrating. Case management goals fall into two categories, those that are primarily client focused and those that are aimed at potential change in delivery systems (Applebaum and Austin, 1990). Although these goals are discussed separately, they are interdependent.

Goals that are Primarily Client Oriented
1. To assure that services are appropriate to the needs of a particular client.
2. To monitor the client's condition in order to guarantee the appropriateness of services.
3. To improve client access to the continuum of long term care services.
4. To support the client's caregivers.
5. To serve as bridges between institutional and community-based care systems. (Applebaum and Austin, 1990, p. 7)

The needs and circumstances of each client are individualized in the case management process. This emphasis is present throughout, from assessment to care planning and re-assessment. Care plans, in theory, are really individualized service prescriptions, unique to each client. Monitoring allows the case manager to identify changes in a client's circumstances and to change the care plan to more accurately reflect currently assessed needs.

Case managers are responsible for enhancing access for individual clients to the continuum of long-term care services. The sheer complexity of programmes and agencies, coupled with bureaucratic procedures, are daunting barriers for clients seeking service. This is particularly the case for the most impaired whose needs are substantial and who often experience the most difficulty accessing the system. Case managers function as the single contact point for client, have knowledge of community services and resources, and are responsible for making the delivery system more responsive to the clients' needs.

The presence, willingness and capacity of informal caregivers are among the most critical considerations in the development of care plans. Indeed, the quality and strength of a client's support system can be the difference between remaining in the community and being institutionalized. In some instances, caregivers also become clients, as they become more vulnerable themselves when faced by the continuing demands of continuing to provide care. A case manager's intervention on behalf of the caregiver, with additional services and respite, can be crucial for those families whose resources have been depleted.

Continuity is critical in the provision of case management services. Ideally, a client will work with the same case manager regardless of at what point in the delivery system they may be residing. This means that the same case manager follows the client from home care, to community services, to acute care, to nursing home care and back to home. The involvement of multiple case managers, each assigned at different points in the delivery system and by various service providers, is neither effective from the client perspective nor efficient from a delivery system perspective. Case management will not be as client centred as it should be if multiple case managers are involved with the client.

Goals that are Primarily System Oriented
1. To facilitate the development of a broader array of non-institutional services.
2. To promote quality and efficiency in the delivery of long-term care services.

3. To enhance the coordination of long-term care service delivery.
4. To target individuals most at risk of nursing home placement in order to prevent inappropriate institutionalization.
5. To contain costs by controlling client access to services, especially high cost services. (Applebaum and Austin, 1990, p.7)

In the development of care plans, case managers make decisions about how much of which services will be provided to the client by which provider. In the care planning process, the case manager can identify service gaps in the community, facilitate the development of new services and may discover the presence of costly duplications. Case managers are also in the position to foster coordination among providers in the local delivery system. *The NASW Standard for Social Work Case Management #6* states, "the social work case manger shall intervene at the service system level to support existing case management services and to expand the supply of and improve access to needed services" (NASW,1992, p.15).

In many communities, the direction of system development is toward the expansion of the scope and volume of community-based services that are present. Such delivery system expansion provides a significant opportunity for case managers to influence the quality and efficiency of newly developed as well as existing services. "By working with providers and monitoring services that clients receive, case managers are able to evaluate the quality of providers' care. In the care planning process, case managers can also offer incentives to providers by directing the flow of referrals, thereby promoting quality and efficiency" (Applebaum and Austin, 1990, p.9). Case managers also have major responsibility for coordinating services to clients, a responsibility that can be particularly challenging when the client is receiving multiple services from different provider agencies.

The combination of case management and community-based services has been advanced as the programmatic strategy for preventing or delaying premature or unnecessary admission to nursing homes. One of the goals of this approach is to divert clients from institutional placement. From a systems perspective, it has been asserted that effective and efficient targeting and close attention to cost in the care planning are necessary for case managers to fulfil their responsibilities regarding cost containment. "Case management, whatever setting in which it is applied, should be accountable so that costs are as streamlined as possible and that public and private financing of case management is spent in a way that protects consumers, payers of case management and direct services and the general public" (Connecticut Continuing Care Inc., 1994, p.69).

V. Role Conflict

These goals create a major dilemma. Can case managers function as client advocates and agents of the system simultaneously? Are the goals of clients and the delivery system consistent? A single service delivery role that can actually address such a broad range of goals is attractive but may be limited by insufficient authority. Most often, the major focus in the delivery of case management services has been on clients. This emphasis suggests that the basic service delivery problem is a lack of information on the part of clients. That is, if only clients had sufficient accurate information about how services were organized and where to access the system, entry into the system and receipt of services would follow smoothly. Access to community services, from the perspective of adequate information about client services, becomes the primary concern of case management services.

Another view is "... case management has enjoyed such widespread acceptance because it has not been viewed as a systemic reform, but as a function that can be incorporated into ongoing delivery systems without changing structural relationships among providers" (Austin, 1983, p.17). Over the last 20 years there has been growing recognition that a key to the effectiveness of case management, in terms of systems development and cost containment, is the extent to which case managers have authority to directly purchase services in the implementation of care plans. The nature of the resource allocation authority dramatically shapes case management activity. The mix of client centred and system oriented activity in the practice of case management reflects the way it is defined and operationalized in a given programme.

VI. Models of Case Management

Case management has evolved across time, organizational settings, programmatic fiscal limitations and public policy directions. What is clear is that past, present and future methods of organizing and financing long-term care services include some form of case management. Numerous models of case management have been offered. Cline (1990) identified three case management practice models: medical care case management (hospital-based); catastrophic care case management (insurance company based) and long-term care case management (community-based). The central defining variable in these models is the primary location from which the case management services are provided.

Another critical variable in the specification of case management models is tied to the nature of a programme's funding. As indicated, fiscal considerations become more critical in case management practice. Three case management models have been identified, each of which can be specified by the extent to which case managers possess direct authority to purchase service in the care plan development process.

First, case managers function as *brokers* when they do not have service dollars to spend on behalf of their clients. Brokers develop care plans and make referrals to providers. Brokers cannot guarantee the provision of service and frequently clients will end up on waiting lists, waiting for services to be delivered by the provider agency. In this situation, the case manager has little leverage with the provider agency and cannot ensure that services will be provided. Here the case manager is primarily passive, following up with the client and provider once a referral has been made, attempting to influence the provider to serve the client quickly through personal persuasion and influence. Brokers cannot directly purchase services since they do not have specific service funds, which are used to buy services prescribed in the care plan. (Much of this activity is conducted on the telephone.) Clearly, when time is a critical issue, brokers cannot be very responsive to client need since service provision cannot be assured. Brokered case management is weak in that it is not optimally responsive to clients' assessed needs and will not produce changes at the delivery system level. Since they are not spending their own programme funding, brokers do not systematically calculate the cost of their care plans. Normally, they are not aware of the cost of their care plans, reflecting the programme's limited attention to tracking costs.

The source of programme funding typically determines the extent to which case managers are fiscally responsible. The power to authorize services is the critical feature of the *service management* model. Here, a case managers' care planning activities are limited by the kinds and amounts of services available in the local delivery system and by budget caps placed on the costs of individual care plans. Once the care plan has been developed, the case manager's functioning in the service management mode determines which providers to contact and orders specific services to be delivered at a defined frequency. In this model, the case manager develops care plans within pre-determined cost caps, frequently within a specified percentage of the cost of nursing home care. Service management case managers can affect the shape of the local delivery since they develop care plans and decide which providers to contact in order to arrange for services. In turn, these resource allocation patterns can influence unit costs, service quality and the supply of services in the local delivery system.

The third model, *managed care*, has emerged most recently. It has developed directly from service management and adds another critical dimension, prospective financing. Here, case managers develop care plans within a fiscal environment where the case management agency receives a specified amount of funding for each client served; this is often called capitation. Prospective payment or capitation creates a so called 'provider risk,' where financial responsibility and liability for expenditures are shifted to the provider agency. Thus, provider agencies must keep costs below the aggregate capitation payment or they are at financial risk for expenses exceeding the prepaid amount. Thus, prospective payment puts additional emphasis on the care planning process, creating pressure on case managers to control total costs, provide and promote prevention oriented services and substitute lower cost services without sacrificing quality or underserving clients. Loomis (1988) noted:

> if case managers control the funds for care provided in all settings, then case managers exert significant influence when service providers decide if clients should be treated in a hospital, a nursing home, or under hospice or home care. Case managers can decide what additional services, in what amount, are necessary or unnecessary to care adequately for the client.... (p.164)

A central feature of managed care case management involves contract negotiation with providers. These negotiations centre on service costs and agreement on the volume of referrals a provider can expect to receive. At the system level, cost containment is the driving force. In the context of provider risk, the questions are — should certain services be provided internally and not contracted out? If so, which ones? From a systems perspective, the managed care approach most dramatically provides incentives to keep clients at the least costly level of care, which appropriately meets clients' assessed needs and assures quality. In managed care, the case manager may be most conflicted in terms of the juxtaposition of client centred and system oriented goals. The danger here is to underserve clients in the name of fiscal management and/or cost containment. Thus far, the evolution of case management indicates the overall trend is away from brokering, more into service management and recently into managed care. This trend suggests that case managers will continue to function with more authority and fiscal responsibility for care plan development and implementation.

VII. Client Centred Issues

Much of case management practice involves direct work with elders, their families and caregivers. Case managers will perform tasks for, collaborate with and/or facilitate services at various times for clients. A familiar criticism has been that clients are not cases and do not need to be managed. As in other social work practice settings, there is the danger of objectifying clients, particularly when caseloads are high and service supply is inadequate. Relationship is a core concept in case management as it is in the more generalized practice of social work. As well, theory and practice may diverge in case management as it does in social work.

Burack-Weiss (1988) suggested several ways the theory and practice of case management are discrepant. Case management practice is frequently discussed in a sequential, linear fashion. Ideally, one task follows the last smoothly, apparently without a hitch. Yet, practice experience indicates that 'smooth' is sometimes the least accurate adjective to describe case management interactions with clients, the families and caregivers. Indeed, many clients are 'non-compliant,' and they may not cooperate even if they have been involved in the development of their care plans. However participatory, clients may perceive the case management process as directive — i.e., telling them what to do. Further, clients may want services that are not available because of inadequate service supply, excessive costs or unrealistic expectations. As well, they may only be willing to accept part of the care plan, rejecting other services. Similarly, as one may surmise, families are not always facilitative. In short, some are willing but not capable of caring for their relatives, while others are capable but not willing.

There is also a tendency to view elders as homogenous, when in fact this age group is just as much if not more heterogeneous than others (see Chapter 1). This is a reflection of ageism, where elders are viewed as the same, except for their various functional disabilities and needs for supportive service. One manifestation of ageism is stereotyping of all members of a group as the same, ignoring cultural, social class, educational, ethnic and economic influences (see Chapter 2 for more elaboration on ageism). Individualizing case management practice is a core practice commitment. Unfortunately, overworked case managers who are asked to manage unmanageably large caseloads may be in danger of treating clients as stereotypes. Here agency pressures can adversely affect the quality of service provision. In turn, client self-determination and individualized care plans can be sacrificed in programmes that are not committed to quality service delivery.

The theory of case management is frequently articulated in technical terms, while in practice it is emotional. Case management terminology includes: comprehensive assessment, providers, care plans, budget caps, care planning, systems, networks and monitoring, among others. The language of practitioners is affective, not abstract, including anxiety and depression. This is another reflection on the dual focus of case management. Case management theory is not client centred in the counselling sense and care planning is individualized within the larger context of programme, costs and delivery system. In an effort to move away from a psychotherapeutic orientation, case management theory has obscured the relationship focus in the role. More specifically, the reciprocal relationships among the elderly, the family and the case manager over time are also significant features of case management service.

Burack-Weiss (1988) astutely noted that "with the advent of case management, practice with the aged has inexorably moved from looking at the person-in-situation to looking for the situation in the person" (p.24). The danger here is that assessment and care planning will dwell on where the client fits into the system, rather than on her individual needs and the development of a tailored care plan. Even when care plans are developed from a client centred rather than a system focused perspective, clients may not follow through, perhaps reflecting an underdeveloped relationship between the case manager and the client. Since assessment is ongoing, case managers and clients determine those interventions that are most appropriate given the client's functional ability over time.

Mainstream case management for the elderly has not emphasized clinical mental health aspects. It is interesting to note that recent books on case management practice have devoted little attention to clinical mental health issues (Applebaun and Austin,1990; Quinn, 1993). Their focus has been on pragmatic problem-solving and coordination within the context of community-based care planning. Indeed, clinical case management is more relationship and psychotherapeutically oriented. Clinical case management has a two-pronged thrust: it is more focused on the changes, options and pacing of relationships than 'broker' models and it weaves clinical understandings throughout the process of dispositions planning, service referral, advocacy and follow-up (Radol-Raiff and Shore, 1993, p.85).

Mental health concerns normally have been addressed as part of the case management process, a process that is not particularly clinically oriented. It should be noted, however, that the increasing prevalence of Alzheimer's disease and other dementias has affected care planning dramatically. In these cases, the focus of care planning is often the caregiver and her or his needs for support and respite. Thus, the focus here is not psychotherapeutic in nature.

Case management is not an orderly sequence of tasks that unfolds effortlessly. It inevitably gets caught up in clients' feelings and reactions, responses that well-organized care plans may not adequately address. If clinical aspects of case management are not adequately addressed, there is the risk that the client will be lost within the larger delivery system, when in fact the client is its centre. The risk is major goal displacement, a risk that creates additional vulnerability for the client and significant ethical problems for social workers.

VIII. Caregiving

A further note on caregiving is necessary at this point. Case managers know that the presence, strength and capacity of the informal caregivers is a critical component in the development of a care plan. Consistently, programmes have stated that a primary goal is to support, not supplant, the care provided by family, friends, neighbours, volunteers, church members and other community contacts. Some elderly are fortunate to have a network of support, which might include an adult daughter, a neighbour, a local friend and friends or relatives who are in touch by telephone. Others are more isolated, lacking in support from any of these sources. Informal caregivers can provide assistance with a wide range of activities including: meal preparation, errands and shopping, transportation, medication management, home maintenance, house cleaning, financial management, financial contributions, laundry, personal care, emotional support and companionship and advocating for services and benefits (Scharlach, 1988; Sterthous, 1986). In the absence of caregivers to provide these services, more formally delivered care will be necessary and more public funding will be required to address the needs of isolated elders.

A significant assumption in public policy regarding community-based, long-term care is that families and other informal caregivers are present, willing and able to perform this critical role. In fact, some elderly do not have caregivers and others have potential caregivers who are neither willing nor able. Family care is not always the best choice. Some families are abusive, while others are not interested. Here the case manager may be caught between the assessed capacity of the informal network and programme policies regarding the involvement of caregivers. In fact, in some programmes the presence of a caregiver may be the basis upon which services are denied.

IX. Ethical Issues

In a recent study of 251 case managers, Kane, Penrod and Kivnick (1994) asked respondents to identify ethical issues they had experienced in their practice. Forty-nine percent of respondents, the largest group, reported that conflicts between the family and the client or case manager regarding nursing home placement was the ethical issue they encountered most frequently. The second most frequently encountered (37 percent) was family and client with differing views, excluding the issue of nursing home placement. The most frequent solution reported by the case managers was providing support for client preferences if the client was competent. This study also included ethical problems that emerged as a result of a discrepancy between client needs and wants. Here, case managers reported two issues that were familiar as conflicts with so-called 'non-compliant' clients. "The most frequently (32 percent) mentioned ethical issues in this category were: 1) the client wants an unsafe or unhealthy lifestyle; and 2) client conflict (for 28 percent of the sample)" related to the client needing home care and does not want [it] (p. 7).

While the universal value of participation in care planning decisions is asserted, it is also necessary to recognize that preferences differ regarding involvement of families and clients in decision-making and the nature of decisions being made. The question here becomes, *who is the client?* All family members are not necessarily involved in decision-making and planning for a vulnerable relative. Knowledge of family history is critical for determining which family members are in the best position to constructively participate in such decision-making.

Protecting client autonomy includes two basic steps. First, the client expresses her or his wishes. Second, those wishes are carried out. Even though a client has articulated her choices, there is real cause for concern that those preferences will actually be carried out. Case managers need to be knowledgeable about the variety of advanced directives (i.e., living wills, power of attorney for health care, etc.) that may prove useful and how to skillfully plan for their timely and successful implementation.

Social workers and other human service professionals are ethically bound to provide quality services. Indeed, in recent years the discussion has shifted from what is case management to what is quality case management (Kane,1988; Applebaum and McGinnis, 1992; National Institute on Community-Based Long-Term Care, 1988; NASW, 1992; Kane and Kane, 1987). Increasing attention is being paid to the design and implementation of quality assurance systems in case management programmes. This represents a significant challenge since there are at least two layers of activity that require qualitative review and assessment. First is case management itself. As a distinct service, case management must meet criteria to demonstrate the quality of its service delivery. As well, case management itself functions as a case management mechanism, focused on improving the quality and suitability of community-based, long-term care services.

A comprehensive quality assurance programme is based on consensus regarding desired outcomes of case management services at both the client and community levels. Quality goals include attention to multicultural realities and demonstrate a commitment to comprehensive quality outcomes in the agency's functions and activities. Consumer empowerment, through direct participation in care planning as well as feedback through client satisfaction surveys is a crucial element of quality. Case managers' competencies and clinical skills should also be routinely assessed in order to determine how well they are performing core case management tasks.

Quality case management service delivery is one of several ethical considerations. Another fundemental concern is client self-determination. "Intrinsic to case management practice is the principle that consumers have the right to self-determination and autonomy. Case management strives to promote the highest level of independence consistent with the consumer's capacity and prefrences for care, allowing consumers to maximize self-directed care to the extent possible" (Connecticut Continuing Care Inc., 1994, p. 6). This is a commitment at the core of professional social work practice. The enhancement and protection of client self-determination are significant challenges for clients in this population.

X. Concluding Remarks

There can be little doubt that case management will continue to be a central function and service in the provision of community-based, long-term care services. The intrinsic stress between the client oriented and system focused responsibilities will not disappear. Social work involvement in case management will vary from one location to another depending on how the role is defined and the presence of other professional groups competing for the designation. Wherever social workers provide case management services, it is necessary to demonstrate three core competencies: psycho-social assessment, skilled intervention, as well as professional accountability within the context of programme and policy commitments. All are central to social work practice and are built upon extensive professional experience. Social workers choosing to become case managers will be challenged to learn and continue to be current about a broad range of knowledge and specialized skills. A larger and older population is the demographic reality in North America, and case management in community-based, long-term care programmes is a predictable component of future service delivery.

References

Applebaum, R. and Austin, C. (1990). *Long term care case management: Design and evaluation:* New York: Springer

Applebaum, R. and McGinnis, R. (1992). What price quality? Assuring the quality of case-managed in-home care. *Journal of Case Management,* 1(1), 9-13.

Austin, C. (1983). Case management in long term care: Options and opportunities. *Health and Social Work,* 8 (1), 16-30.

Beck, A., Ward, C., Mendelson, M., Mock, J. and Erbaugh, J. (1961). An inventory for measuring depression. *Archives of General Psychiatry,* 4, 53-63.

Bergner, M., Bobbit, R., Pollard, W. and Gilson, B.S. (1976). The sickness impact profile: Conceptual formulation and methodology for the development of a health status measure. *International Journal of Health Services,* 6, 393-415.

Burack-Weiss, A. (1988). Clinical aspects of case management. *Generations,* 12(5), 23-25.

Capitman, J., Haskins, B. and Berstein, J. (1986). Case management approaches in coordinated community oriented long term care demonstrations. *The Gerontologist,* 26, 398-404.

Cline, B. (1990). Case management: Organizational models and administrative methods. *Caring,* 9(7), 14-18.

Connecticut Continuing Care, Inc. [CCCI] (1994). *Guidelines for long term care case management practice.* A report of the national advisory committee on long term care case management. Bristol, CT.

Duke University Center for the Study of Aging and Adult Development. (1978). *Multidimensional functional assessment: The OARS methodology.* Durham, N.C.: Duke University.

Grisham, M., White, M. and Miller, L. (1983). Case management as a problem solving strategy. *Pride Institute Journal of Long Term Health Care,* 2(4), 21-28.

Gwyther, L. (1988). Assessment: Content, purpose and outcomes.*Generations,* 12(5), 11-15.

Kane, R. (1988). Introduction, *Generations,* 12(5), 5-6.

Kane, R., Dobrof Penrod, J. and Kivnick, H. (1994). Case managers discuss ethics. *Journal of Case Management,* 3(1), 3-12.

Kane, R. and Kane, R. (1987). *Long term care: Principles, programs and policies.* New York: Springer.

Loomis, J. (1988). Case management in health care. *Health and Social Work,* 13, 219-225.

National Association of Social Workers. (1992). *NASW standards for social work case management.* Washington, D.C.: National Association of Social Workers.

National Institute on Community Based Long Term Care, affiliate to the National Council on the Aging, Inc. [NCOA] (1988). *Care management standards: Guidelines for practice.* Washington, D.C.

Nelson, G. (1987). *Effective social work practice and management in adult services.* Chapel Hill, N.C., School of Social Work, University of North Carolina at Chapel Hill.

Pfeiffer, F. (1975). A short portable mental status questionnaire for the assessment of organic brain deficit in elderly patients. *Journal of the American Geriatrics Society,* 23, 433-441.

Quinn, J. (1993). *Successful case management in long term care.* New York: Springer.

Radol-Raiff, N. and Shore, B. (1993). *Advanced case management.* Newbury Park, CA.: Sage.

Scharlach, A. (1988). *Survey of caregiving employees.* Los Angeles: TransAmerica Life Companies.

Schneider, B. (1988). Care planning. The core of case management. *Generations,* 12(5), 16-19.

Schneider, B. and Weiss, L. (1982). *The channeling case management manual.* Prepared for the National long term care channeling demonstration program. Philadelphia, PA.: Temple University Institute on Aging.

Steinberg, R. and Carter, G. (1983). *Case management and the elderly.* Toronto: Lexington Books.

Sterthous, L. (1986). *Informal services and supports in the national long term care channeling demonstration: A collection of practice oriented papers.* Philadelphia, PA.: Temple University Institute on Aging.

Weil, M., Karls, J. and Associates. (1985). *Case Management in human service practice.* San Francisco: Jossey Bass.

SECTION 2

SELECTED PRACTICE SETTINGS

CHAPTER 9

SOCIAL WORK PRACTICE
WITH INSTITUTIONALIZED FRAIL ELDERLY[1]

LEN FABIANO, R.N.
RON MARTYN, M.A.

*T*he dramatic increase in the number of older people in recent years and on into the next century has heightened awareness of the need for increased and improved institutional services for the elderly. The field of social work has changed and will continue to change to meet the new demands placed on it by the system and by the older frail clients. This chapter focuses attention on the changes and expectations of social workers in response to the special needs of the frail elderly in both generic and age-specific institutions. The skills required of the social worker for this specialized area are presented, along with strategies for future development in the field.

The Clientele

I. The Numbers

In recent years, the dramatic increase in the number and percentage of people over 65 years of age in both Canada and the United States has been a major focal point for demographers and service providers alike. Expectations of an ever-increasing cohort of senior adults have heightened concern for the demands that will follow in the health care sector. The reality is that the percentage shift of elderly persons has already begun. The number over 65 years of age will peak to over 20 percent of the total population (as compared to an average of 11 percent in 1986) by the year 2020 (Marshall, 1987).

The institutionalized frail elderly account for between three percent of the population over 65 years (eg., United States) and eight percent of the population over 65 years (Canada, Sweden) (Berg, Branch, Doyle and Sundstrom, 1988; McPherson, 1983). This major variation in percentage terms reflects a combination of several factors. Where there are insufficient affordable institutional services, the rate of institutionalization is lower. Similarly, where there is an availability of extensive home support services, the rate of institutionalization will be decreased. Conversely, where there are limited home supports, combined with affordable available institutional services, the percentage of institutionalized frail elderly will be increased.

A further consideration is that the major increase in this age group falls into the category of the 'old-old' — those over the age of 85 years. This age group is the fastest growing segment of the older population and represents the larqest portion of the institutionalized frail elderly (Atchley, 1980).

The implications for the future are obvious. Not only will the numbers of older persons increase significantly, but the number of 'old-old' (and consequently, the frail institutionalized elderly) will increase even more dramatically. This shift has already resulted in changes to the health care delivery system, and it will force even more dramatic changes over the next 30 years.

II. Profile of Institutional Care Settings

The institutionalized frail elderly are found in both general population or generic health care settings and age-specific facilities. General or generic settings include acute care hospitals, psychiatric facilities and special treatment centres. Age-specific settings include nursing homes, homes for the aged and, to some extent, retirement facilities. The roles and functions of social workers in relation to the frail elderly will be examined relative to both types of settings.

III. General Population (Generic) Care Institutions

By their very nature, general population institutions were never specifically geared to a particular age group. The intent of such service agencies has been to provide care to all regardless of age. However, as a result of the recent surge in the numbers of older adults, such institutions have increasingly recognized that this segment of the population constitutes a disproportionately high number of the total clients being served.

The impact of an increasingly older client has presented new challenges for the generic facilities. Not only do the special needs of this clientele place special demands, but there are also increased operational pressures on the system that impact the entire organization. Older clients require longer recovery times for most treatments, and as a result the turn-around time from admission to discharge increases significantly (Novak, 1985). Generic settings today are finding that their costs are increasing as more and more clients become long-term in nature — not only is there added cost for the longer treatment programme, but there is added pressure for more bed capacity to resolve the shortage of bed space for those awaiting admission. To increase the bed capacity puts added pressure on an already financially taxed system.

Social workers are employed in most generic settings. They provide services to the broad range of clients within such institutions, but they too feel the impact of encountering more older clients. The need for more time to serve these long-term-stay patients adds pressure to the job that was not there until recent years. Likewise, this segment of the population requires from the professional new skills and knowledge to effectively deal with their complex problems. Some generic facilities have responded accordingly by providing an increased psycho-geriatric perspective in treatment plans, by upgrading staff, and hiring gerontological specialists within each discipline area (Becker and Kaufman, 1988).

IV. Age-specific Care Institutions

Up until the early 1970s, few social workers were employed in age-specific care institutions. The focus of care in such settings was quite limited. Further, programming, supports and resources were at a minimum. The average age of resident populations was typically mid-to-late 70s, and although the clientele were frail they were provided few supports.

In the late 1980s, a different resident profile has emerged. The average age of the resident population is now late 80s, with a new mandate for care that employs concepts such as quality of life, individualized care and home-like environments (Novak, 1985).

There now exists two distinct groups of long-term care facilities. There are those that are preparing for the next decade. These are facilities that have a clear and progressive focus in their philosophy, programming, staff supports and resources. Looking toward the next decade, they have become the forerunners in establishing innovative ideas for the service industry.

The other group of long-term care facilities are those which are still trying to figure out how to get into the 1980s. This group fits the stereotypes of such settings. They have been delinquent in keeping up with the knowledge, trends and expectations within this specialized area. Such facilities are struggling to continue functioning, let alone provide quality of life for unique clientele (Grossman and Weiner, 1988).

Long-term care is very diverse, not only in its progressiveness but in its configuration. For example, working in a 600-bed facility creates different demands than working in a 60-bed facility. A facility located in a major urban setting is quite different than one located in a remote rural setting. Likewise, the configuration of the resident population within any one facility can vary dramatically. Many facilities have three distinct groups: those clients who are cognitively and physically well; those who are cognitively well but physically disabled; and those who are mentally impaired.

Furthermore, one cannot guarantee a homogeneous age group even in what are usually considered age-specific institutions. Some facilities in some regions have individuals as young as 14 mixed with others as old as 105, all under the same roof. Some even have a mixture of seniors with long-time institutionalized mentally handicapped individuals of a variety of age ranges.

When one speaks of becoming involved in age-specific, long-term care institutions, there are many options from which to choose. Without national guidelines, there are no guaranteed standards of services and supports within any long-term care facility across the country. Direct care staff in most long-term care facilities consists mostly of nurse's aids, with registered nursing staff generally assuming management functions. Recreation staff play an integral part in direct care provision in this setting as well. In the typical age-specific, long-term care setting, every member of the facility, from housekeeper, to aid, from maintenance person to administrator, is an integral part of the care process and team (Fabiano, 1989). This is especially important when one considers that the majority of staff comes from a variety of backgrounds and disciplines and possess minimal training in this speciality. This is an approach that is not generally encouraged in the acute care or generic setting.

Presently, the majority of age-specific, long-term care facilities do not employ social workers. Even though the need and desire may be present to have such a specialist on hand, most generally do not receive the necessary funding to add that position to their staff complement. Fortunately, this is changing as pressures within the industry to increase funding, allowing for flexibility to integrate a social worker position within the majority of long-term care facilities.

What is evident to this point in the evolution of the social workers' role within long-term care is that the limits and scope of the role within any one facility depend very much on the initiative and creativity of the individual social worker involved. The challenge for the field of social work is to anticipate the changes before they happen and incorporate new and innovative strategies in response to the increased demands and changes.

V. The Frail Elderly Clientele

The institutional setting in which the older adult is located determines to some extent the problems that they present. In other words, the differences associated with the social, psychological and physical environment of different institutions may result in varied responses in any one client. Therefore, it is important to consider the frail elderly in relation to the type of settings in which they are found.

The elderly admitted as short-term-stay patients (a few days) in the generic settings do not create the same problems as those who become long-stay patients (a period of weeks or months) in an acute care setting. The older adult seldom exhibits one distinct impairment. Rather, he or she typically demonstrates a variety of disabilities. When placed in a setting that includes younger clients, the differences can cause problems.

The contrasting profiles of the younger versus the older person, their premise for being in generic settings and the impact and prognosis of their diagnosis are contributing factors to difficulties they will inevitably encounter.

For example, a younger person may be admitted to the hospital with a leg fracture suffered in a football game at school. In the bed next to him is an elderly man who fell at home and broke his hip. While the injuries are of the same general nature, the individual needs and responses can be quite diverse. The energy, resilience and recuperative powers of the young man may result in his fracture having little more impact than restricting him to bed. His cognitive and physical energy level is still intact, resulting in his need to be active and occupy his time to relieve the boredom. As a result he does those things he likes to do — play his radio (loudly), watch television, do his homework and visit with his friends (which periodically seem to occur all at the same time!)

Meanwhile, the effect of the fractured hip on his elderly roommate is much more severe. This older gentleman is not so quick to 'bounce back' to his normal self. The demands now placed on him both physically and emotionally may be taxing his remaining resources to the limit. In fact, the combination of the injury, its restrictiveness and the effects of the medication given for pain may cause bouts of confusion and disorientation. Any added noise or disturbance in his room represents further stress that he cannot easily deal with at this time. Hence, the conflict. Both patients become increasingly frustrated and agitated with each other. This places demands on staff to resolve the conflicts and smooth over the differences in this imposed relationship.

Furthermore, the pace that staff normally maintain can be constantly challenged by the older client. As a person ages, his or her functioning levels decrease. Reflexes, muscle strength, coordination, cognitive processing, etc., are still intact and working, but are not as fast nor as resilient as when they were younger. This does not create a handicap to any older person in their life course, they simply learn to adapt to the gradual changes as they occur. But when that older person experiences a disability, that limitation now taxes those resources to their limit.

Adding further to such problems may be the approach, perception and focus of the facility and staff toward the long-stay older adult in the general population care centres. In a setting that is focused on treatment and recovery, and measures its successes by major positive changes in a person's condition, performance or behaviour, working with the long-stay older patient may be seen as counter-productive to the organization.

The improvements of the older patient experiencing multiple long-standing problems associated with a decrease in physical energy, stamina and recuperative power are often less dramatic than what such staff are accustomed. When the prognosis shows little gain, those staff who are trained to 'cure' are frustrated in what they perceive as the benefits of intense and aggressive efforts.

For facilities and staff who are geared and trained under the medical model of care, the older client can be seen as a source of frustration. Such frustrations are manifested both overtly and subtly. Overtly, the facility can point to the back-up of treatment and long waiting lists as evidence of the negative impact older people have on the care system and the reason for the institution's inability to cope. In a way, the older clients are often seen as the source of institutional paralysis.

Negative consequences of staff frustration with older clients can be more subtle, and consequently more difficult to identify. Seldom will staff openly express their frustration about the older long-term patient. However, it becomes difficult to contain one's frustration over a long period of time. Eventually, staff may not be able to control their feelings and frustrations when performing care with this client. Although it is hoped that the quality of physical care is not jeopardized, the emotional and psycho-social components may be. The older client will often find the staff's time spent with him or her becomes less and less.

In some settings this can be understandable. Generally, the majority of generic institutions are not environmentally equipped to handle a long-stay patient. The best example is an acute care hospital. Many medical floors where such a patient will be found do not have lounges, dining areas, etc. The patient is then restricted to his or her room for extended periods of time because there is really no where else to sit. The general expectation is that the patients will wear hospital gowns rather than being dressed, perpetuating for the older patient the sick role. Staff on such units do not normally consider how a patient must occupy his or her day. The usual expectation in the generic setting is that patients are too ill to be concerned about fulfilling their time or are well enough to occupy it themselves. The older long-term patient is usually not ill enough that he or she can be oblivious to the hours passing, nor well enough to be independent in filling those hours. This boredom and isolation can only complicate the patient's frailty, resulting in withdrawal or behaviour outbursts in order to break the pattern and routine of this setting.

The care of older clients in generic institutions will not only continue in the future but will be accelerated. The implications for such settings are that both the institutional and staff approaches to care for the frail elderly will require significant changes in order to best serve this clientele.

VI. The Age-specific Institution and the Frail Elderly

One of the most common stereotypes of aging is that all 'old people' are alike. In actual fact there are as many differences among the older population as there are between the young and the old (Keith, 1982). This is perhaps easier to appreciate when one thinks in terms of age spans. It is easy to accept that the needs and interests of the 15 year old are different from that of the 35 year old. (They don't even know who the musical performers are that each other prefers, let alone like each others music!) On the other hand, there can be an expectation that the person who is 70 years of age has a great deal in common with the person who is 90. Just as there is a 20-year span and differences in interests and needs in the younger age comparison, there are similar differences between these older groupings. They don't all like the same old tune. The difficulty for staff in an institution for older clients is to not only recognize and support these differences, but also be aware that over time the institution must change as the age cohorts change.

One problem that may be perpetuated in an age-specific, long-term care facility is that if all clients are older and disabled to some degree, then the range of expectations made of the clientele, by the institution, its staff and the clients themselves, can be less. The obvious detriment of such a setting is that there can be this 'age-ghettoization' process. There are few, if any, younger people within the facility (other than the caregivers themselves), and the older clients become isolated and surrounded by a diminished level of expectation — a 'what else can I expect at my age' response (Fabiano, 1989). This becomes a self-fulfilling prophecy of course — because the client does not expect to be able to do more, it becomes difficult to motivate the client to try harder, to go beyond the current functioning level. And while the personal lifestyles of the younger population can pose frustrations and difficulties for the older client in the institutional setting, the older person can also long for some contact with age groups other than the elderly. It is common in an age-specific setting to hear an older client comment about visitors 'breathing some life into this place' following a visit by a group of young persons or family members.

Upon entry to the age-specific, long-term care facility, the person does become a 'resident.' The name itself is indicative of the institutional expectation of the person's tenure — this is not for recovery, rehabilitation and return home — this is for recovery and rehabilitation to the point where the person will be able to function at his or her maximum level given the circumstances he or she is experiencing. This perception and expectation is reinforced by the operating norms (most people stay long term, and the staff reinforces the person's settling in and making this home). Residents are encouraged to bring in mementos and some furnishings from home. There are no restrictions on visiting hours, and there are more offerings of seemingly non-therapeutic recreational activities, much like what one would find in the outside community.

The net result of this process has the potential of reinforcing the client's loss of control and choice. Now that the person is in an institutional setting, there generally is little discussion or acceptance of the idea of a return to home. The negative responses (fight or submission) may be heightened in response to this new environment (Fabiano, 1989).

Social workers within the age-specific institutions face many problems that are similar to those experienced in generic settings. Both client (now referred to as resident) and family members are the key target groups for the social worker's efforts. Residents in the long-term care settings exhibit the same responses of resignation, unrealistic anticipation and a realistic acceptance combined with the determination to try to deal with the disability as well as possible. However, there may be differences in the intensity of the response now.

The converse of the resident's acceptance of his or her functioning level provides the social worker with the next challenge. Once the resident has accepted the status of 'resident,' the problem of resignation and giving up may become more of an issue. The social worker now must work to provide encouragement for the person to continue to try to be involved in the face of recognizing that things may not get a whole lot better.

Again, the client must come to understand that making the choice to do nothing also has consequences. By doing nothing there will be change — there will be further deterioration. As bad as things may seem now, the resident must understand that they can get worse if nothing is done and there is withdrawal from the surrounding people and activities of the facility. The social worker provides both individual and group supports for residents in the long-term care environment. While the bulk of such interactions may take place in the early stages following admission, there will also be the need for ongoing support for different residents at different times (Burnside, 1984).

The function of helping residents understand their own responsibilities in their personal care plan is an important element in the process of motivating residents. It is one in which the social worker plays a key role, but not the only role. The social worker must function as a team member, coordinating approaches and strategies with all members of the care team. Not only does this have implications for the obvious functioning areas in the facility, such as nursing, O.T., physiotherapy, and recreation, but also the not so obvious areas such as housekeeping and dietary. The social worker must work with all other team members as equal partners in the care process. The dietary aide can either reinforce or undermine the team's efforts simply by casual comments or actions in the course of serving a meal. Similarly, the housekeeping aid can have a dramatic impact on the resident's outlook and approach to life. Most people who work in long-term care generally concede that residents will often disclose more to the housekeeper who comes into their rooms every day than to any other member of the care team. Without encouragement and recognition that they have such valuable insights, the housekeeping staff will often not be aware that they have this exceptional vantage point and will not come forward with their observations. The social worker must not only be open to talking to the housekeepers about what they have seen and heard, but they must also reinforce with them the important role they can serve and encourage them to share this input with others.

Times have changed in long-term care. It used to be that the main concern centred around physical issues — programming to prevent bedsores and contractures and deal with bowels and bladder. The field then progressed to centre attention on social issues such as activation and activities. Now the industry is beginning to focus on the socioemotional concerns.

Nothing less than 100 percent of the clientele within long-term care are candidates for depression, one of the predominant disorders of the frail elderly (Butler and Lewis, 1982). Given the variety and severity of losses experienced within a short period of time, from widowhood, to a change in lifestyle, to relocation, disability and so on, it is no wonder that these individuals experience what can aptly be termed 'compounded grieving' (Fabiano, 1989). The challenges of dealing with the emotional side of these people are only now being recognized in long-term care, and the role of the social worker is crucial to this care process and approach.

Practice Roles and Responsibilities

The roles and responsibilities of social workers in generic and age-specific institutions are different in the configurations of job responsibilities. However, for the most part, their functions are similar in terms of the specific components that make up the job itself. Therefore, the practice roles and responsibilities are examined here from the broad perspective, rather than from a facility-type perspective.

One problem confronting individual social workers is that they face the same moral dilemmas as other health care professionals when confronted by the prospect of working with the elderly in long-term care. For many, the reasons for getting into the field are the same as those that repel them from working with the institutionalized frail elderly.

Individuals are drawn to the social worker field for a variety of reasons, but at the heart of the decision there is generally a desire to help those who are in need. However, the frail elderly can present too much need. Some care providers find it difficult to deal with people with so many impairments and limitations as those living in long-term care. When confronted with a client whose prognosis presents only short-term marginal gains before their condition is further eroded or they are eliminated by death, the care provider's need for personal gratification may take precedence over the desire to assist the client.

The reality is, most professionals believe that working with other populations in the health care sector is seen as more attractive, glamorous and exciting, where the clients have more potential for improvement over a longer period of time. In a society that highly values designer clothes, exotic foreign cars and life in the fast lane, and where people are inundated by a media blitz focused on drugs, alcohol, sexually transmitted diseases and child abuse, the realities of the needs of the frail elderly are lost. People working in the health care sector, including social workers, are obviously influenced by such societal values and focuses. It is difficult for health care professionals to be motivated by wrinkles, sagging body parts, incontinence, memory loss and the constant presence of death.

The frail elderly represent one of the social worker's greatest challenges. Not only must the social worker help the client overcome her or his response to the various impairments and obstacles, but the social worker must overcome her or his own personal notions and prejudices about the elderly, growing old and the relationship of this to the professional role of the social worker to be effective.

Social workers can perform a variety of functions when serving the older adults in institutional settings. The differences vary depending on both the type of setting and the individual expectations of the specific institutions themselves. In some instances, the social worker is hired to perform typical social work functions, not unlike those that would be performed with a non-age-specific group. At other times, the social worker might be hired into an age-specific position where social work skills are seen as a benefit, but where there may be an expectation of many other non-social work functions to be performed. In either situation, the social worker is seen as a key player in the provision of care.

The philosophy of age-specific institutions is on holistic care, which is consistent with the mandate of the social work profession. The skills the social worker brings to the setting are viewed as not only fitting within the philosophical perspective, but are seen as being as important as the provision of physical care for the clients. The social worker in a non-age-specific institution is usually seen as a member of the larger health care team. In its legitimate form, the social worker has as much input and importance as any other member of that team — be it the physician, nurse, occupational therapist or whomever (Edelson and Lyons, 1985). The reality is that this often falls short in actual practice. The social worker may find that the 'hard facts,' such as patient temperature, blood pressure and bowel movements, carry more weight within the medical model of health care than the less measured and calibrated observances of the social sciences. There are realities about the degree of how holistic the care might be, given such restricted perspectives. The placement of the social work department and personnel within the organization should help to shed some light on the status of the program within the facility. If it is located under the medical umbrella, then there may be a realistic expectation that there will be a dominant role to be played by the medical staff.

The social worker in long-term care takes on a more diverse role than in other settings. The social worker generally has an eclectic approach — counselling residents, family and staff, assessment and placement coordination of prospective residents, policy development, leading support groups, educating — almost anything can be expected in this setting. The range of responsibilities and duties of the social worker depends very much on the size and progressiveness of the facility in which that person works and the ability and drive of the individual social worker in each setting. Such a professional may be expected to cover any or all of the following components:

1) Working with the client
   — direct counselling
   — behaviourial assessment and intervention
   — support group
   — education
   — advocacy
   — resource utilization
2) Working with the family
   — direct counselling
   — support group
   — education
   — integration into care
3) Working within the organization
   — assessment and placement
   — employee assistance programme

— policy development
— volunteer coordination
— research
— coordination with psychiatric services
— staff training
— community outreach coordination

I. Working with the Client

1) Direct Counselling

There are no easy solutions to the problems and dilemmas of those living in long-term care. The social worker is challenged in this setting to broaden one's expectations beyond the curative role to a qualitative one — qualitative in the sense that the quality of life for the individual is enhanced to the highest possible level given the losses and impairments that will not go away. There is a major limitation in the social worker fulfilling this role in a long-term care setting — limited time. One social worker in a facility of 200 residents cannot invest much time to do one-to-one counselling for all residents and still perform the range and variety of other duties that would be expected. In this environment, it is important that the social worker not concentrate her attentions on all residents, but to focus on those who the staff cannot handle or who are having the greatest problems.

The social worker takes on a more challenging and creative role in such a setting that can be almost consultative in nature, required to provide the guidance and support for the psycho-social component of care within the entire setting.

Again, some social workers in long-term care will say that their time is so limited that they cannot counsel any residents. As identified earlier, it is the creativity of the social worker that often dictates job priorities and performance. The effective social worker in such a setting learns to take advantage of and utilize all the available resources. This involves completing the initial and ever important assessment, defining the problems, breaking the ground with specific counselling interventions and then assigning specific staff or volunteers to provide that listening ear (Edelson and Lyons, 1985). The utilization of other residents (Scharlach, 1988) and individual staff (Moss and Pfohl, 1988) as 'buddies' for new and troubled residents is proving to have considerable success in the institutional treatment programme.

2. Group Support

Group support in long-term care is not, as yet, a well-developed area (Burnside, 1984). The wide age range, responses and degrees of impairments do not make it easy to have a group of residents interact well in such a setting. The trend has been to move from a restricted group (i.e., only stroke victims or arthritic victims) to general resident support groups (Scharlach, 1988). This allows small groups of residents to discuss and resolve some of the problems of living in a communal setting.

3. Behaviourial Assessment

The skills and insights of the social worker may be most important in getting to the heart of the problem experienced by the resident. It is too easy for untrained staff to see the superficial behaviour of the resident as the problem, rather than identifying the underlying factors that may be causing that behaviour. By not understanding the complexity and interrelationship of this person's circumstances, it is easy for such staff to become critical and impatient with what their client demonstrates, only further compounding the problem (Fabiano, 1987). Providing all staff with a clearer picture and some direction to deal with the problem is probably the most rewarding facet for any social worker's efforts. Tapping the sensitivity and compassion of the staff in long-term care, and steering their efforts to a successful conclusion, represents a significant positive role for a social worker in this setting.

4. Resident Advocacy

Our society is inundated with concerns about human rights. Long-term care is an industry under that pressure. It is the social worker who is often called upon to become the resident advocate. The social worker represents the individual resident's wishes and desires on any decisions made by the care team. The social worker's assessment skills and counselling abilities provide the opportunity for the most objective perception, ensuring that the freedoms and rights of the resident are respected.

5. Education

A very limited area of development in resident supports in the long-term care industry is in resident education. It is important that those who are able do understand their disability, circumstances, rights within the facility and how to relate to others living within the same environment with a range of disabilities and limitations. Such perceptions are essential for quality living within such an institutional setting. The social worker, through both individual and group interactions, can be the primary catalyst for such insights.

II. Working with the Family

The other side of the social worker's responsibility within long-term care has to do with the families of the older clients. There exists a strong stereotype that families abandon their older parents in long-term care settings. In actual fact many families are very involved with their family members (Butler and Lewis, 1982). The major problems that are encountered by families are the same as the residents — the sense of helplessness, not knowing how to deal with mom or dad and what their role is in relation to the changing needs of the parent. These feelings of helplessness and undeveloped interactional skills can keep families away over the long term. In many cases, by the time the family member is admitted to long-term care the family is exhausted.

Typically, the older client will have support from family members, and particularly from daughters. This group has traditionally provided the greatest degree of support for older parents, and the trend continues even as more women enter the workforce and share in the provision of the family income. The social worker is confronted by children who are determined to do what is best for their parents, and while well motivated, they are not always well directed.

Family members are often driven by feelings of inadequacy regarding their availability for support for their aging parents. One hears the lament, 'If only . . .' implying they have been negligent in their support or selfish in their decision to place the parent. With these feelings of inadequacy come feelings of guilt — guilt that they could have or should have done more (Hansen, Patterson and Wilson, 1988). In actual fact, families are left in a 'damned if you do and damned if you don't situation.' No matter what decision they make, 'bad feelings' are associated with it (Fabiano, 1989).

While the family members may have done everything possible, given their time constraints, personal and family commitments, this does not alleviate the immediate feelings of guilt that something more could have been done. The family members' expressions of this guilt may manifest itself in less than obvious ways, such as staying away and rarely visiting, or displacing their negative feelings on the caregivers. The care providers can frequently encounter extreme hostility, unrelenting demands and suspiciousness when dealing with family members.

The social worker must be prepared for 'real feelings' to be expressed by family members, and these can include not only present circumstances but factors that may stem from long-standing relationship problems with their parents — such as old hurts that have not been resolved or complex family dynamics. Families in long-term care can present the full gambit in terms of family counselling needs. This can include dealing with family issues, relationships and emotions that have been in place for 50 years or more and are now complicated by current compounded losses and changes within the family structure. Such situations call not only for the social worker to listen carefully to what is being communicated, but to also recognize that such long-standing problems usually cannot be resolved through short-term interventions.

The social worker plays an important role in helping the family members face the realities of their parents' present situation and helping them to establish legitimate expectations for the future evolution of treatment for their aging parent. Ideally, the family members should become an integral part of the care plan process (Hansen, Patterson and Wilson, 1988). If they are involved in the process, they can become important facilitators in the efforts of enhancing their parent's quality of life, rather than becoming deterrents when their dealings with the older client run contrary to the institutional care plan (Shulman and Mandel, 1988).

Family members are usually open to suggestions for helping their parents adjust to their situation and progress beyond their current functioning level. The social worker can work with the family members through inservice sessions and special family gatherings. Not only do the families gain a better understanding of the social worker's plan, but they can be given specific training and suggestions on how to be more effective visitors. This client group is likely to be dealing with the existing impairments over an extended period of time, and the family will need all the resources it can find to make the visits worthwhile for the client and enjoyable and meaningful for themselves.

Just as knowledge about options and consequences is crucial for the client, the same holds true for the family. And just as the social worker must leave as much control and choice in the hands of the client as possible, the family too must understand the importance of this approach on their part as well when dealing with the parent.

II. Working within the Organization

There are a wide range of roles that can be filled by the social worker. They can include any one or combination of the following:

1. Pre-admission Assessment and Placement

Probably the most universal and long-standing role of the social worker in long-term care is in the area of assessment and placement. This involves interviewing potential clients for admission, determining whether their admission is appropriate and defining the individual's needs in relationship to the facility and making recommendations to an admission committee. This function involves assessing the potential client at home or in another health care facility, meeting and interviewing available family members, coordinating the medical assessment and developing the subsequent report and recommendations.

2. Policy Development

In recognition that the social worker in this setting is probably the most knowledgeable person with respect to the psycho-social needs of the client, the social worker is involved in almost all aspects of organizational growth and development that pertain to such concerns (and these concerns impact almost all elements in the care process).

3. Staff Education

Many social workers are required to augment the staff training programme by providing regular inservice sessions for staff on aging, emotions and grief, death and dying, behaviourial management, communication skills, etc. Staff within the facility can range from individuals with little or no formal education in the people caring field to highly skilled health care professionals. Staff training by the social worker must meet the wide range of needs of this diverse staff group.

4. Employee Assistance Programmes
Employee assistance programmes have not been well developed in many long-term care facilities. It has become the social worker's responsibility in many facilities, especially the smaller rural settings, to provide staff with assistance with personal problems, from family issues to drug and alcohol abuse and so on. In many cases this may involve some counselling to determine the problem and then linking that staff member with available community service agencies for follow-up.

5. Volunteer Coordination
In some settings the role of overseeing volunteer utilization is assigned to the social worker, either being part of her job directly, or having a full- or part-time volunteer coordinator assigned to her, depending on the size of the facility. The rationale for the social worker to have this under her umbrella rather than any other department head has to do with the skills required to direct the volunteer on interacting with the residents and staff, and the importance of linking the volunteer with residents requiring the appropriate support.

6. Community Outreach Coordination
Many facilities assign community outreach programmes to the social worker's jurisdiction. These programmes can range from day centres, respite care and walk-in clinics to community meals support programmes (meals-on-wheels). The attempt is to link the social worker with the community in utilizing the resources available through the facility with contacts made for potential admission. Individuals placed on a waiting list for admission are often those who can best utilize these services on an interim basis. The social worker is often required to maintain that waiting list and ensure it is updated, and therefore it is appropriate for this person to link the services provided by the facility with these individuals while they remain in the community.

7. Coordination with Community Services
The social worker is usually the contact person for external non-medical services needed for resident care. This involves psychiatric assessment and consultation with the available psychiatric institution or unit, social service programmes such as family counselling to link family and staff, drug and alcohol counselling and treatment centres.

8. Research and Publication
Probably the least developed area for involvement by the social worker (and most other team members as well) in long-term care is in the area of research. More and more facilities are monitoring their progression and results as they develop their strategies in caring for an increasingly complex clientele. This is becoming one of the ways to justify increased funding for new and innovative projects. The skills of the social worker make this area a necessary component of their role. The result can not only be recognition for the individual and the facility but also enhanced service opportunities through increased funding.

Potential for Role Development

The social worker's roles and responsibilities within institutional settings seem almost limitless at this point in time. In the generic settings, there will be opportunities to facilitate the organizations' attempts to come to grips with serving an increasingly elderly dominated clientele. In the age-specific settings, there are limited standards or expectations of the social worker role, and there will be tremendous latitude for development of the field in this setting. It will depend primarily on the individual facility, the perception of the need and benefits of such a professional, the philosophy and progressiveness of the facility, the resources and time made available to the individual social worker and the initiative and personal drive of the individual fulfilling the role.

The reality is that the numbers do not match the need. In a relatively new area of specialization such as long-term care, each facility is pressured to evolve in multiple directions at the same time in order to keep up with the increasing demands and expectations placed on it. In the planning of some facilities, the social worker role is seen as a part of that progression. In others facilities it has been a long-established and integrated role, while yet others cannot see the position being of high priority in their immediate growth. The reality is the changing clientele (changing in terms of needs and numbers) will force the requirement for the increased availability of social workers within such settings.

The future older adults that will be served are the 'me' generation, the post war baby boomers. This cohort has been a dominant group throughout their lives in our society and one which has been comfortable and successful in dictating policy directions. There is no doubt that they will probably continue to do so into the future as well. Therefore, there is greater likelihood that services for older adults will increase in magnitude and there will be increased demands for quality services as the baby boomers approach their own old age and see the need for better services. There is also less hesitation on the part of many in this age group to seek out professional help in dealing with emotions and relationship issues as compared to those who are presently over 75 (Lasoski and Thelen, 1987). It will be an expected service by those entering institutional care settings.

As has already been identified, areas such as resident advocacy and community outreach and coordination are being recognized as crucial in the health care continuum. These are areas that are ideally suited to the skills of the social worker, and there will probably be opportunities to develop and be involved in such services.

Much of the impetus for the increased utilization of social workers in the age-specific institutions is likely to come from within such organizations in the future. This can only help to reinforce the need for the expansion of services to include social work as a discipline unto itself in the future. This self-advocacy on the part of social workers should be facilitated by networking among both practicing social workers and non-practicing social workers who are functioning in related capacities (Karuza et al., 1988). If social workers recognize the pioneering role that they can assume in the age-specific institutions, the need and value of networking will be obvious, and this will become an increasingly important area of involvement for them in the future.

Concluding Remarks

Throughout this chapter focus has been on the current and future role of social workers in institutional settings. At times, the role appears quite established and clear. In other instances it is seen as being buried or almost non-existent — social work practices and skills being implemented through the auspices of other disciplines and functions. Both scenarios are visible in the workplace today. The challenge for social workers of the future is to determine where in this scenario they will be able to function most effectively. Some will personally find the established positions to be what they are seeking, and they will benefit most by moving in that direction. Others will be excited by the crusading nature of becoming involved in the less well-defined areas of service and will embark on this more uncertain career path. Either route offers tremendous scope and opportunity for the social workers of the future.

Case Example

Mr. Jones has had a history of relative affluence. He was a bank manager for 42 years until he was forced to retire (with many misgivings) at the age of 65. In retirement he initially had considerable difficulty filling his time and defining his role. He interpreted retirement as 'being old.' He believed he had little purpose. His pre-retired life was predominantly occupied by his job, and without it he had difficulty defining his personal self-worth and identity.

His relationship with his wife was always strong. In retirement that relationship only intensified. She filled the void, challenging him to become involved, becoming his main companion. For three years she directed him into rewarding activities, with much of their time spent travelling. He was beginning to enjoy his changed status and the freedom it provided him.

At the age of 68 Mr. Jones experienced his first stroke. Although the residual effects of that stroke were minimal, it hit him hard, only further reinforcing his previously held misconceptions of 'being old' and his changing role. Again it was his wife who became his main motivational support. It was her encouragement and persistence that drew him away from the abyss of emotional collapse. Two years later he experienced his second stroke. The residual effect this time was much more severe. He lost movement on his right side, as his right arm and leg were completely paralysed.

He was devastated. His time in hospital was a difficult one. His emotional response was expressed in chronic aggressive behaviour. He resisted physiotherapy, activities and almost everything he needed in order to effectively cope and achieve his maximum independent state. The result was that there was little progression beyond being able to transfer himself to a wheelchair. Within a short time, he was ready for discharge. The options given to his family were home or admission to a long-term care facility. His wife decided she wanted to take him home.

Within three months she worked with him to the point that he was able to walk with a quad cane. She had him active to a certain degree. Her constant support became the catalyst to move him through his grieving state to a point where he began to see a light ahead in the tunnel. Within a year of his second stroke he still presented angry outbursts but maintained a more liveable state. It was at this time that his wife died suddenly.

His inability to care for himself resulted in immediate placement in a long-term care facility. He was allowed only to bring in minimal personal belongings. To him each item he sold or gave away represented a permanent separation from his past — a further loss of his wife and a part of himself.

He now not only had to deal with the loss of his wife, his companion and his mentor, but he also had to forfeit the lifestyle to which he was accustomed. As someone who was used to being in control, he would not accept nor participate willingly now when confronted by directives and routines. The only accommodation available was a semi-private room. He was required to share this room with another man in his 90s who was very frail and noncommunicative due to a recent stroke.

Mr. Jones's daughters were beside themselves as to what to do. Their mother was the dominant figure within their family and the only one who 'controlled' Dad. Dad's aggressive response not only made them feel hopeless but frightened them. They had never encountered the full extent of his emotional outbursts before. Mom had always buffered his emotions so they never totally saw this side of him.

Staff in the facility found themselves with an increasingly difficult resident. His aggressive outbursts resulted in an avoidance behaviour on their part. Staff spent only as much time with him as they had to. The more Mr. Jones was left alone, the deeper he sank into his depression and grief.

His involvement within any functions of the facility was almost non-existent. From admission, he sat himself in a wheelchair and refused to walk or even to stand on his own. He would not transfer from bed to chair and back without assistance. Whenever he did receive help, he was belligerent and vulgar, making accusations that staff moved him the wrong way or were not quick enough to respond. Some nursing staff suggested that he be administered sedation to make him more manageable. There was concern that Mr. Jones's frustration and aggression might be taken out on other residents if they disturbed him.

The social worker became the intermediatory factor within the facility. Her initial assessment of Mr. Jones consisted of reviewing his past history, lifestyle, family dynamics and his response to his two strokes. She started working with him in one-to-one counselling. Initially her attempts to establish any rapport were thwarted. As she got closer to any delicate issues, his aggressive response became more intense. During this initial work-up, she met with the daughters to help them understand their father's behaviour and to assist them in learning how to cope with his outbursts and emotions.

With the background information in hand, the social worker began working on establishing a positive relationship with Mr. Jones. During the same period, contact was made with another long-established resident who had indicated an interest in participating as a 'resident buddy.' The social worker discussed Mr. Jones with the other resident buddy, and he agreed to start visitations with Mr. Jones in the hope of making him feel more a part of the facility. After a period of four weeks of resident and social worker visitations, Mr. Jones was encouraged to attend a 'new resident' support group intended to assist new admissions to understand and deal with the transition to long-term care. At the encouragement of the social worker, he was also assessed by a psychiatrist and placed on an antidepressive agent.

In conjunction with these efforts, the social worker worked with the staff during the care conference to help them understand his behaviour and to develop some techniques to deal with his outbursts.

A 'staff buddy' system was established, which identified two direct care staff and a volunteer who were willing to work with the social worker in assisting Mr. Jones to work through his grieving.

The result of these efforts was that Mr. Jones's behaviour and emotional state became tolerable for both staff and family. A year after admission, Mr. Jones was walking again with a quad cane. His depressive episodes flared at increasingly less intervals. Even though he still had frequent periods of anger, he was able to control his outbursts. His involvement within the activities of the facility was minimal, but he would participate in a few general events. On speaking with him he would state that he felt he could not enjoy life anymore, but it was tolerable.

Endnotes

[1] The original version of this chapter was published in *Social Work Practice in Health Care Settings*, M. Holosko and P. Taylor [eds.], Canadian Scholars' Press Inc., 1989, pp. 303-333.

[2] The focus in long-term care is a different one than what most are accustomed to in an acute care setting. The question always arises — What do you do for the person who has virtually lost all of the major components that provide him or her with the desired level of quality of life? The client who experiences compounded grieving is one who has gone from one major loss to another without the opportunity to resolve the initial loss. This has a domino effect, where the emotional experience of the first loss only compounds the second, weakening the person's coping skills and support systems (Fabiano, 1989). In such a situation, there is often little opportunity to re-build a person's life. Rather, there is only the potential to patch it together with what is remaining — probably one of the greatest challenges for any in the 'people professions.'

References

Atchley, R. C. (1980). *The social forces in later life*. Belmont, CA: Wadsworth Publishing Company.

Becker, G., and Kaufman, S. (1988). Old age, rehabilitation and research: A review of the issues. *The Gerontologist*, 28(4).

Bennett, R. (ed). (1980). *Aging, isolation and resocialization*. Toronto: Van Nostrand Reinhold Company.

Berg, S., Branch, L. G., Doyle, A. E. and Sundstrom, G. (1988). Institutional and home-based long-term care alternatives: The 1965-1985 Swedish experience. *The Gerontologist*, 28(6).

Burnside, I. (1984). *Working with the elderly*. Monterey, CA: Wadsworth Health Sciences Division.

Butler, R. N. and Lewis, M. I. (1982). *Aging and mental health*. Toronto: C.V. Mosby Company.

Edelson, J. S. and Lyons, W. H. (1985). *Institutional care of the mentally impaired elderly*. New York: Van Nostrand Reinhold Company.

Fabiano, L. (1987). *Supportive therapy for the mentally impaired elderly*. Seagrave, ON: Education and Consulting Service.

Fabiano, L. (1989). *Working with the frail elderly*. Seagrave, ON: Education and Consulting Service.

Grossman, H. D. and Weiner, A.S. (1988). Quality of life: The institutional culture defined by administrative and resident values. *Journal of Applied Gerontology*, 7(3).

Hansen, S. S., Patterson, M. A. and Wilson, R. W. (1988). Family involvement on a dementia unit: The resident enrichment and activity program. *The Gerontologist*, 28(4).

Karuza, J., Calkins,E., Duffey, J. and Feather, J. (1988). Networking in aging: A challenge, model and evaluation. *The Gerontologist*, 28(2).

Keith, J. (1982). *Old people as people*. Toronto: Little Brown and Company.

Lasoski, M. C. and Thelen, M. H. (1987). Attitudes of older and middle-aged persons toward mental health intervention. *The Gerontologist*, 20(3).

Marshall, V. W. (ed). (1987). *Aging in Canada: Social perspectives*, (2nd ed.). Markham, ON: Fitzhenry and Whiteside.

McPherson, B. (1983). *Aging as a social process*. Toronto:Butterworth's.

Moss, M. S. and Pfohl, D. C. (1988). New friendships: Staff as visitors of nursing home residents. *The Gerontologist*, 28(2).

Novak, M. (1985). *Successful aging*. Markham, ON: Penguin Books.

Scharlach, A. E. (1988). Peer counselor training for nursing home residents. *The Gerontologist*, 28(6).

Shulman, M. D. and Mandel, E. (1988). Communication training of relatives and friends of institutionalized elderly persons. *The Gerontologist*, 28(6).

CHAPTER 10

SOCIAL WORK PRACTICE
IN NURSING HOMES

MICHAEL A. PATCHNER, PH.D.
LISA S. PATCHNER, M.S.W.

*D*espite the focus on the health care needs of elderly people entering nursing homes, social work plays an integral role in the overall care of these persons. As a member of an interdisciplinary team, the social worker is responsible for attending to the psycho-social and familial needs of the elderly. Such tasks include: conducting psycho-social assessments; providing intake services; discharge planning; providing information and referral services; facilitating the resident's adjustment; facilitating resident councils; assisting in effecting treatment plans; and, conducting in-service programmes. Certainly tasks and functions vary from nursing home to nursing home, however, the importance of social work to nursing home care cannot be questioned. The future holds unlimited potential for role development in this area of practice.

Social work is probably the least understood profession in nursing homes that care for the elderly. For instance, nurses care for the medical needs of residents, physical therapists rehabilitate, dieticians plan menus, administrators manage, recreation therapists plan and implement activity programmes, but the role of social workers is often as varied as are the facilities in which they work. Yet, the role of social workers is as vital to the health and well-being of a nursing home resident as any of these mentioned. Indeed, social work is an essential component of long-term care from the time a plan is being made for a person's admission into a facility until the person is discharged or expires.

The Clientele

The 1980 United States Census reported that 1.2 million elderly, or approximately five percent of those over the age of 65, resided in nursing homes (U.S. Bureau of Census, 1980). This statistic can be misleading and at one level implies that there is a five percent chance of an older person going into a nursing home. However, research has shown that approximately 20 to 25 percent of the elderly will spend some time in a nursing home (Kastenbaum and Candy, 1973; Palmore, 1976). It is a fact that the older a person becomes, the greater the likelihood of nursing home placement. In 1985, 16 percent of the nursing home residents in America were within the age group of 65-74, 39 percent were 74-85 years of age and 45 percent were 85 and older (Hing, 1987).

Based upon the type of sponsorship, nursing homes fall into three categories: proprietary, non-profit and governmental. Proprietary homes, owned by corporations or private individuals, are in the nursing home business to make a profit. Non-profit homes are operated by religious or fraternal groups and are primarily intended for use by members of those groups. Governmental nursing homes are those run by federal, state or local governments (e.g., county nursing homes and those operated by the Veterans Administration). According to the most recent data available on nursing home characteristics there are 19,100 nursing homes in the United States. Of these, 14,300 are proprietary, 3,800 are non-profit and the remaining 1,000 are governmental (Strahan, 1987).

Depending on the type of care that is given, American nursing homes that receive Medicare and Medicaid funds are certified as skilled nursing facilities (SNFs) or intermediate care facilities (ICFs).

SNFs provide continuous nursing care on a 24-hour basis. Registered nurses, licensed practical nurses and nurse aides provide services prescribed by the patient's physician. Emphasis is placed on medical nursing care with restorative, physical, occupational and other therapies also provided (American Health Care Association, 1981). Patients receiving skilled nursing care generally are seriously ill. ICFs provide regular medical, nursing, social and rehabilitative services in addition to room and board for people who are not capable of independent living (American Health Care Association, 1981). According to a national survey of nursing homes in the United States, 76 percent of all nursing homes have federal certification, and, of these, 64 percent are certified as either SNF or both SNF and ICF, while 36 percent are certified as only ICF (Strahan, 1987).

Not only do nursing homes vary according to their type of sponsorship and certification, but they also vary according to their size. With respect to bed size, 33 percent of the nursing homes have less than 50 beds, 33 percent have 50 to 99 beds, 28 percent have 100 to 199 beds and 6 percent have 200 beds or more (Strahan, 1987). Generally, government and non-profit facilities tend to be larger than proprietary nursing homes.

Nursing homes have approximately 66 employees per 100 residents (Beaver and Miller, 1985). In general, skilled nursing facilities have more employees per resident than ICFs. Nearly half of all nursing home staff are nurses's aides (Beaver and Miller, 1985) and they provide 80 to 90 percent of the direct patient care. Further, one in ten employees is a nurse (RN or LPN) and about five percent are other professionals such as administrators, activity directors, social workers, physical therapists and occupational therapists (Beaver and Miller, 1985).

Persons enter nursing homes for a variety of reasons. Ten out of every 13 residents are admitted for reasons related to poor physical health. Of the remaining three persons, two are admitted because of mental or behavioural problems and one for reasons not related to health, usually due to lack of alternative community services more appropriate to the person's need or due to family abandonment (American Health Care Association, 1981).

More than 71 percent of the elderly nursing home residents are female (Kart, Metress and Metress, 1988). Women outnumber men in nursing homes not only because there is a disproportionate number of elderly women than men, but in general women live longer than men and a greater proportion of elderly men tend to be married as compared to elderly women.

Further, non-whites comprise approximately eight percent of the institutionalized elderly population (Kart, Metress and Metress, 1988). One may speculate that this low utilization of nursing homes by the non-white populations occurs because elderly non-whites live in states that have relatively low rates of institutionalization. Further, non-whites may not have access to nursing home care or are being institutionalized in other types of facilities, and socioeconomic economic factors, such as the ability to pay for nursing home care, influence this statistic (Kart, Metress and Metress, 1988).

Most nursing home residents are functionally impaired and elderly. Only seven percent of all nursing home residents can independently perform the activities necessary for daily living (i.e., eating, dressing, bathing, grooming, ambulating and toileting) (Hing, 1981). The typical nursing home resident is "an 82-year old widowed female suffering from an average of four illnesses" (American Health Care Association, 1981). Nationally, the health problems of nursing home residents include (Haber, 1987):

- 39.7 percent with diseases of the circulatory system;
- 20.4 percent with mental disorders and senility without psychosis;
- 5.5 percent with endocrine and nutritional metabolic diseases;
- 2.2 percent with neoplasms, including cancer; and,
- the remainder have other diseases proportionately represented.

The nursing home has long been stereotyped as a place to go when persons could no longer take care of themselves and their families were unable to care for them. Often, it was seen as a place to go and wait to die. However, the median length of stay in a nursing home in 1985 was 614 days. For a 12-month period spanning portions of 1984 and 1985 there were an estimated 1,223,500 discharges, of which 72 percent were live discharges (Sekscenski, 1987). Today's nursing homes are also for convalescents who expect to receive treatment and often recover. The emphasis is on living and helping a person to be as independent as possible in order to return to one's own home or community whenever feasible.

Practice Roles and Responsibilities

Nursing home services are directed at promoting, restoring and facilitating the independent functioning of each resident and assuring that quality care is being provided. Social workers, as part of an interdisciplinary team that addresses a resident's physical, medical, psychological and social needs, have a unique role in the nursing home even though their tasks and activities may vary from one facility to another. A number of authors have written about social work practice in long-term care facilities and have described the role and functions of social workers in these settings (Brody, 1976; Conger and Moore, 1981; Getzel and Mellor, 1982; Jorgensen and Kane, 1976; Peckham and Peckham, 1985). Although varied, the social worker's role is essential and will most often include the following tasks.

Social workers in nursing homes spend much time working directly with the residents and their families. From admission to discharge, the social worker is involved in making assessments, counselling, conducting psycho-social evaluations and carrying out care plans. Social workers often have the first contact with the resident and their families at the time of admission. If a nursing home is small and does not have a director of admissions, it is often the responsibility of the social worker to admit persons and facilitate their transition into the nursing home. Entering a nursing home can be traumatic for both the resident and family. Families often feel very guilty about not being able to care for the person at home and having a loved one placed in a nursing home. The resident, too, makes numerous adjustments. Having to deal with loss of health and independence and being removed from their own, familiar home is very stressful. No one ever wants to go to a nursing home as a patient but often has to out of necessity. The social worker, therefore, has to be particularly sensitive to the feelings of the resident, his or her family and the dynamics among them. It is the social worker's responsibility to help make the transition to the nursing home as smooth as possible by being in tune with the fears, expectations and anxieties of all concerned and addressing the particular needs of the person and his or her family. Social workers help facilitate the admission process by showing the resident, when possible, and her family around the facility, introducing the resident to staff, other residents and her roommate, and explaining schedules and policies (e.g., meals, bath times, laundry, smoking regulations, etc.). The idea is to acquaint the resident and family with the facility, without overwhelming them, and making the new resident feel as comfortable as possible.

There are a number of documents that a social worker must complete at the time of admission, which include the admissions form, social history, a contract and patients' rights form. The admission form is designed to provide some pertinent data, which will be helpful to all staff. It acquaints the professional staff with many particulars about the new resident. It includes information such as the resident's preferred name or nickname, age, gender, next of kin, name of physician, medical diagnosis, religious affiliation, funeral home preferred (if needed), guardianship status or power of attorney, financial information, etc. The admission form provides information that is read by nursing, dietary and other departments before they conduct their assessments of the resident.

The social history, which can be completed on a form or done as a narrative, includes general demographic information (e.g., birth date, birthplace, ethnic background, education, etc.), family composition, legal information (e.g., responsible person for the resident, if any, power of attorney, etc.), a general medical profile (e.g., previous hospitalizations and nursing home placements, use of appliances, eye glasses, dentures, hearing aid, etc.), pre-admission data (e.g., prior living arrangements, incidents and conditions leading to admission, etc.), involvement in the community and religious organizations, psycho-social functioning, personal likes and dislikes, reactions to nursing home admission and discharge potential. The social history is used to provide staff with the background and special characteristics of a resident and it allows staff see the resident as a unique person with a particular history and not just as another patient. The contract is a signed document, which states the general services provided by the nursing home and the charges for these services. It makes the resident and/or a family member responsible for paying the bills unless third party payment is appropriate. Also, at the time of admission residents' rights are read and residents are asked to sign the document acknowledging that they are aware of their rights as nursing home residents. If residents are unable to understand their rights as nursing home patients, then the social worker makes sure that a family member or responsible person is informed of them. The appended endnote is a condensed summary of residents' rights in the state of Illinois.[1]

These residents' rights are not only intended to outline the specific entitlement of the residents, but they also identify the facilities' responsibilities and obligations to each resident. It is the social worker's function to inform the residents and their families of these rights, make sure that they understand them, and to assure that the residents' rights are protected. The social worker must serve as an advocate of the resident if his or her rights are violated and if there is any indication of abuse, neglect or poor quality care.

Once the resident is admitted to the facility, the social worker has the responsibility of facilitating the resident's adjustment. Although a few residents welcome being admitted to a nursing home because they soon find that they generally get good care, good food and can interact with staff and other residents, most residents take several weeks or longer to adjust to their new living arrangements. Social workers help residents adjust by frequently visiting with them during this period and by allowing them to express their fears, anxieties and feelings of loss. The social worker may introduce the resident to other residents to try to facilitate some socialization and friendships. During this adjustment period, the social worker may also accompany the resident to some of the activity programmes. The social worker also works closely with the family at this time. Indeed, the family, too, is adjusting and the social worker listens to their concerns and may provide some counselling.

Social workers are also responsible for addressing the psycho-social problems of the residents. For example, if a resident is confused and cannot find her room, if a resident is lonely and feels like she wants to die or if a resident is bedridden or isolates herself in her room, it is the social worker's task to address these problems. These kinds of psycho-social problems are identified by doing an assessment of each resident. This is a psycho-social assessment and it evaluates such things as a resident's orientation, memory, attention, self-image, sociability, initiative, relationships with family, staff, and other residents, etc. Problems in these areas can be addressed by working with the residents either individually, often referred to in a nursing home as working 'one-on-one' or 'one-to-one,' or by working with residents in groups. Common types of groups used by social workers to address particular psycho-social problems include reality orientation, validation therapy, reminiscence groups and socialization groups. Depending on the type of psycho-social problem a resident has, one-to-one interventions can include counselling, sensory stimulation, reality orientation or just friendly visiting. Having one-to-one and group interventions with residents require good generic casework and counselling skills and often require the social worker to work with other departments within the nursing home to help coordinate the logistics of the interventions and also to have all departments follow through with the approaches being utilized by the social worker. This requires the social worker to train other staff to monitor a resident's psycho-social functioning and to intervene as appropriate when necessary.

Providing information and referral services is another important social work function in a nursing home. Specifically, the social worker informs residents and their families of particular services that they may be eligible for and links them to these services. For example, if a resident is developmentally disabled, the social worker can refer her to a sheltered workshop; if residents have low incomes, the social worker can make sure that they are aware of any assistance they may be eligible for; if a resident desires spiritual guidance, the social worker can get her connected to a minister, priest or rabbi; or if residents need to get new eyeglasses, hearing aids or have dental work done the social worker can arrange for these services. The social worker generally takes a very active role in providing information and referral services to the nursing home resident because the residents are often dependent and require assistance in obtaining immediate and needed services. Thus, the social worker will not only have to provide information, but most of the time will have to make appointments, arrange transportation and either personally accompany the resident to an appointment or arrange for the resident to have an escort and often help the resident complete any paper work.

Social workers may also get involved in resolving conflicts that occur with residents. A resident can have a conflict with another resident, a staff person or with a family member, and the social worker generally has the task of trying to remedy such situations. Indeed, interpersonal conflicts between residents are not uncommon in nursing homes. More specifically, most conflicts between residents occur between roommates. Sometimes the personalities of roommates are incompatible and the social worker intervenes to resolve any disputes. When such conflicts cannot be resolved, the social worker will usually arrange for a room change. When conflicts arise between a resident and staff member, the social worker provides suggestions to both the resident and staff member on ways of eliminating such conflicts. For example, if a resident does not want to take a bath and (constantly) argues with a nurse's aide about having a bath, the social worker may instruct the aide on appropriate ways of approaching the resident at bath time. The social worker can also work with the resident to understand the resistance and to alleviate the resident's fears and concerns about taking a bath. Most staff members involved in resident-staff conflicts are the aides because they provide between 80 and 90 percent of the direct care in a nursing home and generally they are not trained to handle such situations. The social worker may also get involved in conflict resolution between a resident and her family. For example, if a resident resents her family because she was placed in a nursing home and makes her family feel very guilty about placement, the social worker usually intervenes. In such instances, the social worker can work individually with the resident and the family members involved or the social worker can work with them as a group. In resolving such conflicts the social worker needs to have good listening, counselling and crisis intervention skills, and the social worker needs to be aware that many conflicts are not easily resolved.

If a resident is not a permanent resident and will be discharged, it is the responsibility of the social worker to plan for this discharge. Discharge planning is defined as, "the process of activities that involve the patient and a team of individuals from various disciplines working together to facilitate the transition of that patient from one environment to another" (McKeehan, 1981, p.3). The social worker coordinates a resident's discharge by working with the resident, family, physician and nursing home personnel (i.e., nurses, physical therapists, dietician, activity director, etc.), and assures that proper services will be in place to permit the resident to make the transition from being in the nursing home to having other living arrangements. If a resident is being discharged to her home, to live with her family or to another independent living situation in the community, the social worker makes sure that all necessary and appropriate services will be provided. For example, a resident might need meals-on-wheels, a visiting nurse or therapist, assistance with housework, shopping, and laundry, and transportation for physician visits. Sometimes residents are discharged to another nursing home or other type of facility. In these cases, the social worker assures that all the necessary information is passed along to the other facility and that the needed services will be offered to the resident. Regardless of where a resident will be living once she leaves the nursing home, the social worker makes arrangements so that appropriate services from all available resources will be provided. Even though a resident leaves the nursing home, the social worker's responsibilities do not end. The social worker follows up to assure that all of the services that were arranged for are being delivered and the social worker evaluates if there are any further needs that are not being met.

Every resident in a nursing home has a care plan that specifies particular treatment and care to be given to each resident. This plan identifies resident strengths and problems, specifies approaches to address the problems and establishes goals for residents to achieve. For example, if a resident had a stroke and is learning to walk again, a portion of the care plan would address this problem. The plan would state that a resident is unable to walk without assistance. The approach for staff to address this particular problem would be for the resident to walk with the assistance of a walker, be accompanied by an aide when walking and receive physical therapy daily. The goal could be for the resident to walk 25 feet with a walker by the next care plan review (usually done every 90 days or less). This would be just one problem addressed in the care plan; others may include that the resident is depressed because of having had the stroke, not able to speak or eat properly, etc. The purpose of care planning is to provide the best possible care for each resident; care that will address each resident's specific needs and maximize his or her rehabilitative potential.

The care planning process involves systematic, coordinated and planned procedures for the development and delivery of necessary care (Patchner and Balgopal, 1987). Care planning is an interdisciplinary process, which staff from all departments within the nursing home meet to discuss and plan the care to be given. Sometimes a resident and family members attend these meetings as well. Within seven days of being admitted to a nursing home a care plan is developed for the resident. Care plans are then reevaluated and revised every 60 to 90 days or whenever a resident's condition changes. A social worker is intimately involved in this process by identifying a resident's particular psycho-social problems, assessing resident strengths and potential and developing a plan of care to address the psychological and social needs of each of the residents. Although most nursing homes have a nurse as the coordinator of the care planning process, it is not uncommon for a social worker to be assigned this responsibility. As coordinator of the care plans, the social worker would then schedule all care plan meetings, ensure that all care plans were done in a timely manner, conduct the interdisciplinary care plan meeting and ensure that all care plans were completed in such a way that they meet all of the governmental and, where appropriate, corporate regulations. As one may surmise, this is a very demanding and time-consuming responsibility, but good care plans usually translate into good resident treatment and care.

As an avenue for residents to have input into the functioning of the nursing home and as a forum to air complaints, many nursing homes have a 'Resident Council.' Such councils are organizations within the nursing home, which are comprised of residents who can formally express their opinions on matters that affect their daily lives. Usually, officers are elected by their fellow residents and regular meetings are held. The resident council works in conjunction with the administration, staff and families to promote better care within the facility and to better address the needs of the residents. It is often the responsibility of the social worker to organize and facilitate the resident council and work directly with its officers. Resident councils should be self-directed and as independent as possible, subsequently the social worker involved must be careful not to be too directive. Such councils work best when: there is a commitment by the administration and staff to the council; regular, well-publicized meetings are held; there are written minutes of all council and committee meetings and these are made available to the residents; there is prompt attention by staff and administration to problems and suggestions voiced by the council; there is a specific meeting place; and some financial resources are available for the council.

Finally, social workers may also conduct in-service training programmes to better educate the nursing home staff and volunteers for the purpose of improving the overall quality of care, which is delivered to the residents. Nursing homes are required to by federal and state regulations to have a continual programme of in-service training for all staff. These can include such issues as fire safety, CPR and proper techniques for cleaning up spills of body fluids, etc. However, the social worker also plays a role in training and is responsible for conducting in-services that address the psychological and social aspects of care. Some common topics for in-service training conducted by social workers include: resident rights, confidentiality, remotivation of residents, stress management, conflict management, techniques for working with confused or disoriented residents and handling death and dying. Because of workers' schedules, most in-service training programmes in nursing homes are rather focused and last for no more than one hour. By conducting these in-services, the social worker needs to be explicitly aware of the educational levels of the staff and care must be taken to give good practical information, which can be readily utilized.

Potential for Role Development

It is very likely that the number of nursing home residents will continue to grow very rapidly primarily because of the large increases expected in the elderly population. One study projected a 70 percent increase in the number of persons requiring long-term care between 1980 and the end of the century (Hing, 1981), and another study estimated that approximately 650,000 additional elderly will be in nursing homes in the year 2000 in the U.S.A. (Fox and Clauser, 1980). Thus, with the increase in the number of institutionalized elderly, the number of social workers needed by nursing homes will also increase.

Social workers will have a unique role in admitting and discharging nursing home residents and developing and implementing programmes and interventive methods to best address their psycho-social needs and those of their families. The greatest potential for the expanded role of social work in nursing homes will result from the growing view that a nursing home is no longer a place to die but a place to live and be a part of the larger community. Thus, social workers will be much more involved in programmes that integrate the community into the nursing home and the nursing home into the community. Working more with volunteer groups, taking groups of residents into the community to volunteer, shop, dine, and be involved with various community efforts, and generally promoting the nursing home as one integral part of the community rather than an institution within the community will take on increased importance in the future. Thus, the social worker will become more of an advocate for the needs of the elderly and may have to work against some deeply ingrained ageist attitudes.

Another growth area for social workers in nursing homes will be increased efforts toward more psycho-social programming for the residents and their families. Although social workers are currently involved in these efforts, more attention will be given to these functions. In this regard, a greater portion of the social worker's time will be spent in developing and implementing more and better psycho-social programmes for the residents.

Finally, social workers in nursing homes will have to learn to deal with some younger clientele. For instance, AIDS is of epidemic proportions and many of its victims will ultimately become nursing home residents. This has tremendous implications for social workers who have a part in educating all staff in the nursing home to work with victims of this disease and to develop meaningful interventive strategies for supporting and working with this group of residents.

The traditional functions of the social worker will continue, but there will also be many new opportunities for role expansion. As new situations present themselves, and with initiative and some creativity, social workers can expand their roles and functions within nursing homes to address the future needs of the residents. As indicated earlier, a social worker's job varies from facility to facility, and many times it is the social worker who is responsible for defining a fair portion of his or her own job description.

Concluding Remarks

Entering a nursing home does not alter the basic needs of an individual. Nursing homes are not only responsible for addressing the physical and medical needs of their residents, but they also have the responsibility for responding to residents' psycho-social needs. Social workers in nursing homes function as part of an interdisciplinary team and are responsible for addressing the psycho-social needs of the residents and their families. Although the social work role may vary from one nursing home to another, a social worker's duties are aimed at facilitating each resident's independence and maximizing his or her rehabilitative potential.

Social work is an essential component of the total care that is delivered to residents. To ensure that social work practice in nursing homes contributes to the well-being of residents and their families, the National Association of Social Workers (NASW) developed a set of standards for social workers to follow (Long Term Care facilities Standards Task Force, 1981). The standards are:

1. The long-term care facility shall maintain a written plan for providing social work services designed to assure their availability to all residents, their families and significant others. It shall be developed by a qualified social worker experienced in long-term care.
2. The plan for social work services shall be guided by a written statement of philosophy, objectives and policies.
3. The social work services plan shall provide for administrative accountability and direction by a social work director who is a qualified social worker responsible to the administrator of the long-term care facility or to the chief executive officer.
4. The functions of the social work programme should include but not be limited to direct services to individuals, families and significant others; health education for residents and families; advocacy; discharqe planninq; community liaison and services; quality assurance; development of a therapeutic environment in the facility; and consultation to other members of the long-term care team.
5. A sufficient number of appropriately trained and experienced social work and supportive personnel shall be available to plan, provide and evaluate all social work services.
6. Social work personnel shall be prepared for their responsibilities in the provision of social work services through appropriate education and orientation specific to long-term care facilities and through education and training programmes.
7. A written statement of the personnel policies and procedures of the agency, the social work programme, and the NASW Code of Ethics shall be available to each staff member.
8. Adequate documentation of social work must be provided in the health care record. Confidentiality must be safeguarded.
9. The quality and appropriateness of social work services provided shall be regularly reviewed, evaluated and assured through the establishment of quality control mechanisms.

10. There must be adequate budget, space, facilities and equipment to fulfil the professional and administrative needs of the social work programme.

Social work practice in the homes can make a radical difference in the quality of care that is provided to the residents. Unfortunately, the general public has an unfavourable image of nursing homes and many older people have negative feelings about nursing home placement even when it is absolutely necessary. Yet, once admitted to a nursing home, many residents feel comfortable, safe and cared for. Social workers must promote their practice and help create an atmosphere of hope, love and compassion.

Case Example

Helen had noticed that she was having some difficulty with walking. She had seen her doctor and was referred for some medical tests at the local hospital. It was discovered that she had had a small stroke. Nearly a year later she had another stroke, which completely affected her left side and caused her to lose control over her left arm and leg. Her speech became slightly impaired, but she could still communicate fairly well. After being hospitalized for this second stroke, it was determined that she would receive better care in a nursing home rather than returning home. She was married and lived with her husband of 45 years, but she could not return home because her husband was in poor health and not able to properly care for her. She had four children; two lived out of state and the other two lived in the same town, but they both worked and had families of their own. So, her children were unavailable for home care. Her income and medical insurance were limited and, as a result, she could not afford the home health care she required if she were to return to her own home.

The social worker at Pleasant Manor Nursing Home received a telephone call from the social worker at the local hospital who was planning Helen's discharge. The hospital social worker knew that Pleasant Manor Nursing Home had an excellent physical therapy department and hoped that Helen could be admitted. Fortunately, Pleasant Manor had a bed available. The social worker at Pleasant

Manor made arrangements to visit Helen at the hospital. At the hospital the social worker talked with the nurse, the hospital social worker, Helen and Helen's family. The purpose of this visit was to assess Helen's appropriateness for the nursing home and to gather as much information as possible about Helen and her particular needs. Upon her return to Pleasant Manor the social worker met with the director of nursing, the administrator and the physical therapist to inform them of Helen and her particular needs. She also met with the dietary supervisor so that Helen could start having meals upon her arrival and she informed the housekeeping department so they could be available to put Helen's clothing in the closet and prepare labels for her clothing.

Helen's family came to the nursing home and was shown around the facility by the social worker who showed them the room where Helen would be staying as well as the physical therapy room with all of the specialized equipment. Later that day Helen was admitted. The social worker handled the admission and made Helen and her family feel very comfortable. The family seemed a bit overwhelmed at all of the paper work and all of the questions that were being asked. However, the social worker explained every form and why the questions were being asked. She took Helen, along with her family, and showed them around the nursing home and introduced them to staff. She took them to the room where Helen would be staying and introduced them to Helen's roommate. The social worker stayed for a while and got Helen settled. She then left to let the family have some time together and later checked on her several times that day. On one occasion she found Helen crying. The social worker reassured her that it was alright to feel sad about being in the nursing home and, because of the medical prognosis, gave her hope for improving.

Helen's care plan was discussed two days after her admission. A plan was developed for physical therapy, nursing care, dietary and activities. The social worker addressed her adjustment to being in a nursing home and noted her slight depression, which could interfere with her motivation to work with physical therapy and to eventually improve. It was decided that the social worker would provide one-to-one counselling to address these problems.

After six months of paying nursing home bills, it came to the attention of the social worker that Helen and her husband's savings had been almost eliminated to pay the nursing home bills of nearly

$2,500 a month. The social worker met with Helen's family about their financial situation and referred them to the state department of public assistance where they applied for Medicaid, which would cover the nursing home bills. The family was grateful to the social worker because even though Helen was making very good progress, she was not ready to come home and the family, exhausting all savings, was not able to pay the nursing home bill.

Finally, after a year and a half of being in the nursing home, Helen's physician said that she had improved enough for her to be able to return home. She made enough progress that she would not be overly dependent on her husband and could take care of most of her activities of daily living. The social worker made plans for her to be discharged. She arranged for meals-on-wheels to be delivered to both Helen and her husband and a public health nurse would visit weekly to assure that the physical therapy exercises were being done properly. Helen's family would assist with grocery shopping, laundry and transportation. Helen was very pleased to be home and felt appreciative of all the good care that she received at Pleasant Manor.

Endnote

[1]   A condensed summary of nursing home residents' rights in the state of Illinois:

Each resident has all rights guaranteed by law, including the right to equal access to appropriate care regardless of race, religion, color, national origin, sex, age or handicap.

Each resident has the right to considerate and respectful care and to treatment with honesty and dignity without abuse or neglect.

Each resident has the right to respect, privacy and confidentiality both in personal and medical affairs.

Each resident has the right to retain and use their personal clothing and possessions as space permits.

Each resident shall be permitted freedom of religion.
No resident shall be required to perform services for the facility.

Each resident is permitted to retain a personal physician at the resident's expense or at the expense of any applicable third party payor.

Each resident is entitled to participate in planning his (her) medical treatment and to receive comprehensible information concerning his (her) condition, health needs and the alternatives for meeting these needs.

Each resident has the right to refuse treatment to the extent permissible by law and to be informed of the consequences of such refusal.

Each resident has the right to be free from physical or chemical restraints except as authorized by the attending physician and documented in the resident's record.

Each resident has the right to be involved in his (her)discharge planning, including the right of self-discharge.

Each resident has the right to the confidential handling of his (her) medical and personal records.

Each resident has the right to manage his (her) own financial affairs.

Each resident shall be informed, at the time of admission and during his (her) stay, of available services and the charges for these services.

Each resident has the right to associate with any person of his (her) choice.

A resident may meet with his (her) attorney or the representative of a public agency charged with supervising the facility or with a member of any other community organization during reasonable business hours.

Married residents in the facility are entitled to share a room, unless none is available or it is medically contraindicated by the attending physician and so noted in the medical record.

Each resident has the right to communicate with any person of his (her) choice.

Each resident has the right to exercise his (her) rights and privileges as a citizen and resident of the facility.

Each resident is entitled to information regarding policies and procedures for the initiation, review and resolution of complaints.

Each resident shall be fully informed of the facility's patient rights policies.

References

American Health Care Association. (1981). *Facts in brief on long term health care*. Washington, D.C.: American Health Care Association.

Beaver, M. L. and Miller, D. (1985). *Clinical social work practice with the elderly*. Homewood, IL: The Dorsey Press.

Brody, E. M. (1976). *A social work guide for long term care facilities* (DHEW Publication No. ADM 76-177). Washington, D.C.: U.S. Government Printing Office.

Conger, S. A. and Moore, K. D. (1981). *Social work in the long-term care facility*. Boston: CBI Publishing Co.

Fox, P. D. and Clauser, S. V. (1980). Trends in nursing home expenditures: Implications for aging policy. *Health Care Finance Review*, 2(Fall), 65-70.

Haber, P. A. L. (1987). Nursing homes. In G. L. Maddox (ed.), *The encyclopedia of aging*, (pp. 489-492). New York: Springer Publishing Co.

Hing, E. (1981). Characteristics of nursing home residents: Health status and care received. *Vital and health statistics* (Series 13, No. 51). Rockville, MD: National Center for Health Statistics.

Hing, E. (1987). Use of nursing homes by the elderly: Preliminary data from the 1985 national nursing home survey. *Advance data form vital and health statistics* (No. 135, DHHS Pub. No. PHS 87-1250). Hyattsville, MD: Public Health service, National Center for Health Statistics.

Getzel, G. S. and Mellor, M. J. (eds.). (1982). *Gerontological social work practice in long-term care*. New York: The Haworth Press.

Jorgensen, L. A. and Kane, R. (1976). Social work in the nursing home. *Social Work in Health Care*, 1(4), 471-82.

Kart, C. S., Metress, E. K. and Metress, S. P. (1988). *Aging health and society*. Boston: Jones and Bartlett Publishers.

Kastenbaum, R. and Candy, S. (1973). The 4 percent fallacy: A methodological and empirical critique of extended care facility population statistics. *International Journal of Aging and Human Development*, 4, 15-21.

Long-Term Care Facilities Standards Task Force of the NASW Committee on Aging. (1981). *NASW standards for social work in long-term care facilities* (NASW Policy Statement 9). Washington, D.C.: National Association of Social Workers.

McKeehan, K. M. (1981). Conceptual framework for discharge planning. In K. M. McKeehan (ed.), *Continuing care: A multidisciplinary approach to discharge planning*. St. Louis: The C.V. Mosby Company.

Patchner, M.A. and Balgopal, P.R. (1987). *The care planning process in nursing homes*. Urbana, IL: University of Illinois at Urbana-Champaign School of Social Work.

Palmore, E. (1976). Total chance of institutionalization among the elderly. *Gerontologist*, 9, 25-29.

Peckham, C. W. and Peckham, A. B. (1985). *You made my day*. Lebanon, OH: Otterbein Home.

Sekscenski, E. S. (1987).Discharges from nursing homes: Preliminary data from the 1985 national nursing home survey. *Advance data from vital and health statistics* (No. 142. DHHS Pub. No. PHS 87-1250). Hyattsville, MD: Public Health Service, National Center for Health Statistics.

Strahan, G. (1987). Nursing home characteristics: Preliminary data from the 1985 national nursing home survey. *Advance Data From Vital and Health Statistics* (No. 131, DHHS Pub. No. PHS 87-1250). Hyattsville, MD: Public Health Service, National Center for Health Statistics.

U.S. Bureau of Census. (1980). *Current population reports* (Series P-25, no. 80). Washington, D.C.: U.S. Government Printing Office.

Chapter 11

Social Work Practice
in Geriatric Assessment Units[1]

Patricia MacKenzie, M.S.W.

T *he gradual deterioration of function with increasing age is so widely perceived and so expected that all difficulty experienced by an elderly person tends to be attributed to age. Geriatric assessment units are built upon the premise that it is disease not senescence which leads to disability in the elderly. GAU programmes provide an environment where it becomes routine for an older person with problems of mobility, mental change or functional disturbance to be assessed for disease and remedial action taken. Composed of social as well as medical and functional investigations, geriatric assessment can address the complexities that accompany many acute and chronic conditions of old age. It is within this investigative environment that social work finds a natural home and the opportunities for creative and challenging practice.*

From the widowed world traveller in Nova Scotia to the 80-year-old marathon runner in Calgary and the 'Raging Grannies' of the West Coast, the older population in Canada uses imagination, energy and creativity to use retirement and aging as an opportunity to accept new challenges and master new skills. These individuals engage in such activities with a zest and passion for life that was beyond their grasp when saddled with ties to jobs, families and the other trappings of the 'productive years.' There are presently more than three million Canadians over the age of 65 and there is every indication that this number will increase in the ensuing years. Projections by Health and Welfare Canada estimate that by the year 2021, Canadians in the 65-plus age group will make up one-fifth of the total population (1988). Skelton (1986) predicts that the 65 and older age group will enlarge more rapidly than any other segment of the population and those in their ninth decade will increase by more than 200 percent in the next two decades.

Despite the 'joie de vivre' and independence of the majority of aging Canadians, society as a whole tends to hold fast to negative stereotypes of the older population and to equate 'old' with debilitated.' Social workers often join other helping professionals, economists, statisticians and politicians in alarmist reactions over the doom and gloom predictions of the greying of our society. As a result, we tend not to see the old realistically. Part of the problem might be that the word 'old' conjures up images of brittle bones, wrinkled skin, fragile health and forgetfulness, all of which serve to obscure the strengths and abilities of the majority of aging Canadians. Seniors advocacy groups have begun to challenge societal perceptions, and acceptance, of the equation that relates chronological age with infirmity and dependence. These new cohorts of the aging population are beginning to question the ministrations of helping professionals and social scientists and suggest that society must recognize and appreciate the political and economic power of a large segment of this group (see Hooyman and Kiyak, 1988).

Although the trend is reversing, academics continue to obtain considerable professional mileage from the study of the aged as if this group were comprised of some strange new species of being. Recent research on the biological, health and social correlates of aging as described by Cox (1988) indicates that the lives of older persons are not nearly as foreboding or as unhappy as the literature may have led the public to believe. As a society, we need to redefine our perceptions of exactly what the aging of our country is all about. Indeed, McDaniels (1988) points out:

The aging of Canada is not new and alarmism about aging fails to recognize some very important points. Societal aging is the unexpected consequence of successful planned parenthood. The average age of the population has increased because of declining numbers of babies and young children. What is new will be the aging trend in the Twenty-First Century as the baby boom generation swells the ranks of the elderly.

Neugarten (1974) has distinguished the young-old from the old-old and fortunately gerontologists, social scientists, helping professionals and economists have begun to listen and recognize that chronological years alone do not an old person make!

It remains, however, that we cannot make broad assumptions about the elderly as being a completely homogeneous group. Each person's lifetime experiences are widely dissimilar and responses to these experiences results in important variations in personality. Consequently, aging enhances our individuality. It is this uniqueness that adds an attractive and challenging dimension to working with elderly people.

Perhaps another reason for our inability to see the elderly in a more positive and differentiated light is that the media and other interested groups limit their focus on that part of the experience of aging that results in the fiscal responsibility of providing increasingly scarce resources to this segment of the population. The sheer business of living weakens the body. As people begin to age and fail to recover quickly from the insults of illness or injury, they often present for care and treatment in a health care facility. It is this entrance into the service delivery system that requires expenditure of public funds and this financial burden seems to be the issue that causes great distress for policy-makers, economists, politicians and health/social service agency personnel. As a society, we worry about the *raging geriatric tide*, which supposedly threatens to bankrupt the health care system. Hertzman and Hayes (1985) question this fear and suggest that an economic redistribution of health and social resources would help to better prepare the state for the interventions required in the coming years.

Caring professionals often neglect to give credit for the benefits this group has conferred upon society and need to adopt a critical review, not only of some of the negative stereotypes of aging but also of the pessimistic predictions regarding the costs of caring for an elderly population. Negative stereotyping of the elderly must be eliminated and education and experience can serve as effective means to that end. Gaitz (1974) points out the necessity for relieving ourselves of repressive attitudes towards the aged when he states:

> If one mistakenly assumes that psychiatric disorders of the aged are beyond treatment, then neglect of elderly persons with remediable conditions may occur. If one assumes that an elderly person is only waiting for death to relieve him, his family and society of a burden, a practitioner may become the instrument of implementing the unwitting inadequate treatment plans of a society unwilling to invest the time, energy, and money to obtain the best resources available to all citizens.

The Clientele

It has been pointed out that old age is not a monolithic, static condition that guarantees dependency. However, while it is true that the majority of persons over the age of 65 enjoy reasonably good health and independent function, what of the elderly who do suffer a health crisis that is sufficiently complex or severe to compromise both their physical and psycho-social functioning?

One of the great economic and social frailties of the present health care system is a failure to respond in such a way as to provide services tailored to meet the specific needs of the elderly. Rathbone-McCuan and Levenson (1977) have suggested that our society has been ineffective in generating strategies for providing preventive or restorative health care to the elderly. When an older person is thought to be coping poorly, there is a tendency to focus on appropriate facility-based care rather than on creative alternatives and helping strategies. As Watson stated (1984), "too often, the individual is made to fit the system, rather than the system being adapted or modified to meet the needs of the person" (p.659). It is, therefore, essential that before any action is taken, every frail elderly person has a proper assessment and review of potential alternate resources and ways of coping.

I. Assessment

This assessment process is described by Rubenstein et al. (1982) as one which "can lead to the discovery of new important and treatable problems, simplification of overly complex drug regimes, arrangements for needed rehabilitation and development or remediation of a supportive physical and social living environment to enhance patient functioning" (p.519).The goal of any assessment procedure is to maximize the abilities and minimize the dysfunction that might result from an insult to an elderly person's vitality.

Therefore, when health crises strike, it is important that the elderly person has available to her or him a continuum of care, which includes programmes designed to treat the treatable, reverse the reversible and maintain a state of physical, functional and psycho-social well-being. Novak (1988) suggests this continuum should range from programmes that have maximal institutional support such as hospitals and long-term care facilities to those with little such support as exemplified by adult day programmes, senior's centres, etc.

This goal of maintaining, enhancing and restoring both the physical and psycho-social vitality of the elderly receives little real criticism from any sector. The challenge, however, involves the actual development of creative and broad-based care delivery systems that can provide the care continuum required. An inherent difficulty in this task is described by Skelton (1986) when he cautions that:

> The present strain the elderly impose on the health and welfare services will not be relieved simply by the provision of more beds. Too frequently the problem is addressed by hasty and thoughtless provision of larger and more expensive long-term care institutions, or by suggestions that favour rationing health and welfare services to the elderly. Better basic planning and the development of integrated and comprehensive geriatric services offer the only viable long-term solutions. (p.21)

II. Geriatric Assessment Units

One of the components of this integrated and comprehensive geriatric service delivery system involves formal geriatric assessment programmes, and, before one can successfully examine the clientele, it is necessary to describe the parameters of these particular practice settings.

Geriatrics is that branch of gerontology that studies pathology, treatment and prevention of disease amongst the elderly. Specialized geriatric assessment units (GAUs) have been established in major urban centres across Canada, patterning trends established in the UK, the USA and Europe. These programmes have developed in response to the growing recognition of the many unmet needs of the frail elderly and are motivated by the conviction that GAUs can have major beneficial impacts on the health and well-being of elderly patients. GAU programmes trace their origins to Great Britain and were pioneered by the work of several people including Dr. Marjory Warren and Sir Ferguson Anderson. Geared to specific local needs and available resources, these programmes vary in many of their structural and functional components including; how the programme is financed, institutional affiliation, which types of patients are accepted, staffing composition, etc.

Rubenstein (1987) defined geriatric assessment as a "multi-dimensional and interdisciplinary diagnostic process designed to quantify an elderly individual's medical, psychosocial, and functional capabilities and problems with the intention of arriving at a comprehensive plan for intervention and follow-up"(p.109). Kane reviews the growing body of literature that outlines the different types and purposes of GAU programmes and also describes the positive health care outcomes of GAU intervention (1987). Wooldridge et al., (1987) point out the need for more cautious and inclusive programme evaluations when measuring programme effectiveness arguing that,

> Successful treatment of severe cardiac congestive failure in an 85-year-old woman which leads to successful discharge home may lead to frustration for all if the presence or absence of family or other caregiving support, the possibility of drug compliance, or the suitability of the patient's housing are not taken into account. (p.121)

This example demonstrates the social parameters that must be taken into account when dealing with the frail elderly and lends credibility to the increasing involvement of social workers in GAU programmes.

Elderly patients typically present with complex and interrelated medical and psycho-social problems that often do not fit into a limited biomedical model of care. The focus, therefore, needs to be expanded beyond the description of the impact of physical disease to encompass the effect of functional, psycho-social and financial problems on the health and happiness of elderly persons and their subsequent ability to remain independent. The interrelationship between the biological and behaviourial aspects of human existence, important for all ages, is no less important for the elderly. Medalie (1986) expanded the traditional approach of assessing the elderly, which generally focuses on the biological changes of the aging process, to include a review of the multiple, interrelating factors associated with the patient, her or his intimate associates, cultural sub-groups and society.

Rubenstein et al. (1982) identify the three major services of geriatric assessment units as assessment, interventions and/or placement of the frail elderly patient. Studies reported by Flathman and Larsen (1976) have noted that patients involved in such programmes improved their physical, mental and social well-being. It is well known that elderly patients have more varied problems and health care needs than younger patients, although Barer et al. (1986) suggest that the reason for the increased utilization of health care resources by the elderly has less to do with the intensity or frequency of disease and more to do with the way the health care system responds. Schumann (1984) also identified the challenge of designing new interventions to meet these needs.

In order to address the multiple problems of the frail elderly, most geriatric assessment units are designed to provide intensive, comprehensive assessment and therapeutic planning by an array of health care professionals. This expanded system of care reflects a broader concept of health and illness than is included in the strictly biomedical model. Central to GAU programme philosophy is the belief that careful assessment of frail elderly patients can often reveal remediable conditions and help to better match services with needs. The GAU social worker, therefore, finds it possible to follow the principal social work objective described by Rosenfeld (1983), "the aim of social work is to match resources with needs and increase the *'goodness of fit'* between them by harnessing potential provider systems to perform this function" (p.189). It is within the GAU environment, then, that social work can find a natural home as this setting offers the opportunity to participate in a system of care that is congruent with the commitment of the profession to person-in-environment interactions. The subsequent intervention strategies (possible in a social model of health care delivery) involve efforts to keep people in their own homes when appropriate.

Since no single professional group is capable of meeting all of the elderly patient's needs, teamwork is essential. Interdisciplinary GAU teams typically consist of geriatricians, other medical consultants, nurses, social workers, occupational therapists, physiotherapists, speech therapists, dietitians and psychologists. Each team member is responsible for patient assessments in her or his field of expertise. Usually the entire team monitors patient progress and continually plans and re-evaluates therapeutic goals for individual patients. Social work is comfortable with Brill's (1976) definition of the team approach to patient care, which suggests that:

> There needs to be a mix of professions each of whom possess particular expertise; each of whom is responsible for making individual decisions; who together hold a common purpose; who meet formally and informally to communicate, to collaborate, and to consolidate knowledge from which plans are made, actions determined and future decisions influenced. (p.42)

Practice Roles and Responsibilities

As Westberg (1986) points out, shifts in the age of a client group do not require the abandonment of all generic or specialized social work skills but do require that those skills be tailored to a new client group whose needs and resources may have special features. This is most certainly the case for the social worker employed in a GAU. For example, it is essential that the social worker acquire a familiarity with medical terminology enabling her or him to understand the common physical ailments and medical interventions performed with this population.

While it is true that social work alone cannot begin to harness all the resources needed by the frail elderly GAU patient, it remains that the principle feature of social work practice in this setting requires the worker to meet the objectives of social work practice outlined by other authors. The required 'tailoring of skills' can be demonstrated by taking the liberty of inserting the appropriate adjectives into Hepworth and Larsen's (1986) stated *Objectives for Social Work Practice*. This process helps to lend additional relevance to this practice setting allowing one to re-write that GAU social workers:

1. Help (frail elderly people) enlarge their competence and increase their problem solving and coping abilities;
2. Help the (elderly patient) obtain resources;
3. Make health care and other social service organizations responsive to (frail elderly people);
4. Facilitate interactions between (older individuals) and others in their environments;
5. Influence interactions between organizations and institutions that serve (elderly people); and,
6. Influence social and environmental policy to respond to the health and social needs of the (older person).

Social work practice in GAUs can be described by using the concepts of primary, secondary and tertiary intervention as outlined by Beaver and Miller (1985). A discussion of the application of these concepts to GAU social work practice follows.

I. Intervention

Primary intervention suggests that it is best to try and identify problems before full manifestation occurs and to design strategies to either eliminate or minimize the potential harmful effects. Primary intervention, therefore, leads the GAU social worker into a role of both consultant-educator and advocate. As such, energy is focused on a review of the conditions necessary for healthy and satisfactory lifestyles of all citizens including the elderly person. The social worker is also responsible for identifying harmful influences and scarcity of resources in the physical and social environment, which may have deleterious effects on the clientele served.

This practice role is easily adhered to in GAU settings as the social worker strives to provide early education of patients/families about the resources available to enhance coping. In the combined consultant-educator role, the GAU social worker is called upon to interpret agency/hospital rules and regulations and to teach or transmit information about a host of services to patients, families and other caregivers.

The social worker in a GAU must also act as consultant/collaborator with other health care professionals, both within and without the GAU, to design effective care plans for individual patients and thereby ensure quality service to the clientele. Virtually all types of GAU programmes have some interrelationship with community services. As Williams (1987) points out, "it is obvious that, if the geriatric assessment is to contribute to the further care of the patient, its results and recommendations must reach the appropriate community services" (p.68). Maintaining this community communication network is often the responsibility of the GAU social worker.

GAU social workers in the advocate role are usually 'client-focussed.' Not only does the advocacy role of social work direct the worker to help patients cut through bureaucratic red tape and other systems related problems, but it has expanded to encompass a conscious movement on the part of the worker to address inequities in social and health policy decisions, which adversely impact upon clients. For GAU social workers then, advocacy is an inherent feature of practice as efforts are made to challenge, among other things, ageist discrimination, limited or rationed health and social services and the assumption that to be old is to be sick and that sickness is to be expected and beyond treatment.

The main emphasis in secondary intervention is on early diagnosis and treatment and it is at this level that the bulk of direct practice responsibilities are found. The GAU practice setting offers opportunity to participate in strategies that are designed to improve and enhance the older person's well-being. In order to bring about a resolution of the patient's problems, or to prevent exacerbation of same, intervention is offered in the form of standard clinical casework. The goal of such intervention includes patient recovery and restoration of the previous level of social functioning. This involves the social worker and patient in problem assessment and problem-solving exercises, all of which are designed to enhance coping abilities.

As social workers assess the presenting problems of geriatric patients, it is helpful to reflect on a modified version of the psycho-social systems perspective as outlined by Beaver and Miller (1985).

This approach offers a set of generic guidelines for the following: engaging the client; conducting the assessment; formulating the intervention plan; and finally, evaluating outcomes. These concepts can be easily transcribed to GAU social work practice and offer a broad overview of the total physical-psychological-social functioning of the patient. Another assessment tool that the reader may find helpful and which can be readily adapted to GAU social work practice is the 4 Rs of medical-social diagnosis as described by Doremus (1976).

Yet another way to assess areas of the patient's life that may have been affected by current difficulties involves a review of several key 'arenas' or 'spheres of influence' which describe aspects of healthy, productive human functioning. These have been described by Gilmore (1973) as vitality, community, identity, accountability, activity and frivolity. An adaptation of these ideas provides a conceptual framework for understanding the depth and breadth required for a complete gerontological social work assessment. It is reasonable, for instance, to suggest that any depletion of the patient's vitality will have an impact upon how capable she or he is of continuing her or his level of involvement in her or his social world or community. As well, a limitation in the activity of the patient may change that for which the individual patient is accountable, i.e. that which gives her or him identity and a sense of frivolity, (defined as accomplishment/ purpose in life). This situation may hasten feelings of loss of self-worth, self-doubt and depression. The following case example illustrates the interconnectedness of the spheres of influence concepts.

> Mrs. B was referred to the GAU for consultation after a recent mild CVA and subsequent problems with erratic blood pressure. The GP and visiting Home Care nurse were concerned about Mrs. B's apparent total disregard for her medication regime/diet. She was described by the family physician as mentally intact but depressed. While talking with Mrs. B during the home visit, the social worker discovered that her husband had died just one month previous. Her only child, a daughter in Toronto, had made a quick trip to Victoria after her father's death and found her mother "incapacitated with grief." The daughter made all the arrangements for her father's funeral, saw to the details of the estate and, just before

returning to Toronto, convinced Mrs. B to put the large home she and Mr. B built 15 years ago up for sale. Arrangements were also made by the daughter for Mrs. B to visit a new senior's condominium complex and put a deposit on the purchase of a suite. She also contacted the lawyer to draw up power of attorney forms for her mother to execute in her daughter's favour. Mrs. B mentioned to the daughter just after the funeral that she was feeling apprehensive about learning to manage the family finances as that was "always your father's responsibility." With that information, the daughter contacted an accountant and made arrangements for all cheques and other finances to be managed by his firm with consultation from Mrs. B.

The tragedy in this case study involves the well-intentioned but misdirected effort of a concerned daughter to make major decisions on mother's behalf and, 'in her best interests,' which had serious negative impacts on her mother's feelings of self-worth, control and competence. By making the assumption that mother was either not capable of or interested in learning how to manage money and other business dealings, the daughter did her mother a great disservice.

By applying the spheres of influence concepts, the social worker recognized that Mrs. B had a recent insult to her physical vitality, (mild stroke with complications), which compromised her ability to cope with some of the social problems of a recently bereaved widow. The resources in the environmental system, i.e. the daughter, failed to recognize the importance for Mrs. B of maintaining a sense of identity, accountability, community, activity and frivolity. Time, and a system of instruction and support, were required to help her learn or re-learn to perform the activities that enabled her to continue to function in the mainstream of life, meeting the usual opportunities for success or failure present for all.

Fortunately, Mrs. B recovered well from her bereavement and stroke episode and, through counselling by the social worker and other members of the GAU team, recognized that many of the arrangements made by her daughter were unnecessary. A team meeting with the daughter on her next visit West helped to clarify and allay some of her very real fears ('mother is all alone and I'm so far away') and when she was able to understand that her mother was in fact capable of continuing to make decisions and call for help from various sectors when required, the situation for both mother and daughter was much more relaxed.

Social workers must expand their perception of the nature of the patient's clinical condition to include a view of the person as being in transaction with their environment. It is this ability to bring an ecological perspective to GAU settings that provides social work with an important and distinct role in these particular practice settings.

II. A GAU Example

It was the author's experience and good fortune to be employed as a social worker in a geriatric assessment unit in Victoria B.C. This GAU operates adjacent to both an acute care hospital and a long-term care facility. Funding for the unit is from the continuing care branch of the Ministry of Health. Wooldridge et al. (1987) list the main purposes of the programme as: 1) to diagnose and treat those elderly who were failing at home for uncertain cause; 2) to diagnose and treat those elderly at home or in long-term care facilities who manifested behaviourial problems, based on the well-recognized premise that much disturbed behaviour has a basis in physical disease; and later, 3) to admit from the acute hospital, including the emergency department, those elderly presenting with multiple diagnoses who had been admitted for an acute illness. This latter group of patients was accepted in recognition of the fact that elderly patients frequently remain in hospital longer than is optimal and develop conditions that make their discharge difficult.

Most referrals are telephoned into the unit medical director and an initial screening process occurs to determine which particular area of the GAU service would best meet the needs of the patient in question. This GAU offers service to patients in three main areas — a 50-space geriatric day hospital, a 28-bed inpatient unit and an outpatient/domiciliary visit service. Social work service is available to patients in all three service areas via a blanket referral system. It is important to note that this particular GAU functions as a 'whole' with interrelated components. This structure was developed with the conviction that only with a broad range of flexible services, available at the moment of referral, can the patient be helped to reach his or her best level rapidly and cost effectively. Patients are often admitted to one particular branch of the programme and later transferred for treatment to other branches as their care needs change.

In this particular programme, the medical director conducts a preliminary review of the patient's condition to assess the acuity/urgency of the referral. On occasion, requests are made by the referring agent to admit patients to the inpatient unit when it is clear that their needs are chronic in nature and would best be met by either expanded home supports or admission to some form of long-term care facility. Continued vigilance has to be maintained to ensure that only those patients with some remedial condition are admitted to the inpatient unit. An active community education programme by the GAU staff aids in the clarification of objectives and purposes of the GAU for physicians and other community caregivers, i.e, the assessment and treatment of episodes of recent and reversible illness.

MacKenzie (1982) confirms that all provinces and territories in Canada now have some type of home care nursing and community support service. British Columbia began a comprehensive long-term care programme in 1978, which has expanded to coordinate both home help/nursing service and the waiting list for all government funded long-term care facilities in the province. Before any individual can be placed in a government funded LTC facility, she or he must have her or his physical and psycho-social care needs reviewed by a staff member from the local LTC office. Needless to say, many patients referred to the GAU require either a complete re-direction to the local LTC office for service and direction or a consultation by the GAU social work staff and LTC about the types of community or facility supports that can be offered to the patient while she or he is rehabilitated or treated through the efforts of the GAU programme. This liaison work between the GAU and the local long-term care office is a principle and vital role of the GAU social worker.

Although there may be variations in the practice styles, modalities and procedures to be found in GAU social work departments, most casework intervention in these settings begins with a review of what is known about a patient. Since most GAUs operate on a referral basis, information is provided to the unit by the attending physician or other referring agent. Equipped with this knowledge, members of the GAU team are invited by the unit director to become involved with the process of helping the patient regain, or compensate for, what was lost.

Considerable emphasis is placed on maintaining the elderly person in her or his home environment. To this end, the majority of the patients seen in this GAU service become patients in the day hospital branch of this GAU service. As reported by Wooldridge et al. (1987), the majority of patients referred to this programme (> 95 percent) are usually seen at home by the social worker. The remainder comprise a patient group whose physical needs are sufficiently acute to require an urgent house call by the geriatrician, usually followed by a direct admission of the patient to the geriatric inpatient ward or transfer to the acute care hospital.

III. Social Work Assessment

For the majority of the patients referred, the social work assessment process begins with the practitioner visiting the patient in her or his own environment. This makes it possible to truly begin where the client is at. A relationship is established with the patient on the patient's home turf and is facilitated by the social work practitioner demonstrating an interest and desire to understand the nature of the patient's present difficulties, as well as her or his interests, goals and strengths. All of this is done in the reflective light of the patients personal, family and community support systems.

IV. Home Visits

Mary Richmond (1917) summed up this aspect of practice well when she observed that we make home visits not to, "find our clients out but rather to find out how to help them better" (p.24). Home visits afford the opportunity for the GAU social worker to perform three very important but often overlooked duties. The first involves preparing patients for GAU intervention by outlining the nature and the types of services offered. It is sad fact that many elderly patients are referred for various health treatments/interventions but are seldom prepared for the rigours of these encounters. Not surprisingly, these processes are met with anxiety and reluctance by many individuals. Just as is the case for the younger patient, an elderly patient also needs to know what the helping process will contain, what will be required of her or him, and receive answers to more practical questions such as cost, transportation, etc. Provision of clear and concise information about the complexities of the process will assist in reducing anxiety and potential feelings of powerlessness.

A second essential duty of the social worker conducting the home visit is the review of the patient's presenting problem. Although the social worker has had some idea of the reasons for the GAU referral, often this information has come via the attending GP and/or family and other caregivers. Although this information is valuable, it requires supplementation by the patient. There are instances, of course, where the very nature of the patient's difficulties may preclude her or him from having the ability to communicate their problems accurately i.e., speech difficulty cognitive, failure or denial/resistance, but it remains that engaging the patient in a discourse about her or his perceptions of the problem(s), thereby coming to an understanding of what the problems *mean* to the patient, is an essential element of good social work practice!

The third duty involves an analysis of the personal and environmental resources available to the patient. The availability of intrapersonal, interpersonal and environmental resources is a significant part of any social work assessment. It is important to try and obtain a perception of what the personal coping strategies of each individual patient are, including a review of personal strengths such as the motivation for getting well.

The role that formal and informal caregivers play in the ability of the older patient to mobilize the appropriate resources to regain their independence is also extremely important and must be included in the social work assessment. Considerable literature is available outlining some of the special roles and characteristics of formal and informal caregivers of elderly patients (see Chappell et al., 1986; Snider, 1981; Fengler and Goodrich, 1979).

V. Assessment Stages

In the beginning stages of geriatric assessment, the social worker may find it helpful to reflect on the eclectic theoretical orientation of crisis intervention as described by Golan (1986). Patients who are seen for geriatric assessment are usually responding to the impact of internal stressors such as injury or illness and/or the external stressors of recent intra- or inter-personal losses. This can create disruptions in the person's equilibrium or homeostatic balance and often thrusts the patient into a state of crisis. The significance of these events for social work practice is that when problems occur and the physical and psycho-social resources of this clientele cannot return them to a state of equilibrium, functioning may become more impaired. Such setbacks result in the elderly person developing feelings of loss of control or purpose, which may lead to depression, increased dependency, lack of motivation for getting better and followed perhaps by the need for institutional care.

After the home visit, the social work case notes are shared with the medical director and other members of the interdisciplinary team as all prepare to admit the patient to the programme. Thus, the information collected by the social worker during this pre-admission home visit provides a solid baseline from which to begin to plan therapeutic interventions with the individual patient. An example of GAU social work intervention is outlined in the case study presentation at the end of the chapter.

Upon admission of a patient, the social worker continues to maintain contact with both the patient and her or his caregiving constellation by providing the social casework services identified earlier i.e., patient and/or family counselling, liaison and referral to community resources, participation in case conferences with other members of the GAU team, etc.

Interventions at the tertiary level stress prevention or delaying the possible consequences of illness or other dysfunctional processes, which may already be occurring. Aging is often accompanied by decline and threats to vitality have consequences that impact negatively on all aspects of an elderly person's personal and social world. The preventive efforts of the GAU team encourage early diagnosis and, hopefully, treatment that will remedy some of the acute problems and chronic conditions of age. This can lead to renewed interests, new hope and a re-vitalized lifestyle for the elderly patient. Typical preventive intervention strategies offered to patient's in GAUs are expanded beyond the treatment of the presenting problem to include suggestions for improved diet, home renovations leading to increased safety, access to expanded home or community supports such as adult day care and medical alert systems, programmes to improve medication compliance, individual and family counselling, etc.

The very essence of a discussion about prevention needs to go beyond superficial strategies however. For preventive or restorative efforts to be successful, it is necessary to know the root cause of certain functional or social problems. This requires a diligent examination of many factors. As Hepworth and Larsen (1986) point out, "direct social workers should not limit themselves to remedial activities but should also seek to discover environmental and other causes of problems and sponsor or support efforts aimed at enhancing the environments of people" (p.89). For example, the difficulty of getting patients and their families to admit that they have some unresolved interpersonal problems, and then believe that these can be resolved with professional guidance and support, presents an interesting, exhilarating, but occasionally frustrating challenge for social work practitioners and other team members. As well, depression is too frequent a diagnosis in the elderly and requires careful assessment and creative treatment approaches. The availability of psychological and geriatric psychiatry services to patients of GAUs is extremely important but often not available, although research findings document that elderly couples and family units frequently need and can benefit from individual, marital, sex and family therapy (see Sander, 1976; Toseland, 1977; Butler, 1975). Social work needs to advocate for the expansion of these and other services and make continued efforts to influence social policy decisions, which affect this group.

Potential for Role Development

As the provision of health care moves into the community and away from the constraints of institutional medical care, the role of the social worker may become less tied to institutional demands, thereby freeing the profession to respond to the broad range of social factors that shape the health of individuals, family and communities. Social work must be prepared to assume this responsibility as both direct practitioners and as health and social service policy planners/ analysts.

At the same time, however, caution must be used not to embrace the concept of community care so tightly as to restrict access to diagnostic and treatment services, which will continue to be offered in institutional settings. Rather than designing the service delivery system based on concerns over cost or programme ideology and then trying to fit the target population into the system, social work, and other service providers, need to ensure that all health agencies continue to identify and respond to the needs of the population to be served. Opportunities for creative and rewarding social work involvement with the frail elderly population should exist in every component of the health care continuum; from the acute care hospital to early rehabilitation and convalescent care centres such as geriatric inpatient units, to ambulatory care programmes such as geriatric day hospitals, to community support programmes i.e., adult day cares, home help agencies, senior's centres etc. and to long-term care facilities. These practice opportunities have become more available within the last decade and will grow as the country continues to respond creatively to the challenge of caring for our aging citizens. Social workers need to educate themselves to the particular needs of the frail elderly and focus on ways to empower this population to use its strengths and resources in mastering the difficulties associated with illness and disability.

The ideal service delivery system of the future will acknowledge that the accumulated impairments and chronic conditions of the older patient should be seen comprehensively and attention must be given to the structure or flavour of the helping agency or institution. Hospitals take great pride in becoming centres of excellence for neonatology, pediatrics, cardiology, etc. Social workers should encourage hospitals and health care centres to recognize the need to elevate the care of the elderly person to the level where we can also identify this population as deserving care from such centres of excellence, which would guarantee a programme of care offered to every elderly patient rather than labelling this entire population of health care consumers as 'bed blockers'!

As the health care system becomes more responsive to the needs of the elderly patient a focus on more comprehensive models of health care will help to redefine and refocus energies and resources away from institutional, disease-related concepts of health and illness to more community-based services, which stress the social and health promotion models of health care service. Social work has much to contribute to this movement and can be on the leading edge of programme and policy initiatives, which will help to make health care organizations more responsive to the people. All health care professionals should be delighted with the statement made by the Canadian federal minister of Health, Perrin Beatty (1989), when he suggested that strategies need to be developed which "promote the independence and quality of life for senior's as this is what they are entitled to as citizens." Representatives of government need to be reminded of the promises in this statement and since such strategies do not come cheaply, nor from mere rhetoric, be persuaded to support new and creative strategies for caring for society as we all age, releasing the resources needed to enhance the existing programmes of care.

The relatively recent development of geriatric assessment programmes in this country makes it difficult to cite examples of research about the efficacy and health/social benefits to patients reviewed. Follow-up studies would provide much information relevant to social work practice with this population and would also provide support and direction to those individuals currently involved with the design and operation of GAUs. Obviously, a tremendous practice opportunity exists for social work research and publication in this 'new' field.

Concluding Remarks

As life is a progression of events that requires individuals to make transitions, there is no better way to perceive old age than to think about continuing change. GAU social workers, as 'agents of change,' find the frail elderly struggling to adapt rapidly to change with diminished personal and environmental resources. The recognition of multiple disabilities, particularly psycho-social disability, is of particular interest to social work in this practice setting. The social work practitioner in these programmes has much to offer as efforts are made to understand the interrelationship of all factors that lead to dysfunctional change and then to design interventions to return the elderly patient to good health and as much independent function as is possible or desired.

Since reversible health problems and individual problems in social functioning may incorrectly be attributed to the infirmities of age, continued efforts must be made by social workers to ensure that stereotypical perceptions of elderly persons do not distort assessments, limit goals, nor restrict interventions. Unless such efforts are made, the elderly of today, and we as the elders of tomorrow, will have to endure the final years of life with services that are designed to provide less than adequate support and opportunities to compensate for human frailties.

Case Example

Pre-admission visit — Mr. Joe Bloggs
Mr. Bloggs is an 83-year-old gentleman who was visited today in his home on Main Street where he lives with his well and active 81-year-old wife. He has been referred to the GAU by his attending physician at the urging of his son, George. George lives in Calgary but manages to visit his parents every three to four months. On a visit last weekend, he was alarmed to note a rapid deterioration in his father's physical and mental functioning. He is concerned that his mother is becoming exhausted with caring for Mr. Bloggs and 'wants something done.'

Mental Function and Mood
Mr. Bloggs appeared listless and depressed during the home visit. Efforts to engage him in conversation were difficult and most questions were answered by his wife before he had opportunity to respond. A gentle direction was given to Mrs. Bloggs to allow Mr. Bloggs to respond in order to allow an assessment of how well he was processing information. On further questioning, Mr. Bloggs appeared oriented to person and place but disoriented to time, but his poor response may be related more to his feelings of poor physical health than a dementing process.

Ambulation
Mrs. Bloggs reports that her husband has been having difficulty walking lately and has had many falls. He gets up often at night to use the bathroom and frequently stumbles en route. His most recent

fall was four days ago when he suffered a severe 'bump' on the head from the edge of the bathtub. She feels his condition has become worse since then.

Medical Background
    Appendectomy — 1923
    Prostatectomy — 1987
    Hiatal Hernia
    Borderline Diabetes
    Hypertension
    Recent Falls

Medications
    Tagamet 300 mg. tid
    Dalmane 30 mg. @ hs
    Diabeta 0.5 mg. OD
    Moduret 25 mg. bid

Social History
Mr. Bloggs is a retired accountant who moved to Victoria from Calgary with his wife 11 years ago. He is described by his family as a shy and quiet gentleman who kept to himself and had few interests outside the home, save his woodworking hobby. Even though Mr. Bloggs has a fully equipped workshop in the basement of their home, it seems he lost interest in this pastime some six to seven months ago. He takes great pride in his business competence but had his ego sorely bruised last spring when he made a number of errors in preparing the tax returns of several friends from their bridge club. Mrs. Bloggs reports that he has appeared depressed and withdrawn since that time and rarely responds positively to social invitations with the individuals he feels he wronged.

Patient/Family Perception of the Presenting Problem
Mrs. Bloggs appears to be very perplexed by her husband's behaviour and confided that she really does believe that he has the beginnings of senility. She states that she is desperate for some assistance or will have to make arrangements to place her husband in a long-term care facility.

Social Work Impression and Plan
It appears this gentleman was having some problems with depression

over that past several months but was otherwise functioning relatively well. His behaviour has changed significantly in the past week. His wife is his primary caregiver and is quickly becoming exhausted. The nature of the geriatric assessment programme was explained to both Mr. and Mrs. Bloggs and after some gentle persuasion and coaxing by his wife, Mr. Bloggs agreed and arrangements were made for him to be seen in the geriatric day hospital in two days' time.

Social Work Case Notes — Mr. Joe Bloggs

Mr. Bloggs was seen in the geriatric day hospital in December, 1988. The geriatrician noted a number of neurological deficits during his physical examination and arranged for an immediate CT scan after learning of Mr. Bloggs recent fall and head injury. The CT scan showed a subdural hemotoma. Mr. Bloggs was admitted to the geriatric inpatient unit for further observation and transferred the next day to the acute care hospital for surgery to release the intracranial pressure from the hemotoma. He returned to the geriatric inpatient unit after a six-day stay on the acute care ward for further investigation of some other physical problems (borderline diabetes, urinary tract infection) and where his medication regime was restructured (including an anti-depressant) and a physiotherapy programme begun to restrengthen him. Both Mr. and Mrs. Bloggs were seen by the nutritionist for counselling for his diabetic condition.The social worker arranged to have the local long-term care office send homemaker help once per week to help Mrs. Bloggs with the heavy cleaning. Both Mr. and Mrs. Bloggs rejected the idea of any home help coming to assist in the personal care needs of Mr. Bloggs such as assistance with bathing.The occupational therapist arranged to visit the Bloggs at home to install railings around the bathtub and a raised toilet seat. Mr. Bloggs responded well to the music programme while on the inpatient ward and was encouraged by the OT to return to his long neglected hobby of restoring musical instruments. The staff reported at case conference that he was thinking more clearly although his mood remained somewhat depressed. Mr. Bloggs remained on the inpatient ward for three weeks and was then discharged home to the care of his wife with the understanding that he would continue his rehabilitation by attending the geriatric day hospital programme of the GAU three days each week. His attendance at the GDH programme was somewhat sporadic as he often would find excuses not to be ready when the GDH bus came to call for him.

The social worker made subsequent house calls to follow up on the concerns of the geriatrician and other members of the team that Mr. Bloggs continued to be depressed and unmotivated.

With some reluctance Mr. Bloggs began to discuss his feelings of apprehension, despair and uselessness. He stated that he felt ridiculous having to depend on his wife for assistance with his personal care as he had been rarely ill and needy of this type of care before. He was very fearful that he might become ill again and that caring for him would be too much for his wife. A subsequent exploration of the sense of failure he experienced when making errors on the tax forms for his friends was structured around helping him to modify his negative self-thoughts and subsequent sense of embarrassment and frustration. Further sessions with both the social worker and the visiting psychiatrist allowed Mr. Bloggs to ventilate some of these feelings and come to some resolution over disappointments he had experienced both in the past and recently. Mr. Bloggs also responded well in group settings with the social worker and other patients of the GAU. He admitted coming to the realization that many other older people like himself struggled with similar feelings of depression over the dependency sometimes associated with ill health. Mrs. Bloggs was seen both separately and conjointly with her husband as the team attempted to help her understand her husband's care needs as well as recognize her need for support in dealing with the situation. Mrs. Bloggs was initially very resistive of the idea of accepting home help as she was very proud of her own homemaking abilities. After some discussion with Mr. Bloggs, the son and the GAU team, Mrs. Bloggs recognized that relinquishing some of the more mundane and exhausting household duties would free her time and energies to allow more opportunities for Mr. and Mrs. Bloggs to become re-involved in a social world they had neglected for some time. The Bloggs were referred to a local senior's activity centre and encouraged to participate in the organization as one way of re-developing a sense of activity, community and frivolity. Mr. Bloggs was encouraged to redefine his sense of identity, which to this point had always told him that he 'must be in control at all times.' Mrs. Bloggs and the son, George, had a tendency to mistakenly assume that Mr. Bloggs would not recover from his recent illness and were about to make arrangements with the bank and the accountant to take over their financial affairs. Fortunately, staff were able to convince Mrs. Bloggs and the son that this potential insult to Mr. Bloggs's sense of accountability and identity was not necessary as his vitality returned.

Mr. Bloggs was discharged from the geriatric day hospital programme of the GAU after an eight-week stay.

Discharge Note — Six Month Follow-up
The Bloggs were contacted by the social worker for follow-up information. Mr. Bloggs recovered well from his numerous physical problems although he continues to struggle with feelings of depression. He is seen monthly by his family physician for re-evaluation of his anti-depressant medication. Mrs. Bloggs reports that they have taken a number of short day trips with a group from the senior's centre and hope to participate in a six-day tour of the Southern United States next month. Mrs. Bloggs cancelled the homemaker help as she found she had plenty of free time since Mr. Bloggs had returned to his woodworking hobby.

Endnote

[1]   The original version of this chapter was published in *Social Work Practice in Health Care Settings*, M. Holosko and P. Taylor (eds.). Canadian Scholars' Press Inc., 1989, pp. 353-381.

References

Barer, M. L., Evans, R. B., Hertman, C. and Lomas, J. (1986). Toward efficient aging: Rhetoric and evidence. Paper presented at the Third Canadian Conference on Health Economics, Winnipeg, Manitoba.

Beatty, P. (1989). Notes from an address to the Canadian Club. Ottawa, Ontario.

Beaver, M. L. and Miller, D. (1985). *Clinical social work practice with the elderly.* Illinois: The Dorsey Press.

Brill, N. I. (1976). *Team work: Working together in the human services.* Philadelphia, PA: W.B. Saunders Co.

Butler, R. (1975). *Why survive? Being old in America.* New York: Harper and Row.

Calkins, E., Davis, P. and Ford, A. (1986). *The practice of geriatrics.* Philadelphia, PA: W.B. Saunders Co.

Chappell, N. L., Strain, L. and Blandford, A. (1986). *Aging and health care.* Toronto, ON: Holt Rhinehart and Winston of Canada Ltd.

Cox, H. G. (1988). *Later life — The realities of aging* (2nd edition). Englewood Cliffs, NJ: Prentice Hall.

Doremus, B. (1976). The four R's of medical social diagnosis. *Health and Social Work,* 1(4).

Fengler A. P. and Goodrich, N. (1979). Wives of elderly disabled men: The hidden patients. *Gerontologist,* 19, pp.175-183.

Flathman, D. P. and Larsen, D. E. (1976). An evaluation of three geriatric day hospitals in Alberta. Calgary, Alberta. Unpublished report, Division of Community Health Services, Faculty of Medicine, University of Calgary.

Gaitz, C. M. (1974). Barriers to the delivery of psychiatric services to the elderly. *Gerontologist,* 14, pp. 210-214.

Germain, C. B. (1973). An ecological perspective in casework practice. *Social Casework,* 54, pp.323-330.

Gilmore, S. K. (1973). *Counsellor-in-training.* Englewood Cliffs, NJ: Prentice Hall.

Golan, N. (1986). Crisis theory. In F. J. Turner (ed.), *Social work treatment: Interlocking theoretical approaches* (3rd edition). New York: The Free Press.

Health and Welfare Canada. (1988). Health Promotion Directorate, Health Service and Promotion Branch, 27(2).

Hertzman, C. and Hayes, M. (1985). Will the elderly really bankrupt us with increased health care costs? *Canadian Journal of Public Health,* 76, pp. 373-377.

Hepworth, D. H., and Larsen, J. A. (1986). *Direct social work practice: Theory and skills* (2nd edition). Chicago, IL: The Dorsey Press.

Hooyman, N. R. and Kiyak, A. (1988). The importance of social supports: Family, friends and neighbours. In *Social gerontology — A multi-disciplinary perspective.* Needham Heights, MA: Allyn and Bacon.

Kane, R. (1987). Contrasting models: Reflections on the pattern of geriatric evaluation unit care. In L. Z. Rubenstein, L. J. Campbell, and R. L. Kane (eds.), *Clinics in geriatric medicine.* Philadelphia, PA: W.B. Saunders Co.

MacKenzie, J. A. (1982). Aging in Canadian society. *Issues in Canadian social policy: A reader, II,* Canadian Council on Social Development.

McDaniels, S. A. (1988). Prospects for an aging Canada: Gloom or hope? *Transition,* pp.9-11.

Medalie, J. H. (1986). An approach to common problems in the elderly. In E. Calkins and A. Ford (eds.), *The practice of geriatrics.* Philadelphia, PA.: W.B. Saunders Co.

Neugarten, B. (1974). Age groups in American society and the rise of the young-old. In *Political consequences of aging*. The Annals of the American Academy of Political and Social Science, 415 pp.187-198.

Novak, M. (1988). *Aging and society*. Scarborough, ON: Nelson Canada.

Rathbone-McCuan, E. and Levenson, J. (1977). Geriatric day care: A community approach to geriatric health care. *Journal of Gerontological Nursing*, 3(4), pp.43-46.

Richmond, M. (1917). *Social diagnosis*. New York: The Russel Sage Foundation.

Rosenfeld, J. (1983). The domain and expertise of social work: A conceptualization. *Social Work*, 28, pp.186-191.

Rubenstein, L. Z., Abrass, I. and Kane, R. L. (1981). Improved care for patients on a new geriatric evaluation unit. *Journal of the American Geriatrics Society*, 29, pp.531- 536.

Rubenstein, L. Z., Rhee, L. and Kane, R. L. (1982). The role of geriatric assessment units in caring for the elderly: An analytic review. *Journal of Gerontology*, 37, pp.513- 521.

Rubenstein, L. Z. (1987). Geriatric assessment: An overview of its impacts. In L. Z. Rubenstein, L. J. Campbell, and R. L. Kane (eds.), *Clinics in geriatric medicine*. Philadelphia, PA: W.B. Saunders Co.

Sander, F. (1976). Aspects of sexual counselling with the aged. *Social Casework*, 58, pp.504-510.

Skelton, D. (1986). The future of geriatric medicine in Canada. *Gerontion: A Canadian Review of Geriatric Care*, 1, pp. 19-23.

Schumann, J. Z. (1984). Maintaining ability in the elderly. *Canadian Family Physician*, 30, pp.607-610.

Snider, E. L. (1981). The role of kin in meeting health care needs of the elderly. *Canadian Journal of Sociology*, 6, pp. 325-336

Toseland, R. (1977). A problem-solving group workshop for older persons. *Social Work*, 22, pp.325-326.

Watson, M. (1984). Alternatives to institutionalizing the elderly. *Canadian Family Physician*, 30, pp.655-660 .

Westberg, S. (1986). An aging population: Implications for social workers in acute hospitals. *The Social Worker — Journal of the Canadian Association of Social Workers*, pp. 107- 109.

Williams, T. F. (1987). Integration of geriatric assessment into the community. In L. Z. Rubenstein, L. J. Campbell, and R. L. Kane (eds.), *Clinics in geriatric medicine*. Philadelphia, PA: W.B. Saunders Co.

Wooldridge, D. B., Parker, G. and MacKenzie, P. (1987). An acute inpatient geriatric assessment and treatment unit. In L. Z. Rubenstein, L. J. Campbell and R. L. Kane (eds.), *Clinics in geriatric medicine*. Philadelphia, PA: W.B. Saunders Co.

Chapter 12

Social Work Practice with Dementia Patients in Adult Day Care

Patricia MacKenzie, M.S.W.
Irene Beck, B.S.W.

he stage is set for the development of alternatives to the existing health care delivery system for the elderly. Adult day care is one of the most frequently cited components of an expanded and comprehensive service delivery system, which is aimed at keeping the impaired elderly in their own homes for as long as possible. Adapting adult day programmes to meet the needs of adults with dementia presents an additional challenge to programme planners. The Luther Seniors Centre adult day programme in Saskatoon, Saskatchewan has been selected to demonstrate that social workers in such settings perform varied and important roles. Tasks range from administrative duties to direct clinical casework. The social worker, with a person-in-environment perspective, has much to offer participants and primary caregivers. Given the growing demand for such services, it is important that members of the social work profession take up the challenge in meeting this need in various communities that serve the elderly.

The delivery of care and services to dependent seniors is one of the major challenges facing contemporary social planners (Jutras, 1990). There is growing recognition that the 65 and older age group will increase more rapidly than any other segment of the population over the next two decades. As the population of frail elderly rises, including an increase in the number of people who suffer from some form of dementing illness, recent efforts to develop a system of community supports will continue. Adult day care forms a portion of the range of such service requirements and is one of the most frequently cited ways to provide support to participants and respite for caregivers (Mace, 1984; Chappell, Strain and Blandford, 1986; Aaronson, 1983). Although day programmes for the chronically ill originated in Europe and became more well defined in Britain during the early 1940s, the evolution of adult day care in Canada has been considerably slower. Many major Canadian cities remain without this important resource.

Adult day care differs from the type of programming usually available through a typical seniors centre. Although generic senior citizen centres have expanded to become multipurpose settings serving a wide range of people, these centres continue to focus their energy and resources on activities for the well or independent senior. Before one can adequately describe the nature of the clientele in adult day care programmes for the cognitively impaired, it is necessary to provide a short review of the history, goals and structure of these service settings.

Ohnsberg (1981) suggested that adult day care programmes share the common goal of providing non-institutional support to those unable to remain in the community without it. Wish (1980) defined adult day care as:

> primarily a social program for the frail, moderately handicapped, slightly confused older person who needs care during the day for some part of the week, either because he lives alone and cannot manage altogether on his own or, by sharing with his family some of the responsibility for his care, to relieve his family to help them to keep him at home. (p. 92)

Weissert (1977) has identified two types of adult day care programmes and describes them according to service objectives and target populations. The first type are those that serve a homogenous group who share some specific health-related concerns. The second type serves a more varied clientele whose principal need is for social stimulation/reintegration and caregiver relief. Huttman (1985) identified three types of adult day care programmes; those considered to be based on the so-called 'medical model,' 'the social model' or the 'mixed model.' Most Canadian adult day care programmes fit into Weissert's (1977) second category or are based on a social or mixed model. The medical model adult day care programmes described as such are usually referred to in Canada as geriatric day hospitals and the social work practice roles in these programmes are well described elsewhere (MacKenzie, 1989).

Thus, adult day centres provide programmes aimed at meeting the needs of those persons who require assistance to maintain their social and physical functioning while living in the community. Their programmes are intended to serve those individuals whose mental and/or physical health no longer allows them to remain in the community without the support of a family (or family surrogate), as well as other home supports. In the absence of these supports, many would be at risk for institutionalization (Rathbone-McCuan and Elliot, 1976).

Adult day care is a generic term for a variety of programmes. These range from the provision of structured social activities to those which offer active rehabilitation or physical and mental health intervention for a broad range of ambulatory, chronically ill or disabled adults who do not require 24-hour-a-day inpatient care. Rathbone-McCuan and Elliot (1976) suggested that adult day care is primarily a social programme for frail, moderately handicapped or confused older persons who need care during the day for some part of the week. Some clients live alone while others seek day care services to relieve families of the total responsibility for their care in the home. It is not surprising that an important service goal is the provision of respite and support for the caregivers of participants. The services of a social type of day care in which the socialization aspect is supplemented by availability of personnel to help with some physical care (e.g., bathing, incontinence care, medication supervision, etc.) has been found to be helpful in maintaining functioning and preventing precipitous admissions to permanent care environments (Chappell, 1985).

Many adult day care programmes are related to other agencies and services such as seniors centres, home care programmes, long-term care facilities or institutional and hospital care. Still others are independent and exist as free-standing programmes in the community. As well, most adult day care programmes in Canada receive funding on a global budget or fee-for-service arrangement from the relevant public health or social service agency, although some rely on monies from charitable agencies. In general, adult day care programmes operate only during the day and client attendance is determined by need and usually ranges from once every few weeks to daily visits. The staffing of adult day care programmes varies accordingly and may include registered nurses, occupational therapists, physiotherapists, recreation workers, care aides and social workers. The actual numbers of Canadian adult day care programmes that employ social workers has not been determined. It is our opinion that social work, with a natural orientation to the importance of the interaction of the client within his or her social environment, has significant expertise to offer such programmes.

The Clientele

Sally Jones, a stroke victim who now needs a walker for stability, would not miss her two days each week at the adult day centre for the world. She claims that going to the centre gives her a reason to get up in the morning and have something to do.

Sally's story is a common one across the nation. Her friends at the centre usually share her experience of physical disability, but for many the disability is more invisible although equally difficult. Her disability is cognitive impairment caused by of one of the dementing illnesses. Dementia arises from cerebral disease, which is often progressive in nature. Such conditions often result in the loss of intellectual abilities of sufficient severity to interfere with social or occupational functioning. The deficit is usually multifaceted and involves memory judgment, impairment and abstract thought (Pearce and Miller, 1973). Disturbances of higher cortical functions may lead at times to aphasia, apraxia and agnosia. For many older people, dementia involves a deterioration in intellectual performance and memory loss, which eventually becomes severe enough to interfere with the performance of activities of daily living (Fasano, 1986).

Although these cognitive functions might be impaired due to disorders of the central nervous system such as Alzheimer's disease, multi-infarct disease or related conditions, there are other conditions that may also account for poor brain function. These may be toxicity due to medication or other noxious agents, tumours pressing on the brain tissue or a profoundly depressed affect. Indeed, depression very closely mimics the symptoms of dementia and can fool the most astute observer (Gurland et al., 1984). Cognitive dysfunction, then, is *not* a diagnosis, but instead points to a serious underlying cause, which requires a careful and comprehensive assessment to uncover and possibly treat. As one can surmise, defining the elderly as confused, demented or cognitively impaired, presents something of a challenge.

Clients who have been labelled senile or 'demented' often wear these labels due to the presence of some overt symptomatology such as confusion, agitation or forgetfulness, rather than because of a careful assessment of a client's condition. It is well known that many older adults suffer from the reversible dementias that may clear up if the offending cause was eliminated (Skelton, 1987; Wooldridge et al., 1987). Others suffer from the non-reversible dementias such as those induced by Alzheimer's, multi-infarct disease or other organic brain disorders. Alzheimer's disease is a little known but remarkably common disorder that directly affects the cells of the brain. While experts formerly believed that the disease occurred mainly in persons under the age of 65, this disorder is now recognized as the most common cause of severe intellectual impairment for those over 65 years of age (Health and Welfare Canada, 1984).

Due to the difficulty in making differential diagnoses between reversible and non-reversible dementia among the elderly, it is important that the family and the formal caregiving system ensure that every older person has access to a regular comprehensive assessment to guarantee that each individual functions to his or her optimal level. (Later on, this chapter will illustrate how social workers in adult day care programmes for the cognitively impaired participate with other health care professionals in conducting such assessments.)

For our purposes, the client population described and served will be those persons who have a 'working diagnosis' of irreversible dementia from organic or chemical changes to the brain. The impairment of cognitive function for these individuals may be sufficiently extensive as to disrupt a person's capacity to carry out the activities of daily living, which require uninterrupted access to the cognitive functions of logic, reason, memory, perception, judgment and motor control.

These clients may live alone but often cohabit with family or friends in the community. The caregivers for adults with irreversible dementia often find the responsibility to be onerous at times and a stress on their physical and emotional health (Robinson, 1983; Kane, 1987). As the disease progresses and the burden of care increases, caregivers often request some sort of respite from what has been described as the 36-hour day (Mace and Rabins, 1981). Studies have generally found that the burden of caring for the cognitively impaired person often falls upon a single household member, often the elderly spouse or adult female child (Pratt et al., 1985). The adult day centre is one community support available to provide caregivers with some time out from their responsibilities as well as complementing the goal identified as one of the reasons to keep the client at home — a sense of community or belonging.

Huttman (1985) found that many adult day care programmes are reluctant to accept cognitively impaired clients for service and only a few programmes specialize in treating this group. In addition, service utilization of adult day care programmes by families caring for cognitively impaired clients has been a concern for many (Aaronson and Lipkowitz, 1981; Ory et al., 1985). As Caserata et al. (1987) pointed out, knowledge and access to adult day care programmes does not guarantee eager utilization of the service. Preventing potential breakdowns in the community care of the cognitively impaired elderly requires that those persons charged with the responsibility of linking clients to adult day care programmes are prepared to help caregivers overcome or resolve any feelings of denial, guilt, apprehension or anxiety about requesting service. Identifying and dealing with these potential patterns of resistance is of particular interest to social workers. For example, the possibility that those persons most in need of the respite care available through adult day care may be the very people most reluctant or recalcitrant to seek out such support is very real concern. Springer and Brubaker (1984) suggested that many caregivers have difficulty identifying or articulating their own needs for support and relief in this regard. Harel et al. (1985) also identified the level of caregiver burden, and the amount of 'other resources' available to the caregiving constellation, as factors that need to be considered when linking clients and caregivers to adult day care programmes. Indeed, dealing with resistance issues is a principal social work concern in these settings, which will be discussed later on.

Adapting adult day care programmes to the differing needs of adults with dementia is challenging, but programmes are increasingly being developed that serve only demented adults (Cherry and Rafkin, 1988; Mace, 1984). Of particular concern in this regard are those clients who are incontinent, wander or exhibit aggressive or disruptive behaviour. Managing problem behaviours requires a careful review of each case and a thorough understanding of the antecedents and consequences of each behaviour. Most adult day programmes use a problem-solving approach as their overriding treatment framework. This involves the programme staff (with appropriate inclusion of the caregiver as expert) working to determine causal relationships and potential management techniques. Many participants who enter adult day care programmes struggle with the major role losses of old age and the functional limitations of their disabilities. Programme participants, helped to recapture their socialization skills, have been found to be less agitated or distressed and perform activities of daily living more successfully while attending such programmes (Wish, 1980; Cherry and Rafkin, 1988).

Thus, it appears that adult day care programmes not only play a significant role in maintaining function in the participants, but also provide significant benefit to the caregiving constellation. To this end, both the cognitively impaired person and the caregiver(s) can be considered to comprise the clientele for social workers in these settings. The experiences of working with such a programme has enabled the authors to focus on the specific needs of both adult day care participants and informal caregivers, and also expand on the interventions used in the remainder of this chapter. The rewards of working in such a programme are many and the client population is interesting, appreciative and delightful.

The Luther Seniors Centre programme in Saskatoon, Saskatchewan is similar to other adult day centres in the country but considers the principal target population to be those older persons who are experiencing problems of daily living due to an irreversible dementing illness. The main aim of the Luther Seniors Centre adult day programme is to improve the quality of life for the participants and their primary caregivers. This involves the provision of safe, compassionate care and meaningful activities for participants, and relief and support for caregivers. Participants in the Luther Seniors Centre adult day programme include those individuals with 'mild' dementia through to those in advanced stages of the disease.

Practice Roles and Responsibilities

Social workers play a vital part in meeting the care needs of both participants and family members of adult day care centres from initial intake to discharge, a period of time that may span weeks to several months.When working with a client who has been identified as having a dementing illness, the adult day centre social worker must recognize both the client's needs for attention and support as well as those of the primary caregiver(s).

At the Luther Seniors Centre adult day programme, contact between the social worker and client system begins with the initial referral. The social worker is responsible for receiving applications for service. Applications can be made by anyone, however, the principal sources of referral are the local coordinated assessment unit — home care, the geriatric assessment unit, hospital social workers or family physicians. Some clients/families are self-referred and some are referred from other adult day care programmes in the city who cannot manage to meet the needs of the cognitively impaired.

Once an application has been received, the social worker arranges and completes a home visit. A great deal can be gleaned during these visits concerning the ability of the prospective participant to sustain himself or herself in the home environment, particularly if she or he is living alone. Two major objectives of the home visit are to gather information to complete an initial assessment and to establish rapport. Since many caregivers are severely stressed by the time they begin to consider adult day care, the social worker must be careful not to confuse apprehension or protectiveness with resistance. The need for an empathetic and sensitive approach, coupled with a working knowledge of normal aging and dementia, is required as the worker begins to explore needs and offer support. Establishing a trusting relationship with both the caregiver and prospective participant can help to reduce guilt, anxiety and fear of the unknown, thereby easing entry into the programme.

Effective interviewing skills, important for all social workers, are particularly essential during contacts with caregivers and cognitively impaired adults. How the cognitively impaired person responds to the social worker often determines whether or not the caregiver(s) will pursue day centre attendance. It is essential that the worker be friendly, make appropriate use of self and demonstrate superior listening and communication (both verbal and non-verbal) skills. Although it may be desirable to interview each person separately, in many cases this is not feasible. It is important, therefore, to ensure that both the prospective participant and caregiver feel they are included in these discussions. Even though it may appear that the cognitively impaired person cannot comprehend or follow the conversational flow, excluding him or her from the initial discussion limits the worker in the ability to obtain a vital impression of the level of his or her cognitive and verbal functioning. Dealing effectively with an increasingly dependent person, while appreciating that she or he remains an adult whose pride can be easily injured, is indeed a tremendous challenge (Health and Welfare Canada, 1984). Social workers, committed to recognizing the inherent worth and dignity of all people, should use such philosophy to guide interventions with all clients.

If it is not possible to obtain information that may be of a delicate nature or information that the caregiver does not feel comfortable disclosing in the presence of the cognitively impaired person, the worker may have to make a follow-up telephone call. This may help to clarify issues as well as determine the presence of difficult-to-manage behaviours, e.g., wandering, aggression or safety concerns, etc.

Data gathered during the course of the interview include social and medical histories, a description of activities of daily living, a sketch of the living environment and an assessment of the interpersonal interactions between the cognitively impaired person and significant others. Also important is a description of the formal and informal support systems available and used (Bennett and Grob, 1983). As well, the adult day care social worker is often responsible for initiating and maintaining communication among the various support systems caring for the participant.

During the initial home visit, the Luther Seniors Centre social worker is involved in administering the Kingston Dementia Rating Scale (Hopkins, 1983). This tool is used to assess the prospective participant's level of dementia. Once again, the need for a delicate and gentle approach is required during the administration of this test, as some cognitively impaired persons may find the questions intrusive, threatening or insulting. An approach that weaves the Kingston Dementia Rating Scale questions into the course of everyday conversation may help to ameliorate concerns. On these occasions, this particular process may need to be set aside until a later date when the participant feels more relaxed and trusting.

As has been noted, both the participants and the caregivers are considered to be 'clients' for adult day centre social workers. Thus, an additional assessment tool used at Luther Seniors Centre adult day programme is the Family Burden Index (Zarit et al., 1985). This inventory is left with the caregiver to complete and then return to the staff at the centre. The index is designed to indicate the perceived level of stress that the primary caregiver may be experiencing. Studies conducted at the Luther Seniors Centre have indicated that the higher the level of dementia (as demonstrated on the Kingston Dementia Rating Scale), the greater the stress for the primary caregiver (Beckett, 1987). The significance of this correlation for service delivery certainly warrants further review.

The final responsibility of the social worker prior to the participant beginning the programme occurs at a twice weekly case conference. This involves the social worker giving a clear, concise and accurate description of the history, current functioning and relevant support systems for the new participant.

Once admitted to the Luther Seniors Centre adult day programme, the social worker's direct service work with both participants and caregivers continues. Direct service to participants includes the initial assessment, one-to-one counselling, group work, crisis intervention and referring the client to other resources. A critical factor that needs to be determined early on is the participant's willingness to participate in the adult day care programme. Cognitively impaired persons who are not content or compliant to become involved in what is essentially a group activity will usually be distressed and potentially difficult to manage. Non-compliance may also add to, rather than detract from, the stress experienced by the caregivers. In turn, this may lead to premature withdrawal from the programme as caregivers may be unable to 'force' their family member to attend the programme if it makes them unhappy. Non-compliance on the part of the caregiver due to misperceptions about the nature of the programme, fear of 'letting go' or other concerns may also be issues requiring intervention. Thus, the social worker needs to be astute in determining the level of compliance in the participant (and caregiver), and do as much as possible to make him or her feel comfortable, involved and secure with the arrangements.

Another important direct service for adult day centre participants is orientation to the programme. At the Luther Seniors Centre, the social worker is involved in providing this orientation to both the participant and caregiver. This usually occurs on the first day of attendance and includes a tour of the centre, introduction to staff and other day centre participants and a review of the activities available. If the caregiver has accompanied the participant on that first visit, she or he is then encouraged to return home, leaving the participant to complete the day. Transportation arrangements home on the first day and in future visits are made by centre staff if the caregiver is unable or does not wish to drive. The provision of transportation to and from the centre is an absolutely essential component to guarantee access and utilization of the service.

One-to-one counselling with participants may either occur on an impromptu basis during the course of the week or may be initiated by another staff member who identifies a psycho-social need in the participant. Such needs may arise due to separation anxiety, sadness about some real or perceived loss, a need for information and/or problem behaviours such as wandering or striking out. Or it may simply be a request from the staff to involve the participants in some quiet time, which will permit the participant to express their feelings. Maintaining personal contact with each participant as such enables the social worker to assess the progression of the participant's disease, his or her level of comfort and involvement with the programme, and the participant's concerns about the future. With this information, the social worker is more knowledgeable and in touch with the client's functional ability. This permits the worker to be better able to offer insights and suggestions for strategies to help the participant retain optimal functioning both at the centre and at home.

In communicating with cognitively impaired persons, it helps to remember that, by the very nature of their disease, such individuals may often function more on an emotional rather than an intellectual level. Although the participant may not seem fully cognizant of the world around them, they are, of course, continuing to experience the world. Due to a faulty receptive ability, however, their world may appear confusing, foreboding or foreign. The reaction to these skewed interpretations of the world may cause the participant to demonstrate confused, disoriented or aggressive behaviour as she or he grapples with a reality that does not appear to make sense. Other emotive behaviours may be depression, fear and frustration. Thus, it is essential that the social worker is aware of the nature of the emotional and behavioural reactions the cognitively impaired person may suffer. The social worker who, by careful and attentive listening, attends to the feelings of the cognitively impaired person is helping to preserve his or her dignity and self-respect.

Group work is another direct service social workers may provide to participants. The focus of such groups may be reminiscence, reorientation, re-socialization or just plain fun! As flexible team members, social workers in adult day centres often try out new (or revisit old) skills by conducting physical exercise sessions or by leading a current events group or directing a sing-a-long. This may not fit the usual job description, but the involvement of the social worker in the day-to-day activities of participants affords one more opportunity to keep abreast of client progress and interaction with others.

As well, crisis intervention may be required of the social worker at various times. Examples of crisis intervention in an adult day centre usually occur when clients become aggressive or develop an anxiety attack. Other instances that require instant attention occur during the occasional times participants wander away from the building and perhaps refuse to return when found. Although wandering can be minimized by environmental design and vigilance on the part of staff, such occurrences do happen and are legitimate cause for concern. Preventative measures such as decreasing environmental stimuli and keeping in touch with participants who may be becoming increasingly agitated are helpful in this regard. Using a calm, reassuring approach when persuading a participant to remain at the centre, or to return if wandering has occurred, may help to minimize both the frequency of these events and the consequential stresses for all concerned.

Other crisis intervention is required if the primary caregiver becomes ill or is otherwise unable to continue to care for the cognitively impaired person in the home environment. The adult day centre social worker maintains close liaison with other community services such as long-term care facilities or home support programmes. These may need to be quickly mobilized to provide alternate care arrangements.

A. Family Support and Service to Caregivers

As was mentioned, provision for around-the-clock care for cognitively impaired people places a tremendous burden on the entire caregiving system. It is not surprising, therefore, that an important and time-consuming responsibility of the social worker involves the provision of family support services. These generally include one-to-one counselling, family conferences and facilitation of a caregivers' support group, crisis intervention, education and referrals to support services in the community. Contrary to the popular opinion that cognitively impaired older people are abandoned by their families to long-term care facilities, it has been estimated that families provide at least 80 percent of the home care for persons with chronic disabilities (Hooyman and Lustbader, 1986). Caregivers of cognitively impaired people are usually under tremendous stress, and this makes it difficult for them to see a way out of a situation and their usual problem-solving abilities may be diminished (Zarit et al., 1985). Thus, in addition to the respite offered by the adult day care programme, caregivers require a combination of information, education and opportunities for emotional ventilation and support. Social workers often find it necessary to point out to caregivers the importance of maintaining their own health, a realistic perspective on life and a sense of humour. The appropriate use of humour is a valuable therapeutic tool, which can be used to relieve stress and promote well-being. By helping the caregivers come to terms with their situations and accept that they have limits in their abilities to meet all of the needs of the cognitively impaired person, the social worker fulfils an important duty.

In most cases, the relationship between the adult day centre staff and the caregiver is a positive one, but tensions may arise at times. For instance, the caregiver may feel caught in the middle as she or he tries to follow the instructions of the professionals while at the same time meeting the needs and desires of the care receiver. The caregiver may often feel, "I know this person better than anyone," and this is usually beyond question. Thus, inclusion of the caregiver in discussions about case planning, listening to his or her point of view and working to ensure a mutual decision-making process happens between all parties is an important social work responsibility.

Assisting the caregiver to deal with the emotional strain of caregiving involves the social worker in individual counselling with the caregivers and significant others, education and information brokerage and referral to other support agencies. Although the primary goal is always to keep the impaired person at home for as long as possible, it may be that this objective is no longer feasible. Helping the caregiver to recognize when the home environment can no longer provide the care needed without the sacrifice of the caregivers own health is a responsibility of the social worker. For carrying out all these roles, the adult day centre social worker requires a solid background in family systems theory, counselling skills and an expert knowledge of community resources with the ability to help the client to access the same.

B. Caregivers Support

Caregivers can benefit from group sessions in which they discuss common problems and develop supportive links. Sharing problems and solutions with others in similar situations enables them to gain insight and strength from one another (Weiler and Rathbone-McCuan, 1978). At the Luther Seniors Centre adult day programme, the social worker facilitates such groups twice each month.

The value of mutual support cannot be over emphasized. Caregivers of cognitively impaired persons often feel helpless, misunderstood and alone (Powell and Courtice, 1983). They may have difficulty accepting the changes in their loved one or in recognizing that many of the behavioural problems that occur are manifestations of the disease not intentional contrary mindedness on the part of the impaired person. Friends and relatives who see the impaired person only on rare occasions may suggest that the primary caregiver is fussing about nothing or that 'things are not that bad.' Indeed, in the early stages, many people with dementia maintain sufficient superficial social skills fooling family and professionals alike. Only the primary caregiver, living under the same roof 24 hours each day, sees the faulty cognition and can view the whole picture. Caregivers often feel bereft of support and believe friends and relatives do not want to listen to their concerns.

Adjusting to a diagnosis of irreversible dementia can be like adjusting to an imminent death (Gruetzner, 1988). It is not surprising, therefore, that caregivers experience a range of emotions. For example, denial is a defence mechanism that may serve to help the caregiver adjust to the diagnosis. In the beginning stages, it may help to buffer pain or fear. However, unresolved denial may be a stumbling block to caregivers seeking help for themselves and the impaired person. By not accepting that a problem exists, the caregivers may put their own health in jeopardy. As well, such a reaction may deny the impaired person the opportunity to participate in programmes and services for their benefit.

As a normal reaction to disappointment, helplessness or frustration, anger is one of the more problematic emotional reactions. It should not be surprising that caregivers may feel angry. Caregivers may understandably feel angry and resentful for having to devote large portions of time and energy to the care needs of the impaired person. Resentment may also be directed at other family members for not helping with the task of caregiving. Assessing and attending to such dynamics within such family units is an area of expertise for the social worker.

As well, feelings of guilt are common for many caregivers of participants in adult day centres. Interactions that end with the caregiver becoming angry or frustrated with the impaired person may lead the caregiver to castigate himself or herself afterward for being impatient. Caregivers may also feel guilty about placing their loved one in an adult day centre rather than keeping him or her at home where they feel most comfortable. A gentle reminder by the social worker that they are human and do have limits to their caregiving can be of help in alleviating some of the guilt.

Sorrow and grief are other emotions expressed by many caregivers in this regard. For spousal caregivers, the cognitive impairment may be such as to preclude the impaired person from continuing to function effectively as friend, confidante, sexual partner and someone to talk to. The grief at losing someone to a dementing illness begins long before the impaired person actually dies. Buchanan (1984) aptly described this state of emotional or social suspended animation as 'half-widow/half-wife.' Many caregivers also grieve the loss of leisure time and the social opportunities they always thought the golden years would hold for them. To compound such losses, many times friends stop visiting. Going out to strange environments may become too distressing for the impaired person. The world suddenly becomes a very small space for the cognitively impaired and his or her caregiver. Sharing these feelings of grief, loss and isolation with others in the support group or with the social worker on an individual basis can give some comfort.

Some degree of depression is usually present in caregivers as a natural reaction to the events that have transpired. Social work intervention with caregivers on an individual basis and in the group setting is helpful to encourage ventilation about the feelings experienced and offer suggestions for resolving them. Occasionally, depressive reactions may reach such a degree as to suggest the social worker refer the caregiver for additional service or attention for himself or herself from the family physician or others.

Fear of what the future holds can be very disturbing to all. Caregivers are concerned about what might happen to their loved one should they themselves become ill. Other family members may be apprehensive about possible genetic predispositions to the disease. Children of impaired persons need to be given factual information about the nature of the disease in such a way as to minimize their concerns but not discount them. The social worker should ensure that caregivers and significant others are knowledgeable about the disease and fully aware of the resources that are available in the community.

Love and hate are contradictory emotions that are closely related. All human beings need to be loved and the cognitively impaired are certainly no exception. There are instances, however, when loving too much may be counterproductive. An example might be the caring, sensitive daughter who gives up her career to care for her cognitively impaired mother. Unless the daughter has established a system of respite from the 24-hour-per-day burden of this task, she may become quickly exhausted, frustrated and distressed as her best efforts are not able to meet all of her mother's care needs. Thus, what began as a loving gesture may turn to resentment and anger as the daughter is confronted with the enormity of the task at hand. An alert social worker may be able to spot such a problem and encourage the daughter to relinquish some of the care to others. In turn, this effort may preserve as much of the warmth of the mother-daughter relationship as possible and avoid dysfunctional patterns of interaction from developing. The reports of elder abuse occurring as a consequence of the exceptional care demands of cognitively impaired persons are beginning to be recognized (Beckett, 1987) and certainly warrants further study.

It is also important for the social worker to realize that dementing illnesses often lead to major role changes within family units, and adjusting to role changes can be very painful for everyone. For example, a son may find it difficult to explain to his father why he can no longer drive the car or go out for a walk alone. The same son may find helping with the physical care, such as bathing his father, very embarrassing. While the social worker certainly does not have easy answers to these difficult situations, encouraging caregivers to be open in their communication with each other and with the impaired person as much as possible may help to prevent misunderstandings. Such an approach may also lead to a greater spirit of cooperation in what must surely be 'a joint effort' among all concerned. Thus, the social worker needs to help the primary caregiver to learn to give clear messages to other family members about the kind of assistance that is both needed and beneficial. For many members of the caregivers' social constellation, not helping is often a case of not knowing *how* to help. Recognizing that other caregivers in the support group struggle with the same issues can alleviate some of the feelings of isolation. At the same time, such sessions provide the opportunity to share and receive helpful hints for managing caregiving responsibilities.

As a result, a great deal of learning occurs at the caregiver support meetings. Much of this happens on an informal basis as caregivers learn from each other. No amount of textbook reading can replace the helpful hints caregivers provide each other as they share stressful, frightening and occasionally humorous accounts of their efforts to provide a safe and comfortable environment in the home for their impaired loved one. In their struggle to live one day at a time, these people inadvertently become experts with innovative solutions to everyday problems that occur with cognitively impaired people. Caregivers of newly referred participants, concerned about sending their loved one to the adult day centre, are often relieved to hear that others experienced similar apprehensions. The social worker who facilitates caregiver support groups needs to be aware of the power and strength available to caregivers through this kind of sharing and encourage it.

At other times, caregivers require more factual information. For example, medication dispensing, management of incontinence or problem behaviours and effective communication techniques are topics of interest to caregivers. Other practical information the social worker can help the caregivers to obtain (via individual contact or on a group basis) includes legal and financial counselling or housing and home care services. Through these and other activities, the social worker is called upon to act as educator and information broker.

C. Interdisciplinary Team Involvement

The responsibilities assumed by social workers in adult day centre programmes range from administrative tasks through to direct clinical duties. The social worker considers the role at the Luther Seniors Centre programme to be primarily one of direct service to the entire client group. The social worker is part of a team consisting of a manager, registered nurse, recreation/care staff, pastoral care, dietary aide, housekeeper and secretary. The social worker is involved in twice weekly care conferences, which involve participating in the formulation of individualized care plans for each participant, providing input into daily programming and presenting new admissions. The social worker is seen as the principal liaison between caregivers and staff.

As an active participant in educational programmes for staff, the social worker plays a vital role in helping the team to cope with the stressful nature of this type of work. Avoiding the possibility of overextending oneself, recognizing the necessity of accepting limitations to caregiving and dealing with the limited verbal feedback given to staff from participants are issues that may be addressed by the social worker with individual staff or in-group, in-service sessions. The social worker works with other staff to build morale and create the kind of warm and friendly environment conducive to fostering good function for both staff and the clientele.

The social worker also provides an important educational resource to the larger community. Participation in community education programmes, which describe both the type of service offered by the adult day centre programme, as well as the particular needs of the cognitively impaired person and their caregivers, is an area of expertise the social worker needs to be prepared to share. Supervision of social work students from university social work programmes also involves the social worker in teaching. Activities of this nature hopefully capture the interest and commitment of a new generation of social work practitioners to enter this emerging field of service to the aged.

As with any professional committed to lifelong learning, it is the responsibility of the adult day centre social worker to keep abreast of current literature and research about care of the cognitively impaired elderly and their families. As a result, a willingness to invest the time and energy in attending conferences and updating knowledge and skills is requisite.

Potential for Role Development

There are increasing opportunities for broadening the practice roles for social workers with the aging population. The profession needs to respond to both the direct and indirect service needs of the aging population generally, and the cognitively impaired and their caregiving networks specifically. One of the most significant aspects about the needs of this client group is the 'information vacuum' in which many clients and their caregivers initially find themselves. Many families referred to the Luther Seniors Centre adult day programme appear to be 'at their wit's end.' It is obvious that, for many, a referral to this type of a support service could have happened much earlier. What would be helpful in the community is some sort of an early warning system, which could allow for early identification of caregiving families at risk of breaking down. One of the first social work duties that has considerable room for development is to provide the community with information about various services available. This responsibility is based on an early social work premise, which accepts the clients' right to know and then how to use available social services. As Toseland (1981) pointed out, client self-determination, a historical social work objective, is increased by providing alternative resources for problem-solving. Hence, the information broker and outreach role of the social worker in both the larger community and in adult day care programmes is valuable and needs expanding.

In addition to the information vacuum facing many older people and their caregivers, there continues to be a dearth of resources in the community for helping to maintain cognitively impaired older people in their own homes. Unfortunately, current adult day centres are frequently deluged with long waiting lists. Until additional services are developed, early identification of families who could benefit from adult day care may not be of much utility. It could, however, help to obtain a true picture of the need for service. This suggests that social workers participating in needs assessment surveys and other research activities would be able to gather information pertinent to the development of social and health policy.

As well, Brody and Brody (1974) suggested a neglect in the provision of health service to the elderly population must be met by social workers with a commitment to advocacy. With an increasing ability to document the benefits of adult day care programmes in maintaining functional ability and mental functioning for recipients of these programmes, social workers need to advocate for the enhancement in both quantity and quality of such programmes (Chappell, 1985). As Canada's population increases, we can expect an increase in the number of persons with dementing illnesses. Our already inadequate resources to relieve the primary caregivers of these individuals will become even more overtaxed. Social workers committed to influencing environmental and social policy concerns need to lobby for continued development of adult day centres and related programmes for the elderly. Research conducted by social workers either alone or in concert with other disciplines on the efficacy of adult day care centres for the cognitively impaired is sorely needed to substantiate the plea for services of this nature.

The inevitable fiscal battles, which occur as community-based services to the elderly compete for increasingly scarce human service dollars, require the presence of stalwart social work practitioners committed to developing sound social policy. Once again, the need for creativity and cooperation is apparent. The present federal Minister of Health, Perrin Beatty (1989) suggested that strategies need to be developed that promote the independence and quality of life for seniors, as this is what they are basically entitled to as citizens. One may assume that such apparent commitment on the part of government would create considerable momentum for potential change in this area. Social workers, as well as other professional and non-professional groups, can continue to identify needs of the cognitively impaired and develop comprehensive service delivery systems designed to create opportunities for such independence and quality of life.

The actual social service needs of caregivers of the cognitively impaired elderly also warrant some attention. Although some caregivers find opportunities to have their own psycho-social and emotional needs met by social work personnel in adult day centres and other programmes as such, the availability of counselling services for the elderly, their caregivers or significant others is grossly inadequate. Social workers in family service agencies, private practice or government programmes will eventually be required to meet the direct and indirect service needs of the aging population. It is really not yet well understood what therapeutic interventions or counselling modalities are helpful in relieving psycho-social distress in the elderly (Weiler and Rathbone-McCuan, 1978). Thus, there is a need to expand the conceptual frameworks that guide interventions with older people. Social workers with an interest in psychotherapy and family work need to be urged to focus clinical and research efforts on appropriate and effective intervention techniques for multi-generational family systems.

Further, to be effective practitioners with the elderly and their caregiving network, we (the profession) need to eliminate earlier erroneous assumptions that social work with the aged means placing old people in nursing homes, arranging funerals and tending to practical but boring tasks such as procurement of dentures, eyeglasses and/or pension cheques. Attending to such practicalities is required, but the profession needs to go beyond this limited view of practice if it is to develop in this area. A belief in the capacity for growth and change throughout the entire life-cycle is essential for the gerontological social worker. A review of the 'fit' between current social work counselling theories and skills and the needs of the cognitively impaired and their caregivers is, therefore, required. Responding to the service needs of this population will also require creativity, an expanded view of the nature of individual counselling and multi-generational family work and a philosophical view that considers the older segment of the population to be a group worthy of respect and attention in our society.

Seniors groups have begun to lobby for expanded community supports, and social work should be firmly supportive of their efforts. Peer counselling service is an idea that has become recently popular. Social workers could do much to help educate such counsellors thereby increasing the availability of counselling support to those requiring such services. Another potential resource to the cognitively impaired and the caregiving network would be volunteer support. Specifically, social workers could help to enhance the informal support networks of the cognitively impaired by recruiting and educating a core of capable volunteers equipped to assist in alleviating caregiving tasks.

It is not realistic to suggest that all cognitively impaired people will be able to remain in their own homes until their dying days. Some will, but others will continue to need admission to long-term care facilities. Efforts to develop social policies that are supportive of developing facility-based care, which provide enhanced programming and a 'maintenance of function' orientation programme for the cognitively impaired, need to continue to be a social work goal. As well, the expansion of short-term, planned and emergency 24-hour respite care must also continue. The group home concept developed in Sweden is an additional caregiving arrangement that has some merit and requires further investigation (Beck-Fiis, 1988). Alternate forms of care must be developed that provide the cognitively impaired person with an environment that is as home-like and stimulating as possible. Social work consultation in planning, implementation, and provision of such services, are essential.

The education of helping professionals equipped to care for the needs of the elderly in the next decades has been identified as a major challenge. Faculties of social work and other health related disciplines have been urged to incorporate course work of aging into the curricula (Matthews, 1989). This is important, but such initiatives could be taken a bit further. Specifically, due to the interdisciplinary nature of most practice environments that serve aging populations, social work practitioners would be correct in urging faculties of social work to join others on the leading edge of a movement to educate helping professionals interested in the aged in interdisciplinary settings. Certainly, there is much each discipline can learn from the other in this field. The opportunity to obtain both an understanding and a healthy respect for the practice orientation and particular skills each discipline brings to the practice environment would only be of benefit to future clients.

Concluding Remarks

The multi-faceted needs of the cognitively impaired participants of adult day care programmes and their caregivers require that the social worker provide many different types of service. These roles may be described as enabler, programme worker, advocate, information broker, educator, liaison, therapist and confidante. In addition to direct service to the participants and caregivers, the social worker holds an important role in the planning, development, implementation and administration of unique service delivery systems such as adult day care centres. As an innovative addition to the spectrum of care provided to the cognitively impaired person, adult day care programmes bring together a variety of services in one setting: social, recreational, counselling and educational programmes, meals, information and referral and, for many, a sense of belonging and restored purpose in life. For the caregivers, adult day care provides a break from the caretaking routine, the opportunity to focus on their own needs and the chance to recapture the energy required to sustain the nature of the relationship between themselves and the impaired person. The social worker should be skilled in helping people to access resources, resolve interpersonal and family conflicts and work toward growth and change throughout the entire lifecycle. Social work, with an emphasis on the 'person-in-environment,' a commitment to enhancing the quality of life for all and a belief in the inherent worth and dignity of all persons, has much to offer such programmes.

Case Example

Mrs. A, an 80-year-old widow with mild dementia, has lived in a one bedroom apartment in a senior's highrise since the death of her husband ten years ago. His death and the move from a farm to a city apartment was difficult for her. Fortunately, a daughter and son-in-law live nearby and visit frequently. These family members assist her with household chores, take her shopping, look after her finances and include her in larger family social functions. A few months ago, the daughter and son-in-law left town on an extended holiday. During their absence, arrangements were made for Mrs. A to fly to Toronto to stay with her son and his family. The local family members had begun to worry about Mrs. A's increasing confusion and did not feel she could be left alone. The son in Toronto had not seen his mother during the preceding two years. Although warned by his sister that she had begun to have significant memory problems, he and his family were completely unprepared for his mother's behaviour. During her stay in Toronto she was unable to find the bathroom unaided, did not want to put her purse down for fear that it would be stolen and at one point struck her daughter-in-law when she was prevented from leaving the house in the middle of the night in her dressing gown. Unable to cope with Mrs. A's anger, agitation and confusion, her son sent her back to her home city in the care of her granddaughter, a young mother with a full-time job.

Without the support and reassurance from her usual caregiver, (her vacationing daughter) Mrs. A was totally lost. She began to haunt the hallways of her apartment building, often disturbing neighbours at all hours of the night. Eventually, the local home care office was alerted by the granddaughter and an urgent referral to the adult day centre made. The social worker visited Mrs. A in her apartment and after some initial reluctance, Mrs. A agreed to attend the programme in order to 'have something to do.' Due to the need to provide extensive care and supervision for Mrs. A during her daughter's absence, arrangements were made by the adult day centre social worker for her to attend the day programme from Monday to Friday. Home care was contacted to supplement the granddaughter's care by providing meal time support and a sitter service during some evenings and weekends. When the daughter returned from her holiday, home care involvement was reduced although her daily attendance at the adult day care programme continued. A routine call by the adult day centre nurse to the family physician discovered a medication error, which was corrected. This led to a slight improvement in Mrs. A's mental functioning.

Mrs. A, a very sociable woman, settled well into the adult day programme. She enjoyed the routine group activities and found particular pleasure in singing, participating in the reminiscence group led by the social worker and visiting with other participants. She especially loved to dance. These opportunities to socialize with others were identified by her family as providing great benefit to her in retaining some of the interpersonal skills for which she was previously well known. Having a hot meal at noon relieved her daughter's concern about her diet and freed her from having to prepare full evening meal for her mother on those days.

Mrs. A continued daily attendance at the adult day centre for several months. One winter night she was found in her pyjamas 'lost' in front of her apartment building. The next day the adult day centre social worker held a family conference to discuss the risks involved in allowing Mrs. A to continue to live alone. Since the family was opposed to moving Mrs. A to a large institution the social worker helped them to find a compromise situation. A vacancy at a small ten-bed private care home was located and arrangements were made for Mrs. A to be admitted. Admission to this type of care environment did not interfere with her continued attendance at the adult day centre, as would a move to a large government institution. The move did not go at all well as Mrs. A had a great deal of difficulty adjusting to a new environment. This fuelled the daughter's already considerable guilt at not having her mother in her own home. Frequent counselling sessions with the day centre social worker allowed the daughter to resolve some of her concerns.

Continuing her attendance at the adult day centre two days each week, allowed Mrs. A to maintain some sense of continuity and to see old friends. The presence of this routine helped her eventually settle into her new environment. Some months later, a further deterioration in Mrs. A's physical health led the family to seek help from the adult day centre social worker in arranging a placement in a higher level of care. Mrs. A was subsequently transferred to a government subsidized long-term care facility. As government policy mandates that residents of such facilities are ineligible to attend community-based programmes such as adult day care, Mrs. A was discharged from the programme after an 18-month contact. On her first morning in the government facility, Mrs. A was seen walking down the corridor arm in arm with a friend she had known at the adult day centre.

The above case illustrates the appropriate use of an adult day centre in meeting the urgent need of an elderly cognitively impaired person who had begun to fail in the community. Although she did have family support, individual circumstances made it difficult for family to meet all her care needs. The adult day centre provided meaningful social and recreational opportunities for Mrs. A, respite and a supportive resource to family members, as well as allowing a delay in the institutionalization of Mrs. A. The social worker was able to assist both Mrs. A and the family to move through a range of emotions from guilt to acceptance, as all realized that admission to a long-term care facility became the only option. It is suggested that adult day centres, designed to delay institutionalization, can also provide time for the family to adjust to the loss, perhaps making 'letting go' less traumatic.

References

Aaronson, Linda. (1983, Spring). Adult day care: A developing concept. *Journal of Gerontological Social Work*, 5(3).

Aronson, M.K. and R. Lipkowitz. (1981). Senile dementia, Alzheimer's type: The family and the health care delivery system. *Journal of the American Geriatrics Society*, 29, 568-571.

Beatty, Perrin. (1989). Notes from an Address to the Canadian Club. Ottawa, Ontario.

Beck-Fiis, Barbro. (1988). At home at Balzargarden: Caring for the geriatric senile in a small scale group environment. *Bokforlaget Libris-Orebro*.

Beckett, J. (1987). Adult day care for the cognitively impaired: Are we meeting the needs? An address presented to Shaping the future: New direction and intervention models. *National Forum on Long term Care*, Ottawa, Ontario.

Bennett Clare J. and G. Grob. (1983). The social worker new to health care: Basic learning tasks. *Social Work in Health Care*, 8(2).

Brody, E.M. and S. Brody. (1974). Decade of decision for the elderly. *Social Work*, 19(5).

Buchanan, Karin. (1984). *Coping when life is threatened*. Regina: Weigl Publishers.

Caserata, M.S., Lund D.A., Wright, S.D. and Redburn, D.E. (1987). Caregivers to dementia patients: The utilization of community services. *Gerontologist*, 27(2) 204-214.

Chappell, N. L. (1985). Who benefits from adult day care: Changes in functional ability and mental functioning during attendance. *Canadian Journal on Aging*, 2(1).

Chappell, N.L., Strain, L.A. and Blandford, A. (1986). Aging and health care: A social perspective. Toronto: Holt, Rinehart and Winston of Canada, Ltd.

Cherry, D.L. and Rafkin, M. (1988). Adapting day care to the needs of adults with dementia. *The Gerontologist*, 28(1).

Fasano, Marie A. (1986). Creative care for the person with Alzheimer's. A brady book. New Jersey.

Gruetzner, Howard. (1988). Alzheimer's: A caregiver's guide and source book. New York: John Wiley and Sons Inc.

Gurland, B., Golden R., Leaf P. et al. (1984). The SHORT-CARE: An efficient instrument for the assessment of depression, dementia, and disability. *Journal of Gerontology*, 39, 166-169.

Harel, Z., Noelker, L. and Blake, B.F. (1985). Comprehensive services for the aged: Theoretical and empirical perspectives. *The Gerontologist*, 25, 644-649.

Health and Welfare Canada. (1984). *Alzheimer's disease: A family information handbook*. Health and Welfare Canada - Health Services Directorate in cooperation with the Alzheimer's Society of Canada.

Hooyman, Nancy R. and Lustbader, W. (1986). *Taking care: Supporting older people and their families*. New York: The Free Press; A division of Macmillan Inc.

Hopkins, R.W. (1983). *Kingston dementia rating scale*. Kingston, Ontario: Kingston Psychiatric Hospital.

Huttman, Elizabeth D. (1985). *Social services for the elderly*. New York: The Free Press; A Division of Macmillan, Inc.

Jutras, Sylvia. (1990, March). Caring for dependent senior's in Quebec: A family responsibility? *Transition*, 20(1).

Kane, Rosalie. (1987, February). Assessing social function in the elderly. In L. Z. Rubenstein, L. Y. Campbell and R. Kane (eds.), *Clinics in geriatric medicine*, 3(1), Philadelphia, PA: W. B. Saunders Company.

Mace, Nancy. (1984, October). Day care for demented clients. *Journal of Hospital and Community Psychiatry*, 35(10).

Mace, Nancy and Rabins, Peter. (1981). *The 36-hour day: A family guide to caring for persons with Alzheimer's disease*. Baltimore, MD: Johns Hopkins University Press.

MacKenzie, Patricia. (1989). Social work practice in geriatric assessment units. In M. J. Holosko and P.A. Taylor (eds.), *Social work practice in health care settings*. Toronto, Canada: Canadian Scholars' Press.

Matthews, Charlotte. (1989). *Educating health professionals to the care of the elderly*. Notes to an address at a Conference cosponsored by the Canadian Medical Association and Health and Welfare Canada, Ottawa, Ontario.

Ohnsberg, D. W. (1981, Jan./Feb.). Burgeoning day care movement prolongs independent living. *Perspective on Aging*, pp. 18-20.

Ory, M.G., Williams, T.F., Emr., M., Lebowitz, B. et al. (1985). Families, informal supports and Alzheimer's disease: Current research and future agendas. *Research on Aging*, 7, 623-644.

Pearce, John and Miller, Edgar. (1973). Clinical aspects of dementia. London, England: Bailliere, Tindall and Cassell.

Powell, Lenore S. and Courtice, K. (1983). Alzheimer's disease: A guide for families. New York: Addison Wesley Publishing Co.

Pratt, C., Schmall, V., Wright, S. and Cleland, M. (1985). Burden and coping strategies of caregivers to Alzheimer's patients. *Family Relations*, 34, 27-33.

Rathbone-McCuan, Eloise and Elliot, M. (1976-77, Winter). Geriatric day care in theory and practice. *Social Work in Health Care*, 2(2).

Robinson, B. (1983). Validation of a caregiver strain index. *Journal of Gerontology*, 38, 344-348.

Skelton, David. (1987). *Grapes or raisins: A geriatrician's reflections upon the future of health care for the elderly.* An annual paper presented to the Alberta Hospital Association Annual General Meeting.

Springer, D. and Brubaker, T. (1984). *Family caregivers and dependent elderly: Minimizing stress and maximizing independence.* Beverley Hills, CA.: Sage Publications.

Toseland, Ronald. (1981, April). Increasing access: Outreach methods in social work practice. *Social Casework, 62,* 227-234.

Weiler, Philip G. and Rathbone-McCuan, Eloise. (1978). *Adult day care: Community work with the elderly.* New York: Springer Publishing Company.

Weissert, W.G. (1977). *Adult day care programs in the United States: Current research projects and a survey of 10 centers.* Public Health Reports, 92.

Wish, Florence. (1980). Day care: Its value for the older adult and his family. *Journal of Jewish Communal Care, 52*(2).

Wooldridge, D.B., Parker, G. and MacKenzie, P.A. (1987). An acute inpatient geriatric assessment and treatment unit. In L. Z. Rubenstein, L. J. Campbell, and R. Kane (eds.), *Clinics in geriatric medicine, 3*(1). Philadelphia, PA: W.B. Saunders Co.

Zarit, S.H., Orr, N.K. and Zarit, J.M. (1985). The hidden victims of Alzheimer's disease: Families under stress. New York: New York University Press.

Chapter 13

Social Work Practice with the Frail Elderly in Adult Day Care

Rhoda Kopstein, M.S.W.
Sorele Urman, M.S.W.

*T*his chapter describes a non-medical, community-based service designed to meet the differential psycho-social needs of the frail elderly. The goal of this service is to help older persons stay in control of their situation by using basic contracting principles with them and their family system. The functions of social worker both as case worker and group worker are emphasized. The main assumption put forward is that by acknowledging dependency and focusing on strengths, older adults may be helped to achieve their potential.

The Clientele

The National Institute of Adult Day Care (N.I.A.D.C.), established in the United States in 1979, defines adult day care as "a community-based program that is a structured, comprehensive program that provides a variety of health, social and related support services in a protective setting during any part of a day but less than 24 hour care" (p. 42). This definition embraces all day care services whether they serve the frail elderly, Alzheimer's victims and/or employ a social work model, a health-based model or a combination of both (Weissert 1989).

The day care programme (DCP) at Baycrest Centre for Geriatric Care in Toronto, Ontario, uses a unique social work model for serving a community-based population of 120 frail elderly people, with an average age of 83. The actual programme expects a planned attendance of 60 people daily. It has its own physical structure (e.g., rooms) in a separate section of the adjoining Jewish Home for the Aged, and also has access to the proximal Baycrest Hospital, a chronic care and rehabilitation hospital.

In the well-staffed DCP, virtually all of the participants are vulnerable and suffer from one or more of the following disabilities: physical, emotional, social or cognitive, i.e., some 'forgetfulness' or mild Alzheimer's. Without exception, applications to the DCP are accelerated by a specific crisis in an older person's life. Such crises have the familiar mixture of losses to spouses, physical vitality, friendships, employment, family roles, income and/or familiar environment. Regardless of what combination of such losses are experienced, the results are usually the following: 1) feelings of uselessness because of lack of meaningful socially based roles; 2) feelings of loss of control, engendering fear, anger and various forms of defensive behaviour; and/or, 3) severe lowering of self-esteem. Since most participants are in their 80s or 90s, their family caregivers are usually in their 50s or 60s. As a result, respite for caregivers is part of the mandate of the programme (Miller, 1989).

The combined deficits usually experienced by this population are reflected by its auspices, that of a home for the aged and an adjacent hospital. Thus, DCPs in free-standing facilities may have fewer physically handicapped elderly than in a facility connected to a hospital such as this programme (Weissert et al., 1989).

The litany of losses and deficits of the programme participants are balanced by the strengths that such people retain. For instance, most have lived very full and long lives and take much pride in the families and social networks they have created. Further, many come with obvious or latent skills in such activities as crafts, creative writing or drama. All have lived through momentous events and usually have decided opinions about issues such as politics or emotional memories of their past lives. As well, some have other skills in making and keeping friends and many are blessed with a sense of humour (Miller and Solomon, 1980).

Meeting the psycho-social needs of this clientele for a regained sense of community, relationships, new experiences, self-esteem and control over decisions that affect their lives is the primary responsibility of the social work staff. Thus, the social worker relates to their strengths and builds supports into the programme to acknowledge and compensate for their existing deficits (Miller and Solomon, 1980). Further, arrangements to meet health care needs and other case management issues such as help to the families in supporting their relatives are important social work responsibilities, which attempt to provide service to the whole person.

The actual term 'day care' is welcomed by older adults as a true description of a service that meets their daily needs for care. Unlike younger adults, participants generally don't find the term infantilizing or demeaning. The concern of some (usually younger adults) is that the concept of day care may serve to reinforce non-functional dependency. Thus, what may appear as dependency "may be a reaction to the actual absence of needed supports, and when these are in fact provided, dependency decreases rather than increases" (Miller and Solomon, 1980, p.76). However, when non-functional dependency occurs, it is explored and dealt with by staff.

All of the members live in the adjacent community in their own apartment or with their families or in group homes. Each participant retains his or her own personal physician in the community and is required to have a medical examination every six months. Referral by the DCP physician to some clinics in Baycrest Hospital are facilitated by the DCP social worker.

Each participant is assigned to a social worker who carries a caseload of up to 30 individuals and their families, in addition to leading groups, supervising volunteers, educational supervision of students in practicum, programme development as well as attending to some of the management tasks of the DCP. As well, case management and complex discharge planning involving the family are important aspects of the job (Burack-Weiss, 1988). Integral to the provision of optimal service are: 1) social work intake staff who assist individuals and their families to enter into the programme; 2) a DCP staff of a director, social workers, part-time specialists, health care aides and clerical staff; 3) volunteers and specialists (paid by local boards of education) who enrich the service and who are supervised by DCP social workers; 4) a reliable personalized transportation system; 5) two meals a day and snacks prepared and served by the food services staff of Baycrest Centre; 6) an activity schedule that permits individualized choice and is changed four times a year; 7) access to a beauty shop and barber shop, podiatry clinic and a psychiatric consultant; 8) the use of F.M. hearing assistive devices for discussion groups; and, 9) first aid on-call service by the nursing staff of Home for the Aged.

Practice Roles and Responsibilities

A. Intake Function

In order for the programme to meet the psycho-social needs of the individual she or he must participate in the decision-making process. For instance, even if a professional (e.g., doctor, social worker, public health nurse, etc.) determines that the programme would be good for them, if they does not agree or is not facilitated in helping to overcome their fears of participation they will not enter the programme.

I. Steps in Intake
The intake process requires full family participation, both together with and separate from the applicant.
1. Enquiry — Initially a client, family member or a referring agency calls or personally comes in to discuss the need for this service. Subsequently, an enquiry is written up by the social worker on duty. Information and support is provided if the service is not deemed appropriate and/or there is crisis requiring immediate attention.
2. Initial Screening — The enquiry is passed on to the intake supervisor who then assigns it to the appropriate social worker for processing.
3. Initial Assessment — This includes a formally structured meeting with the client and his or her family jointly to establish the needs of the client and determine whether day care service should be provided. Basic information about the day care services are given to the client and family on the understanding that neither we (the DCP) nor they are making a commitment

that the client will enter the DCP. The purpose here is to: 1) ensure that the person does not feel she or he is being rushed into something; 2) that she or he still retains control over their situation; and, 3) assure the client that she or he will have adequate opportunity to look around and test out the programme before making a decision. This initial assessment usually involves about two interviews but may frequently take more, depending upon what we meet in the situation and how quickly the family and the applicant can move along in their considerations.

4. Initial Orientation — Once the DCP staff have established the person's need for and readiness to become involved, the social worker arranges for the client to visit individual programmes. Scheduled times and transportation must also be arranged with the applicant and his or her family as DCP transportation is not used until later on in the process. The idea here is to help the client feel that she or he has potential for self-determinism and can cope with the pending situation. For instance, if the client knows he or she has the capacity for more demanding programmes after the first visit, a further orientation to another programme is usually arranged, e.g., she or he may then stay for the afternoon. If all goes well during this process, the applicant moves on immediately to the next stage.

5. Specific Orientation and Introduction — The basic task here is to help the client enter the regular DCP by offering the following services:

   a) This is the stage where the applicant obtains formal medical clearance for the programme from her or his own physician (this includes a chest x-ray). The client then formally completes a DCP membership form. Payment for services is discussed with applicants and family and if need be, their children are asked to fill out a financial form if their help is needed and if they (the clients) are unable to pay the full programme costs. The social worker determines with the client and family the amount of the payment and the method of payment of fees.

   b) The social worker then prepares a summary outlining what she or he knows about the applicant's characteristics and needs, information about past and present social relationships, occupational information and family background data. The worker submits this to the director of day care who then arranges a joint meeting with the applicant, family members, the intake social worker and the assigned day care worker.

B. Admission and Contracting Function

The DCP director then begins the process of helping to provide the transition from intake to full day care trial visits for the applicant. Tasks in this regard include the following:

- Prepares for the admission interview by studying the social summary provided by the intake worker.
- Consults regularly with intake worker and may meet the applicant during programme visits.
- Makes a preliminary decision about which day care social worker and group to assign the applicant to, based on the information provided to date, e.g., language spoken, social skills, etc. are carefully considered here.
- Negotiates a time for the intake worker to have a meeting with the applicant and the family.
- Invites the assigned day care worker to the interview.

The purposes of this interview are: 1) to contract with the applicant for a mutually agreed upon number of trial visits of full day attendance; 2) to contract about mutually agreed upon expectations that the applicant may have of DCP and expectations that the programme will have of him or her; and, 3) to begin the transition to the new worker of the applicant and his or her family (e.g., the client system).

I. Elements of the contracting interview following introductions (not necessarily in order):
- A statement of the purpose of the meeting.
- Reach for feedback on applicant's overall understanding and clarify the agenda for the meeting.
- Convey that the applicant is in charge of the decision after the agreed upon number of full-day trial visits.
- Encourage the applicant to describe her or his own need

for the programme and expectations of it. In this context, respond honestly as to which expectations can be met by the programme and also those which cannot be met.

- Describe the expectations that the DCP has, i.e., to learn to take help in the beginning; to give help when she or he is comfortable; to look around for people with whom she or he might like to become friends with; to attend the daily meeting with the day care social worker in the morning every time that she or he comes.
- Describe the supports and help that she or he will receive from both the intake worker and the day care worker. For instance, the intake worker will meet him or her when she or he first arrives and make sure that she or he attends the early morning activities and the morning meeting; the day care worker will make sure the client is seated at a compatible table in the dining room. Also, the client will be reminded of the activities to go to and receive help in going to them.
- Negotiate the days she or he will attend (minimum two per week).
- Reassure the client that she or he will not have to remember everything as staff will write it down and 'help remember for her or him.'
- Acknowledge the help the client has been given by his or her family in attending programme visits and attending this meeting. Encourage the client, if it seems appropriate, to express feelings to those members of his or her family who are present re: the help they have provided.
- Describe to family members those programmes that they will be invited to, i.e., the annual birthday party, the family meetings, family support groups, etc. Assure the family that they will continue to receive counselling or help if they require it.

This type of systematized contracting with the individual who has identified her or his own needs, who has a beginning understanding of the service and what she or he can get from it, and what she or he can give to it, is a powerful incentive to many, and enables many individuals to stay in control of their programme participation every step of the way. Social work's role in contracting and recontracting as such facilitates both individualized programming and safeguards the overall self-determinism of all clients in the DCP.

If the applicant decides, after the contracted number of visits, to remain in the program, the transition is formally completed approximately six weeks later, at a meeting of the day care social worker, the intake social workers, the applicant (now a member) and her or his family. For this 'transfer meeting,' the intake worker prepares a summary updating information and noting additional information that will be useful to the day care worker in taking over the case.

This contract interview is essentially where the programme's purpose and the applicant's needs come together (Schwartz and Zalba, 1971; Gitterman and Shulman, 1986). The idea that there will be expectations of her or him is both thrilling and fear inducing for the individual. Thus, most applicants need reassurance that the social worker will be available to help them.

C. Activity Planning and Management Function

The DCP activity schedule is designed and re-designed four to five times a year by social work and programme staff with input from programme members. The schedule is very structured, offering a minimum of three activity choices every hour in the afternoon. Offering choices as such is necessary not only to take into account for varied interests and abilities but also in helping people retain their uniqueness and dignity through having personal choices. As well, the structured day plans help members to stay oriented to time.

The various small group activities offered provide opportunities for mutual aid and the development of friendships. Some 'mass' activities are also held, which provide for welcome anonymity, e.g., concerts, bingos, etc. The activity schedule is routinely evaluated as to whether it contains the right mix of physical fitness, music, discussion groups, opportunities for gaining new knowledge and other intellectual challenges, and opportunities for personal growth and self-expression. Inherent in such activities are the opportunities for development of social relationships and self-esteem building.

The so-called management tasks include providing support so that people can meaningfully participate. That is, making arrangements for hearing assistive devices, which help the hearing impaired stay connected in discussion groups; arranging for people to be taken in wheelchairs to the dining room for those who find it too exhausting to walk there; and staff taking turns as programme reminders to help individuals get to programmes they have previously selected.

D. Group Work

The task of each social worker is to assist in establishing a culture of a community of mutual aid and support (Gitterman 1989; Miller and Solomon, 1980). In the DCP, this culture is operationalized by each of the staff with members of their own caseloads in a meeting called 'the morning meeting group.' While this morning meeting group has seemingly loose cohesion, its boundaries are very clear. Specifically, everyone in the DCP belongs to a morning meeting group led by their social worker and is entitled and expected to attend. The introduction of a new member to the group is the beginning of the socialization process to the culture of the therapeutic community.

As with traditional groups, the morning meeting group has certain rituals, e.g., taking attendance and reporting by the staff and members on absent members, plans for visiting people who are ill by members of the group, opportunities for members to congratulate one another on happy events in their lives, i.e., birth of a new great-grandchild, etc. In those groups where there are persons with short-term memory problems or beginning Alzheimer's, the worker announces the day, date and time.

Day care social workers also lead groups for members who may not be on their caseloads. In discussion groups, such as reminiscence programmes and current events, frequent synopses of content by the group leader compensates for short-term memory loss by some members. In all of the groups a strong leadership role is played by the social worker. This is usually different from group work done with other age groups where the worker normally acts as a resource person and, through process, the group develops ownership of itself (Weisman and Schwartz, 1989). Acknowledgement of dependency of older adults by the worker 'pays homage to the principle of beginning where people are' (Miller and Solomon, 1980).

E. Supervision

Not all the activities of the DCP require leadership by a social worker. Some activities are more suitable for recreation workers, adult educators and specialists in areas such as arts and crafts, horticulture, music, etc. (Briggs et al., 1973). The role of the social worker in supervising specialists and group leaders then becomes: 1) to act as a resource person; 2) to provide them with materials that they need to carry out the programme; 3) to establish expectations of involving everyone in the group; and 4) to ensure that they use appropriate supports so that members can have a sense of achievement and purpose they value. All group leaders (as well as bus drivers) are expected to report any changes they may see in participants to alert social workers and staff who may need to discuss such concerns with staff and family members.

F. Casework and Case Management

All participants in the DCP require 'private time' with their social worker to discuss concerns and issues that have arisen in their lives. For some people, the providing of individual attention is enough. Often, however, a counselling relationship is required wherein the social worker may assist a client, for example, to come to grips with attitudes and behaviours that may be preventing them from finding acceptance or friends in the DCP (Gitterman and Shulman, 1986). As well, frail adults in the programme may be concerned about their future living arrangements and may require help in planning for institutionalization.

The role of the social worker is to help sort out immediate needs with the individual, his or her family and to enable the family to provide additional supports for the individual when needed. Thus, the social worker deals with differences and conflicts within the family, ambivalence around plans and generally helps the individual and family sort out together what their next steps will be. As such, the worker provides casework for the individual and family within the context of the DCP.

As a case manager, the social worker ensures that the living arrangements for the individual are satisfactory and that the client has the financial resources to live with dignity. For those who have no family, the social worker makes arrangements for community supports such as welfare, meals-on-wheels, medical services or the involvement of the public trustee (Burack-Weiss, 1988). Finally, in this regard, the day care social worker may not be the individual's case manager. Some individuals may have case managers in other agencies and this then involves the day care social worker in periodic inter-agency consultations. By referring members to other services in the community as such, the social worker acts as an advocate for the client.

Potential for Role Development

An increasingly frail and medically unstable clientele will inevitably involve the DCP in providing some nursing services. Presently, members attend certain out-patient clinics in the hospital referred to by their personal physicians and facilitated by their social worker. The trend toward meeting both health and social needs of older adults will require social workers in this setting to become skilled in interdisciplinary and holistic treatment, which is needs driven. It sounds simple but it is not, as both the service delivery system and changing client needs present enormous challenges to social workers attempting to provide the best services possible. As well, it is our perception that the demand for day care will increase as there is a strong preference in the community for community-based care over institutional care (Wood, 1989).

Finally, one of the objectives of any day care programme is to provide respite to families. Families report that the DCP does provide some respite for them but not enough. The agency as a whole does not provide for weekend, evening or holiday care, or provide a bed for a relative who needs care while the caregiver has to go to hospital. It appears then that social workers will need to conduct more research on the hours of day care needed and other types of respite care required by families in an age when many caregivers are working and under stress (Capitan, 1989).

Concluding Remarks

Very briefly, in working with the very old the roles, functions and activities of a worker differ from those used with younger age groups. Specifically, the salient features are:

- A longer pre-affiliation process with 'mini-contracts' with the worker and assurance of retaining control over the decision (on behalf of the client).
- Full and active involvement of the family in the process.
- A structured programme.
- Proactive involvement of the worker in providing support for participants to use the programme and interact with one another.

The challenges and opportunities for social work in this field are many and varied and require a social worker who has a humanistic touch and competent skills. Only then can the rewards in working in this field be truly realized.

Case Example

1. Intake

Respecting the client's right to make her or his own decision often produces serious problems for families who must also be helped to trust the process and allow for the careful working through of the decision. This example illustrates this point.

Mrs. Smith was referred by the social service department of a local hospital where she had been briefly hospitalized. The family had been referred by her physician because of their concern about the mother living alone and their frustration in dealing with her. An overweight, alert and strong-willed person, Mrs. Smith had been insistent on living alone, even though she was unable to cope in many areas of functioning and was increasingly dependent upon her four children, especially her two daughters. At the same time she was becoming increasingly more resistive to her children's suggestions and directions about her life situation.

The family eagerly accepted referral to Baycrest Day Care Service. We first saw Mrs. Smith once in her own apartment to demonstrate our interest to her. However, it took a long period of very careful work with the family (and between the hospital worker and the DCP) and with Mrs. Smith to get her into the office for an appointment.

Fearful of engagement, she contended, against all evidence, that she could manage well on her own in her one-bedroom apartment. She also indicated that she was not isolated or lacking the company of friends or relatives. She even claimed her children told her that she did not need day care, much to her children's consternation. One by one we began to deal with Mrs. Smith's many fears. She believed agreeing to day care was consenting to the first step in a dreaded admission to the home for the aged, which she could correctly sense her children wanted. Thus, we initially needed to help the children realize that admission to the home was not needed and to assure their mother that they were not making any arrangements for her 'behind her back.' Mrs. Smith also seemed surprised to learn that over 50 percent of the members in day care at that time were not applicants and did not want the home, nor were we (the programme) interested in either their business or hers.

We then began to systematically confront some of Mrs. Smith's distorted ideas about the people who attended the DCP. In her mind, they were all old and 'senile.'

In reality, very frightened by her obvious decreasing ability to function, she tried to cope by denying this both to herself and her family. This, of course, would provoke her children into furious and frustrating arguments with her. Attacking this defence only made her more unreasonable and suspicious of their efforts. On their part, they thought she was becoming 'senile,' making her feel that they regarded her as childish and incompetent. In helping to realize that she was frightened and comforting herself by her pretence enabled the children to back off, not necessarily changing their minds about what was good for her but simply giving their opinions and leaving their mother room and time to think through and decide what she wanted to do. As well, they were instructed not to attempt to answer her questions or criticisms about the DCP, but to refer them to us directly.

At the same time, Mrs. Smith was encouraged to come and see for herself what day care was and then make up her own mind about the programme. The fact that coming to the office for an appointment did *not* obligate her to the programme was an important component in this early process.

Subsequently, she did come in to discuss and then to see part of the programme, being constantly assured that she would not be pushed into doing or deciding anything until *she* was ready. She was, however, challenged to see and to test out some of the programmes. Thus, she went to a concert, tried crafts, an indoor gardening group and a current events discussion group. When she met some people whom she knew, she extended her testing time to finally participate in an admission interview with the director of day care and then included whole day visits in the DCP, on a trial basis.

Alert, intelligent and very able to socialize, she met and made friends in the programme, and agreed that she enjoyed it. It took somewhat over four months from the time the hospital first called us until Mrs. Smith began to come regularly to the DCP. She needed to be seen regularly although not frequently. Periodically, she questioned whether she needed day care or whether physically it was too much for her or whether it wasn't a step into the home after all.

Her relationship with her children and, in particular, with her two daughters, improved greatly. Mrs. Smith was no longer angry with them and they were relaxed and more comfortable with her. She now has some part of her life that is pretty well under her control and about which she can talk when they come. Everyone seems satisfied to leaving her living situation as it presently is.

2. Group Orientation

The intake worker brought Mrs. Smith into my morning meeting on her first full day visit. I settled the other members (of the programme) into the circle and proceeded with the taking of attendance. I placed Mrs. James beside me because she appreciates it when I cue her when she is wandering off topic. This is an arrangement that she and I have because she finds it embarrassing but sometimes can't help herself.

I told the group that Mrs. Simpson, who had fallen ill, was getting better and was now ready to receive visitors. Mrs. Berger said, "I want to go, but I can't go today because there is something I'm supposed to be doing." Mrs. Johnson, who is very shy, signalled to me that she wanted to say something. I asked everyone to listen to her. She said, "today is the day that we are selling daffodils for the Cancer Society and you are supposed to help." Mrs. Berger said, "Oh, that's right, I knew there was something." I brought everyone back to the subject of visiting Mrs. Simpson. Mrs. Green then said, "I want to go too, to visit her, but I want to hear that speaker on the new tax, I don't know what it's all about." I said that today is a problem for everyone and its probably too soon to visit anyway. Mrs. Berger said, "Well you know we can go next Monday," and three ladies, Mrs. Berger, Mrs. Johnson and Mrs. Herman, asked me to make the arrangements for the visit.

I turned to Mrs. Deven and said, "You were saying something about the new tax." Mrs. Deven said, "I know there is going to be a new tax and they are even going to be taxing funerals." Everyone in the room gasped. Mr. Goldberg said, "You don't have to worry about it right away, they're not putting the tax on until next year. If you die this year you don't have to pay it." Mrs. Deven said, "That's good, if we don't want to pay the tax we will either have to live forever or die this year." Everybody laughed and I was delighted to see that Mrs. Smith 'got the joke' and was looking with interest at Mrs. Deven who did not fit Mrs. Smith's image of a 'senile' day care member at all.

At this time I said I wanted to introduce the new visitor to the members. I introduced Mrs. Smith, as a first-time full day visitor to our morning meeting group. The members immediately responded by applauding with some smiling and nodding their heads in welcome.

Since this was Mrs. Smith's first full day, I asked the group if they would help her understand what day care was all about. Several of the members talked about their favourite programmes. Mrs. Ray told Mrs. Smith that day care was important because some people needed help, and she could help them by showing them where arts and crafts were when they couldn't remember, or sometimes by pushing somebody in a wheelchair when they were tired. This was an important statement for Mrs. Ray who, in making it, reaffirmed her contract with day care.

Everybody joined in and as the discussion warmed up several people stated that it was very lonely at home. Many said that coming to day care was wonderful because they made friends here and felt they were with their 'family.'

Mrs. Smith appeared to feel a response was expected of her at this time. She said that she had a wonderful family, but they were pushing her to come to day care and she was sure that they were trying in this way to get her into the home for the aged. Mr. Kane hadn't quite grasped what Mrs. Smith had said so I repeated it. Mr. Kane laughed, he said, "Listen, I have been waiting to get into the Home for nearly two years, it's not so easy to get in and they aren't going to take you if you don't want to go, so don't worry."

Mrs. Deven said, "What's it like for you at home anyway? You've got lots of company and you are busy all day?" Mrs. Smith's eyes filled and she said, "No, it really is very lonely." She had promised her family that she would try day care. The members rushed in their eagerness to assure her that she would love day care. After all she would be in their group with their social worker, Jane, who was "wonderful and does everything for us, so you don't have to worry." I assured Mrs. Smith that I was there to help her, but that was only part of what happens in day care. I turned to the group and said, "Please explain to Mrs. Smith how you help each other." Mrs. Berman said, "We help each other by listening to people who get sad." She looked pointedly at Mrs. Lee who said, "Yes, Mrs. Berman listens to me when I'm not feeling well and it makes me feel better." Mr. Goldberg said, "Jane can't do everything. We come to day care to help each other. I myself, am helpful to everybody and I have met some nice people here." Mrs. Davis, eager to be included among the helpful said, "I phoned Mrs. Simpson and she was happy to hear from me. She sends everybody regards." I intervened at this point and said, "Mrs. Smith you hear what the members are saying, I am here to help you, but they are explaining what day care is all about, it is helping each other. If you decide to become a member, you will want to help others and welcome their help when you need it." Mrs. Smith nodded and said, "You know, it would be nice maybe to have a life of my own, away from my kids, and it may be good to do something for somebody else and feel like a person again, but I don't know anybody here really, and everything seems so strange." I turned to the group and asked them to think back to their first full day in day care. The members started to compete with each other about who felt worse on their first day. "Mrs. Smith, when you get to know us," said Mrs. Gould, "you will want to become a member." I said we all hoped she would join the programme and that she would be in charge of that decision herself.

I told Mrs. Smith that she would be seated at the same table with Mrs. Deven and Mrs. Lee, and I wondered if the ladies would like to show her where the table was. I also explained that she would be at that table every time she came to day care, if she liked it. Mrs. Smith said, "I'm still not sure, but I am going to try it anyway."

In summary, the two-sided struggle (for Mrs. Smith) involved in both owning her need and risking the pursuit of help is necessary to enter the increasingly more demanding 'mini-contracts' used for appointments and for programme visits, admission interview and then for full day trials. Specifically, owning one's needs and 'risking trying' are necessary pre-conditions if the applicant is to derive the ego-supportive social experiences she or he requires from the programme. As indicated many times in this chapter, our goal is to empower the client and her or his family system to achieve a fuller balance in their lives.

References

Adler, B., Baltzan, N. and Smyth, S. (1987). Is there anything in it for you? Helping an elderly client explore a group oriented day program. Older people in groups: The social work focus. *Proceedings of 9th Social Work Clinic Day*, Baycrest Centre for Geriatric Care.

Adult Day Care A Mutual Support Community. (1982). *Proceedings Social Work Clinic Day*, Baycrest Centre for Geriatric Care.

Briggs, T.L., et al. (1973). An overview of social work teams, the team model of social work practice. *Manpower Monograph, 5*, Syracuse University, School of Social Work.

Brunnington, H. and Huffington, C. (1985, July). Altered images: Role overlap, professional rivalry and poor communication can all lead to conflict between professionals in a multidisciplinary team, *Nursing Times*, 81(31).

Burack-Weiss, A. (1988, Fall). Clinical aspects of case management. *Generations*, 12(5)

Capitan, J.A. (1989, October). Day care programs and research challenges. *The Gerontologist*, 29(5).

Clark, P.G., et al. (1987). Challenges and barriers to interdisciplinary team training in the academic setting. *Gerontology and Geriatrics Education*, 7(3/4).

Gitterman, A. (1989). Building mutual support in groups. *Social Work with Groups*, 12(2).

Gitterman, A. and Shulman, L. (1986). The skills of helping individuals and groups (2nd ed.). Itasca, IL: F.E. Peacock Publishers Inc.

Kane, Rosalie, A. (1975). Interprofessional teamwork. *Manpower Monograph*, 8, Syracuse University, School of Social Work.

Miller, B. (1989). Adult children's perceptions of caregiver stress and satisfaction. *Journal of Applied Gerontology*, 8(3), National Institute of Adult Day Care, Washington, D.C.

Miller, I. and Solomon, R. (1980). The development of group services for the elderly. *Journal of Gerontological Social Work*, 2(3).

National Institute of Adult Day Care (1979). An update on gerontological services for the elderly in America. U.S. Council on Aging, Washington, D.C.

Scharlach, A. (1989). Social group work with the elderly: A role theory perspective. *Social Work with Groups*, 12(3).

Schwartz, W. and Zalba, S. (eds.) (1971). *The practice of group work*. New York: Columbia University Press.

Shulman, L. (1984). *The skills of helping individuals and groups*. Itasca, IL: F.E. Peacock Publishers Inc.

Weisman, C. and Schwartz, P. (1989, November). Worker expectation in group work with the frail elderly: Modifying the models for a better fit. *Social Work with Groups*, 12(3).

Weissert, W. et al. (1989, October). Models of adult day care. *The Gerontologist*, 25(5).

Wood, J. (1989). The emergence of adult day care centres as post-acute care agencies. *Journal of Aging and Health*, 1(4).

Chapter 14

Social Work Practice with Family Caregivers of Frail Older Persons[1,2]

Ronald W. Toseland, Ph.D.
Charles M. Rossiter, Ph.D.

*T*his chapter begins with a review of the major issues and concerns facing family caregivers of frail older persons. Described next are generic social work roles and responsibilities, as well as consultation, coordination and management, three specific social work roles that are commonly used in work with family caregivers and frail older persons. Opportunities for social workers in outreach, supervision, coordination and delivery of services, particularly as they relate to the needs of underserved family caregivers are also described. The chapter ends with three case examples illustrating the three previously discussed social work practice roles.

Family caregivers represent a large and growing clientele whose needs for social services will increase dramatically in the coming decades. In America, it is estimated that nearly 5.1 million older persons living in the community need assistance with some aspects of personal care or home management activities (AARP, 1986). These needs range from occasional assistance with specific tasks, such as shopping or household chores, to around the clock monitoring of serious health problems. Because chronic and acute health problems increase in frequency and intensity with advancing age, and as the population itself ages, the number of older people needing assistance will increase dramatically in future years and family caregivers will provide most of this care.

The Clientele

Close family members, particularly spouses and adult daughters, are the most likely to assist frail elderly with physical and emotional needs. Shanas (1968) suggested that the decision about who will provide care follows a 'principle of substitution.' If a spouse is available, he or she is most likely to provide care. If a spouse is unavailable, an adult daughter is most likely to become the primary caregiver. In the absence of adult daughters, daughter-in-laws, sons, son-in-laws or other relatives, neighbours or friends are most likely to provide care.

A recent national survey (Stone, Cafferata and Sangl, 1987) has provided helpful data about family caregivers. Most caregivers are female and between the ages of 40 and 65. Their average age is 57.3 years. One third are over 65. Many have some chronic health problems themselves. Most are wives (29 percent) or adult daughters (23 percent). Most are white, although 20 percent are non-white. A majority (57 percent) report low or middle incomes, and nearly a third (31.5 percent) report income at poverty or near poverty levels.

The average age of the frail elderly who are the recipients of family care is 78. Twenty percent are over 85. The majority (60 percent) are female. About half are married (51.3 percent), but many (41.3 percent) are widowed. Only 11 percent live alone. The remainder live with spouses, children or other family members.

I. The Effects of Caregiving

The effects of providing care for a frail older family member are many and complex, yet caregiving can be a rewarding and fulfilling experience. Whether done out of love, a sense of responsibility, perceived obligation to restore equity in interpersonal and inter-generational relationships, compassion, guilt, the expectation of reward or a complex combination of reasons, caregiving can have a variety of beneficial effects.

Caregiving provides a meaningful role and an important purpose for some caregivers. There is often a heightened sense of self-esteem and self-worth because caregivers feel they are 'doing the right thing,' and are doing it with altruistic motives. Caregivers take pride in their efforts and feel good about being able to help. Pride and satisfaction are enhanced when caregivers are praised for their efforts by family members, friends and others whose opinions they hold in high regard.

At the same time, social workers should be aware that caregiving can be extremely demanding and extremely stressful. Caregiving often involves a long-term commitment, which taxes the resources of the caregiver. The average caregiver devotes four hours each day to caregiving. Twenty percent of all caregivers in the previously mentioned national survey provided care for five or more years, 80 percent provided care seven days a week and virtually all spousal caregivers reported daily caregiving (Stone, Cafferata and Sangl, 1987).

Caregiving demands can create stresses that overburden caregivers and endanger their well-being. Stress is "a relationship between the person and the environment that is appraised by the person as taxing or exceeding his or her resources and endangering his or her well-being" (Lazarus and Folkman, 1984, p. 21). A number of elements of the caregiving situation contribute to the stress experienced by family caregivers.

Uncertainty is a major factor. Frail elderly needing care are usually in a condition of declining health. As the care receiver's health status worsens, new demands are made on the caregiver, which, in turn, often necessitate changes in the relationship between the caregiver and the care receiver. For example, an adult child may have to learn new ways to relate to an increasingly dependent parent. Spouses may have to learn to live without some pleasurable aspects of their marriage relationship, which ailing partners can no longer provide. To be effective in working with caregivers, social workers in health care settings should be sensitive to the shifting dynamics of the caregiver-care receiver relationship and the profound psychological adjustments that have to be made as the care receiver's health status changes.

Middle-aged women, a group that includes the majority of caregivers, are particularly vulnerable to the stresses of caregiving (Brody, 1981; Fengler and Goodrich, 1979). In addition to the changing nature of their relationship with the care receiver, adult children often have to cope with the demands of work and their own family. Many caregivers are employed outside the home either full-time or part-time (Stone, Cafferata and Sangl, 1987; Toseland, Rossiter and Labrecque, 1992). Employed caregivers must make adjustments in their work schedules to fulfil their caregiving responsibilities. Stone, Cafferata and Sangl (1987) found that nine percent of caregivers quit their jobs in order to provide care, and over half said the demands of caregiving required them to reduce the hours they work, to rearrange their work schedules or to take time off without pay.

Stress from caregiving can have a negative effect on caregivers' psychological, social and physical well-being. Depression, the most frequently cited symptom of caregiver stress, has been estimated as high as 52 percent (Sanford, 1975). In addition to depression, some caregivers are troubled by anxiety, anger, frustration and excessive guilt and self-blame. In a recent study, when caregivers were asked what problems resulting from caregiving troubled them the most, psychological problems were mentioned more than twice as often as any other type of problem (Toseland, Rossiter, Labrecque and Beckstead, 1988).

The sources of emotional distress for caregivers are complex. Many caregivers feel guilty about how they are performing their caregiving duties. They believe they are not doing enough for the care receiver. Others feel guilty about the feelings they have about caregiving. For example, they may feel anger or frustration because of demands made by the care receiver and then, later, feel guilty for their anger.

A general sense of anxiety and worry often permeates the caregiving situation (Hasselkus, 1988). Caregivers worry about the health of the care receiver. Little changes, such as the development of a small sore or refusal to eat a meal, can be frightening, as any small change may be an early warning of further decline in the care receiver's health. Caregivers worry that a decline in their own health might interfere with their ability to fulfil essential tasks for a frail family member. Social workers can help caregivers reduce their feelings of worry and anxiety by enabling them to ventilate their concerns, to sort out realistic and unrealistic fears and to develop plans for coping with emergency situations that may arise.

Caregiving can also contribute to social and interpersonal problems. Leisure and recreational activities are often restricted. Caregivers frequently feel socially isolated, lonely and trapped (Farkas, 1980). Conflicts with other family members about caregiving responsibilities are common (Cantor, 1983). For example, some caregivers express resentment toward siblings for 'not doing their fair share.' Others experience interpersonal conflicts with their own children or spouses as increasing demands are placed on their time by a deteriorating care receiver. Caregivers sometimes express this latter problem to social workers by stating that they are in a 'no win situation,' caught between the competing needs and demands of different family members while feeling that they have no time for themselves. At such times, it can be helpful for social workers to suggest one or more family meetings in which concerns are shared, conflicts are de-escalated and family members are helped to work together to improve problematic aspects of the caregiving situation.

Disturbance of normal sleep patterns, lack of appetite and psychosomatic complaints are also frequently experienced by overburdened caregivers (Golodetz, et al., 1969). In addition, lifting, transporting and other physically demanding aspects of certain caregiving situations can cause physical injuries. Many caregivers have little or no prior experience in providing care and are not aware of the most effective or efficient home care techniques. Social workers can assist caregivers with the physical demands of caregiving by encouraging them: 1) to develop a plan for taking better care of themselves, 2) to obtain periodic respites from caregiving, 3) to acquire the knowledge and skills necessary to perform home health care tasks without endangering their own health and 4) to utilize available home health care resources to supplement their own caregiving efforts.

Practice Roles and Responsibilities

Social work practice roles and responsibilities with caregivers are similar to those engaged in with other client groups. For example, social workers establish therapeutic relationships, assess needs and plan, implement and monitor intervention plans as they would with other client groups (Pinkston, et al., 1982; Rubin, 1987). However, specific adaptations in these roles and responsibilities are needed when serving caregivers.

I. Engaging the client

Making initial contact with caregivers is sometimes difficult. Caregivers are often reluctant to ask for help. Some believe it is their responsibility to provide care and that relinquishing that responsibility would be like abandoning the person for whom they are caring. This is particularly true in certain ethnic groups where family bonds are strong and normative expectations prescribe family caregiving as a duty. Caregivers may never have had to ask for help before and pride may become an obstacle. In other situations, it is the frail older person who resists or refuses 'outside help.'

For all these reasons, it is important for social workers to engage in active outreach efforts, which make information about services and resources for family caregivers available throughout the community. In-person telephone contacts with health, social service, religious and civic organizations, press releases, newspaper stories, appearances on talk shows, public service announcements on radio and television and educational forums and workshops sponsored by community planning agencies are all useful ways to reach out to caregivers (Toseland, 1981).

Social workers must be particularly careful in designing outreach strategies for particular groups of caregivers. For example, black and Hispanic caregivers rarely respond to traditional avenues of publicity used in recruiting participants (Toseland et al., 1988). Extensive personal contacts through established and trusted religious and service organizations in the community are a much better approach to engaging this client group (Garcia-Preto, 1982; Roberts, 1987).

Male caregivers are also difficult to reach. Davies, Priddy and Tinklenberg (1986) found that even though men from a larger caregiver programme had requested a smaller, male-only support group, these men were only willing to participate when they were told that the group was part of a pilot programme to test a new intervention. They were unwilling to join the group for the sole purpose of gaining help for themselves as caregivers.

II. Establishing a Relationship

Once initial contact has been made, the primary job of the social worker is to develop a trusting and supportive relationship with the caregiver. Research suggests that many caregivers are reluctant to admit to difficulties with caregiving, even though they may be nearly overwhelmed by them (Toseland, Rossiter, Labrecque and Beckstead, 1988). We have interviewed caregivers who break down and cry during interviews and say they have not slept well in weeks. Yet when asked about their stress levels, these same caregivers say they experience 'a little' stress. Many caregivers would rather bear their burdens in silence than risk being seen as complaining or uncaring. To make it possible for caregivers to acknowledge and accept their thoughts and feelings about the caregiving situation, social workers should be attentive and empathic listeners.

Caregivers have a strong tendency to believe that those who have never been in their situation cannot possibly understand what they are going through. If the worker has had direct experience with caregiving, appropriately timed self-disclosures can be helpful for universalizing the experience and for increasing trust and promoting client self-disclosure.

In addition to providing an opportunity for ventilation, the worker should be a supporter and an enabler. As a supporter, the worker provides encouragement and validation. Many caregivers are unnecessarily critical of themselves. They believe that they are not doing all they could do in the caregiving role. They also tend not to take as good care of themselves as they could, foregoing their own needs for those of the care receiver and other family members. As a supporter, the worker applauds any indication that the caregiver is taking better care of herself or feeling better about how well she is providing care. The worker also validates and elucidates more fully the caregiver's experiences so that the caregiver can better accept negative feelings such as anger or frustration with the care receiver.

As an enabler, the worker encourages change by helping the caregiver to become motivated to mobilize social resources to improve a problematic situation. To function effectively as an enabler, the worker must be aware of available community services that caregivers and care receivers are likely to need. The worker should also be aware of eligibility requirements and other difficulties in accessing services.

The worker may help a client complete necessary paperwork to obtain services or go to an agency with the client to provide support and assistance during the application process. In some situations, the worker may also act as an advocate for the client, helping her to obtain services that are not readily available.

III. Assessing the Situation

As the caregiver discloses information about herself and her situation, the worker assesses her needs. Assessment of the caregiving situation includes not only understanding the caregiver and the care receiver but also their relationship to each other, to other family members and to the larger society. Ideally, social work assessments should include a thorough examination of the current physical, psychological, emotional, social, financial and environmental status of the caregiver and the care receiver and their life situation. Any pertinent historical data bearing on the current situation should also be ascertained. For a detailed discussion of comprehensive assessment techniques for the frail elderly see Kane (1985) or Kane and Kane (1981).

In many health care settings, it is important for social workers to coordinate their assessments with allied health personnel. For example, important information about the course of a specific illness, the effects of medications and the physical limitations and abilities of the care receiver may be provided by doctors, nurses and physical therapists. For this reason, comprehensive assessments of the caregiving situation are sometimes best made by a health care team.

As team members, social workers may be expected to focus their assessment on certain dimensions of the caregiver or care receiver functioning. For example, the social worker may be the member of a team who is responsible for gathering pertinent data about the caregiver's social support networks. To gather such data, the social worker might inquire about the individuals who comprise the caregiver's support network and the quality of existing relationships with these individuals. The social worker might also assess the extent to which the caregiver is satisfied with existing informal social supports and whether the caregiver is motivated to reach out for additional support. The social worker uses this information, with information obtained from other team members, in the development of a comprehensive assessment of a caregiver's situation.

IV. Developing an Action Plan

Based on the needs and desires of the caregiver and the care receiver, an intervention plan is developed. A major decision in developing an action plan is what mode of intervention would be most beneficial. For caregivers with very high levels of psychological stress, those with very personal issues or those who are not ready to share their experiences with a group, individual counselling may be most appropriate. In contrast, family or couple counselling may be most appropriate in situations where interpersonal tensions and conflicts predominate (Horowitz, 1985). Recent research indicates that support groups may be particularly useful for reducing feelings of loneliness and isolation and for increasing social support (Gallagher, Rose, Rivera, Lovett and Thompson, 1992; Greene and Monahan, 1987; Montgomery, 1988; Toseland, Rossiter, Labrecque and Beckstead, 1988). Participation in a support group helps caregivers to feel understood and supported by others in similar situations.

Another important decision when developing an action plan is determining the most appropriate role to take in a particular situation. A social worker may play three primary roles: consultant, coordinator and manager. Each of these roles requires different actions and responsibilities on the part of the caregiver and the worker, which are summarized in Table 1.

Table 1 was developed to distinguish and highlight the differences in the three roles. In actual practice, in many health care settings social workers are expected to move comfortably from one role to another depending on the changing needs and evolving health status. At one point in time, the worker may act as a consultant. Later, the worker may act as a manager. With some family caregivers, the social worker may actually play different roles with the same person. For a particular concern, a family caregiver may only need consultation to be able to cope with or resolve a problem. However, for another concern, the caregiver may need the social worker to act as a coordinator.

Table 1 — Social Work Roles and Responsibilities when Working with Family Caregivers

Selected Decision Criteria	Consultation	Coordination	Management
Type of Caregiver	An independent, responsible, dedicated, informed caregiver with time, energy and competence to cope with the situation and to meet the care receiver's needs.	A competent caregiver seeking assistance because she is becoming overwhelmed with duties and responsibilities and needs help on a regular basis.	Unable to fulfil many caregiving duties; e.g., caregiver out-of-town and unable to take care of many of the day-to-day needs of the care receiver.
Need for Outreach	Greatest.	Intermediate.	Least.
Responsibility for Care	Primarily with the caregiver.	Shared between caregiver and social worker.	Primarily with social worker.
Assessment	Caregiver plays a major role by providing information about the care receiver's condition.	Social worker and caregiver jointly access situation.	Social worker plays a major role in determining accuracy of information.
Development of Action Plan	Caregiver in consultation with social worker.	Social worker in consultation and collaboration with the caregiver.	Social worker responsibility in consultation with caregiver/receiver.
Implementation of Action Plan	Social worker maintains occasional contact on an 'as needed' basis.	Social worker provides some services and helps caregiver and care receiver to utilize other community services as needed.	Social worker delivers or arranges for the delivery of services to the care receiver.
Monitoring Action Plan	Caregiver monitors situation and requests support, information and help gaining access to services as needed.	Caregiver monitors care plan day-to-day, social worker maintains regular contact monitoring situation and the delivery of services.	Social worker monitors day-to-day situation of care receiver, co-ordinates services and arranges for services as needed.

V. Consultant Role

The social worker should consider adopting the consultant role in situations where the caregiver is an independent, responsible, dedicated person who: 1) prefers to take primary responsibility for the care receiver's needs without deferring to outside help, 2) is coping effectively and 3) has been assessed by the social worker as in need of relatively little assistance. When deciding on whether the consultant role is most appropriate, the social worker assesses the caregivers' capacities and abilities, as well as their current level of functioning. The social worker should also assess the client's willingness to ask for help when needed. Because of heavy caseloads, social workers may not be able to contact the client very frequently. Therefore, before assuming a consultant role, social workers should assess whether or not they can rely on the client to acknowledge a need and request appropriate help.

The worker must also consider the ethical issue involved in deciding whether to adopt the consultant role or a more active role. Ethical issues often arise when, in the worker's judgment, clients could benefit from more help than they think they need. A general practice principle that applies in this situation is that, unless caregivers or care receivers are in jeopardy of endangering themselves or some other third party, the client's request for autonomy should be respected. The worker should also guard against adopting a consultant role because of caseload considerations.

Because caregivers who are independent and competent feel the least need for assistance, active outreach is often needed to inform them about community resources and services that may be helpful to them in their current situation or in the future. But no matter how this group of caregivers comes into contact with social workers, Table 1 clearly indicates that the responsibility for providing care and ensuring the well-being of the care receiver remains primarily with the caregiver.

When social workers adopt a consultant role, the caregiver is expected to play a major role in the assessment process. The worker recognizes that the caregiver is intimately familiar with the situation and can provide information about the care receiver's functioning in a variety of areas. Because caregivers in this category are responsible and competent, they are relatively reliable and accurate sources of information on which the social worker heavily depends.

As a consultant, the social worker may be asked to help the caregiver and the care receiver with a wide variety of environmental, social, behaviourial and emotional problems. Tonti and Silverstone (1985) indicate that some of the more frequent are helping with: 1) the nursing home placement decisions, 2) adjustments in living status such as when a frail older person moves from her own home to her daughter's home, 3) behaviourial and emotional problems, 4) resistance to some aspect of what the caregiver believes is in the best interest of care receiver, 5) alcoholism and 6) mental impairments such as Alzheimer's disease.

When developing and implementing action plans, social workers who are acting as consultants rely heavily on caregivers' input. For example, a caregiver requests information about a day care centre that the worker had mentioned during a previous contact. When the worker provides the information, the caregiver indicates that she will contact the centre and enrol her mother. As consultant, the social worker supports the caregiver and informs her that she is available should any obstacles be encountered when attempting to obtain the service.

Social workers may adopt a consulting role following a period of more active intervention. In the consultant role, social workers sometimes maintain occasional contact to assure that the situation remains stable, to offer information and advice or to help the caregiver connect with needed services. At other times, workers respond on an 'as needed' basis with information, advice and other help that is requested by the caregiver.

VI. Coordinator Role

Because of the care receiver's situation or the caregiver's ability or willingness, more assistance may be needed than can be provided by a consultant. Some caregivers have provided care for many years without the need for the assistance of a coordinator but then become overwhelmed by their duties and responsibilities. The care receiver's physical or mental condition may deteriorate or the caregiver's abilities may become diminished by health problems or increased responsibilities at work or at home. For caregivers who are overburdened and finding it difficult to cope with increasing stress, the social worker should consider adopting the role of coordinator.

Table 1 indicates that outreach efforts can be a little less active with this group of caregivers than with those who can benefit from consultant services only. Stress resulting from feeling overburdened is more likely to motivate caregivers in this group to seek services for the care receiver or for themselves. Another reason why outreach does not have to be as active with this group of caregivers is that they are more likely to be receiving services, and referrals from health care and social service providers are likely to be more frequent.

In the coordinator role, the worker and the caregiver share responsibility for ensuring that the care receiver is receiving needed services in a well-planned fashion. In assessing the situation, social workers should gather as much data from the caregiver as possible. However, they are more likely when acting as a consultant to make independent assessments of caregivers' and care receivers' abilities.

In the coordinator role, the social worker may provide needed services such as individual, family or group counselling. For example, the worker might provide brief family counselling to reduce conflicts about caregiving responsibilities in the family and to develop a more complete and coordinated plan of care.

The social worker helps to arrange for whatever services the caregiver needs by being an enabler, a broker or an advocate. The worker also helps the caregiver to arrange for services for the care receiver. This might include helping the caregiver to develop a written schedule of informal and formal services (Toseland, Derico and Owen, 1984). Such a schedule could be posted on a refrigerator or a bulletin board so that appointments for different services will not be confused or improperly scheduled.

Once the services for the caregiver and the care receiver are in place, the worker generally maintains regular contact with the caregiver. However, the caregiver continues to take the day-to-day responsibility for the functioning of the care receiver and for the appropriate provision of services. As coordinator, the worker makes sure that any difficulties the caregiver is having in fulfilling these responsibilities are resolved during their regular meetings.

Since the caregivers and care receivers with whom a worker might function as a coordinator differ greatly in their levels of stress, capabilities and needs, it is important for the worker to consider each caregiver's short- and long-term needs. For example, if the caregiver is an older person who has chronic health problems, the worker might need to maintain more frequent contact than with a caregiver in better health.

VII. Management Role

The management role is differentiated from the coordinator and the consultant role by the degree to which the caregiver is involved in the plan of care for the care receiver and in the implementation and monitoring of that plan. When caregivers are unable to fulfil duties and responsibilities necessary for the care of frail older persons in their family, social workers who are managers ensure that proper care is provided.

As Table 1 indicates, there is frequently less need for outreach with this kind of caregiver and care receiver because many are already in contact with health and social services for chronic health problems before their need for management arises. In other situations, acute medical problems bring older persons who are unable to care for themselves into contact with medical social workers.

In the management role, the worker takes primary responsibility for helping the care receiver live independently in the community. After gathering information from the caregiver and the care receiver, the worker makes independent assessments of the condition of the caregiver and the care receiver and determines what services, if any, are needed. To whatever extent possible, the practitioner involves the caregiver and care receiver in the development and implementation of the action plan. The social worker then either provides the needed services or obtains whatever services are needed and sees to it that these services are administered in a timely, efficient and effective manner.

As a manager, the social worker is expected to: 1) develop a comprehensive assessment of the client without relying solely on the judgments of a family member who may not be able to fully provide what the care receiver needs, 2) develop a comprehensive plan for the care of the frail older person whose needs can not be fully provided for by a care receiver, 3) implement the plan by providing and coordinating health and social services to meet the needs of the caregiver and the care receiver, 4) monitor the situation to ensure that the caregiver and the care receiver are receiving services that are appropriate (Steinberg, 1985; Steinberg and Carter, 1983; Johnson and Rubin, 1983).

In the management role, workers maintain frequent and regular contact with care receivers to make sure their needs are being met.

Continuous monitoring is important because, unlike in the coordinator or consultant role, the manager can't rely on a family caregiver to monitor the day-to-day situation or to take appropriate action should problems arise in the delivery of services. As manager, the worker either provides all needed services for the care receiver or ensures that they are being provided by informal caregivers or by professional health care and social service providers.

Potential for Role Development

There is great potential for the development of social work with family caregivers, particularly in the following areas: 1) home health care, 2) collaborative work with peer helpers, 3) outreach and 4) the development and management of caregiver support programmes.

The anticipated increase in the elderly population, particularly the old-old, in the next 40 years, means that there will be a greater need for home care services in the future. Social work services are an important component of comprehensive home care. Therefore, as the population ages, the social work role in home health care should increase dramatically, unless social work services are performed by other professional helpers. This is a real possibility as nurses and psychologists trained in community work are now performing many of the tasks traditionally considered to be a part of the social work domain.

Working with peer helpers is a second expanding area for social workers. There are thousands of self-help support groups for caregivers sponsored by organizations such as the Alzheimer's Disease and Related Disorders Association. Working with peer helpers requires a relationship that is based on mutual respect. Social workers can build such relationships by reaching out to peer helpers and developing a relationship with them. Ideally, these relationship should be based upon social workers' appreciation of the experience that peers can bring to the situation, the therapeutic benefit of self-help efforts for both the person giving help and the person receiving help and a respect for the autonomy of peer helpers.

There is a also a need for innovative outreach and culturally sensitive intervention programmes in minority ethnic communities.

Cultural differences may influence how minority caregivers respond to efforts to inform them about services and also how they respond to intervention efforts (Haber, 1984; McGadney, Goldberg-Glen and Pinkston, 1987; Taylor and Chatters, 1986). Therefore, development of appropriate, culturally sensitive outreach and intervention programmes is an important, albeit neglected role for social workers.

Fourth, there is an expanding role for social workers in the development and management of caregiver programmes. In future years, there will be an increasing recognition of the importance of family caregivers to the welfare of frail older persons. With this recognition, social workers will be called upon to develop and implement programmes of support to assist caregivers. This, in turn, will require social workers to be familiar with the array of administrative, supervisory and direct service skills that are necessary to develop and manage a social service programme.

Concluding Remarks

The typology of social work roles outlined in Table 1, and described in this chapter, is intended as a heuristic device to elucidate the range of social work practice roles in health care settings with caregivers of frail older persons. In actual practice, the roles may not be so clearly differentiated. The changing needs of caregivers and care receivers, the availability and receptivity of different referral sources, the degree of emotional burden experienced by caregivers in relation to specific caregiving tasks and responsibilities and a host of other factors often necessitate the use of a mix of roles and practice strategies in a particular situation. Still, the typology that has been presented should serve as a useful guide for social work practitioners deciding on the most appropriate mix of roles and strategies to employ in the complex caregiving situations they confront in many health care practice settings.

Case Example

Social Worker as Consultant

Marie, at 43, is energetic, capable, well educated and in excellent health. She works as a freelance artist and has a self-defined work schedule. Her husband, Earl, owns a small business and his responsibilities allow him to take time off from work when necessary. Since he works only five minutes from home he is available to respond to emergencies that may arise at home.

Marie's mother, Theresa, aged 83, had lived at Marie's brother's house for seven years. While visiting Marie during her son's annual winter Florida vacation, Theresa experienced stomach pains and was taken to the nearby hospital where she was diagnosed as having cancer. Following an operation, which was not able to remove all of the cancer, she moved to Marie's home to be closer to the hospital and to the rest of her family.

The immediate family was highly supportive. Marie's older brother and sister lived approximately a half hour away. Each volunteered to provide respite for Marie and Earl, and each visited with Theresa at least one or two half-days per week while she was in the hospital.

Prior to discharge, the hospital social worker talked with Marie, Theresa and other family members about Theresa's situation. Marie's brother agreed to look after the paperwork, which Theresa had difficulty doing, regarding medical insurance and hospital bills. Marie agreed to have her mother continue to live with her but enquired about a service to 'look in on Theresa' should she suddenly take a turn for the worse.

With the hospital social worker's help, Marie made some phone calls and arranged for services from a local hospice programme. After contacting the hospital social worker and receiving a formal referral, the hospice team initiated regular contact with Theresa. The hospice programme continued to provide services to Theresa, who remained mentally alert and able to ambulate with the assistance of a cane until she died at home, six months later.

Julie is an 82-year-old black woman who is in poor health. Her husband, Jim, has advanced heart disease, diabetes, hearing loss and severe arthritis. The latter problem worries Julie who fears that Jim will try to move about when she is not home, will fall down and hurt himself. Julie has always taken care of Jim and would not consider placing him. Their only child died five years ago in an automobile accident and there are no other immediate family members who live close enough to provide care for Jim. However, Julie has a close friend, Ann, who sometimes watches Jim and is a source of emotional support.

Julie was brought to the social worker's attention by Ann. When Julie refused to go to the community senior centre for their weekly card game, Ann went anyway. She mentioned that Julie seemed as if she was having an increasingly difficult time caring for Jim to a social worker who worked for an affiliated community health centre, which was located directly across the street. The worker contacted Julie who said she was not feeling well and didn't think she had the strength to leave the house. However, since she knew the worker from previous visits to the centre, she agreed to a home visit. During several home visits over the course of a month, the worker concluded that Julie could use some help in caring for Jim. Julie reluctantly agreed to some help as long as she could remain in charge of Jim's care.

In assessing the situation, the worker determined that Jim's increasing deafness was an important problem. The worker consulted a non-profit agency for the deaf and through them arranged for Julie and Jim to acquire a telephone amplifier, a device to allow them to see captioning on television and a light hook-up on the doorbell so that Jim could see that someone was at the door when Julie was not at home.

The couple's financial situation was also problematic. Recently, they had incurred non-reimbursable medical expenses, which their pension and social security cheques did not cover adequately. Accepting any financial assistance was difficult for Julie who had been brought up to believe that a person should avoid being 'on welfare' at all costs. The worker explained to Julie that the taxes she had paid over the years entitled her to financial assistance now that she needed it. With the worker's help, Julie was able to re-frame her situation and realize that to refuse assistance might result in a deterioration of her own health condition or that of her husband's. This, in turn, might cost society even more money in the long term. Therefore, she reluctantly decided to accept the worker's assistance and applied for food stamps and meals on wheels.

Convincing Julie to get out of the house and remain active was another issue that needed to be addressed. Julie's main concern was that Jim would fall down and hurt himself while she was out. The social worker recommended that Julie enrol in Lifeline, a programme sponsored by a local hospital. They fitted Jim with a special device that hung around his neck and connected to the telephone so that he could signal for help at any time.

Julie was also somewhat depressed about her situation. The worker, concluding that Julie was suffering from a mild reactive depression, helped Julie and her friend Ann, who was also a caregiver, to enrol in a support group programme for caregivers sponsored by a nearby family service agency. These sessions, and the other services that were arranged, proved to be very helpful, and soon Julie began going to the senior centre again. The social worker continued to monitor the situation by meeting with Julie at the senior centre on a regular basis but provided no other active support for the three years she remained working for the agency.

Social Worker as Manager

Mary, aged 79, began living independently again after 32 years of hospitalization with a DSM-3 diagnosis of bipolar disorder, depressed. In the early 1970s she was given a trial of lithium, which stabilized her mood swings.

Sarah, Mary's social worker from a social health maintenance organization (SHMO), first met Mary while she was an inpatient. Together with the discharge planning team in the hospital, a small one bedroom apartment was located for Mary with a landlord who had previously rented to former psychiatric patients and was tolerant if not sympathetic to their plight.

Sarah helped Mary to contact her niece, Gwen, who lived about a mile away and who had not seen Mary in about 13 years. Gwen offered to assist Mary in any way possible, although it was clear that Gwen, who worked part-time and had her own family, would not be able to provide a great deal of assistance.

Sarah helped Mary to pay bills and deal with other paperwork, which Mary was not familiar with because she had lived so long as an inpatient. Gradually, Mary learned to handle most of her own affairs, except for complicated paperwork that she sometimes encountered when applying for or receiving health and social services.

Sarah encouraged Mary to enrol in a seniors-only day treatment programme at the health centre. She also helped to arrange for transportation to and from the programme. This arrangement worked quite well. Mary did not experience any difficulty until about 18 months after leaving the hospital. She stopped taking her lithium and soon became quite depressed.

Sarah, who had continued to see Mary on a monthly basis after setting up the day treatment programme, went to see Mary in the hospital and arranged a plan with Mary and Gwen to keep Mary's apartment for one month until she could be stabilized and returned to the community.

Once Mary returned home, Gwen agreed to monitor Mary's medication. Every other day Gwen stopped by to see Mary. She watched while Mary took her medication and she checked on the remaining pills to make sure that Mary was taking the correct dosage when she was not present.

Sarah arranged for Mary to have more frequent checkups to monitor her lithium blood level. She also arranged for Mary to attend the day treatment programme again. As Mary's needs change, with Gwen's help, Sarah will continue to help Mary live independently.

Endnotes

[1]   Preparation of this manuscript was funded through grants from the Prevention Research Branch of the National Institute of Mental Health, the Andrus Foundation of the American Association of Retired Persons and the Health Services Research and Development Office of the Veterans Administration.

[1]   An earlier version of this revised chapter was published in *Social Work Practice in Health Care Settings*, M.J. Holosko and P.A. Taylor (eds.), Canadian Scholars' Press Inc., Toronto, Ontario, 1989, pp. 509-533.

References

AARP. (1986). *A profile of older persons: 1986*. Washington, D.C.: American Association of Retired Persons.

Brody, E. (1981). Women in the middle and family help to older people. *The Gerontologist*, 21, 471-480.

Cantor, M. (1983). Strain among caregivers: A study of experience in the U.S. *The Gerontologist*, 23(6), 597-604.

Davies, H., Priddy, J. M. and Tinklenberg, J. R. (1986). Support groups for male caregivers of Alzheimer's patients. *Clinical Gerontologist*, 5, 385-395.

Farkas, S. (1980). Impact of chronic illness on the patient's spouse. *Health and Social Work*, 5, 39-46.

Fengler, A. and Goodrich, N. (1979). Wives of elderly disabled men: The hidden patient. *The Gerontologist*, 19, 175-183.

Gallagher, D., Lovett, S. and Zeiss. A. (in press). Intervention with caregivers of frail elderly persons. In M. Ory and K. Bond (eds.), *Aging and health care: Social service and policy perspectives*. New York: Tavistock.

Gallagher, D., Rose, J., Rivera, P., Lovett, S. and Thompson, L. W. (1992). Prevalence of depression in family caregivers. *The Gerontologist*.

Garcia-Preto. (1982). Puerto Rican families. In M. McGoldrick, J. Pearce, and J. Giordino, (eds.), *Ethnicity and family therapy* (pp. 164-186). New York: Guilford.

Golodetz, A., Evans, R. Heinritz, G., and Gibson, C. (1969). The care of chronic illness: The responsor role. *Medical Care*, 7, 385-394.

Greene, V. L. and Monahan, D. J. (1987). The effect of professionally guided caregiver support and education group on institutionalization of care receivers. *The Gerontologist*, 27, 716-721.

Haber, D. (1984). Church-based mutual help groups for caregivers of non-institutionalized elders. *Journal of Religion and Aging*, 1, 63-69.

Hasselkus, B. R. (1988). Meaning in family caregiving: Perspectives on caregiver/professional relationships. *The Gerontologist*, 28, 686-691.

Horowitz, A. (1985). Sons and daughters as caregivers to older parents: Differences in role performance and consequences. *The Gerontologist*, 25, 612-617.

Johnson, P. J. and Rubin, A. (1983). Case management in mental health: A social work domain. *Social Work*, 28, 49-55.

Kane, R. A. (1985). Assessing the elderly. In A. Monk (ed.), *Handbook of gerontological services* (pp. 43-69). New York: Van Nostrand.

Kane, R. A. and Kane, R. L. (1981). *Assessing the elderly: A practical guide to measurement*. Lexington, MA: D. C. Heath.

Lazarus, R. S. and Folkman, S. (1984). *Stress, appraisal and coping*. New York: Springer.

McGadney, B. F., Goldberg-Glen R. and Pinkston, E. M. (1987). Clinical issues for assessment and intervention with the black elderly. In L. L. Carstanson and B. A. Edelstein (eds.), *Handbook of Clinical Gerontology*. New York: Pergamon.

Montgomery, R. (1988). *Family support project: Outcome and measurement implications*. Paper presented at the annual conference of the Gerontological Society of America, Washington, D. C.

Pinkston, E. M., et al. (1982). *Effective social work practice*. San Francisco: Jossey-Bass.

Roberts, R. (1987). The epidemiology of depression in minorities. In P. Muehrer (ed.), *Research perspectives on depression and suicide in minorities*. Washington, D.C.: HHS-NIMH.

Rubin, A. (1987). Case management. In A. Minahan et al, (eds.),*Encyclopedia of social work* (pp. 212-222). Silver Spring, MD: NASW.

Sanford, K. A. (1975). Tolerance of debility in elderly dependents by supporters at home: Its significance for hospital practice. *British Medical Journal*, 3, 471-473.

Shanas, E. (1968). *Old people in three industrial societies*. New York: Atherton Press.

Steinberg, R. M. (1985). Access assistance and case management. In A. Monk (ed.), *Handbook of Gerontological Services*, (pp. 211-239). New York: Van Nostrand.

Steinberg, R. M. and Carter, G. W. (1983). *Case management and the elderly*. Lexington, MA: D. C. Heath.

Stone, R., Cafferata, G. L. and Sangle, J. (1987). Caregivers of the frail elderly: A national profile. *The Gerontologist*, 27, 616-626.

Taylor, R. J. and Chatters, L. M. (1986). Church-based informal support among elderly blacks. *The Gerontologist*, 26, 637-642.

Tonti, M. and Silverstone, B. (1985). Services to families of the elderly. In A. Monk (ed.), *Handbook of gerontological services* (pp. 211-239). New York: Van Nostrand.

Toseland, R. W. (1981). Increasing access: Outreach methods in social work practice. *Social Casework*, 62, 227-234.

Toseland, R. W., Derico, A. and Owen, M. L. (1984). Alzheimer's disease and related disorders: Assessment and intervention. *Health and Social Work*, 9, 212-226.

Toseland, R. W., and Rossiter, C. M. (1991). Group intervention to support family caregivers: A review and analysis. *The Gerontologist*.

Toseland, R. W., Rossiter, C. M. and Labrecque, M. (1992). The effectiveness of peer-led and professionally-led groups to support family caregivers. *The Gerontologist*.

Toseland, R. W., Rossiter, C. M., Labrecque, M. S. and Beckstead, J. W. (1988). *The effectiveness of two kinds of support groups for caregivers*. Paper submitted for publication.

Chapter 15

Rural Social Work Practice with Mentally Retarded Elderly

Barbara A. Dicks, Ph.D.
Vincent J. Venturini, M.S.W.

*T**he rural elderly mentally retarded represent a microcosm of the rapidly increasing aged population in the United States. This subgroup has received very limited attention in the social work literature. With the projected escalation of the aged over the next decade, increased emphasis is needed in the areas of service delivery, programming, recruitment and training of social workers to meet the needs of mentally retarded members of this age cohort. A case study illustration of one southern rural retardation centre's approach to service delivery with the elderly mentally retarded is presented after a discussion of social work roles and responsibilities with this group of persons.*

The elderly mentally retarded are a group that have been relatively obscure in the social work literature. Furthermore, there are debates over numerous rudimentary issues such as the size of the actual population and use of a standard of chronological age to classify as elderly (Janicki and Wisniewski, 1985; Seltzer and Selzer, 1985;

Kaufman, DeWeaver and Glicker, 1989; Sison and Cotten, 1989). With the projected escalation of the elderly population over the next decade and increase in migration to rural areas, social workers will be challenged to meet the needs of this group in the 21st century.

Given the nature of issues such as limited availability and accessibility to social service programmes in rural areas, rural values such as self-reliance, extensive use of informal systems (Johnson, 1980) and stereotypes regarding the mentally retarded, the profession has a mammoth task of educating the community and other professionals about the needs of this unique population.

The Clientele

The specific population discussed here are elderly clients served by Boswell Retardation Center, in Sanatorium, Mississippi. Attention will be directed to describing social work practice roles employed with this population, including particular tasks central to each role. Before beginning this discussion, it is important that the reader have a clear understanding of mental retardation. Mental retardation is used to define individuals who possess significantly sub-average general intellectual functioning existing concurrently with deficits in adaptive behaviour manifested between birth and 18 years of age (Grossman, 1977). There are four degrees of mental retardation generally based upon three factors: mental ability, adaptive behaviour and physical development. Based upon one's intelligence quotient (IQ), persons are classified into various degrees of retardation. These are: (1) mild (IQ 53-67); (2) moderate (IQ 36-52); (3) severe (IQ 21-35); and (4) profound (IQ 20 or less). According to Grossman (1977), the percentage ranking for the degree of retardation consists of the following breakdown: mild (89 percent), moderate (6 percent), severe (3 1/2 percent) and profound (1 1/2 percent).

The heterogeneity of persons with mental retardation makes it difficult to assign a specific chronological age as the beginning of elderly status for this population. For instance, some persons with mental retardation in the 30-50 age range often manifest certain physiological changes that produce functional impairments typically associated with the aging process (Kaufman et al., 1989). As a result of these early physiological changes, age 55 best minimizes potential errors in mis-classification of diverse populations of persons with mental retardation (Seltzer and Krauss, 1987). Therefore, age 55 will be used in this context to designate Boswell Retardation Center's elderly clients.

The Boswell Retardation Center was created by an act of Mississippi's legislature in 1976 to provide a less restrictive environment for high functioning adults with mental retardation. The centre is located in Mississippi's rural Piney Woods region, approximately 45 miles south of Jackson. The main campus comprises 80 acres of lush green farmland with a picturesque lake in its midst. Boswell is one of the few institutions in the nation that has several staff members residing on its grounds. Most client activities take place in the nearby small town of Magee (population 5,000). While there is no mass transit system, vans are available to transfer clients to various activities in Jackson and the surrounding environs.

There are currently 301 clients served by Boswell Retardation Center's three components: (1) the intermediate care facility; (2) the independent living skills training; and (3) community services. The intermediate care facility receives Medicaid funding and provides training in self-care survival skills for 84 clients who generally have severe or profound levels of mental retardation coupled with physical handicaps.

The independent living skills training (ILST) serves 151 clients and is a transitional programme between an intermediate care placement and community living. Clients in the dormitory receive training in personal grooming, domestic activities, functional academic skills, yard maintenance and vocational training. The community service centre provides alternative living arrangements for 56 clients in supervised homes, apartments or retirement homes.

The breakdown by race and sex in each component and for the centre at large is indicated in Table 1.

There are currently a total of 37 elderly clients in Boswell's total population of 301. Ten of these clients reside in the intermediate care facility consisting of five white females, three white males and two African-American males. Two white and two African-American elderly males are served by the ILST component. Twenty-three elderly clients are served by Boswell Retardation Center's community services department. These include 13 white females, six white males, two African-American females and two African-American males.

Table 1 — Boswell Program Components by Race and Gender

Race	Intermediate Care Facility		Independent Skills Training		Community Services		Total
	Female	Male	Female	Male	Female	Male	
African American	19	16	16	37	11	4	103
Native American	1	1	1	1	0	0	4
White	24	23	53	43	31	20	194
Totals	44	40	70	81	42	24	301

Other services include specific programmes related to community living, vocational training/placement and leisure education. Pre-retirement training is also offered for clients who are elderly or approaching elderly status, to help them prepare for changes brought on by retirement. These clients have the option of retiring from vocational programming or working fewer hours.

Clients who reside in the retirement homes have the option to spend their time engaging in leisure activities, performing domestic chores, participating in shopping trips and/or preparing meals if they choose. Retirement home clients are also provided the options of continuing to work or participating in volunteer activities. Those who are at least 60 years old can attend a local elderly nutrition centre for meals and socialization with seniors who are not mentally retarded.

Social work activities within the intermediate care facility and the independent living components of the centre are provided by the social services department. This department is headed by a coordinator, who holds an M.S.W. and supervises a staff of four B.S.W. level employees. The community services programme has a separate social work staff of two, one has a master's degree and one is a B.S.W. employee. Both social workers in this unit report directly to the coordinator of community services who is a psychologist. The nature of Boswell Retardation Center's client community and the services rendered to these clients allow for social workers employed at the centre to perform a variety of social work tasks.

Practice Roles and Responsibilities

Numerous authors have addressed the diverse generic roles of traditional social work practitioners (Compton and Galaway, 1989; Germain and Gitterman, 1980; Middleman and Goldberg, 1989), but the literature is very limited regarding social work roles with the elderly mentally retarded. The most comprehensive typology of interventive roles with this population is presented by Kaufman, DeWeaver and Glicker (1989). A case management model of social work practice focusing on the roles of outreach worker, advocate, teacher, therapist, enabler/facilitator and broker/coordinator with the mentally retarded aged who are institutionalized, deinstitutionalized or living in a family unit is outlined by Kaufman, DeWeaver and Glicker (1989). Indeed, case management activities represent the basic social work model of practice with the mentally retarded (DeWeaver and Johnson, 1983; Kaufman, DeWeaver and Glicker, 1989). Given the nature of daily activities at Boswell, the discussion here will focus on the roles previously mentioned.

I. Social Brokerage Role

Social brokerage is a social work function intended to assist a client system to identify, locate and acquire resources necessary to problem-solving. Social brokerage activities assist different segments of the community in the enhancement of their mutual interests by connecting them with one another (Middleman and Goldberg, 1989; Germain and Gitterman, 1980; Barker, 1987). Assisting elderly clients in acquiring transportation necessary to perform essential daily tasks or linking them with an elderly community service project are examples of social brokerage. At Boswell Retardation Center, social brokerage activities may be divided into four categories: 1) community-based services, (2) placement activities, (3) employment, and (4) social interactional activities.

For clients in the institutional setting, social brokerage services are largely directed at linking them with age-specific programmes and residential living arrangements. In this regard, the institutional social worker is part of the interdisciplinary team that makes decisions concerning a client's individual programme plans and living arrangements. Social brokerage activities pertinent to Boswell's community service clients entails linking them with necessary community-based services. Such services include medical/dental, nutritional, religious, recreational, shopping, employment and voluntary activities.

Social brokerage services undertaken to provide clients access to volunteer or employment activities are primarily provided for on an individual basis. Not all of the elderly clients served by the programme possess the necessary cognitive or social skills to adequately perform employment or voluntary tasks in a community setting. Therefore, efforts are made to enable access for those clients capable of performing such roles in the community, should they desire to do so. As well, other elderly clients who choose to continue working are permitted to do so in Boswell's work activity centre or adult activity centre, depending upon their individual skills levels.

Another unique and integral part of social brokerage activities at the centre entails providing elderly clients opportunities for social interaction with other elderly persons who are not mentally retarded. In the institutional setting, this function is largely carried out through adopt-a-friend activities. Thus, institutional social workers coordinate activities with local churches, civic organizations and the Retired Service Volunteer Program in order to enlist adopt-a-friend for clients who are isolated and have no family contact. Adopt-a-friend activities can also include receiving letters from a community person or attending church and/or recreational programmes with that individual. Social brokerage activities focus more upon client integration into social settings. Thus, clients are encouraged to participate in all programmes offered for older persons in the community.

Some clients are also active participants in Mississippi's Senior Olympics. Community services department social workers work with other staff in ensuring that their application to participate in the Senior Olympics are completed and mailed and that they are provided transportation and receive proper supervision during the event.

Elderly clients who reside in the community are provided the option of attending church services in the community or at Boswell's chapel. It is an important social brokerage role to ensure that elderly clients have access to the churches of their choice and to link them with transportation services to all church activities. Case managers have also been instrumental in facilitating mid-week services in the retirement homes through volunteer efforts from local churches.

II. Enabler Role

The enabler role is utilized when social workers seek to assist clients to discover coping strengths and resources within themselves to achieve desired ends (Compton and Galaway; 1989). This definition has been expanded through identification of specific skills employed by the social worker in the execution of this role (Middleman and Goldberg, 1989; Shulman, 1979; Barker, 1987). These skills include conveying hope, reducing resistance and ambivalence, recognizing and managing feelings, identifying and supporting personal strengths and social assets, breaking down problems into manageable parts to facilitate problem resolution and maintaining a focus on therapeutic goals and the means of achieving them. In this regard, the social worker seeks to direct clients in accomplishing positive changes through their own efforts. Social work intervention utilizes the enabler role in assisting clients to effect both personal and environmental changes.

Very few Boswell clients possess such deficient cognitive skills that they are unable to draw upon personal resources to accomplish a needed and desired change. While some changes sought for Boswell's elderly clients appear rudimentary, such as understanding the importance of waiting one's turn during a conversation or learning how to offer constructive criticism to peers, they signify important social skills for persons with mental retardation, especially when they interact in the wider community. Therefore, social workers frequently utilize the enabler role in assisting clients to acquire these or similar skills.

Institutional social workers frequently utilize the enabler role when implementing written training programmes. In this regard, the social skills alluded to previously are taken from this assessment. The social worker identifies and prioritizes the client's deficient social skills and presents them at the annual staffing on the client. The interdisciplinary team collectively decides upon the deficient skills that should be addressed by the social worker. The enabler role is utilized by the social worker to assist the clients accomplish objectives of the individual programme plan. An example is an individual programme plan designed to reduce episodes of volatile behaviour in a client. Social work activities in this context are directed at helping the client to identify and understand the causes of his or her volatile behaviour, the consequences of such behaviour and the more appropriate responses to these causes. The social worker does not provide the client with answers, but rather guides the client in identifying and implementing steps she or he can take in reducing such volatile episodes. Through these activities, the client is, therefore, enabled to express his or her anger in more socially appropriate ways.

Social workers in the community setting generally have more flexibility in designating certain areas in social functioning as problematic and implementing enabling activities with clients. Here, the social worker has the advantage of allowing clients to practice appropriate responses in a 'real world' social setting. It should also be noted that elderly clients residing in a community setting often have greater personal and environmental resources available to them.

Employing enabling activities with elderly clients, however, is more difficult in the area of effecting environmental changes. An example of enabling activities directed at altering the environment may include steps undertaken to assist elderly clients who reside in the community and attend an elderly nutrition centre, in understanding the reluctance of other elderly persons to interact with them. Once a client can recognize environmental cues that influence her or his social interaction with non-mentally retarded elderly persons, she or he can then identify positive actions that may facilitate enhanced social interactional opportunities with other elderly persons in the community. In short, the client may be enabled to communicate his or her own personal worth to 'normal' elderly persons and allow them to recognize that a person with mental retardation possesses unique qualities and experiences to share in social interactions. The performance of volunteer tasks by elderly persons with mental retardation is an important function for engendering environmental changes. It informs community citizens that elderly persons with mental retardation can be providers as well as receivers of vital services. This, in turn, enables elderly persons with mental retardation to acquire a fuller partnership in community affairs that affect them, and hence it usually enhances their self-esteem.

On an individual level, social work enabling activities with Boswell's elderly clients are employed to assist clients in verbalizing their problems, venting their frustrations and arriving at appropriate, workable resolutions. While it is sometimes necessary for the social worker to take a more direct role in identifying problems or stressing the need for change with this population than would be necessary with most other clients, efforts are still undertaken to assist the client in fostering change as much as possible.

The enabler role demands that the social worker's primary focus and interaction is with the client rather than with external systems (Compton and Galaway, 1989). It is our perception that persons with mental retardation have often led cloistered lives, whether in an institutional setting or with family members. Further, their reduced ability to understand and manipulate the rules of external systems minimizes their potential for acquiring maximum benefits available in such systems. In such instances, the enabling role must be modified to allow the social worker to act on behalf of the client in effecting environmental changes. When vested interests are discovered in the environment that are hostile to client interests, the social worker must intervene and make decisions regarding the course of action to be taken.

III. The Teacher Role

The teaching role entails providing the client with information essential for accomplishing desired objectives. Social work teaching activities can also be directed at assisting clients to gain new skills or to replace negative behavioural patterns with more positive ones (Germain and Gitterman, 1980; Middleman and Goldberg, 1989).

A primary teaching activity employed with clients who have mental retardation is the written training programme. Traditionally, this is known as the rehabilitation plan or individual programme plan (IPP). This programme is an active treatment module implemented to impart new skills to the client in a therapeutic goal oriented way. It entails teaching the client to perform desired tasks independently through incremental steps. Social work written training programmes most often involve teaching social skills or assisting the client in learning how to appropriately utilize social skills in public settings.

Elderly clients who reside in the community have greater interactional opportunities with non-mentally retarded persons in the community than other Boswell clients, through the local council on aging programmes. It is important, therefore, that they acquire skills about how to conduct themselves that will facilitate psycho-social integration. Thus, the social worker directs activities intended to assist the client in acquiring appropriate behavioural patterns within the community setting. Very often, these activities are facilitated with the assistance of home managers.

Boswell Center's pre-retirement curriculum provides another example of teaching activities. While this curriculum is an interdisciplinary effort, social workers, including the current project director, have been instrumental in the development and coordination of this curriculum. The purpose of the pre-retirement curriculum essentially is to teach elderly persons with mental retardation how to cope with this reality. After the centre opened its first retirement home, it became evident that several clients did not know 'how to retire.' They had resided most of their lives in institutions and were unprepared for this newly acquired status. For example, they did not understand that retirement provides new options and choices pertinent to meaningful leisure activities, community involvement, part-time employment opportunities and community support services.

Boswell's social services coordinator developed and still teaches the content concerning such options and choices. Clients are taught that options are those things available to you that you can choose from, and that choices are the selections you make from these options or what you choose to do or have. Learning exercises during classes are very simple using pictures to illustrate options in a specific context.

Such exercises are repeated throughout two hour-long sessions. Thus, clients learn that retirement provides them with such options as attending an elderly nutrition centre or continuing to work part-time. This, in turn, permits them to choose whether they participate in an elderly nutrition programme, continue to work part-time or engage in various leisure pursuits.

The social services coordinator also participates in the curriculum component involving community support services. Here, clients are taught that they are entitled to a host of programmes and benefits in the community, not necessarily because they are elderly and/or carry a mental retardation diagnosis, but because they are people and citizens foremost. They are also taught the responsibilities that such rights carry.

IV. Mediator

The social worker, as mediator, facilitates numerous negotiation processes. In general mediation involves efforts to resolve disputes that may exist between the client system and other persons and organizations (Compton and Galaway; 1989). A useful example of mediation activities employed in the team process involves the client who wishes to work only when she or he wants to. The work activity centre, and centre staff may question the advisability of work hours being reduced. Through mediation, the team agrees that the client can work reduced but regular hours. A schedule is agreed upon whereby the client works half-days or three days per week. The client comes to understand that the work activity centre must have a reliable workforce in order to meet production goals and accepts the responsibility for being a dependable employee. In this context, work activity centre staff come to understand that elderly clients sometimes have special scheduling needs.

Mediation activities tend to be generally less formal and are often directed at resolving disputes between different clients. For instance, tensions may develop between clients residing in a retirement home over what television programmes to watch or over where to eat during shopping or recreational trips. The social worker, in these instances, works with the home manager in enabling clients to compromise with these problems. For example, clients may decide on a television schedule in which each person is provided the opportunity to watch certain programmes.

Similarly, clients may learn how to compromise on selections of dining establishments. For instance, a client who prefers eating at McDonald's may not be able to do so every week but will have the opportunity to do so on occasion. She or he will also learn to accept that they must visit other eating establishments when it is another client's turn to choose.

This raises again the notion of options and choices previously discussed, and points to the interrelationship between social work mediation and teaching activities. Through mediation activities, the client learns that individual options are often limited in a group setting. Thus, the client comes to understand that compromise is integral to the options and choices that are made available in various community settings.

V. Advocacy Role

In this role, the social worker acts as the representative for the client in securing entitled benefits for a single client or group of clients she or he represents (Middleman and Goldberg, 1989). Advocacy activities generally entail ensuring that clients are aware of their rights and are able to exercise those rights. These activities involve ensuring that clients receive appropriate care, are able to maintain family or extra-family contact and can access transfers to less restrictive living arrangements, including community placement, when appropriate.

As well, advocacy efforts entail recommending access to pre-retirement training and retirement opportunities. For instance, in the event that an elderly client is determined to require skilled nursing care, the social services coordinator seeks to place this client in a nursing home close to family. This often entails advocating for a client's admission to a nursing home that does not ordinarily serve persons with mental retardation and may be reluctant to accept such a client.

Advocacy efforts specific to Boswell's community services component generally involve ensuring that clients are able to gain access to the same services afforded to non-retarded elderly persons in the community. This includes both age-specific and generic services. As well, community service social workers are responsible for making sure that clients are aware of their legal, civil and constitutional rights. This requires coordinating activities with home managers to ensure that clients have the opportunity to vote, attend the church/synagogue/mosque of their choice and to see that they are able to utilize public recreational facilities the same as other persons.

One of the most important advocacy activities employed by community service social workers entails the acquisition of social security, supplemental security insurance or other benefits to which a client is legally entitled. In this context, the social worker makes application for these benefits and represents the client's eligibility for and entitlement to these benefits to the appropriate agency. In the event a client is refused these benefits, the social worker argues the appeal in an effort to secure benefits outright for the client. Since this activity is vital to the client, the social worker as advocate must be knowledgeable of the eligibility guidelines of a host of public benefits.

Table 2 summarizes the various roles discussed in this subsection.

Table 2 — Social Work Practice Roles with Rural Mentally Retarded Elderly			
Programme Components			
Practice Roles	**Independent Care Facility**	**Independent Living Skills Training**	**Community Services**
Social Broker	1 Develop written training programmes 2 Ensure access to institutional services 3 Ensure appropriate client placement	1 Develop written training programmes 2 Ensure access to institutional services 3 Ensure appropriate client placement	1 Arrange client access to local community services
Enabler	1 Facilitate client development of coping skills 2 To identify strengths and personal assets	1 Facilitate client development of coping skills 2 To identify strengths and personal assets	1 Empower clients to overcome service barriers 2 To identify strengths and personal assets
Teacher	1 Implement written training programme 2 Assist client development of social skills 3 Prepare clients for retirement	1 Implement written training programme 2 Assist client development of social skills 3 Prepare clients for retirement	1 Assist client development of social skills 2 Assist client development of communication skills 3 Educate community about needs of M.R. persons
Mediator	1 Assist client in resolving disputes 2 Arrange age appropriate programmes for client	1 Assist client in resolving disputes 2 Arrange age appropriate programmes for client	1 Assist client in resolving disputes 2 Negotiating concessions for clients
Advocate	1 Advise client of rights 2 Ensure client freedom to exercise rights 3 Promote client right to less restrictive living situation	1 Advise client of rights 2 Ensure client freedom to exercise rights 3 Promote client right to less restrictive living situation	1 Advise client of rights 2 Ensure client freedom to exercise rights 3 Ensure equitable rights accorded other community citizens 4 Promote slient eligibility for needed services 5 Sensitize community to human qualities of clients

Potential for Role Development

The potential for role development relative to social work intervention with this population is inherent in the broker, enabler, teacher, mediator and advocate roles. It should be a goal in any type of social work intervention to encourage the client's right to self-determination as much as possible. This relates directly to advocacy activities. Unless a protective function must be utilized, the social worker should go no further in advocacy activities than the client wishes to go (Hepworth and Larsen, 1986). Therefore, the social worker involved with elderly persons with mental retardation must assist the client to first realize their rights and to ensure that they understand, as much as possible, potential ramifications in the exercising of these rights.

Promoting self-determination requires employment of the teacher and enabler roles. It is in the capacity of teacher that the social worker imparts knowledge to the client pertinent to his or her rights in a given situation and possible consequences should the client choose to exercise these rights. Thus, the social worker should work directly with the client in helping him or her know just what the exercise of self-determination entails. The social worker should provide simple examples, similar to those employed in the lessons on options and choices. In fact, these teaching exercises should reinforce to the client that the exercise of self-determination involves options and choices relative to the courses of action they may wish to take.

The potential for role development is enhanced by the fact that many of the roles previously discussed (in Table 2) interrelate with each other and positively influence each other. For instance, once a social worker has facilitated the client in a greater understanding and exercise of self-determination, enhancement of the broker and mediator roles will inevitably result as well. The mediator role will be strengthened as a result of an increased bargaining power the social worker will acquire, since the client is more assertive in demanding certain rights and/or services. In short, the social worker would be representing the client in a more effective way. Instead of taking a primary role in determining what the client's best interests are, the social worker would be representing the client's decision as to what his or her best interests are. This applies to the advocacy role as well.

Enhancement of the social broker role should result from the client's increased assertiveness pertinent to desired services. For instance, the social worker and client can list together the various services the client wishes to receive or become involved in. It would be the social worker's primary responsibility in this phase of the activity to suggest services the client may be seeking and explain any pitfalls inherent in potential choices. Once the client has determined desired services, the social worker should then assist them in their acquisition.

The teacher and advocacy roles can also be enhanced on different levels. Teaching activities have previously been discussed solely from the perspective of direct intervention with the client. These activities may also be employed with the personnel of various service agencies and with persons in the community at large. Social workers at the centre have been active in recent years in conducting presentations at conferences about the pre-retirement curriculum and retirement home clients, and at such presentations many of the myths pertinent to elderly persons with mental retardation have been dispelled. It is our belief that more activities of this nature are needed in the future. Concurrently, social workers should endeavour to speak at civic clubs and organizations. It is crucial that community members understand that a diagnosis of mental retardation does not diminish an individual's worth as a person or necessarily significantly decrease skills in all domains.

Through the advocacy roles, the social worker should employ and impart an awareness of the client's individuality and right to be treated with dignity regardless of mental limitations. For instance, when interacting with non-mentally retarded elderly persons in normal life circumstances, they are generally referred to by such titles as Mr., Mrs. or Ms. One generally uses first names with elderly persons only when they request it. Social workers should do the same when speaking to an elderly client who happens to have a diagnosis of mental retardation.

Concluding Remarks

Social work practice with elderly persons with mental retardation residing in rural communities is an area that deserves greater attention from the profession in the immediate future. In the next decade, there will be a considerable increase in the elderly and consequently the potential for a larger subgroup of mentally retarded individuals. Concerns related to this population reflect pertinent service issues regarding all mentally retarded individuals as they struggle for equitable treatment in a society that has difficulty accepting and tolerating such differences. Elderly persons with mental retardation have a dual difficulty in our society due to inherent prejudices against the elderly as well as the mentally retarded.

Given the nature of the various roles undertaken by social workers to provide services to the mentally retarded elderly in rural communities, there is a challenge for social workers and human service providers. Schools of social work should become more active in assuring that they promote education and training with mentally retarded populations and the elderly through curriculum content and field work opportunities. State institutions and local programmes can begin to take a more pro-active role in educating and sensitizing the public to the needs of one of our most vulnerable populations. Finally, as we move toward the beginning of the 21st century, social work must meet the challenge of ensuring that the needs of those clients approaching the end of life who are intellectually unable to advocate for themselves in all arenas can depend on the services of a dedicated profession.

Case Example

Mr. J is a 64-year-old white male client of Boswell's community services department with a diagnosis of mild retardation of measured intelligence concurrent with mild adaptive behaviour deficits. His medical diagnoses includes seizure disorder and a heart condition. Mr. J also has a history of alcohol abuse, although he has not recently demonstrated any problems with alcohol.

Mr. J is ambulatory and verbal and has limited reading, writing and numerical abilities as he only completed the fifth grade. He speaks and understands complex sentences and can integrate past and present events. He has been more successful than other elderly clients served by Boswell's community services department in integrating into social networks of non-retarded elderly persons in Simpson County.

Mr. J was one of five children born to his parents in a rural northeast Mississippi community. He describes an early childhood history of seizures for which he received no medical treatment. He was admitted to the state hospital in 1977 for alcoholism and then transferred to Boswell Retardation Center due to his mental retardation. He progressed to the level of a supervised apartment living arrangement and in 1986 moved into a senior citizen's apartment building in the same complex that he had resided in the previous five years. Although he was no longer a resident of the supervised apartment programme, he continued to receive case management and other support services from Boswell.

Concerns were raised over the condition of Mr. J's apartment by community services staff. Concurrently, reports were made to the social worker by Boswell's work activity centre staff that Mr. J went to work smelling bad and that he apparently was neither bathing nor washing his clothes regularly. An investigation by the staff social worker uncovered several packages of green, spoiled meat in the refrigerator and molded loaves of bread. Mold was also discovered in the bathroom and rats had chewed a hole in a bushel bag of peanuts stored in the living room.

Mr. J initially protested that he was adequately caring for himself and his apartment and accused staff and other clients of lying about him in an attempt to hurt him. When confronted by the social worker, however, he admitted that he needed help.

It was determined that Mr. J required assistance in the performance of domestic duties. The social worker presented this to the community services coordinator, along with the contention that a significant number of professionals and other non-mentally retarded persons are poor housekeepers. Thus, the argument was made that the condition of Mr. J's apartment was not necessarily a consequence of his mental retardation diagnosis. It was decided by the coordinator, social worker and Mr. J that he could hire another community service client to clean his apartment for a fair wage. Therefore, a younger client was hired who supplemented her income by taking domestic jobs in the community.

Mr. J was also counselled about his poor grooming and hygiene skills. The social worker discussed with him the need to bathe daily with a good deodorant soap, use deodorant, brush his teeth regularly and wear clean clothes. He was also instructed in the need to wash his clothes regularly. Mr. J was advised that since he was now in a case management programme he was responsible for performing these tasks on his own initiative. Most importantly, he was told that despite the fact that he now employed a housekeeper once a week, he was responsible for the daily maintenance of his apartment, including sanitary conditions. Mr. J was told that this required placing dirty clothes in a hamper, throwing away spoiled food, properly storing unused food items and taking out his garbage regularly. Furthermore, Mr. J was told that his poor hygiene habits could cause negative responses from citizens in the community toward persons with mental retardation.

Case Analysis

Mr. J's case is a good example of the employment of different social work practice roles and the manner in which these roles mesh together in social work activities at the centre. Interventions with Mr. J intended to ensure the proper upkeep of his apartment operationalized all the roles previously discussed in this chapter. The broker role was employed to assist Mr. J acquire necessary services to keep his apartment clean and meet housing authority standards. Enabling activities were directed toward prompting Mr. J to utilize the skills he already possessed pertinent to his personal hygiene and domestic skills. The social worker also employed the teaching role in activities designed to instruct Mr. J in appropriate shopping skills and proper food storage. The teaching role was then also utilized concerning community expectations relative to personal hygiene.

Distinctions between the mediator and advocacy roles are more difficult to distinguish in this case example. The advocacy role was employed when the social worker stated the position that several non-mentally retarded older persons require assistance in keeping their homes clean and argued that Mr. J should remain in his apartment and acquire the services of a housekeeper. This entailed advocating that the same right accorded other elderly persons to remain in their homes with appropriate support services should be available to elderly persons with mental retardation. Mediation activities involved requesting the landlord to exterminate the apartment.

Brokerage activities were employed when the social worker facilitated arrangements with Mr. J and another client for Mr. J to receive housekeeping services. The two parties were assisted in agreeing on the day and time she would work and the salary she would receive. During this session, delineation of tasks specific to both Mr. J and the housekeeper were decided.

Mr. J did demonstrate some improvement in the areas of concern, as a result of social work intervention utilizing the practice roles described above. His food storage habits improved and his apartment ceased to attract rodents. He also demonstrated significant progress in his personal hygiene and appearance. Hence his competency and self-esteem were also increased.

References

Barker, Robert L. (1987). *The social work dictionary*. Silver Spring, MD: National Association of Social Workers.

Compton, Buellah R. and Galaway, Burt. (1989). *Social work processes* (4th ed.). Belmont, CA: Wadsworth.

DeWeaver, Kevin L. and Johnson, Peter J. (1983). Case management in rural areas for the developmentally disabled. *Human Services in the Rural Environment*, 8(4), pp. 23-31.

Germain, Carel B. and Gitterman, Alex. (1980). *The life model of social work practice*. New York: Columbia University Press.

Grossman, Herbert J. (1977). *Manual on terminology and classification in mental retardation*. American Association on Mental Deficiency. Baltimore, MD: Garamond/Pridemark Press.

Hepworth, Dean H. and Larsen, J. Ann. (1986). *Direct social work practice: Theory and skills* (2nd ed.). Chicago, IL: The Dorsey Press.

Janicki, Matthew P. and Wisniewski, Henry M. (1985). *Aging and developmental disabilities: Issues and approaches*. Baltimore, MD: Paul H. Brookes Publishing Company.

Johnson, H. Wayne. (1980). *Rural human services: A book of readings*. Itasca, IL: F.E. Peacock Publishers.

Kaufman, A., DeWeaver, K. and Glicker, M. (1989). The mentally retarded aged: Implications for social work practice. *Journal of Gerontological Social Work*, 14(1/2), 93-111.

Middleman, R. and Goldberg, Gale. (1989). *Social service delivery: A structural approach to social work practice* (2nd ed.). New York: Columbia University Press.

Seltzer, M. M. and Krauss, M. W. (1987). *Aging and mental retardation: Extending the continuum*. (Monographs of the American Association on Mental Retardation No. 9). Washington, D.C.

Seltzer, M. and Seltzer, G.B. (1985). The elderly mentally retarded: A group in need of service. In G.S. Getzel and M.J. Mellor (eds.), *Gerontological social work practice in the community*. New York: The Haworth Press Inc.

Shulman, L. (1979). *The skills of helping individuals and groups*. Itasca, IL: F. E. Peacock Publishers.

Sisson, Gustave F.P. and Cotten, Paul D. (1989). The elderly mentally retarded person: Current perspectives and future directions. *Journal of Applied Gerontology*, 8(2), 151-167.

CHAPTER 16

SOCIAL WORK PRACTICE IN A PRIVATE RETIREMENT COMMUNITY

VIRGINIA L. FITCH, PH.D.
LEE R. SLIVINSKE, PH.D.
SALLY NICHOLS, L.S.W.

*T*his chapter describes the practice roles and responsibilities of social workers in a private, non-profit continuing care community. Although the interventions and services offered are similar to those offered to elders in other settings, the wide range of client needs and the variety of care options available require innovative approaches to practice; the ability to work with individuals, families, groups, communities and other agencies; and knowledge of the elderly and the relationship of staff to client in a long-term relationship. The social worker plays an integral role in helping residents adapt to the setting and achieve a quality of life that affords them satisfaction.

This chapter describes the roles and activities of social workers in a continuing care retirement community. Rockynol is one of seven facilities operated by Ohio Presbyterian Retirement Services (OPRS) in the state of Ohio. OPRS is a private, non-profit organization with corporate headquarters based in Columbus.

Rockynol is located on 12 campus-like acres in the city of Akron and serves a total of 300 residents. The majority are from Akron and surrounding areas or have returned to live near relatives.

Organizational governance is accomplished through structures that provide for input at many levels. Residents of each OPRS facility participate in councils that meet regularly to provide input on current operations and future plans. Their concerns are transmitted to a local advisory council composed of community leaders and a resident representative. Community members of each of the seven advisory councils are appointed to the volunteer board of trustees of OPRS. The seven resident representatives elect one among themselves to serve on this board. The procedure insures that residents have a voice in planning and policy issues concerning their community and home.

Rockynol provides long-term care. Originally, long-term care referred to a secondary, primarily custodial function of the health care system. As used today, long-term care is broad in nature and includes a range of care sources and settings (Beaver, 1983).

Rockynol has several distinguishing features. Of the estimated 1,000 full-service continuing care retirement communities in the country, it is one of only 91 accredited by the Continuing Care Accreditation Commission. The commission is sponsored by the American Association of Homes for the Aged. Second, a team from OPRS headquarters makes periodic visits throughout the year and conducts an annual quality assurance review. The standards of the OPRS quality assurance programme are more stringent than those required by government regulations. Third, Rockynol functions as a small community within the larger urban community. It has a library, art gallery, banking system, chapel and full-time chaplain, accommodations for visits from family and friends, beauty/barber salon, activities department, transportation, as well as a full complement of services. Finally, four levels of care are offered, including independent living, congregate living, assisted living and intermediate/skilled nursing care.

Admission is based on a formula that includes consideration of the elderly person's income and assets, past and current health and life expectancy. The cost of residency is substantial and varies depending upon level of care. Rockynol does accept some individuals on Medicaid. In addition, OPRS maintains a policy called Life Care. Once admitted, no resident has ever had to leave due to depleted finances. The organization assumes responsibility for the resident's service and supports the Life Care plan through a separate foundation established by OPRS.

The mission of the facility is to provide older adults with caring and quality services to enhance physical, mental and spiritual well-being. The goal is to have every resident living in the least restrictive environment at the highest level of autonomy possible consistent with individual service preference. In practice this means that a resident who could live more independently may prefer to receive help in some activities of daily living.

The Clientele

Rockynol serves a predominantly upper-middle-class, white clientele. Although clients from all ethnic and racial groups are welcomed, the demographic composition seems to reflect the differential socioeconomic conditions and aging patterns that exist between groups.

Greater diversity in religious affiliation is found. Although the organization has historical ties with the Presbyterian Church, 15 denominations, including Protestant, Catholic, Jewish and Orthodox are represented.

Although the residents in this facility tend to be affluent, there is still some diversity in the primary source of funding for their care. Sources of funding include Medicaid, Medicare, Life Care and private pay.

Rockynol residents are predominantly female with an average age of 84. This places the majority in the old-old category, those aged 75 and over. Neugarten (1981) described this group as experiencing the most significant and rapid decrease in health status. They are the most frail and vulnerable and have the greatest need for a wide spectrum of services (Myers, 1989). This is an important consideration for social workers and other staff at Rockynol. With this in mind, Rockynol has developed policies and programmes designed to address quality of life issues for people with these varying problems and needs. As noted in the introduction, a variety of activities and care options are available. The needs and problems of residents vary from one level of care to another and within each care option.

At present, 39 percent of Rockynol's residents are in independent living. These residents are totally autonomous and do not require assistance or supervision from staff in any way. They live in high-rise apartments, engage in all self care, arrange all their own activities and appointments, although they are welcome to attend the activities offered by the facility. Many maintain their own cars and use public and other transportation. Their problems are primarily health-related and may include chronic heart conditions, cancer and similar conditions. They typically require the services of a social worker for temporary crises involving their health. Some utilize walkers and other supportive devices such as a cane, brace, wheelchair, etc., but they require no staff assistance to remain independent.

Congregate living provides a level of service that allows a resident to live independently but with staff assistance with meals, housekeeping and personal laundry. Residents in congregate living make up about 26 percent of the total community and live in one of the towers that comprise the main building. They are usually capable of independent living but choose to have some services provided by the facility.

Many of those in independent living and congregate living are motivated to seek admission because Rockynol residents have priority access to skilled nursing care if needed. Factors precipitating admission often include chronic health conditions that make care of both home and health burdensome, a significant breakdown in the client support system such as the death of a spouse or pressure from adult children to move into a protected environment. Residents who are influenced by others to seek admission usually have the most difficulty adjusting to the community.

Assisted living provides licensed rest home care that is designed to provide a range of services to residents who need assistance and supervision in activities such as walking, bathing, dressing, housekeeping, transportation and taking medications among others. These residents make up eight percent of the retirement community. They do not require constant supervision to carry out the activities of daily living even though some may appear forgetful or confused at times. They have special activities designed to meet their needs and limitations. A health maintenance nurse and an aide are with them daily. They and the social workers serve as their primary on-site contact. Due to their frequent interactions, the social worker is aware when problems arise that require intervention.

Skilled nursing/intermediate care is the highest level of care provided. Residents require a range of service that may include staff assistance and supervision in planning and carrying out all activities of daily living and total care in addition to full professional nursing care. As in the other levels of care, residents present a range of problems and needs. For example, they range from individuals with physically incapacitating diseases, such as rheumatoid arthritis, but who are alert and independent in other ways, to people who are bedridden, confused and unresponsive to their surroundings. The proportion of persons with Alzheimer's and related disorders in this level of care has increased necessitating special management and care plans. A new free-standing health care building for skilled nursing/intermediate care is scheduled to be built next year, replacing the present one. The existing space will be redesigned to meet other needs.

Admission to independent, congregate or assisted living often includes a three-day guest visit. This gives the staff an opportunity to assess the applicant in the setting and allows the individual to make a more informed decision about entering the community. At other times circumstances require an appointment with the applicant and family in the hospital, another nursing home or private residence.

Admission to skilled nursing/intermediate care usually is arranged by someone other than the applicant. When an opening occurs, it is filled quickly by admissions personnel unless it can be filled from within the facility. Level of care change by residents occurs frequently and often in both directions. A sudden illness may necessitate assisted living, intermediate care or skilled nursing. After recovery, the resident may be able to return to a level offering less care. Facility policy allows the individual to retain a place on two levels of care for 42 days if progress is being made toward the more independent level of care. This provides an impetus to recover more quickly. Even after the designated time period, the resident is encouraged to return to a more independent level although the original apartment may not be available. A more complicated problem results when a couple is admitted with vastly different care needs or when one spouse experiences accelerated physical or mental deterioration while the other remains physically and mentally capable. Separate care options may be necessitated.

Residents are assigned to a social worker's caseload based on their level of care. One social worker serves residents in intermediate and skilled nursing care. The other social worker assumes primary responsibility for independent, congregate and assisted living.

Practice Roles and Responsibilities

Unlike many nursing homes and retirement communities, at Rockynol social work is in the programme service department. The department has its own budget and a social worker as director. This extends the range of roles and responsibilities of social workers beyond those filled in many retirement communities. As in many agencies the social worker is a generalist who works with individuals, families, small groups, the community of residents and the larger community context. The variety of social and personal problems and needs experienced by the elderly provide the focus for these roles. In addition, social workers perform major administrative tasks including budgeting, planning and policy-making. Since these may be unique to this organization, this chapter will examine only the direct service tasks, functions, duties and responsibilities of practitioners as they are interpreted in the retirement community setting.

The social worker is involved with all residents from the time of initial contact with the agency when admission is sought and throughout the duration of their tenure in the community. Actual client admission decisions are undertaken by a separate department established for this purpose. The social worker completes a client assessment prior to admission unless client circumstances dictate otherwise. For example, if admission is arranged by a third party for a family member hospitalized out-of-town, the assessment process will be completed within three days after admission. The initial interview by the social worker includes both the applicant and family members. The social worker elicits their feelings and expectations about admission, their perceptions of the facility and the quality of their relationship. Engagement of both begins at this point. As pointed out by Abramovice (1988), excluding the family unit contributes to the development of loss of status and loneliness in the elderly. Thus, efforts are made to reach out to and involve families.

The initial interview includes obtaining a social history and detailed assessment of the resident. The purpose of the assessment is to identify the person's capacity for independent living and self-care and the existence of limitations that would interfere with adjustment to the residential environment. For example, the social worker assesses the client's ability to perform the activities of daily living, including dressing, toileting, bathing, housekeeping, laundry, shopping, meal preparation, mobility and similar concerns. Questions regarding customary behaviour patterns, mental alertness, drug usage, interpersonal relationships, communication skills and ability to seek assistance when needed also are addressed. Areas where assistance is needed or where social work intervention is indicated are noted for immediate follow-up. Appointments for assessment by other staff are scheduled as needed.

Out of this assessment an individualized care plan is developed. A team headed by a social worker and consisting of a chaplain, dietician, nurse and activities person meet to discuss programming needs, services and interventions indicated by the assessment. The team identifies any early indicators of change in the client's current status. They try to anticipate whether the resident will remain at the current level, deteriorate or improve in the next six months. Based on the team's recommendations, the social worker develops a care plan within the first five days after admission. The plan is discussed and reviewed with the client and family.

The team meets twice weekly to review and develop care plans. One meeting reviews residents in nursing and skilled care, and the other, congregate and assisted living. Individualized plans for health care residents must be updated every 90 days but are reviewed more frequently when warranted by a change in the client's status. Social work progress notes are written as change occurs but must be written at least quarterly. The nature of continuing care in a retirement community and the limited size of the client population allow social workers to become very familiar with each resident and family.

The social work practitioner works with residents and families formally, in scheduled office sessions, and informally, in daily encounters. Clients are helped to articulate their needs, identify their problems, explore alternative approaches to problem solving, engage in decision-making and enhance their capacity to meet their needs. Their problems may range in scope from those that are temporary to those that require long-term intervention. For example, the social worker addresses a variety of problems including conflicts between residents, problems adjusting to the facility, unresolved grief and physical and/or mental deterioration. Methods of intervention may include individual counselling, group treatment, family counselling and environmental modifications among others. Clients also may be referred to external resources. A community resource file is maintained and updated regularly by the social workers. This provides prompt access to the community services needed by residents. When a resident needs service from an external source, the social worker assumes the case management role. In this role, the social worker identifies the need, contacts external resources and coordinates services. Generally, the more independent the level of care, the less frequent the need for social work intervention.

Upon admission, the immediate responsibility of the social worker is to assist the individual in dealing with some degree of role loss. With the move into a retirement community, there is shrinkage of the range of roles played by any resident. Having many services provided for them, many experience an increase in unoccupied time and a subsequent decrease in self-esteem. The social worker helps residents identify their interests and abilities and make connections for volunteer opportunities and other activities both in and outside the retirement community.

Level of care change also is the responsibility of the social worker. Initial level of care placement decisions are made by admissions personnel in consultation with the social worker. Thereafter, placement suitability is reassessed by the social worker in the care setting on an on-going basis. When physical or mental deterioration begins to occur, both the resident and family are involved in discussion and decision-making. The family frequently has difficulty perceiving the changes that are occurring and may resist a move from the level of care to which the resident is accustomed. The adjustment of the resident is enhanced when the family is involved and supportive of the move. The social worker tries to anticipate the need for change in advance since adjustment by both resident and family is more difficult when a sudden crisis necessitates immediate change. As part of the formal orientation procedure for new residents, the social worker conducts a seminar on level of care change. Long-time residents also are invited to reacquaint themselves with the procedure and ask questions.

The family is encouraged to maintain close involvement with the resident and to participate in the facility community. Social workers conduct formal group meetings with families and residents at least three times a year. These meetings enhance communication, educate and provide support to families. They also serve as a forum to give and receive feedback on resident care. The social worker takes responsibility for transmitting concerns to the appropriate staff and conducts a follow-up to see that a response is made.

The social worker also is responsible for working with the two resident's councils and linking them with the facility. One council, consisting of those in intermediate and skilled nursing care, requires greater assistance from the social worker in conducting meetings. The residents in more independent levels have their own constitution, elect their own officers and establish committees to deal with all aspects of their lives. In both groups the social worker's role is quite similar. Residents are helped to develop their abilities to effect change in their environment. When their physical and/or mental capacities impose limits, the social worker serves as an advocate.

One of the most important functions of the social worker is in developing facility services and programmes to meet the changing needs of the resident community and to address particular problems as they arise. For example, the increase in the number of residents with Alzheimer's and related disorders has resulted in the development and implementation of a programme designed to enhance involvement with and awareness of their surroundings and to decrease daily anxiety.

Potential for Role Development

After admission, social workers are involved in every aspect of resident care in retirement communities. The unique characteristics of the social work profession make it integral to client well-being and quality of life in this setting. Social work also has been essential in achieving the organizational mission described in the introduction. The role of the social worker is an evolving one that must respond to changes in individual residents and the resident community, the overall organizational context and the larger community. The responsiveness and flexibility of practitioners in meeting a broad spectrum of needs and providing a comprehensive array of services have been noteworthy.

The potential for developing the social work role can be identified in several areas. First, the preadmission phase provides several opportunities for role development. As pointed out by Smallegan (1985), the decision to institutionalize is a decision of last resort, often leaving the family and client feeling trapped. Although retirement communities promote opportunities for independence and autonomy, admission signals a decrease in ability to control one's life and environment. Three possibilities for enhancement of the social work role at this point can be identified:

1. Provision of preadmission support groups for families and applicants;
2. Exploration of and referral to community resources to delay the point of entry;
3. Involvement of applicants in activities provided by the facility prior to admission.

These would support and, perhaps, prolong in-home care and make the transition to the long-term care environment easier when it becomes necessary.

Second, social workers possess a wealth of knowledge and skills that could be shared with other staff. For example, staff with the least amount of education and training provide much of the basic care and many services. This includes nurses aides, dietary employees and maintenance staff, among others. Increasing their knowledge could result in an enhanced quality of care, early detection of problems and more comprehensive assessments.

Third, the social worker's understanding of cultural diversity issues could be utilized to develop programming consistent and supportive of the aging lifestyles and patterns of ethnic and minority groups. This could broaden the composition of the retirement community and draw on the strengths found in a diverse population.

Finally, social workers should continue to expand their current role in increasing opportunities for making choices and taking control. Elders who feel they have control over their lives and environment experience better adjustment, higher morale and satisfaction (Ryden, 1984).

Concluding Remarks

The number of life care communities is small but growing. As noted by O'Shaughnessy and Price (1987), in 1984 the estimated number ranged from 300 to 600, based on the definition used. These facilities offer a quality of care that is inaccessible to many of the elderly. Those who choose this living arrangement are offered a range of long-term care services in addition to basic services.

The nature of the practice setting and client composition affects the roles and responsibilities of social workers in several ways. On the one hand the range of resources available, including financial, personnel and environmental, offer the practitioner an unusual variety of options in planning interventions. By the same token, these factors tend to broaden the scope of duties performed.

In addition, clients vary from the well, active elderly to the frail, bedridden and unresponsive. Developing treatment plans that are truly individualized requires innovation and creativity.

Another feature is the long-term nature of the setting. Although the specific practice roles and responsibilities performed are found in many other settings social workers in continuing care communities come to know each resident and family very well. They observe them interact, identifying strengths and limitations and noting changes as they occur.

Finally, the entire residential community may be termed a type of milieu intervention. Interventions and treatment are an integral part of daily community life. In addition to responding to problems, the facility staff is actively involved in promoting growth and achievement of potential among the residents. The social work practitioner is an integral part of making the community effective.

Case Example

The following case example exemplifies many of the issues addressed by social workers in a continuing care facility. The intervention strategy and associated social work activities are those often required in this type of setting.

Mr. and Mrs. S are a white, middle-class married couple, aged 65 and 63, respectively. They applied for admission to the life care community at the instigation of their two children. Mr. S is a native of Akron, Ohio. He is the youngest of three children and the only surviving member of his family. His family medical history reveals a high incidence of cancer, diabetes and stroke. He was diagnosed as having Alzheimer's disease at the age of 60. He has a master's degree and was employed as a high school teacher until the age of 61 when periods of irritability and disorientation resulted in his early retirement.

Mrs. S is from Cleveland. She has two brothers, who live out of state. Even though she reported a family history of heart disease, she had no serious medical problems. After raising a family, she completed a bachelor's degree and worked full-time as a librarian. She retired at age 59 in order to care for her husband. They own their home and are financially stable despite early retirement. Their, son age 44 and daughter, aged 38, both have families and time-consuming careers. One lives in Columbus and the other in Cleveland.

After retirement, Mr. and Mrs. S became increasingly isolated from their community. As Mr. S experienced a greater degree of confusion and memory loss, Mrs. S became increasingly overburdened with his need for supervision and with household responsibilities. At this point their son and daughter urged admission to Rockynol. An intake interview with Mr. and Mrs. S and their children took place in their home. Since sudden changes upset Mr. S, a guest visit was not recommended. During intake, his family reported that Mr. S was still able to engage in all aspects of self-care and had no problems with mobility. The son and daughter felt he needed a protective environment while she needed relief from her mounting responsibilities. Mr. S was cooperative and friendly during the interview but was unable to respond to questions. The social worker discussed their different needs and abilities to engage in facility activities. All agreed that independent living was not appropriate. Mrs. S, however, expressed a desire to continue performing a number of household tasks.

It was the social worker's impression that currently Mr. S could be maintained in congregate living with supportive programming to provide structure and routine activities. This would allow Mr. and Mrs. S to remain together as long as possible and relieve her of some of her caregiving responsibilities.

Soon after admission, the staff team met to reassess their individualized care plans. Staff observations confirmed that the family had overestimated Mr. S's ability to care for himself. Furthermore, the stress of relocation seemed to accelerate Mr. S's deterioration. He began wandering the halls at night, experienced increasing problems with toileting and began failing in other areas. Although Mrs. S was adapting well to the community, making new friends and finding activities she enjoyed, she was exhausted due to his increased need for supervision.

The social worker met with Mrs. S and the family and discussed the need for a level change to accommodate their differing needs. Mrs. S acknowledged that she could not provide the degree of care her husband required and would like some freedom. Initially, their son and daughter were reluctant to accept the fact that their father's condition was worsening. Finally, after much discussion with the social worker, they became supportive of his move into assisted living. With her encouragement, they made the move a family event to lessen the effects of relocation. They visit both parents frequently.

During the day Mr. S is in a community day care programme for Alzheimer's patients. He can converse in complete sentences and engages in more self care. He also has adapted to assisted living. As his Alzheimer's disease progresses, skilled nursing will become necessary. The social worker has helped his family prepare and plan for this eventuality.

Mrs. S appears relieved and comfortable. After a period of hospitalization following a mild stroke, Mrs. S has returned to congregate living. The social worker continues to monitor their progress, referring them for services as needed, keeping their family aware and involved and helping them build a lifestyle that affords them satisfaction.

References

Abramovice, B. (1988). *Long term care administration*. New York: The Haworth Press.

Beaver, M. L. (1983). *Human service practice with the elderly*. Englewood Cliffs, NJ: Prentice Hall.

Evashwick, C. J. and Weiss, L. J. (eds.). (1987). Managing the continuum of care. There was nothing else to do: Needs for care before nursing home admission. *The Gerontologist*, 25, 364-369.

Myers, Jane E. (1989). *Adult children and aging parents*. Alexandria, VA: American Association for Counseling and Development.

Neugarten, B. L. (1981). Growing old in 2020. *National Forum*, 61, 28-30.

O'Shaughnessy, C. and Price, R. (1987). Financing and delivery of long-term care services for the elderly. In C. J. Evashwick and L. J. Weiss (eds.), *Managing the continuum of care* (pp. 191-224). Rockville, MD: Aspen.

Ryden, M. B. (1984). Morale and perceived control in institutionalized elderly. *Nursing Research*, 33, 130-136.

Smallegan, M. (1985). There was nothing else to do: Needs for care before nursing home admission. *The Gerontologist*, 25(4), 364-369.

CHAPTER 17

SOCIAL WORK PRACTICE WITH GERIATRIC PATIENTS IN A REHABILITATION HOSPITAL

VIRGINIA L. FITCH, PH.D.
LEE R. SLIVINSKE, PH.D.
JANICE GREEN, M.S.S.A.
DEBRA HINKSON, M.S.W.

S *ocial workers have worked with geriatric patients in rehabilitation settings for many years. In the rehabilitation hospital, due to its medical focus, two primary social work contributions are formally recognized: liaison to the patient's family and discharge planning. However, they perform many additional tasks. These include assessment, education, networking, mediation, advocacy, linkage with community resources, team participation, consultation, counselling, case management and discharge planning among others. The entire array of responsibilities they assume allows elderly patients and their families maximum participation in rehabilitation, fosters adaptation to remaining handicapping conditions and enables the disabled elderly to have maximum lifestyle choices.*

Edwin Shaw Hospital is an accredited rehabilitation hospital servicing the needs of people disabled by head trauma, amputations, strokes, spinal cord injuries, degenerative joint and muscle diseases and other disabling illnesses and accidents. It is located in the state of Ohio in southeast Summit County. Although no geographical catchment area is designated, in practice the hospital is viewed as a regional rehabilitation centre serving a 15-county area.

Edwin Shaw is considered a county hospital and receives a percentage of its funding from Summit County. Because of its location and the funding relationship, members of the board of trustees are appointed by the Summit County Executive Director. The appointees are bipartisan and represent different sectors of the community including educators, corporate executives and health care experts among others.

The hospital's mission is to serve as the region's leading centre for comprehensive medical rehabilitation. Its purpose is to reduce the extent of disability and maximize the long-term functional independence of patients physically, emotionally, vocationally and in every other way. The comprehensiveness of the services provided makes it unique. The services include a skilled nursing unit, day hospital for adolescents and adults, chemical dependency unit for adolescents and adults, outpatient services and a 70-bed inpatient rehabilitation programme. This chapter will describe the activities of social workers with geriatric patients in the inpatient rehabilitation programme.

The Clientele

Social work practice in rehabilitation involves both disabled persons and their families as clients. The first part of this section reviews the impact of disability on the elderly. In the second part, the geriatric patients receiving services at Edwin Shaw are described.

A. The Effects of Disability

In general, the most salient factor in the quality of life expressed by the aged is physical health status (Elwell and Maltbie-Crannel, 1981; Markides and Martin, 1979; Milligan, Powell, Harley and Furchtgott, 1985). Ward (1984) has even suggested that being old results not from arriving at a particular age but from a combination of experiences and situations that make elders 'feel old.' A subsequent reduction in quality of life is then experienced.

The incidence of chronic illness and disability among older adults is well-documented. However, declines in physical capabilities do not uniformly lead to decreases in well-being. The degree of decline and its effects on activity level are important considerations. In addition, changes in social conditions, including role loss and loss of important reference groups, may ensue. These deprive the aged of feedback regarding their competencies (Holahan and Holahan, 1987). Certain factors such as having options from which to choose, positive sources of self-validation and social supports serve as mediators between impairment and the impact of the loss (Decker and Schultz, 1985).

For the individual, impairment precipitates a crisis both socially and emotionally. Fear and uncertainty about prognosis and the life change that will be necessitated are aroused. Alterations have to be made in self-image and in social and family roles (Feibel and Springer, 1982). The individual also is likely to experience loss of control over self and environment. In turn, loss of control may lead to further deterioration in physical and psychological well-being (Langer and Rodin, 1976; Schultz, 1976; Slivinske and Fitch, 1987). When a patient comprehends the extent of loss, the grieving process will begin. This point may be reached days, weeks or months after the precipitating crisis.

Most elderly maintain regular contact with their family. Thus, changes in the elder's health status affect the entire family system. Usually the family is the primary provider when an elder needs long-term care (Monk, 1983). A disabling illness places new demands on the family and generally results in some degree of crisis. New stressors are added to those already affecting the family system. Their impact is influenced by family beliefs about disability and health and prior experiences with illness. Roles, approaches to decision-making and other patterned behaviours may need to be modified. Families vary in their ability to make the changes needed in order to cope. Their ability to respond will determine whether the family in crisis is incapacitated. Often an early response to the crisis is denial. A belief in full recovery may be maintained by the family while the patient refuses to accept the degree of life change required (Zarski, DePompei, West and Hall, 1988). Other families become overprotective and overinvolved further decreasing the control and independence available to the patient.

The caretaking is financially, physically and emotionally draining. The caretaking role for the geriatric patient is most often assumed by the spouse, secondly the daughter, followed by the son, female relative and male relative. Where the spouse is caretaker, in addition to the assumption of unfamiliar tasks, loss of personal life and, often, isolation, he or she may have one or more chronic health conditions that require special care. Children who become caretakers are often called the 'sandwich generation.' They find themselves caught between the needs of the parent at the top, their children at the bottom and their spouse in the middle (Myers, 1989; Zarit and Zarit, 1984). These problems are exacerbated by the decreasing size of families, leaving fewer people to provide help, and the increasing tendency for both spouses to work outside the home.

Although a certain level of adjustment to disability may be achieved by the elder and the family, changes in treatment, prognosis and functional capacity inevitably produce further stress. Long-term adjustment will require continuing effort (Zarski, DePompei, West, and Hall, 1988).

B. Geriatric Patients in Inpatient Rehabilitation

With a few exceptions, all geriatric patients at Edwin Shaw are referred from acute care hospitals. They are admitted based on the belief that: 1) they have the potential to improve their level of functioning, and 2) they are medically able to participate in an intensive, comprehensive rehabilitation programme. Therapies are provided based on these criteria. This distinguishes the rehabilitation centre from a skilled nursing facility. The impairment must impact on several of the person's abilities and rehabilitation must include a comprehensive array of therapies. A patient who can benefit from only one therapy, such as an individual with a hip fracture, is not a candidate for admission.

Clientele are admitted by admissions personnel who determine rehabilitation potential and medical status. The patient is assigned to a nursing unit and a social worker is assigned to the patient. Each social worker has a caseload of approximately 17 to 18 patients and is assigned patients on one or two specific units. When possible, patients are assigned to a social worker by diagnosis so that expertise may be developed in working with a particular impairment.

Length of stay is not predetermined since a rehabilitation centre is not subject to the same DRG funding constraints faced by an acute care facility. Some progress or improvement has to occur in order to justify continued hospitalization. Each case is subject to review prior to discharge. The average length of stay is 32 days although this varies somewhat by diagnosis.

Geriatric patients comprise approximately 75 percent of individuals receiving inpatient rehabilitation at Edwin Shaw. Over 60 percent are female. Racial composition appears representative of the proportion of black and white residents in the region. No age limit is placed on rehabilitation potential. In 1989, a number of patients were over 95.

Each client represents unique problems that challenge the skills of the social worker. However, two case scenarios typify often encountered life situations of geriatric patients with disabilities. In the first scenario, the elder lives alone and has chronic health problems. The most recent illness or injury interferes significantly with the level of autonomy and control and precipitates a crisis. Generally, a daughter becomes involved, providing physical, financial and emotional support. She represents the sandwich generation, trying to care for an aging parent while balancing other roles and responsibilities toward spouse, children and work (Myers, 1989). In the other scenario, one member of an elderly couple experiences a debilitating impairment. They live alone and have few informal support systems. They may have some formal supports from community agencies. Often the spouse has health conditions that interfere with the ability to be caretaker.

Practice Roles and Responsibilities

The roles and tasks of the social worker in a rehabilitation centre may appear similar to those found in other settings. In practice, they are enacted in unique ways. Since physical rehabilitation is the main purpose of the centre, the social worker performs roles and takes responsibilities that support this purpose. The hospital formally assigns the social worker two responsibilities: 1) liaison to the patient's family and 2) discharge planning. In addition to these roles the social worker informally takes on many others including those of broker, advocate, educator, case manager, enabler, mediator, team participant and consultant.

In the rehabilitation process, the social worker functions as part of a multidisciplinary treatment team. The team, led by a physician, is composed of representatives from each department including a nurse, speech therapist, physical therapist, occupational therapist, social worker, psychologist, nutritionist and recreational therapist. Each member works with a patient and conducts an assessment based on its disciplinary task. Each assesses whether the treatment provided can benefit the patient. However, throughout the treatment process, from the day of admission until the day of discharge, the social worker is involved with each patient and family. Limited contact may take place after discharge. In general, this involves making referrals to community resources.

The initial contact with patient and family usually is made on the day of admission. Many experience their first contact with a social worker at this point. They often have misconceptions about social work that must be addressed. In addition to role clarification and establishing a helping relationship with the clients, the social worker has several tasks to accomplish. First, a beginning assessment of the patient and the patient's family must be done. Both are interviewed at the same time. Several areas are covered in the assessment. For example, the patient's previous level of functioning, coping skills, formal and informal support systems, home setting, including obstacles to mobility, living situation and expectations for recovery, are explored. This information will help identify obstacles to adjustment after discharge. If the patient is unable to respond, the family will be the primary source of information. The social worker will attempt to include the patient's participation by eye contact or other non-verbal gestures.

For the family assessment, information on each member's sense of the patient's likely degree of recovery, previous roles and interactions with the patient, experience with chronic illness and ability to participate in aftercare is elicited. The spouse's physical health and cognitive level also are important. The social worker needs to determine whether the spouse can participate in rehabilitation and be the caretaker physically, mentally and emotionally. Often the spouse also is impaired and unable to provide care.

A separate appointment with the family may be scheduled if cues indicating conflict or disagreement are noted in the joint interview. At other times the family may request a meeting immediately to discuss a possible nursing home placement after discharge. At this point the social worker will address the issues involved in discharge planning at a preliminary level. Further discussion will occur during the patient's stay.

A second task during the initial interview is to educate the family about rehabilitation. Families are often overly optimistic about recovery and vary in their understanding of rehabilitation. The social worker will attempt to help the family understand that the elderly patient rarely returns to the normal previous level of functioning and will need some degree of support after discharge.

In addition, general orientation to the treatment process and the hospital environment is given. Terms such as OT (occupational therapy), RT (recreational therapy) and PT (physical therapy) among others are explained. The social worker demystifies the process and empowers the client and family to participate effectively and have input in the rehabilitation process.

The third and final task, at this point, is to make an informal contract with the family. The contract will indicate the person(s) to serve as primary contact, how to reach them and their plans for participating in treatment.

After completing the assessment, the information is recorded on a form that is placed in the patient's chart. The assessment is presented at the next team meeting. At the meeting, all information on the patient and family is summarized and developed into a highly individualized rehabilitation programme. A baseline of current status and initial goals is established and tentative plans for projected length of stay are discussed.

Weekly team meetings are held with a review of each patient scheduled every two weeks. The social worker represents the patient and family and advocates for them. For instance, plans for discharge may be postponed if the social worker feels the family is unprepared to provide aftercare. Content from each meeting including all therapy reports, prognosis, projected length of stay, on-going assessments, aftercare needs, equipment requirements and the like are discussed with the family and explained by the social worker. The family in turn is encouraged to provide feedback regarding how the patient is coping and behavioural changes noted since the treatment began. Initial team assessments are revised and updated as new information emerges.

Throughout hospitalization, the social worker is viewed as a liaison. The team expects families to attend therapy training once a week. There they receive education about the patient's activities, kinds of assistance needed and training in continuing therapies after discharge. Through the social worker, the team approaches the family and obtains their cooperation. The family views the social worker as a means of having input into team decision-making.

The mediator role also is often needed. On the one hand, if the rate of physical progress is not consistent with the patient's expectations, anger may be directed toward self, the health care system, hospital personnel or anyone perceived as being at fault. On the other hand, a conflict may arise between team members and the family. The social worker helps facilitate a resolution of the problem.

During hospitalization, a minimum of one formal appointment is made to meet with the family and patient after each team evaluation. Consistent with the concepts of personal assumption of responsibility and self-determination that are basic to rehabilitation, families are encouraged and expected to initiate contacts with the social worker whenever a need arises. The degree to which they do so varies. Each contact is documented in the medical chart and includes comments on the family dynamics observed and the social worker's activities and interventions.

Interventions such as counselling occur informally and often focus on problem solving and provision of social support. The family typically is the focus of many social work interventions. Still in a state of crisis, members require reassurance and help in dealing with role change, establishing new patterns of interaction and in managing stress levels.

Discharge planning begins with the initial social work interview. As the time of discharge approaches, plans are finalized and written in summary form. The discharge plan usually addresses the following: when the patient is leaving and where, the identified caretaker, referrals for services and equipment recommended. The social worker identifies the range of long-term care services available, acts as their guide in choosing services and helps them explore their personal resources. Although discharge planning may appear to be a simple task, it is based on multiple contacts with the patient and family and community resources for the purpose of linking them. At times, discharge planning presents the social worker with a dilemma. A geriatric patient, without a family to provide needed aftercare, may choose to return home to live alone against medical advice. The patient's right to self-determination is held paramount. Aftercare decisions must be consistent with the patient's wishes unless he or she is adjudicated incompetent. A conflict between this principle and the value systems of other professions within the hospital may arise. The social worker will likely make a referral to adult protective services for follow-up. Where indicated, a court referral requesting a guardian appointment may be initiated.

Potential for Role Development

Social work's importance to successful medical treatment has been recognized for many decades (Bartlett, 1975). The process of rehabilitation in a medical setting tends to be very fragmenting with many disciplines making contributions. The social worker performs an integrating function and makes rehabilitation a more cohesive experience for the family and patient. Rehabilitation is placed in context through the social worker's contributions, which include psycho-social assessment, counselling, team participation, linkage of clients with community resources and consultation to the other disciplines involved. The list of contributions is both comprehensive and impressive.

Nevertheless, several areas for role development can be identified. Development of these areas would require the provision of additional resources. First, outreach services providing follow-up to discharged geriatric patients and families would help to ensure continuity of rehabilitation and support. Achievement of an optimal level of functioning would be more likely with the addition of such services. Also, problems could be addressed before developing into a crisis.

Second, patients and families would benefit from support groups during hospitalization and after discharge. Groups are used very effectively in many rehabilitation settings. However, Medicare requirements for a daily therapy regimen in inpatient rehabilitation have eliminated a time for group meetings in many hospitals including Edwin Shaw.

Third, although social workers often provide case management informally, a formal designation as case manager could enhance patient care. As noted by Kane (1981), this would allow them to formally coordinate services and integrate care within the hospital setting and ensure the patient is viewed holistically.

Finally, social work involvement in preadmission screening and assessment or in marketing strategies could result in better informed patients and families. Often patients are admitted with no understanding of what will be expected of them. They are ill prepared to act assertively on their own behalf in the hospital setting.

Concluding Remarks

Social workers in a rehabilitation centre work closely with clients beginning with assessment and through discharge. The roles and tasks are the same regardless of diagnosis. However, the patient's age makes a significant difference in the problems they encounter and the resources available. They apply the principle of self-determination to enable patients with impairments to reach their potential and have maximum life choices. They recognize that the patient is part of a system also affected by the impairment. Interventions are formulated with the entire client system in mind. Physical rehabilitation is meaningful only to the extent that it returns the client system to a functional state. Social workers accomplish this by helping the patient and family fit the rehabilitation process into their lives.

As non-medical personnel, their roles and responsibilities often go unrecognized by other disciplines. The social work knowledge and skills brought to the setting may be less visible than the therapy regimens of other disciplines. Nevertheless, the outcome of rehabilitation would be less than successful without social workers. Although often credited only as discharge planners they do much more. They assess the psycho-social impact of the impairment on patients and families, provide direct services to facilitate adaptation and post hospitalization planning, monitor and evaluate the effectiveness of discharge planning and identify gaps in service in the community. In sum, through effective discharge planning and coordination with formal and informal systems, they see that the progress achieved during hospitalization is maintained after discharge. Rehabilitation succeeds, in large part, through their efforts.

Case Example

The case described in this section illustrates the importance of the social worker's contribution to rehabilitation. The unique problems and life situations of the geriatric patient also are evident.

Mr. M is a 69-year-old white male referred to Edwin Shaw Hospital for rehabilitation following a cerebral vascular accident (stroke). He is a native of Youngstown, Ohio and is the youngest and only surviving one of five siblings. As a result of the stroke, Mr. M was unable to speak during the initial interview with the social worker. He was alert, oriented to place and time but easily distracted. He was accompanied by his daughter, Joanne, age 32, and his ex-wife, age 58. Assessment information was obtained from them in his presence.

Mr. M completed a high school degree and was employed in a steel mill for 45 years until his retirement. He retired at age 63 due to complications arising from diabetes. At that time circulatory problems resulted in amputation of the left leg above the knee. He walks with the aid of a prosthesis and a walker. His income is modest and adequate for his needs until the recent expenses incurred as a result of the stroke.

Mr. M has been divorced 28 years and has one daughter. He remains on good terms with his former wife and her second husband. He is a member of a Greek Orthodox church but rarely attends services. All social activities involve his family. Joanne described him as kind, generous and family oriented with a dislike for change. His lifestyle following the amputation has become a sedentary one. She reported that he coped well following the amputation. She described him in very loving terms and stated that he would cope well with the stroke as long as he could go home.

The social worker found the daughter and ex-wife to be very supportive. Both reside in Youngstown approximately one hour from the hospital. Joanne is married and has three children, ages 14, 13 and 8. The youngest is hyperactive. She works full-time but plans to visit every other night. Both she and her mother intend to participate in therapy education once a week.

Their expectations for his recovery differed. His former wife expressed concern that he would need nursing home placement after discharge. The daughter refused to consider a nursing home and expected her father to live with her and her family until he could return to his apartment.

The social worker's impression was that although the daughter had a high level of involvement, she verbalized unrealistic expectations. In addition to her work and family responsibilities, she refused to acknowledge the physical barriers present in her small rural home. All bedrooms were on the second floor, entries had several steps and the first floor had no bathroom facilities. These would limit the patient's movements and capacity for developing independence. Mr. M's need for 24-hour supervision, equipment for aftercare and outpatient rehabilitation therapy were beyond her physical, emotional and financial capacities. When the social worker talked with Joanne about these concerns, she insisted that she could manage.

Mr. M was hospitalized for two months. Through rehabilitation, his mobility improved although he continued to require assistance getting in and out of bed, bathing, toileting and in other self care. He was able to formulate simple sentences regarding his basic needs but could not engage in conversations.

Joanne visited each week but rarely attended therapy training sessions. She had counted on her mother's assistance. However, her mother experienced a mild coronary and was unable to help. The focus of social work intervention was to help the daughter to explore her roles at home with her family and at work, the resources available to her in the community and from informal supports, and her father's needs. Her anxiety and agitation grew as it became more obvious that she could not provide in-home care for her father. Three weeks prior to his discharge she was able to acknowledge this after his first overnight home visit. With the social worker's support, Joanne told her father that she was unable to provide the care he needed and that a nursing home placement would be necessary. For the first time, Mr. M realized the extent of his impairment and began the process of grieving for his loss. Joanne expressed feelings of guilt. The social worker helped Joanne and her father begin to work through their feelings. Together they developed an aftercare plan and identified options.

Joanne chose a skilled nursing home in the Youngstown area. Staff there were contacted by the social worker and arrangements were made to provide for his special needs. Mr. M was discharged into the facility. Although initially he was very upset, he became accepting of the arrangement. His family visits him frequently.

References

Bartlett, H. (1975). Ida M. Cannon: Pioneer in medical social work. *The Social Service Review*, 49, 208-228.

Decker, S. D. and Schultz R. (1985). Correlates of life satisfaction and depression among middle-aged and elderly spinal cord injured persons. *American Journal of Occupational Therapy*, 39, 740-745.

Elwell, F. and Maltbie-Crannel, A. (1981). The impact of role loss upon coping resources and life satisfaction of the elderly. *Journal of Gerontology*, 36, 223-232.

Feibel, J. H. and Springer, C. J. (1982). Depression and failure to resume social activities after stroke. *Archives of Physical Medical Rehabilitation*, 63, 275-280.

Holahan, C. K. and Holahan, C. J. (1987). Correlates of life stress, hassles and self efficacy in aging: A replication and extension. *Journal of Applied Social Psychology*, 17, 574-592.

Kane, R. A. (1981). Education for teamwork revisited: Caveats and cautions. In J. Brown, B. Kirlin, and S. Watt (eds.), *Rehabilitation services and the social work role: Challenge for change* (pp. 304-315). Baltimore: Williams and Watkins.

Langer, E. J. and Rodin, J. (1976). The effects of choice and enhanced personal responsibility for the aged: A field experiment in an institutional setting. *Journal of Personality and Social Psychology*, 34, 191-198.

Markides, K. and Martin, H. (1979). A casual model of life satisfaction among the elderly. *Journal of Gerontology*, 34, 86-93.

Milligan, W., Powell, D., Karley, C. and Furchtgott, E. (1985). Physical health correlates of attitudes toward aging in the elderly. *Experimental Aging Research*, 11, 75-81.

Monk, A. (1983). *Resolving grievances in the nursing home: A study of the ombudsman program*. New York: Columbia University Press.

Myers, Jane E. (1989). *Adult children and aging parents*. Dubuque, Iowa: Kendall/Hunt.

Schultz, R. (1976). Effects of control and predictability on the psychological well-being of the institutionalized aged. *Journal of Personality and Social Psychology*, 33, 553-573.

Slivinske, L. R. and Fitch, V. L. (1987). The effect of control-enhancing intervention of the well-being of elderly individuals in retirement communities. *The Gerontologist*, 27, 176-181.

Ward, R. A. (1984). The marginality and salience of being old: When is age relevant? *The Gerontologist*, 24, 227-232.

Zarit, S. H. and Zarit, J. M. (1984). Psychological approaches to families of the elderly. In M. G. Eisenbert, L. C. Sutkin and M. A. Jansen (eds.),

Chronic illness and disability through the lifespan: Effects on self and family (pp. 269-288). New York: Springer.

Zarski, J. J., DePompei, R., West, J. D. and Hall, D. E. (1988). Chronic illness: Stressors, the adjustment process, and family-focused interventions. *Journal of Mental Health Counseling*, 10, 145-158.

CHAPTER 18

SOCIAL WORK PRACTICE IN
COMMUNITY PSYCHOGERIATRIC PROGRAMMES

DARLENE H. KINDIAK, M.S.W., C.S.W
JANE L. GRIEVE, M.S.W., C.S.W.

T *his chapter discusses psychogeriatric practice and describes the clinical and administrative roles that have emerged for social workers on psychogeriatric teams. Within these roles, the variety of responsibilities along with the complexities involved are outlined. Discussion is oriented toward future trends and the importance of education and training for social workers working in this field.*

Community psychogeriatric services can be regarded as a relatively 'young' area of speciality within the mental health field. One of the first full-time Canadian psychogeriatric programmes was established at Ottawa General Hospital in 1976 under the direction of Dr. David Harris, with the support of Dr. Gerald Sarwer-Foner (Harris — personal communication, August 18, 1993). Due to an ever-increasing number and proportion of the elderly in Canada, along with an emphasis on maintaining individuals in the community, a growing number of outreach psychogeriatric services have been established across the country.

Within the province of Ontario, there are currently over 40 community psychogeriatric programmes whose mandate is to service the mental health needs of elderly persons 65 years and over. These programmes are primarily based on three types of models: assessment /consultation; assessment/consultation and treatment; and assessment/consultation, treatment and teaching (Grant and Tarswell, 1993). Generally, there is no established norm of service delivery, rather each programme tends to operate idiosyncratically. Further, these programmes tend to differ according to their sponsorship (teaching hospital, non-teaching hospital, community mental health clinic, etc.); location (urban or rural); composition of team members (social workers, nurses, occupational therapists, psychologists, psychiatrists, etc.); and team size (ranging from two to ten members).

Due to the multifaceted biological, psychological and social problems that are frequently presented by elderly clients, the social worker is challenged to broaden his or her clinical knowledge and skills in order to work effectively with this population. There is also a need for social workers to be able to articulate and delineate their roles within the context of the multidisciplinary team. The specific mandate of the programme, the parameters which define each programme model, the blend of disciplines, the history of inter/ multidisciplinary functioning within the organization, plus the amount of flexibility that each social worker is comfortable maintaining, inevitably determines the role that the social worker formulates within each setting.

The role of the social worker in community psychogeriatric programmes has typically had three different components: clinical, administrative and a dual role (both clinical and administrative). While each of these may be clearly outlined in job descriptions specific to each work environment, the overlapping of functions and the degree of support received within the sponsoring organization ultimately affects the range of responsibilities, which are translated into practice.

I. Psychogeriatrics Defined

The psychiatry of old age, otherwise known as psychogeriatrics, has evolved from a movement originating in Britain during the 1960s.

Up until that time, interest in the mental health of old age had been largely confined to clinical research. Arie (1990) identified the following five factors as the basis for the development of this emerging speciality:

- pressure from the increase in the numbers of the aged and particularly the very aged;
- the growth in psychiatry's capacity to treat conditions previously regarded as hopeless (Post, 1978);
- the movement of psychiatry from mental hospitals into people's homes and into the general hospital;
- the effectiveness of geriatrics in British medicine; and
- the writings and teachings in the 1960s of a small group of figures . . . on the epidemiology, clinical features, prognosis, and pathology of the mental disorders of old age. (p.70)

Canadian interest in this area was initially sparked at McGill University in Montreal during the late 1940s, with the establishment of the first gerontological group within a department of psychiatry (Tourigny-Rivard and Reichenfeld, 1989). This original group included Drs. Stenn, Prados, Grad and Kral. The 1970s served as a turning point, with the development of geriatric psychiatry extending beyond the borders of Montreal (Tourigny-Rivard and Reichenfeld, 1989). Specifically, in 1974 the first multidisciplinary psychogeriatric association in Canada — the Ontario Psychogeriatric Association — was formed and contributed to the establishment of services, education and research for various health-related disciplines. Furthermore, during the late 1970s the Canadian Psychiatric Association formed a section on geriatric psychiatry and the University of Toronto established the first division of geriatric psychiatry.

Over the years, the term psychogeriatrics has been used interchangeably with *geriatric psychiatry* and *geropsychiatry* to identify the psychiatric subspeciality that addresses the care of the mentally impaired elderly (Health and Welfare Canada, 1988). At the same time, there has been wide variation in the meaning, with some confining the word to the care of the confused and demented elderly and others applying it where mental and physical disease occurred simultaneously (Pitt, 1982). Although there has not been general consensus, according to Pitt (1982) most refer to psychogeriatrics as:

. . . the assessment, treatment and management of elderly people suffering all kinds of mental disorders. These include depression (which is even more common than dementia), paranoid states, neurosis (mainly manifest as undue anxiety) and troublesome quirks loosely labelled personality and behaviour disorders, as well as acute or chronic states of confusion. (p.1)

While the term psychogeriatrics has often been criticized for being an 'ugly word' (i.e., cumbersome, overtly clinical) as well as denigrating to the individual who is identified as a psychogeriatric patient (Pitt, 1982), its use reflects the broad speciality area that concerns itself with all aspects of care and functioning. As further defined by Health and Welfare Canada (1988),

It comprises a body of knowledge on the psychodynamics and psychopathology of old age, special expertise in the pharmacological and psychosocial treatment and management of the mentally ill elderly, and a unique organization of services. It represents an innovative use of existent resources rather than a new specialty, for it has had contributions from many fields and disciplines. (p.14)

II. Psychogeriatric Services

The provision of psychogeriatric services is quite distinct in that it is premised upon a community-based approach to care. This need, to assess and treat the elderly in the community as much as possible, has been expressed by Gutkin (1985) to include the following:

. . . I believe that the vast majority of patients are best managed in their own environment. This is not to say that in-patient units are not necessary or important, but that well-balanced and relevant services for the elderly must include both facilities. (p.179)

Several reasons for a community orientation have been outlined by Hemsi (1982). First, due to the nature of mental disorders, there is often little to be gained by admitting an elderly person to the hospital. Since older people are integral members of social networks, it is essential to have a good working knowledge of that network as observed in the community. Further, in order to provide the necessary support which may be required, it is important to understand the individual's situation and the psycho-social processes that are having an impact on them. Finally, in this regard, it is not realistic to expect that there will be a large shift toward institutional care in the near future.

The majority of psychogeriatric teams provide assessment and treatment in an elderly person's own home or long-term care facility. Such views have also been reinforced by Health and Welfare Canada (1988), whereby the home is considered the 'optimal setting' for assessment of persons with psychiatric disorders. While this allows greater comfort and privacy for the client, working in the home setting may induce increased stress for the professional. In this regard, the loss of control experienced by the professional needs to be acknowledged and understood.

The approach taken by health care professionals in the assessment and treatment of the psychogeriatric population has evolved over time. Initially, as programmes became established, team functioning often focused upon a multidisciplinary approach to care, whereby several disciplines become involved in the delivery of services. Within this approach, each team member takes responsibility for activities related to their own particular discipline (Halper, 1993).

As team building became an important component in the delivery of service, and there was a greater need to interact among the disciplines, teams often experienced a shift from multi-disciplinary to inter-disciplinary functioning. Compounding the responsibility of the team members working toward a common goal, the inter-disciplinary approach also incorporates group effort and outcomes along with active family involvement (Halper, 1993).

A further shift has also emerged in light of current economic constraints, staffing cuts and limited resources. The so-called trans-disciplinary approach is based upon the premise that:

> ...one person can perform several professionals' roles
> by providing services to the patient under the

supervision of the individuals from the other disciplines involved. Representatives of various disciplines work together in the initial evaluation and care plan, but only one or two team members actually provide the services. (Halper, 1993, p. 35)

This type of approach is becoming more common and is particularly prevalent with programmes operating in rural settings where staffing and/or community resources are frequently limited. In essence, the type of approach that is used within each psychogeriatric programme is dependent upon flexibility and such factors as the number of team members, the types of disciplines, the sponsoring organization's philosophy of care, the degree of psychiatric input, etc.

Despite the orientation taken, the community approach to care requires cohesive teams. Since optional team functioning often means a blurring of roles, each team member must be able to transcend the role of their specific discipline while maintaining their professional uniqueness, in terms of specific knowledge and skills. Obviously, such collaborative processes also involve the learning and incorporation into one's clinical practice of a variety of knowledge and skills from the other disciplines. Thus, the ultimate goal for the team is to enable its members not only to retain the expertise of their specific disciplines, but also to develop a commonality of skills as applied gerontologists (Knight, 1989).

While team functioning and the operations of practice vary from one programme to another, it has become recognized that the expertise needed to conduct home assessments is commonly associated with the professions of nursing and social work (Ramsdell, Swart, Jackson and Renvall, 1989). However, regardless of which practitioners partake in the actual home visit, the basic premise of a team approach is that all the team members have an equal opportunity to contribute to the diagnosis and treatment plan (Health and Welfare Canada, 1988).

The Clientele

The psychogeriatric population essentially refers to seniors experiencing mental health difficulties. Projections of the Canadian population 65 years of age and older are expected to increase dramatically over the turn of the century. Despite such projections, conflicting reports make it difficult to determine the precise incidence of mental health problems among the elderly. For instance, there are studies that suggest that the elderly are particularly vulnerable to mental health problems (Wasylenki, 1980; Blazer, 1980). Yet others, such as D'Arcy (1987), concluded that such a relationship does not exist, as he contended that the incidence of mental illness among the elderly is no greater than among any other age group.

One major exception does exist however. Dementia is undisputedly the most prevalent mental health disorder more common among the elderly population. Health and Welfare Canada (1988) reported that for individuals 65 years of age and older, five percent are thought to suffer from mild to moderate dementia and five percent from severe dementia. Further, for individuals 80 years of age and older the rate of dementia may rise to 20 percent.

In the province of Ontario, the prevalence of dementia has been estimated as being even higher than the reported national figures. For example, in Hopkin's (1990) study, the following dementia rates per 1,000 were estimated for individuals over 65 years of age:

Table 1 — 1990 Age and Dementia Rate Projections in Ontario	
Age Cohort (Yrs.)	Dementia Rate per 1,000 Population
65-69	17.8
70-74	33.4
75-79	62.6
80-84	117.4
85-89	220.2
90+	413.0

Note: Source is R.W. Hopkins (1990), *Dementia projections for the counties, regional municipalities and districts for Ontario*. Unpublished manuscript, Kingston Psychiatric Hospital, Geriartric Unit, Kingston, Ontario.

Dementia is a particularly severe problem because there is presently no cure for it. Furthermore, the course of the disease is one of progressive deterioration, compounded by the onset of difficult behaviours as a result of the cognitive impairment. Consequently, the caregivers for persons suffering from dementia are at risk themselves for the development of mental health problems.

Aside from dementia, depression is the most pervasive and possibly the most frequently underdiagnosed mental health problem experienced by the elderly (Health and Welfare Canada, 1988). To date, epidemiological information about depression has been contradictory, with early studies identifying higher rates of prevalence (Butler, 1975; Weissman and Myers, 1979), yet more recent evidence has challenged this once prevailing view. It has more currently been identified that the proportion of elderly who suffer from 'clinical depression' is not higher among their younger counterparts (Anthony and Aboraya, 1992; Feinson, 1989; Newman, 1989).

Despite these conflicting findings, almost all epidemiologic data demonstrate that depression among older adults is too prevalent a problem to be ignored (Anthony and Aboraya, 1992). In addition, depression in elderly persons is often 'masked' by major symptoms in other areas. For instance, somatic complaints, especially pains of unknown origin, are common along with such presenting complaints as tiredness, fatigue and lack of energy. Depression may also hide behind any alteration in usual behaviour, i.e., impulsive sexual behaviour, outbursts of rage, drug and/or alcohol abuse, etc., (Wasylenki, 1987). Furthermore, the suicide rates among the elderly are higher than among other age groups, with elderly white males having the highest rate for suicides (Butler, 1975; D'Arcy, 1987; Wasylenki, 1987).

Although it is not within the scope of this chapter to detail the problems associated with the diagnosis and treatment of depression in later life, the fact that depression is a common and treatable problem for elderly persons needs to be emphasized. Frequently, depression remains undetected in this age group, due to the misperception that depression is a normal reaction to the losses associated with aging.

Other psychiatric disorders, which are common among the elderly population, include: anxiety, somatoform disorders, personality disorders, paranoid disorders and substance abuse. In addition, there are individuals who developed psychiatric disorders earlier in life, which they carry to their senior years. This subgroup is often not represented statistically in the data, but rather subsumed under 'other diagnoses.' Various disturbances of mental functioning or behaviour in later life, notably confusion or delirium, may also be associated with systemic infections, adverse drug reaction, trauma or surgery (Health and Welfare Canada, 1988).

The identified mental health problems of elderly persons as described in the literature reflect the types of referrals currently received in community psychogeriatric programmes. In particular, two of the more prevalent reasons for referrals to these programmes are depression and dementia/memory loss. Other common presenting problems include: complicated and non-complicated grief reactions, behaviour management and paranoid behaviour. In addition, problems related to retirement, marital conflict and elder abuse are increasingly being identified among the reasons for referral.

Psychogeriatric services are not only targeted to the identified elderly client but also to their spouses and adult children. In particular, family members who are caring for someone who is cognitively impaired are at risk for the development of a range of emotional difficulties such as depression, anxiety, guilt, social isolation, marital/family/interpersonal conflicts and ultimately physical health breakdown (Mace and Rabins, 1991).

In addition to the unique presentation of mental health problems of elderly persons, there are also specific difficulties related to the delivery of service. Traditionally, elderly persons have constituted a disproportionately small percentage of the population receiving mental health services. As noted by Cohen (1976), at the time of his study, the elderly had comprised more than ten percent of the population, yet fewer than four percent of all psychiatric outpatients were seen in private practice or a community mental health clinic.

Barriers to the provision of mental health services are evident not only among this clientele but also with service providers. For example, elderly persons do not tend to perceive of their problems in psychological terms and are inclined to be wary about involvement with mental health services (Waxman, Carner and Klein, 1984). Likewise, service providers may be pessimistic and question the value of the provision of mental health services for elderly persons or feel inadequate in their ability to provide these services (Knight, 1989).

In essence, given the broad range of clinical presentation of mental health problems of elderly persons and the reluctance among this age group to accept help, the approach to treatment requires knowledgeable, skilled, sensitive and creative practitioners. A review of the roles and responsibilities of the social worker will demonstrate the wide versatility required of this discipline in working in community psychogeriatric programmes.

Practice Roles and Responsibilities

Social workers are represented on almost every psychogeriatric team currently functioning in Ontario. As indicated earlier in this chapter, three types of roles characterize social work practice on these teams — clinical, administrative and the dual clinical/administrative. The following discussion provides a description of these clinical and administrative roles, with a caveat that these descriptions are neither inclusive nor definitive.

I. The Clinical Role

The clinical roles includes a composite of both direct and indirect practice skills. Subsumed under direct practice skills are the following competencies: to conduct a comprehensive biopsychosocial assessment; to provide supportive counselling and psychotherapy on an individual, family and group basis; to locate and coordinate linkage with appropriate resources; and to offer case management services (coordination, monitoring and advocacy).

Within the context of these various clinical responsibilities, the process of assessment demands the acquisition of important skills. The significance of the assessment process has been stated emphatically by Health and Welfare Canada (1988).

> Assessment is the cornerstone of good psychogeriatric care. Careful, broad-based, systematic examination of the patient is essential for accurate diagnosis and appropriate treatment decisions. Assessment is necessary for determining priority of needs, for

establishing competency or incompetency, for patient monitoring, for outcome or program evaluation, and hence for resource allocation. (p. 8)

The clinical psychogeriatric assessment extends beyond the psycho-social assessment to include the following components: physical and mental health; behaviour and self care abilities; and the individual's physical environment (Ontario Psychogeriatric Association, 1990). These essential elements are further developed in the assessment report protocol (Figure 2) as developed by West Park Hospital in Toronto, Ontario.

Figure 2 — Assessment Profile for Psychogeriatric Report at West Park Hospital, Toronto, Ontario

Assessment Report Protocol

NAME: FILE #:
ADDRESS: DOB:
PHONE #:   REPORT DATE:

Introduction
 — identifying information (name, age, family status, etc.)
 — brief description of living environment
 — reason for referral and who initiated (when and why)
 — to date, identify worker(s) and number of visits

Presenting Problem
 — client's and family's identification of problem, i.e., financial, functional, family, marital, legal, medical, psychiatric, living situation, emotional or physical abuse, substance abuse, home management
 — description of symptoms and behaviours and their effects
 — comments regarding severity, frequency, timing
 — history of problem development, i.e., when did problem occur? what were precipitating factors?, course of symptom development?, strategies attempted and results?

Health History
 — system review and diagnoses
 — history of illnesses, hospitalizations
 — use of medications, compliance, dosages, etc.
 — alcohol and smoking habits (addressed when appropriate)

Figure 2 (continued)

— nutritional habits (addressed when appropriate)
— psychiatric history, i.e., diagnoses, treatment, admissions to psychiatric facilities (when and where)

Personal History
— date, place of birth
— significant events
— relationships (past and current)
— pertinent family history, i.e., psychiatric, education
— work history
— leisure activities (past and present)

Current Living Status
— family, caregiver, community supports, i.e., extent of involvement
— supports available to caregiver
— financial resources
— ADL functioning
— observations of home environment
— self care, i.e., eating, bathing, grooming, toileting, dressing
— household management, i.e., cooking, laundry, cleaning, maintenance, repairs
— community management, i.e., shopping, banking, telephone, public transportation
— ambulation, i.e., safety, mode, distance
— adapted equipment/devices
— environmental adaptations

Mental Status
— observations re: appearance, behaviour, speech, affect, suicidal ideation, thought content and process, perceptions
— cognition: orientation, memory, language, attention and concentration, abstract thinking, judgment, insight (see Martin 1987)
— results of mini-mental status and geriatric depression (or note reasons not included)

Impressions
— strengths, weaknesses
— brief synopsis of medical, psychiatric, social factors
— diagnostic impressions

Recommendations and Treatment Plan
— identify further consultation, investigation, treatment, services and/or management
— prioritize

Note(*).   Adapted from West Park Hospital Policies and Procedures, Toronto, Ontario, 1993.

In assessing the mental status component, there needs to be an examination of the individual's psychological/emotional state and cognitive functioning. Martin (1987) offered a breakdown of mental status categories, which need to be observed and recorded as follows: 1) Appearance and Behaviour — manner of relating to the interviewer, appropriateness to the interview, gross neglect of hygiene and grooming, inanition and dehydration, mobility and bizarre behaviour; 2) Speech — rate and articulation and vocabulary (command of English); 3) Affect — subjective and objective mood, self-esteem, future orientation and suicidal ideation; 4) Thought Form and Content — coherence and logic, themes with which the patient is preoccupied, obsessional thoughts and delusions; 5) Perception — illusions, hallucinations and depersonalization/derealization; 6) Cognitive Function — level of consciousness, orientation, memory, attention and concentration, language, visual — spatial organization, abstract thinking, judgment and insight (p. 121).

To assist in the assessment of mental status and cognitive functioning, standardized assessment tools are also commonly utilized. For example, one of the most widely used instruments for screening cognitive function is *The Mini-Mental Status Examination* (Folstein, Folstein and McHugh, 1975). Another popular instrument used in assessing the level of depression in the elderly is *The Self-Rating Geriatric Depression Scale* (Yesavage, 1986). (A comprehensive listing of the numerous structured instruments that are available and useful in working with the psychogeriatric population is offered by the Ontario Psychogeriatric Association (1990).)

It is clearly apparent that specialized knowledge and skills are required for direct practice with this clientele. The social worker must be able to understand such features as: the unique presentation of mental health problems among persons over age 65; the progression of dementia and the utilization of behaviour management strategies to deal with difficult behaviours; the necessary adaptations required in communicating with sensory and cognitively impaired older adults; and the issues involved with the provision of multigenerational family intervention.

Furthermore, psychotherapy with older adults also requires subtle changes in one's practice. For example, reminiscence is effective therapy for elderly clients, although this process can be misconstrued as being repetitive story telling rather than 'real therapy.' The location, frequency, timing of sessions, use of self-disclosure and physical touching are also subject to variation in working with the elderly person. However, other therapeutic conditions such as the provision of an atmosphere of safety and trust, skilled listening, awareness and use of transference and counter-transference issues remain constant.

As is evident from the previous overview about the evolution of psychogeriatrics, psychiatry has strongly influenced the development of mental health services for the elderly. Consequently, there has been a reliance on descriptive nomenclature such as the *Diagnostic and Statistical Manual of Mental Disorders, 4th edition (DSM IV)* and its bias toward the medical model of diagnosis and treatment. Within the context of the 'person-in-environment' perspective, the social worker can serve to broaden the domain of mental health services for elderly persons beyond the realm of psychiatric pathology and medical management. In the process of assessment, for example, consideration needs to be given to the political, social, cultural, gender and economic realities and their impact on elderly persons. The current emphasis to pharmacological dispensation, as the primary mental health intervention with older persons, needs to be addressed and consideration given to alternate forms of treatment. Thus, the varying theoretical orientations common to social work practice (i.e., psychodynamic, family systems theory, cognitive behavioural) can serve to broaden the understanding of symptomatic behaviour and the scope of intervention strategies. In addition, the focus to relationship and differential use of self can be helpful for other team members in understanding their work with this clientele. (See Section I of this text for an elaboration of these particular issues.)

Another reason for the medical emphasis in psychogeriatric practice is due to the prevalence of physical illness coexisting with mental health concerns. Consequently, social workers on psychogeriatric teams may find themselves in a similar position as their colleagues working in hospital settings, in that they lack the medical knowledge and skills that are common to the other team members. In addition, as the other team members become more proficient in dealing with psycho-social issues, the social worker may feel threatened and become defensive or succumb to the pressure of the prevailing model. It is important that social workers functioning on community psychogeriatric teams be able to articulate for themselves and the team their unique knowledge that can contribute to understanding elderly persons and their specialized skills in working with this age group.

Nevertheless, social workers on psychogeriatric teams are required to expand their knowledge and skills beyond traditional social work practice to include a familiarization with related areas in pharmacology, psychology and medicine. Teams need social workers who have an understanding and working knowledge of the diagnostic model of medical illness in elderly persons. In addition, social workers need to develop comfort with the use of standardized questionnaires such as mental status tests and depression inventories. In order to incorporate such new knowledge and skills within the social work perspective and to function effectively as a member of the team, one must have a strong professional identity, self-awareness about both their own collaborative style and interpersonal biases (Lowe and Herranen, 1981). Failure to do so may unduly restrict and even jeopardize the role of the social worker on psychogeriatric teams.

In addition to the numerous direct practice skills required of social workers in community psychogeriatric programmes, there are also indirect practice skills. These include such competencies as: consultation to long-term care institutions; collaboration with other community agencies; education to professionals and lay persons; supervision of students; and programme and community development (to identify unmet needs and to promote the development of new resources). Discussion of these competencies will be centred on the area of education.

In working with this clientele, there is a need for the provision of education regarding aging and related problems for professional and personal caregivers. Social workers are skilled in understanding the issues regarding the impact of illness on individuals and family functioning, along with the resulting difficulties that can ensue. Also, social workers have an appreciation of some of the dynamics involved regarding the provision and acceptance of help. The interpretation of these dynamics can be useful for other caregivers who are frequently frustrated with the tendency among elderly persons to resist or refuse assistance. In practice, there is considerable variation among each psychogeriatric programme regarding the focus given to education. For those teams that operate on the assessment and consultation model, a greater emphasis may be given to education. Whereas, for those teams that operate within the assessment and treatment models, there may be less opportunity to provide this service.

Overall, it is evident that the clinical role for social workers on psychogeriatric teams is broad in scope, encompassing both the direct and indirect practice skills. The balance of the emphasis that is given to either direct or indirect practice will depend to a large degree on the nature of the individual team in combination with education, specialized skills and interests of the social worker.

II. The Administrative Role

Another role for the social worker functioning on a psychogeriatric team is the administrative one. Currently in Ontario, approximately ten of the 42 operational psychogeriatric teams have social workers designated in management positions. These job titles can vary anywhere from programme manager to coordinator to team leader.

Similar to the clinical component, the division of administrative responsibilities for these administrators varies with the functioning of each team as well as the structure of the sponsoring organization. While the administrative role is essentially comparable to any middle management positions, such as director/supervisor of social work, there are some unique administrative functions common to psychogeriatric programmes.

The first identifiable feature is the budgetary responsibility. In Ontario, the majority of psychogeriatric programmes are funded by the Community Mental Health Branch of the Ministry of Health (Grant and Tarswell, 1993). Each programme receives separate funding that is funnelled through a sponsoring organization. Hence, the social work manager is often primarily accountable both to the Community Mental Health Branch and the institution. This dual reporting relationship also comes to the forefront in relation to other expectations. For example, the Community Mental Health Branch requires that all funded programmes submit statistical data in accordance with a management information systems (M.I.S.) framework. In turn, these statistics may or may not be sufficient for the institutional requirements and hence further adaptations may be necessary.

Another dual reporting relationship occurs in regard to the evaluation process. Both the Community Mental Health Branch and the sponsoring organization each have specific programme guidelines, standards and expectations that must be adhered to. Thus, it is very common for psychogeriatric programmes to participate in two types of evaluations. For example, one of the author's experiences in a newly funded programme during their three-year probationary period was to undergo three separate evaluations by the Community Mental Health Branch, plus partake in two accreditations by the hospital.

A final dual reporting relationship occurs in relation to the programme advisory committee. Each programme is mandated under the Community Mental Health Branch to establish an advisory body comprised of consumers/family members, service providers, etc., to serve in assessing, developing, guiding and promoting an efficient, effective and progressive community psychogeriatric service. At the same time, this committee is accountable to the board of directors of the institution.

In essence, the social work administrator is thus responsible to two sources — to their respective supervisor within the organization and to the community programme consultant at the Community Mental Health Branch of the Ministry of Health. While some managers are permitted full access and communication with their programme consultant by their institutions, in other cases the responsibility for contact is redirected to other management personnel. Whichever system is practiced, the social work manager is always in the delicate position of having to balance all of the responsibilities and maintain open communication from all avenues.

In addition to the normally expected management responsibilities that a social work administrator would have to fulfil within the organization's expectations, this individual also needs to focus a large amount of energy in their local community. Since community psychogeriatric programmes are mandated to maintain a community outreach focus, the manager is often actively involved in local community services, (i.e., Alzheimer societies, adult day programmes, homecare, V.O.N., etc.,) as well as planning bodies, (i.e., district health councils, long-term care committees, mental health committees, etc.,) which are relevant to psychogeriatric issues.

Overall, the administrative role in psychogeriatric programmes is extremely challenging. The social work manager must be able to balance internal obligations with external community endeavours along with ministry expectations. While the social worker is well equipped to utilize the principles of social work practice at the macro level in managing their tasks, ongoing administrative upgrading and education is required for the individual to meet all these demands.

Potential for Role Development

The opportunity for role development exists within both the clinical and administrative components of social work practice on psychogeriatric teams. Within the clinical role, two areas can be identified that would benefit from enhancement — research and ethical issues.

As stated previously, community psychogeriatric teams tend to be idiosyncratic in structure and function, plus there does not seem to be a consensus regarding an ideal model for delivery of this service. In addition to examining and evaluating the existing models, research also needs to be directed toward the effectiveness of community psychogeriatric teams. There is a need for ongoing research into client problems commonly encountered by social work practitioners such as social isolation, poverty and substance abuse. Traditionally, social workers have tended to ignore research due to the demands of clinical practice. However, it is our opinion that involvement in research serves to enhance the credibility of the role of social work in the overall provision of psychogeriatric services.

Ethical dilemmas are also common to social work practice with elderly persons. For example, issues regarding competency, autonomy, the right to refuse treatment and euthanasia are an integral part of psychogeriatric practice. In particular, referrals to psychogeriatric teams frequently include the request for a recommendation regarding the safety of an individual to remain living in his or her own home. It is important for social workers to gain expertise and comfort with the process of assessing competency and to develop a framework for working through ethical dilemmas.

The potential for role development also exists in the administrative component of social work practice. The most significant area lies in the role of advocacy. Within the past few years, the Ontario provincial government released documents that are intended to serve as a guide for service provision in the areas of long-term care and mental health reform. Both of these reports — *Partnerships in Long-Term Care* (1993) and *Putting People First: The Reform of Mental Health Services In Ontario* (1993) — offer recognition of the problems and needed services for the psychogeriatric population. Hence, social workers in administrative positions need to become actively involved in bringing these concerns to the forefront. Advocacy, at the provincial level, is definitely a role that must be developed if psychogeriatric programmes have a chance for future survival.

Concluding Remarks

Social work practice in community psychogeriatric programmes is emerging as an area of speciality within the social work profession. Thus, in order to prepare social workers for psychogeriatric practice, educational issues need to be addressed. At the present time, graduates from BSW and MSW programmes are not adequately prepared to provide knowledgeable and skilled service in working with the aging population. As a result, social workers in this area tend to have obtained on-the-job training and search out additional courses to gain the required knowledge and skills. Whether it is possible for the inclusion of a significant component of courses on aging within the current curriculum offered by the existing facilities of social work is debatable. Solomon and Mellor (1992) described an innovative post-graduate social work interdisciplinary geriatric education model offered at Hunter/Mount Sinai Geriatric Education Center in New York City. These authors stated ". . . interdisciplinary geriatric education for social workers is best approached after graduation, in the workplace and as a continuing education process" (p.184). Further exploration of the utilization of this education model would seem advisable in order to adequately prepare social workers for practice with this rapidly growing segment of the population.

Finally, the social work profession has been an integral player in the development of community psychogeriatric teams. This specific field of practice has required practitioners to move beyond the traditional social work into an area of speciality where one must work intensely with other disciplines. The demands of team functioning, the blurring of roles between disciplines, the difficulties involved with the shift to conducting home rather than office visits, along with the need to expand one's knowledge base and assessment skills can all contribute in making this type of position very strenuous. At the same time, the challenges and continued growth opportunities offered in community psychogeriatric programmes can also serve to provide the social worker with an extremely rewarding work experience.

Case Example

Mr. G, aged 72, was admitted to hospital as a result of a heart attack. Following the stabilization of his medical condition, Mr. G appeared to be quite depressed and a referral was made to the medical social worker. At the time of discharge, the medical social worker recommended follow-up by the psychogeriatric clinic. When the social worker from the clinic was introduced to Mr. G, he responded to her in a brusque manner stating that he was quite capable of managing on his own. However, he did accept her card with the name and phone number of the clinic. The family physician prescribed an antidepressant medication and Mr. G was discharged home having refused any referrals for community support.

Two days following his discharge home, Mr. G contacted the clinic by phone. He appeared to be in a state of acute anxiety and he agreed to having the social worker make a home visit later that afternoon. A biopsychosocial assessment was completed by the social worker and presented at the team conference. The following problems were identified: 1) reactive depression to cardiac illness, 2) unresolved grief reaction following the death of his wife six years ago, 3) suspected alcohol abuse and 4) refusal of community supports. A concurrent mental status examination revealed mild confusion attributed to his depression rather than the early onset of dementia.

When the social worker met with Mr. G, he was somewhat formal but cordial and he reported that he did not recall meeting her at the hospital. Mr. G stated that he was agreeable to seeing her on a weekly basis only on the condition that she was not to discuss emotional issues. The social worker respected Mr. G's strong need for control in these early sessions and concentrated on establishing a trusting relationship with the client. Mr. G proved to be an intelligent and articulate man and he enjoyed sharing with the social worker aspects of his former career. He also talked about his only child, a son, with whom he appeared to have had a close relationship. Initially, when Mr. G appeared to be overwhelmed with emotion, he would leave the room. However, in time, he was able to disclose and weep openly with this worker regarding some of the painful losses that had occurred during his life.

One day, the social worker was notified that Mr. G had suffered a coronary attack and had been admitted to hospital. When the social worker went to see Mr. G he introduced her to the nurses as his friend. He died the following day.

Case Comments

Due to the multiple nature of problems presented by the elderly, the likelihood that adaptive interventions are required and the lack of other services, social workers can rarely confine themselves to playing a single preferred role, such as therapist. Rather, they will often be required to display a high degree of flexibility geared to the specific needs of the client (Edinberg, 1985). This brief case example has attempted to illustrate this feature of the clinical role.

When the social worker first met with Mr. G he seemed to be a contentious and somewhat confused elderly man. Frequently, elderly people present very differently in hospital and a return to the familiarity of their own home can effect a remarkable improvement in their physical, emotional and cognitive functioning. While in hospital, Mr. G seemed to have perceived of the offer of support as an intrusion into his personal life. His rejection of community resources upon discharge may be interpreted as defence reaction and a need to regain a sense of himself through his refusal to allow others into the privacy of his own home. Nevertheless, Mr. G was able to accept the worker's invitation and did contact the clinic two days later.

Building a relationship — the cornerstone of the social work practice — is crucial to therapeutic involvement with older adults. The core conditions (respect, non-judgmental attitude, genuineness, empathy) are frequently absent in the interpersonal relationships experienced by elderly persons. Their experience, more often, is of being ignored or treated in a paternalistic manner. The social worker allowed Mr. G to set the terms of her involvement and focused on the development of a trusting rapport. It took considerable time for a therapeutic relationship to develop with Mr. G, and, initially, the social worker experienced concern that she was more like a friendly visitor than a professional. These feelings were intensified by seeing Mr. G at his home where they would meet in the kitchen over coffee.

Frequently, older people do not differentiate among professionals or may, as Mr. G did, prefer to perceive the social worker as a friend. This attempt to minimize the status of the social worker may be interpreted as another illustration of the tendency of elderly persons to resist help. Indeed, by perceiving the social worker as a friend may have enabled Mr. G to accept her help. As long as the professional boundaries are maintained, for the worker to dispel the notion of friendship (at least with this particular client) might have been counterproductive. During the course of involvement with the social worker, Mr. G eventually was able to engage in a meaningful and purposeful helping relationship. It was the impression of the social worker that Mr. G had made considerable progress toward the integration of his formerly disavowed painful emotional states.

Death is a reality in working with elderly clients. However, Mr. G's death was unexpected, as he had been managing quite well. The death of a client (expected or unexpected) with whom one has had a significant relationship is a loss and the feelings of grief need to be acknowledged and validated. To be able to experience the intensity of the feelings of loss and grief that are frequently the crux of the problems presented by elderly persons, without the worker becoming overwhelmed, is one of the challenges of working with this population.

References

Anthony, J.C. and Aboraya, A. (1992). The epidemiology of selected mental disorders in later life. In J.E. Birren, R.B. Sloane and G.D. Cohen (eds.), *Handbook of mental health and aging* (2nd ed.). New York: Academic Press.

Arie, T. (1990). Psychogeriatrics, *British Journal of Hospital Medicine*, 44, 70-71.

Blazer, D.G. (1980). The epidemiology of mental illness in later life. In E.W. Buss and D.G. Blazer (eds.), *Handbook of geriatric psychiatry* (pp. 249-271). New York: Van Nostrand Leinhold.

Butler, R.N. (1975). Psychiatry and the elderly: An overview. *The American Journal of Psychiatry*, 132, 9.

Cohen, G.D. (1976). Mental health services and the elderly: Needs and options. *The American Journal of Psychiatry*, 133, 1.

D'Arcy, C. (1987). Aging and mental health, In V.W. Marshall (ed.), *Aging in Canada: Social perspectives*, 2nd ed. (pp. 424-450). Toronto: Fitzhenry and Whiteside.

Desjardins, B. (1993). *Population, aging and the elderly: Current demographic analysis.* Statistics Canada.

Edinberg, M.A. (1985). General considerations in mental health practice with the elderly. *Mental health practice with the elderly* (pp. 140-156). Englewood Cliffs, NJ: Prentice-Hall, Inc.

Feinson, M.C. (1989). Are psychological disorders most prevalent among older adults? Examining the evidence. *Social Science and Medicine, 29,* 1175-1181.

Folstein, M.R. Folstein, S. and McHugh, P.R., (1975). Mini-mental state: A practical method for grading the cognitive state of patients for the clinician. *Journal of Psychiatry Research, 12,* 189-198.

Grant, G. and Tarswell, N. (1993). *Provincial psychogeriatric survey of programs funded by Community Mental Health and Addictions Branch.* Unpublished manuscript. Presented at the 1993 Psychogeriatric Team Exchange, September, 1993, Stratford, Ontario.

Gutkin, B. (1985). Psychogeriatrics. *The Medical Journal of Australia, 143,* 178-179.

Halper, A.S. (1993). Teams and team work: Health care settings. *American Speech-Language Hearing Association, 35* (617), 34-35.

Harris, D.J. (1993). Director, Psychogeriatric Community Clinic, Victoria Hospital, London, Ontario — Personal Interview, August 18.

Health and Welfare Canada (1988). *Guidelines for comprehensive services to elderly persons with psychiatric disorders.* Department of National Health and Welfare, Ottawa, Ontario.

Health and Welfare Canada (1991). *Mental health problems among Canada's seniors: Demographic and epidemiologic considerations.* Department of National Health and Welfare, Ottawa, Ontario.

Hemsi, L. (1982). Psychogeriatric care in the community. In R. Levy and F. Post (eds.), *The psychiatry of later life* (pp. 252-287). Oxford: Blackwell Scientific Publications.

Hopkins, R.W. (1990). *Dementia projections for the counties regional municipalities and districts for Ontario.* Unpublished manuscript, Kingston Psychiatric Hospital, Geriatric Unit, Kingston, Ontario.

Knight, B. (1989). *Outreach with the elderly.* New York: University Press.

Lowe, J. and Herranen, M. (1981), Understanding teamwork: Another look at the concepts. *Social Work in Health Care, 7,* 1-11.

Mace, N.L. and Rabins, P.V. (1991). *The 36 hour day* (Rev. Ed.). Baltimore: The Johns Hopkins University Press.

Martin, B.A. (1987). Clinical assessment. In D.A. Wasylenki, B.A. Martin, D.M. Clarke, E.L. Lennox, L.A. Perry and M.K. Harrison (eds.). *Psychogeriatrics: A practical handbook.* Toronto, Ontario: Gage Educational Publishing Company, pp. 115-137.

Ministry of Health (1993). *Putting people first: The reform of mental health issues in Ontario.* Toronto, Ontario: Queen's Printer for Ontario.

Ministry of Health, Ministry of Community and Social Services and Ministry of Citizenship (1993). *Partnership in long-term care: A new way to plan, manage and deliver services and community support.* Toronto, Ontario: Queen's Printer for Ontario.

Newman, J. P. (1989). Aging and depression. *Psychology and Aging,* 4, 150-165.

Ontario Psychogeriatric Association (1990). *Creating links: Review of assessment for persons with dementia.* Toronto: Ontario Psychogeriatric Association.

Pitt, B. (1982). *Psychogeriatrics: An Introduction to the psychiatry of old age* (2nd ed.). New York: Churchill Livingstone.

Post, F. (1978). Then and now. *British Journal of Psychiatry,* 133, 83-86.

Ramsdell, J.W., Swart, J., Jackson, J.E. and Renvall, M. (1989). The yield of a home visit in the assessment of geriatric patients. *Journal of the American Geriatrics Society,* 37, 17-24.

Solomon, R. and Mellor, M. (1992). Interdisciplinary geriatric education: The new kid on the block. *Journal of Gerontological Social Work,* 18, 175-186.

Tourigny-Rivard, M.F. and Reichenfeld, H.F. (1989). Teaching the psychiatry of old age: A Canadian perspective. In von Hahn, B. (ed.), *Interdisciplinary Topics in Gerontology.* Switzerland: S. Karger, Basel, Chapter 6.

Wasylenki, D.A. (1980). Depression in the elderly. *Canadian Medical Association Journal,* 122, 525-532.

Wasylenki, D.A. (1987). Depression. In D.A. Wasylenki, B.A. Martin, D.M. Clark, E.A. Lennox, L.A. Perry and M.K. Harrison (eds.) *Psychogeriatrics: A practical handbook.* Toronto: Gage Educational Publishing Company, pp. 41-58.

Waxman, H., Carner, E. and Klein, M. (1984). Underutilization of mental health professionals by community elderly. *The Gerontologist,* 24, 23-30.

Weissman, M. M. and Myers, J.K. (1979). Depression in the elderly: Research directions in psychopathology, epidemiology and treatment. *Journal of Geriatric Psychiatry,* 12, 187-201.

Yesavage, J.A. (1986). The use of self-rating depression scales in the elderly. In L. Pivon (ed.), *Clinical memory assessment for older adults.* American Psychological Association, Washington, D.C.

SECTION 3

FUTURE CONSIDERATIONS

CHAPTER 19

GERONTOLOGICAL SOCIAL WORK PRACTICE IN THE 1990S AND BEYOND

MICHAEL J. HOLOSKO, PH.D.
LINDA J. WHITE, M.S.W.
MARVIN D. FEIT, PH.D.

Introduction

Gazing into a crystal ball and projecting what the future will hold for social workers practicing in the field of gerontology is less risky if one examines what is currently known about such practice and then evolves from there. This textbook is rife with rich illustrations of social workers practicing with the elderly in both unique and creative ways. It reminds us that to do so they must utilize knowledge and practice, which transcends conventional social work curricula and localizes itself moreso in the 'art' side of social work practice rather than the skill oriented 'craft' side of the profession. Indeed, all of the chapters in this text serve as testimony to the fact that social work practitioners have important roles to play in helping the elderly in health and human service organizations (HSOs), and they are operationalizing these roles in most efficacious ways.

Three main themes, which require some elaboration at this point, underpin each of the chapters of this text. They are: 1) the social work profession has a decidedly important role to play in practicing in this field; 2) in order to be more effective in the future, the profession will have to adapt accordingly to the many demands, resources and needs of this client group and 3) the future is now.

No statistician, epidemiologist or Malthusian demographer need remind us that the numbers of elderly both with the general population and also in need of services are increasing at an alarming rate. The many practitioners who have diligently described their practice activities in this text have successfully fulfilled their roles within the frameworks of their respective health and HSOs in most adroit ways. Indeed, the various psycho-social, familial, social support and service needs of the elderly described in these various settings require comprehensive social service delivery. Thus social work, moreso than any other profession that helps the elderly (e.g., medicine, nursing and/or any other speciality field) has such a diverse range to its practice repertoire that its service potential is universal to all clients in need of help. It is also complementarily (to some other one) tied to the multiple needs of the vast majority of elderly clients in care. In other words, regardless of what services elderly persons require, they seem to also require social work services, if not immediately, then at some point in the near future.

This reality certainly shifts the importance of many social workers practicing in this field from offering tangential or supporting services to providing cornerstone service delivery. In this regard, the impassioned accounts of the current and future practice roles of gerontological social workers in Section II of this text consistently reiterate the point that social workers hold integral and key roles in serving the needs of the elderly. There is also no doubt that this trend will continue in the future.

In regard to the second theme expressed in this text, that is, social work's adaptation to the changing needs and resources of the elderly, the hallmark of social work's evolution has been characterized by its flexibility. Historically, clients' needs have dictated how the profession has evolved, and the only troubling variable in this equation is whether there will be adequate resources to 'do the job' in the future. To date, policy-makers at both the macro (governmental) and meso (organizational, agency) levels have made sporadic attempts in providing meaningful programmes and services for the elderly, and any consideration of whether the profession can adapt accordingly must be framed contextually in whether resources will be made available for such change. Certainly, not only resources, but policies that promote such services and administrative supports, are equally important factors to consider in this regard. Thus, our ability to adapt is based less on our malleability (which is a 'given') and more on other variables in our external environment, which loom as potential impediments to our adaptation.

The final point about timeliness speaks to the fact that social work practitioners (as was noted throughout this manuscript) have already filled many cracks in various health and human service delivery systems and are primary caretakers for many elderly persons. The future is *now* for the profession in this very exciting and challenging field. Thus, we need to evolve and share our practice knowledge and wisdom through practicing, researching and educating ourselves, if we are to be effective with this client group in the future.

Future practice directions are many and varied and involve both indirect and direct practice concerns. Since front-line direct practitioners have been on the leading edge of working with the elderly, the impetus for understanding where the profession is emerging in gerontological social work practice will be discussed from this perspective. Four areas that are projected as areas for emerging practice include: 1) prevention, 2) community-based initiatives, 3) practice considerations and 4) education and training. Rather than present a prescription for what the profession should do in each of these areas, our intent here is to create some awareness about how we may envision or think about such inevitable practice realities.

I. Prevention

Prevention is a notion that we (the profession) have embraced and have difficulty defining (Bloom, 1981). Not unlike other helping professions, social work practice in North America has been supported by funding agencies who define their fiduciary parameters in quantitative terms, based on 'body count' data. In other words, how many you see, how many you treat and how many return for service are the basis for how much money HSOs and health care organizations receive (Canadian HSOs do not differ significantly from American ones in this regard). Not surprisingly, therefore, prevention programmes or strategies provide a disincentive for HSOs as they 'keep the monthly statistics down' of clients who form the units of service for funding purposes.

Herein lies the rub. As evidenced in Section II of this text, when one examines the various settings of care for the elderly, they are being inundated with demands for service. Indeed, existing structures, institutions or programmes are being 'stretched to the limits' to provide minimal services basic to their organizational mandates. Such programmes and their personnel are already working within their full capability, and guess what — there is no relief in sight. No large chunks of federal, provincial (Canada) or state monies are being earmarked to meet these disproportionately increased demands for service, and guess what — there are more elderly in sight. This only means one thing, that sooner or later prevention must emerge as a reality for future service provision in this area, and because social work, moreso than any other helping profession, can be 'had on the cheap,' we may find ourselves right 'smack dab' in the middle of this issue!

In this regard, we hope that the profession doesn't entrap itself in the long-standing public health and health care dilemma (actually originally conceived in the mental health field) of getting hung-up defining elaborate models of prevention and funding exclusive aspects of primary, secondary or tertiary prevention programmes. Certainly, one of social work's strengths has been its atheoretical orientation and getting to the heart of practice by letting their clients determine their prevention needs. What is required, therefore, is for the profession to sense and act accordingly to these needs and develop low cost strategies to infuse them into their existing programmes and services. What is also required is for a different mind set to emerge (on behalf of funding agencies) about prevention activities and coherent agency policies and procedures to support these activities. For example, it really doesn't cost that much for a social worker who is conducting a psycho-social assessment (in-home or in the office) to call a public health nurse to assist a client with something that we (the under-60 cohort who can touch their toes, or have someone else touch our toes) consider as mundane as podiatric care, which can slowly evolve (if not treated) into a chronic debilitating problem for many elderly persons.

II. Community-based Initiatives

Another area on the horizon for gerontological social work practice involves practitioners taking more community-based initiatives for either providing direct care for elderly persons or supporting service provision in a complementary fashion. As we know, institutional and residential care facilities are costly and needed; however, data about this issue clearly point out that much can be done to support community-based care for the elderly.

At one level, better integration of services using information systems, referral networks, resource sharing and interorganizational models is necessary. This involves a regional conceptualization of health and social services as defined by a community's needs, and implies that communities have a holistic notion of comprehensive community care. As one may surmise, the ability to operationalize such models of service would be complex but not unrealistic. Usually, it takes the initiative of several HSOs to get something like this started, and/or the creativity of funding bodies to envision it (see for example, Holosko and Dunlop, 1989). Certainly, as we venture into the high tech information era, such integration seems inevitable.

At another level, social supports and social networks for helping the elderly need to be defined and utilized more effectively by both helping professionals and lay persons alike. Our current knowledge of social supports and their integral role in service delivery cannot be overstated (see Chapter 14 by Toseland and Rossiter; Gottleib, 1983; Erickson, 1975, 1984) and the potential for practice in this area is both exciting and promising. In sum, it will be a challenge for the profession to evolve in this area in meeting the multifaceted and various needs of the elderly, and such practice can only lead to better community-based service provision.

III. Practice Considerations

A creative shift in how we look at this stage of life flies in the face of our ageist and death-defying culture. The vision of old age as a viable, dignified and hopeful stage of life is met with societal denial, which is intense, pervasive and often unconscious. It follows, then, that the foremost qualification for any practitioner dealing with this age group is a belief in the importance of seeing and understanding the real problems of old age. The obvious issues of disease and frailties are often exacerbated by the stigmatizing, minimizing and general discounting of older individuals.

Not only do practitioners need to be realistic about the problems, they will have to be prepared to highlight issues that our institutions and service agencies have not considered and are not yet ready to consider. Because most of our present services are based on stereotypical and euphemistic thinking about old age, they are often inadequate.

The paradigmatic shift which needs to take place is a 'hard sell.' Other professionals, particularly those who have been the 'experts' in the field and our own colleagues who have practiced in the 'old' system, will present the most resistance. A practitioner needs to be prepared to teach, persuade, cajole and force a different way of 'seeing' the problems on existing service agencies and funders. We will need to develop and use our expertise in advocacy, research, writing, proselytizing and public speaking as well as our clinical skills in order to prove a point such as prevention saves money.

Practitioners who take up this challenge will be unpopular and misunderstood, at times by the families of their own clients. What they have to offer is not a neat package with no loose ends. Rather, it is a philosophy and a style that is open-ended and uncertain, as yet. It involves a capacity to deal with messy, half-baked situations with an open mind and intelligent curiosity. It involves resisting the status quo when things get tough and holding out for recognizing the uniqueness of each new situation. It entails a willingness to learn from clients and their families, as all good social work practice does. However, add to that the absolute necessity of being willing to experiment, take risks, make mistakes and to document what works when it works.

The challenge is obvious. The questions yet to be answered are: Who will meet it and how?

IV. Education and Training

Despite the rather convincing evidence presented throughout this text that social work has a decidedly important role to play in serving the elderly, the profession has had a reticent educational orientation toward moving in this direction. This probably has more to do with its reluctance to provide specialization and training than anything else. The empirical data on this subject are fairly clear, that is, professional social work education in North America is oriented toward generalist practice at both the BSW and MSW levels; however, graduate programmes are more likely to provide any specialized education and training (if it occurs at all).

As noted by legions of social work authors who have debated ad infinitum the generalist-specialist issue, the question of what specifically constitutes a generalist versus specialist curriculum is germane to it. Certainly, one course, a practicum and perhaps a term paper in gerontology, does not make anyone a 'specialist' (Erickson and Erickson, 1989). Also, one must be mindful that speciality courses or speciality fields of practice do not constitute specialized education and training (Brengarth, 1981). Without sinking too deep into the nuances of this issue, the chapters in this text remind us that we have much to learn about how to practice effectively with the elderly and much of this learning is not being offered in most North American schools of social work.

However one perceives this issue, it appears that education and training must go beyond traditional sequenced learning objectives in a curriculum that enhances a students' knowledge, values and skills and move toward developing self-awareness, compassion and a sense of more humanism among social work students. Thus, issues such as death and dying, intergenerational families, intrapsychic awareness, communication skills, tolerance, cultural awareness, attitude shaping and teaching social workers how to become competent in two to three practice interventive repertoires, which are used with the elderly, need to be addressed. The extent to which current formal or continuing professional education and training can provide such learning seems uncertain at this point in time. Within the future, however, we (the profession) must take the responsibility for such educational initiatives if we are serious about our commitment to providing minimally competent care for elderly persons.

V. Concluding Remarks

Gerontological social work practice holds a promising future for our profession. The future directions noted in this chapter are but a few of many challenges we will face in the next decade and beyond. We believe that social work has much to offer. However, it needs to better orient itself to the needs of the elderly, educate and train its entry level professionals in more comprehensive ways and promote and market its skills and competencies in more dynamic ways. Both indirect and direct practitioners will face very real challenges of working effectively in an age of belt-tightening and economic constraint. The time is now for the profession to meet these and future challenges and the sooner we throw ourselves into the foray, the better. We (the authors and editors) feel that we (the profession) have something special and important to offer this field. Let's not get bogged down by conceptualizing it but by proactively going and doing it, and to beat the drum one final time (at the expense of overkill). . . the *future is now*!

References

Bloom, M. (1981). *Primary prevention, the possible science*. Englewood Cliffs, NJ: Prentice Hall Inc.

Brengarth, J. (1981). What is 'special' about specialization? *Health and Social Work*, 5(2), 91-94.

Erickson, G. D. (1975). The concept of personal network in clinical practice. *Family Process*, 14, 487-497.

Erickson, G. D. (1984). A framework and themes for social network intervention. *Family Process*, 23, 187-198.

Erickson, G. D. and Erickson, R. (1989). An overview of social work practice in health care settings. In M. Holosko and P. Taylor (eds.), *Social work practice in health care settings* (pp. 3-19). Toronto, Ontario: Canadian Scholars' Press.

Gottlieb, B. H. (ed). (1983). *Social support strategies: Guidelines for mental health practice*. Beverly Hills, California: Sage Publications.

Holosko, M. J. and Dunlop, J. (1989). *A program evaluation of the interorganizational family violence project*. Chatham, Ontario: The Chatham-Kent Women's Centre.